"This book promises 'an introduction to the study of Paul and . . . an entryway to more advanced study.' It does not disappoint. The authors capably navigate complicated fields of research covering Paul's life, writings, and theology. They clarify without oversimplifying and offer fair judgments on controversial debates. They interact with great names in past scholarship but are attuned to the current state of discussion. Both beginning and advanced readers will love this substantial study and teaching tool for the succinct orientation it provides."

—Robert W. Yarbrough,
Professor of New Testament, Covenant Theological Seminary

"Echevarría and Laird have given us a concise and useful introduction to Paul's life, letters, and theology. They are fair, balanced, and irenic, and introduce readers to current scholarly debates in the matters discussed. Both students and professors will find it to be a very helpful resource."

—Thomas R. Schreiner,
James Buchanan Harrison Professor of New Testament Interpretation,
Professor of Biblical Theology,
The Southern Baptist Theological Seminary

"Miguel Echevarría and Benjamin Laird have written a helpful introduction to Paul's life, writings, and theology. They explore a wide range of topics concisely and carefully, while interacting evenhandedly with contemporary scholarship. *40 Questions About the Apostle Paul* provides an excellent starting point for readers who want to explore any of those questions at greater length."

—John D. Harvey,
Professor of New Testament, PhD Program Director,
Columbia Biblical Seminary of Columbia International University

"No one can read Paul's letters without numerous questions arising about their author. In this volume, Laird and Echevarría address forty such questions, on some of which scholars provide clear answers, whereas on others scholars either disagree among themselves or acknowledge the limitations of our knowledge. Readers are certain to appreciate the authors' informed, balanced, and accessible treatments of what we can, or think we can, or wish we could know about the apostle."

—Stephen Westerholm,
Professor Emeritus, McMaster University

"Professors Echevarría and Laird have succeeded in packing a lot of succinct information about the cultural context, biography, missionary work, and theology of the apostle Paul, including an evaluation of Paul's older and recent interpreters, into a very accessible volume. Their focus on the text of Paul's letters and Luke's Acts is consistent, their assessments of scholarly debates are fair, and their prose is lucid even when describing exegetical conundrums. Students and general readers are in their debt."

—Eckhard J. Schnabel,
Mary F. Rockefeller Distinguished Professor of New Testament,
Gordon-Conwell Theological Seminary

T0312498

"Sometimes when you read Paul's letters, it can seem as if you are trying to put together a puzzle without having the box. This helpful volume takes the pieces and gives a comprehensive picture of Paul's life, writings, and theology so you can understand how things fit together. In addition, each essay is short and accessible, so you get the main idea without getting lost in the details."

—Ben C. Blackwell,
Professor of Early Christianity, Houston Theological Seminary

"Drs. Miguel Echevarría and Benjamin P. Laird have written a helpful book asking and answering forty important questions about the apostle Paul. Even when readers disagree with either their questions or answers, they will still learn important things about Paul, his theology, and his letters."

—Jarvis J. Williams,
Associate Professor of New Testament Interpretation,
The Southern Baptist Theological Seminary

"In three well-conceived sections covering forty key questions, Echevarría and Laird have produced an important and sure-footed guide to the apostle Paul. I enthusiastically recommend this volume for anyone—both the novice and the veteran alike—who wants to gain or regain their 'sea legs' as they engage Paul, his writings, and his theology. It will repay rich dividends. Kudos to Echevarría and Laird for this superb work."

—Jay E. Smith,
Department Chair and Professor of New Testament Studies,
Dallas Theological Seminary

"Anyone who has read Paul's letters comes away with a lot of questions. Where did Paul come from? How was Paul transformed? Why did he write so many letters? What is his central teaching? Thankfully, Miguel Echevarría and Benjamin Laird have gathered the most important of these questions and provided balanced, readable, and genuinely insightful answers. This little volume represents a concise compendium of scholarship on a wide variety of issues—historical, theological, and pastoral—and is packed with charitable, judicious evaluation. This is a must-read primer on the apostle to the Gentiles!"

—Moyer Hubbard,
Chair and Professor of New Testament Language and Literature,
Talbot School of Theology, Biola University

"These forty questions and the superb discussion that follows are not focused on tangential matters, but lay an essential foundation for interpreting and understanding Paul and his letters. Where there are major interpretive issues (e.g., the role of women in the home and the church, the continuation of spiritual gifts, and more), the authors provide a fair and balanced discussion. Their discussion of each question is well-written and the Q&A format makes this a delight to read. This volume would make an excellent textbook for a course on Paul or the basis for a Bible study series on the apostle and his letters."

—Clinton E. Arnold,
Research Professor of New Testament,
Talbot School of Theology, Biola University

40 QUESTIONS ABOUT
The Apostle Paul

Miguel G. Echevarría
Benjamin P. Laird

Benjamin L. Merkle, Series Editor

40 Questions About the Apostle Paul
© 2023 Miguel G. Echevarría & Benjamin P. Laird

Published by Kregel Academic, an imprint of Kregel Publications, 2450 Oak Industrial Dr. NE, Grand Rapids, MI 49505-6020.

This book is a title in the 40 Questions Series edited by Benjamin L. Merkle.

For a complete list of titles in the 40 Questions series, go to 40questions.net.

All rights reserved. No part of this book may be reproduced, stored in a retrieval system, or transmitted in any form or by any means—electronic, mechanical, photocopy, recording, or otherwise—without written permission of the publisher, except for brief quotations in printed reviews.

All Scripture quotations, unless otherwise indicated, are from The Holy Bible, English Standard Version, copyright © 2001 by Crossway Bibles, a division of Good News Publishers. Used by permission. All rights reserved.

The Greek font GraecaU and the Hebrew font New JerusalemU are from www.linguistsoftware.com/lgku.htm, +1-425-775-1130.

Maps of Paul's journeys on pages 56, 66, and 67 were designed by Shawn Vander Lugt, Managing Editor for Academic and Ministry Books at Kregel Publications.

ISBN 978-0-8254-4752-5

Printed in the United States of America

23 24 25 26 27 / 5 4 3 2 1

For our students

Contents

Part 3: Questions About Paul's Theology

Abbreviations

AB	Anchor Bible
BBR	*Bulletin for Biblical Research*
BDAG	Frederick W, Danker, *A Greek-English Lexicon of the New Testament and Other Early Christian Literature*, 3rd ed. Chicago: University of Chicago Press, 2000.
BECNT	Baker Exegetical Commentary on the New Testament
BETS	*Bulletin of the Evangelical Theological Society*
BNTC	Black's New Testament Commentaries
BSac	*Bibliotheca Sacra*
BTNT	Biblical Theology of the New Testament
CBQ	*Catholic Biblical Quarterly*
ConcC	Concordia Commentary
DPL	*Dictionary of Paul and His Letters*
IBC	Interpretation: A Bible Commentary for Teaching and Preaching
ICC	International Critical Commentary
JBL	*Journal of Biblical Literature*
JETS	*Journal of the Evangelical Theological Society*
JGRChJ	*Journal of Greco-Roman Christianity and Judaism*
JSNT	*Journal for the Study of the New Testament*
JSNTSup	Journal for the Study of the New Testament Supplement Series
JSPL	*Journal for the Study of Paul and His Letters*
JTS	*Journal of Theological Studies*
LBS	Linguistic Biblical Studies
LCL	Loeb Classical Library
LEC	Library of Early Christianity
LNTS	Library of New Testament Studies
NACSBT	NAC Studies in Bible & Theology
NDBT	*New Dictionary of Biblical Theology*
NICNT	The New International Commentary on the New Testament

NIDNTTE	*New International Dictionary of New Testament Theology and Exegesis*
NIGTC	The New International Greek Testament Commentary
NPNF	Nicene and Post-Nicene Fathers
NSBT	New Studies in Biblical Theology
NTS	*New Testament Studies*
OECS	Oxford Early Christian Studies
PAST	Pauline Studies
PNTC	The Pillar New Testament Commentary
SBJT	*Southern Baptist Journal of Theology*
SBR	Studies of the Bible and Its Reception
SSEJC	Studies in Scripture in Early Judaism and Christianity
TDNT	Theological Dictionary of the New Testament
TNTC	Tyndale New Testament Commentaries
TynBul	*Tyndale Bulletin*
WAWSup	Writings from the Ancient World Supplement Series
WGRW	Writings from the Greco-Roman World
WJT	*Westminster Journal of Theology*
WUNT	Wissenschaftliche Untersuchungen zum Neuen Testament
ZCINT	Zondervan Critical Introductions to the New Testament
ZECNT	Zondervan Exegetical Commentary on the New Testament
ZNW	*Zeitschrift für die neutestamentliche Wissenschaft und die Kunde der älteren Kirche*

Introduction

The author of Ecclesiastes once said: "Of the making of many books there is no end." We would be hard-pressed to disagree with this conclusion, especially when we consider the current state of Pauline studies. The sheer number of works on topics such as the authenticity of Paul's epistles, Paul's use of the Old Testament, the New Perspective on Paul, the interpretation of *pistis Christou*, and the role of faith and works in salvation can be overwhelming for the average professor—let alone for a student or layperson. We can only imagine what the author of Ecclesiastes might think about the number of volumes on Paul. Perhaps he would be so overwhelmed (as many of us are) that he would qualify his observation: "Of the making of many books 'about Paul' there is no end!" And who would dare disagree with him?

All this begs the question: Why write *another* book on the apostle Paul? Is there really anything else to say or anything new to explore? We would argue that the question itself speaks to the need for the present volume. For many, it is unrealistic to wade through the large number of books, articles, and monographs about Paul that continue to be published on an annual basis. We can certainly sympathize with college and seminary students who may feel intimidated by the ever-expanding body of literature devoted to one aspect or another of Paul's life, writings, and theology. The number of publications devoted to the study of Paul is nothing short of staggering. In fact, it is safe to say that a well-rounded bibliography on Paul would well exceed a hundred pages. One could spend an entire lifetime devoted to the study of only a portion of Paul's writings or a single element of his teaching, let alone the entire body of his writings or the sum of his teaching.

With these practical concerns in mind, we have condensed into one volume a wide-ranging discussion about Paul's life, writings, and theology. In writing this book, our aim was not to be comprehensive in scope or exhaustive in our treatment of a particular subject. There are several additional subjects that could have easily been added. In fact, it would have not been a stretch to write a volume titled *One Hundred Questions About the Apostle Paul*. Rather than covering all possible subjects related to Paul's life and teaching or offering the most robust treatment possible of specific topics, our aim has been to provide readers with concise and accessible responses to a variety of questions that are foundational to our understanding of Paul. We encourage readers to use our book as both an introduction to the study of Paul and as an entryway to more advanced study.

As readers make their way through the volume, they will become acquainted with the background of Paul's life and letters, his teaching on a number of issues, subjects at the center of contemporary debate, and the viewpoints of a number of Pauline scholars. Throughout the process, readers will become familiar with contemporary scholars such as N. T. Wright, Morna Hooker, Thomas Schreiner, and Douglas Moo, notable figures from previous generations such as F. C. Baur, Albert Schweizer, and Rudolf Bultmann, and even how certain perspectives may be traced back to leading figures of the Protestant Reformation such as Martin Luther and John Calvin.

Before delving into our study of Paul, it will be helpful to briefly outline the layout of the volume. The book is divided into three major units. Part 1 addresses subjects related to Paul's background. In these initial chapters we consider a variety of questions related to Paul's early life, education, his opposition to Christianity prior to his conversion, his missionary activities, the final years of his life, and what we know about his death. Our treatment of these subjects relies primarily on Acts and the relevant information contained in Paul's writings. References to noncanonical sources are also made when appropriate.

Part 2 answers questions about Paul's writings, such as the historical context in which Paul penned each of his letters, how they were composed and delivered, how a single canonical collection of his writings was likely assembled, what may have happened to his lost letters (an exact location is not provided!), arguments both for and against the authenticity of the canonical works attributed to him, his possible role in the composition of Hebrews, whether he regarded his letters as authoritative Scripture, and the sources that he may have consulted. As many readers are well aware, historical subjects related to the background of Paul's letters present modern interpreters with several confounding questions. These chapters will enable readers to become conversant with the various perspectives on these matters and to become more familiar with Paul as a writer.

Part 3 addresses questions related to Paul's theology such as his view of the atonement, the nature of Christ, the relationship between law and gospel, the role of faith and works in salvation, miraculous gifts, church ordinances, slavery and racial division, eschatology, and several additional theological subjects. We will also consider matters of contemporary debate such as the New Perspective on Paul. The responses in this section deal with some of the most heated debates in Pauline studies—some that go back centuries, and some that have only recently become a matter of debate and controversy.

Words of Thanks

There are many people we would like to thank for helping us bring this book to completion. We want to thank Benjamin Merkle, the series editor, for accepting this book into the 40 Questions series and for his insightful comments and keen editorial eye. We are also grateful for all our friends at Kregel who were involved in the acquisition and publication of this book.

I (Miguel) would like to thank my former administrative assistant at Southeastern Seminary, Owen Kelly, who read an early version of the work and provided feedback. His careful, theological eye sharpened my arguments. I would also like to thank my coauthor, Ben Laird, for his substantive feedback on the manuscript. My work is stronger because of his comments. My current administrative assistant at Southeastern, Hayden Fleming, provided helpful advice on the New Perspective section. Last but not least, I would like to thank my family for their love and support. Not that I have arrived (as I am sure Paul would agree), but my work on Paul is far more gracious, and I take myself far less seriously, because of the influence of my wife Hollie and my four daughters Miriam, Esther, Eunice, and Lilias.

Ben would like to thank Miguel Echevarría for, as Paul might say, serving as a valuable *synergos*, a fellow worker, throughout the process of writing and editing this volume. While we share the same enthusiasm for the study of Paul, our specific interests and areas of expertise have complemented each other very well and have enabled us to cover a wide spectrum of subjects that would have been much more difficult to cover alone. I (Ben) would also like to thank my wife Margaret and our children Meredith, Jonathan, Lydia, Nora, and Charles for their support and encouragement throughout the process.

Above all, we would like to thank the Lord Jesus Christ for calling the apostle Paul to testify to the saving work of God to the ends of the earth. Paul's testimony has spurred many to preach the Lord Jesus in places where many have never heard—from indigenous communities in the jungles of Brazil to the inner cities of North America, from nomad communities in the Middle East to the streets of London. Wherever Jesus is preached, we have the example of Paul as the forerunner of generations of missionaries, evangelists, and pastors. May this book lead to a better understanding of the apostle Paul's cosmic vision of salvation, resulting in many going to those who have never heard of the redemption God has accomplished through the life, death, and resurrection of Jesus Christ.

PART 1

Questions About
Paul's Life

Paul's Pre-Christian Life

Where Was Paul Born and Raised?

R eaders of this book may be tempted to skip chapters related to the background of Paul in order to begin with questions about his writings and his treatment of various theological subjects. We agree that it is rewarding to read Paul's discussions about topics such as the righteousness of God, the atonement, and Jesus's second coming. That Paul writes with a warmth and exhilaration not found in other New Testament authors makes skipping ahead in this book especially tempting.[1] Nevertheless, to fairly treat questions about Paul's letters and writings, it is necessary to first consider a number of historical questions related to his life and background. The more acquainted we become with his Jewish upbringing, his earliest influences, his education, and his former life as a persecutor of the church, the better prepared we will be to address matters related to his writings and his treatment of various theological subjects. In this first section, then, we will address several questions related to Paul's life.

The primary sources for Paul's life are Acts and his extant letters. Of the two, Acts provides the majority of the information about the historical Paul. Yet, neither was intended to serve as a biographical work on the apostle. We must therefore take extra care to piece together an accurate portrayal of his life. While relevant sources outside the Bible, such as those of Strabo and Jerome, are useful, we will mainly rely on the historical facts that can be derived from Acts and his surviving writings. We will depend on sources outside the Bible only in places where Scripture is silent.

Answering questions related to the apostle Paul's life will hopefully acquaint us with the man whose writings have been so profitable for Christians

---

1. F. F. Bruce captures this sentiment: "Of all the New Testament authors, Paul is the one who has stamped his own personality most unmistakably in his writings" (*Paul: Apostle of the Heart Set Free* [Grand Rapids: Eerdmans, 1977], 15).

throughout the centuries. We will start by answering the important question about where the apostle Paul was born and raised.

Born in Tarsus

Luke records that Paul was from Tarsus (Acts 9:30; 11:25; 21:39; 22:3), where he was likely born in the first decade CE.[2] Sources from antiquity describe Tarsus as a flourishing city. Some might even call it a metropolis. Paul's description squares with what we find in contemporary literature—that it was "an important city" (Acts 21:39). Tarsus's reputation was largely centered around its economy and devotion to philosophy.

The city's economic repute dates back to the fourth century BCE. Xenophon notes that Tarsus was a "large and prosperous city."[3] One of the main reasons for Tarsus's favorable economy was the Cydnus River, which flowed through the city. Merchants so frequently traveled along the river that it was considered "one of the great trade routes of the ancient world; the easiest and most frequented land route from Syria and the east to Asia Minor and the Aegean crossed the Amanus by the Syrian Gates, and the Taurus by the Cilician Gates."[4] Tarsus also benefited from being the first stop on a major business route that connected the Mediterranean with the Black Sea.[5] The city was thus a center of trade and business, making it a major commercial center.

Tarsus also benefited from being the capital of the Roman province of Cilicia. Dio Chrysostom (40–115 CE) attributes the economic station of Tarsus to both its great river and its status as a capital city: "The fact is . . . your home is in a great city and you occupy a fertile land, because you find the needs of life supplied for you in greatest abundance and profusion, because you have this river flowing through the heart of your city, and because, moreover, Tarsus is the capital of all the people of Cilicia."[6] During the reign of Mark Antony, in 42 BCE, Tarsus was declared a free city and released from paying taxes to Rome—benefits that continued well beyond Paul's lifetime.[7]

The success of the economy allowed the study of philosophy to thrive. Tarsus was a well-known center of Stoic philosophy where famous philosophers

---

2. We can only approximate a date for Paul's birth. In Philemon 9, Paul calls himself "an elderly man." Paul's first-century contemporaries considered a man around the age of sixty to be "elderly." If Philemon was written during Paul's first Roman imprisonment in the early sixties, Paul would have likely been born sometime in the first decade CE. See Jerome Murphy-O'Connor, *Paul: A Critical Life* (Oxford: Clarendon, 1996), 2–4.
3. Xenophon, *Anabasis* 1.2.23 (Brownson, LCL 90).
4. A. H. M. Jones, *Cities of the Eastern Roman Provinces*, 2nd. ed. (Oxford: Clarendon, 1971), 191. Cited in Murphy-O'Connor, *Paul*, 33.
5. Udo Schnelle, *Apostle Paul: His Life and Theology*, trans. M. Eugene Boring (Grand Rapids: Baker Academic, 2003), 58.
6. Dio Chrysostom, *Tarsic Discourse* 1.17 (Cahoon, LCL 358).
7. Appian, *History* 5.1.7.

such as Antipatrus of Tarsus (140 BCE) were based.[8] In the early part of the first century CE, Strabo observes: "The people at Tarsus have devoted themselves so eagerly, not only to philosophy, but also to the whole round of education in general, that they have surpassed Athens, Alexandria, or any other place that can be named where there have been schools and lectures of philosophers."[9] Strabo acknowledges that it was mainly the natives of Tarsus who studied in its schools, and that its citizens often began their learning in the city and then went elsewhere to complete their education.[10] From this observation we gather that though the city was known for its devotion to philosophy, its schools did not have an international reputation, and that its students often finished their education at more prestigious centers of learning.

The city of Tarsus, then, into which Paul was born, was a thriving and prosperous city known for its economy and its pursuit of philosophy. This background would have proved helpful when Paul stood before Stoics and Epicureans at the Areopagus and quoted the philosopher Aratus: "We are indeed his offspring" (Acts 17:28). The Stoics would have recognized Aratus as one of their own. From our brief look at Tarsus, we assume that the philosophical air at Tarsus would have blown Aratus's treatises in Paul's direction—knowledge he would later use to call those who were "listening to the latest ideas" to repent and worship the true God (Acts 17:16–34).[11]

Raised a Jew

The biblical record clearly indicates that Paul was raised in Tarsus as a Jew (Acts 21:39). The apostle identifies himself as a "Hebrew of Hebrews" from "the tribe of Benjamin" (Phil. 3:5; cf. Rom. 11:1). According to Jerome (347–420 CE), Paul's family likely relocated to Tarsus from Gischala (modern Jish) in Galilee.[12] How they got there is debated. Once again Jerome may provide some insight—for he indicates that Paul's parents arrived as prisoners of war.[13] Regardless of the circumstances surrounding their relocation, they would have joined the Jewish community in Tarsus and continued worshipping in their ancestral religion of Judaism. The religious freedom that the Jews of Tarsus enjoyed may be attributed to Julius Caesar, who exempted Jews in the Roman Empire from practices that contradicted the requirements of their

---

8. Schnelle, *Apostle Paul*, 59.
9. Strabo, *Geography* 14.5.13 (Jones, LCL 223).
10. Strabo, *Geography* 14.5.13.
11. Paul also quotes the Greek poet Meander (1 Cor. 15:33) and the Cretan philosopher Epimenides (Titus 1:12).
12. Jerome, *Commentary on Philemon*, vv. 23–24.
13. As Murphy-O'Connor notes, in his *Commentary on Philemon* (*Paul*, 36–37). Jerome states that Paul's family arrived in Tarsus as prisoners of war. However, in his *De Viris Illustribus* 5, he notes that they arrived voluntarily. Of the two, Murphy-O'Connor argues for the reliability of the former (*Paul*, 38).

religion.[14] Thus, Roman law granted Paul's parents the freedom to raise their child in accordance with their ancestral faith.

We evidence his parents' devotion to Judaism in Paul's claim to have been "circumcised on the eighth day" (Phil. 3:5).[15] Their piety is also demonstrated by their naming of Paul after the most famous Benjamite, Saul. Charles Quarles makes the thought-provoking connection that the name could have expressed hope in the Messiah.[16] According to Quarles, it is possible that Paul's parents "hoped their Saul would be a forerunner to the Messiah, 'the son of David,' much like Saul was the predecessor of King David."[17] Like many Diaspora Jews, Paul's family may have hoped that the Messiah would return to end the exile and restore the kingdom. And how great would it have been to imagine that God might use their son to deliver his people? Of course, the New Testament records that God did use Paul in a mighty way—to announce the Messiah's arrival to the nations. Like Isaiah and Jeremiah centuries earlier, Paul became aware that God had separated him from the womb for this mission (Gal. 1:15; cf. Isa. 49:1; Jer. 1:5).

The last important fact we must mention is that Paul was a born a Roman citizen (Acts 22:28). His Roman citizenship would have granted him the same rights as other citizens of the empire, such as the right to appeal after a trial, exemption from military service, and the right to choose a local or Roman trial.[18] In Acts we find Paul benefiting from his Roman citizenship on several occasions: when he is released from jail in Philippi (16:37–39), when Roman soldiers protected him from an angry mob (22:25–29), and when he appealed for a trial before Caesar (25:7–12; 26:32). These benefits were first available to him in his hometown of Tarsus.

In Tarsus, then, Paul would have been raised in a Jewish community with the right to worship the God of Abraham, Isaac, and Jacob. By naming him Saul, his parents displayed their devotion to the God who they hoped would return to save his people from the very Gentiles in their midst. Paul's Roman citizenship granted him valuable rights and protections afforded to other residents of the empire. Later in life, Paul would exercise his citizenship privileges when gospel ministry put him in precarious situations.

---

14. Josephus, *Antiquities* 14.10.8 (Marcus and Wikgren, LCL 489).
15. Bruce W. Longenecker and Todd D. Still, *Thinking through Paul: A Survey of His Life, Letters, and Theology* (Grand Rapids: Zondervan, 2014), 25.
16. Charles L. Quarles, *Illustrated Life of Paul* (Nashville: B&H, 2014), 5.
17. Quarles, *Life of Paul*, 5.
18. Mark Reasoner, "Citizenship, Roman and Heavenly," in *Dictionary of Paul and His Letters*, eds. Gerald F. Hawthorne, Ralph P. Martin, Daniel G. Reid (Downers Grove, IL: InterVarsity Press, 1993), 140.

Summary

We have begun our study of Paul's life with a discussion on where he was born and raised. We have just begun, then, to become acquainted with the historical experiences and influences that shaped the apostle whose letters and theology have had such a profound influence on Christians throughout the centuries. We know thus far that Paul was a Roman citizen born in Tarsus who was reared in his family's ancestral Jewish faith. We have also discovered that he would have been exposed early in life to the philosophical treatises which he would later use in his ministry to Gentiles.

REFLECTION QUESTIONS

1. What were two factors that contributed to the flourishing life Paul would have experienced in Tarsus?

2. How did the philosophical climate in Tarsus aid Paul's later ministry?

3. Who codified into law the religious freedoms the Jews experienced in the Roman Empire?

4. What biblical evidence points to the likelihood that Paul's parents were devout Jews?

5. What were some of the benefits of citizenship that Paul initially experienced in Tarsus and later exercised in his ministry?

What Do We Know About Paul's Family?

As a central figure in the book of Acts and the author of roughly half of the New Testament writings, a considerable amount of insight may be gleaned about Paul's missionary activities and his perspective on a variety of theological subjects from the biblical writings. Historical information relating to his personal background is very limited, however. While we would naturally like to know more about Paul's early years and family connections, we are left with only a few passing references in the New Testament that offer insight about his personal life and his family's heritage. Although references in Acts and the Pauline Epistles to members of Paul's family are few in number and offer only limited insight, it will be helpful to briefly consider what they may reveal about his background.

Paul's Father

Paul's father is not mentioned by name, but it is often thought that Paul refers to him as a Pharisee in Acts 23:6 in his address to the Sanhedrin. Interestingly, there are two different ways in which the major English translations render this passage. According to the KJV and NKJV, Paul claimed not only that he was a Pharisee, but that he was a "son of a Pharisee," implying that his father was also a member of the Pharisees. In contrast, the majority of modern translations render Paul's statement as something like "a son of Pharisees" or "a descendent of Pharisees." The primary difference, of course, relates to whether the word Pharisee (*Pharisaios*) is translated as a singular or plural. Those who prefer the singular tend to recognize Paul's father as the Pharisee, a deduction that seems quite natural in light of Paul's description of himself as a "son" (*hyios*) of this individual. Understanding the term "son" in a physical sense becomes more of a challenge, however, when the word "Pharisee" appears in the plural. In what sense could he be regarded as a son or descendent of Pharisees? Is it possible that he was making the claim that both his father and perhaps even his grandfather were Pharisees?

To reach a satisfactory conclusion to this subject, we must briefly comment on two issues: one textual and the other hermeneutical. Textually, we find that the majority of early Greek witnesses to Acts contain the plural *Pharisaiōn* but that a number of later manuscripts contain the singular *Pharisaiou*. How might we account for this discrepancy? It would seem likely that a shift from the plural to the singular was introduced into the textual transmission of Acts at some time after it had been in circulation in order to provide clarity. One can imagine that a scribe may have been conflicted by the phrase "son of Pharisees" because of the difficulty of accounting for multiple Pharisees in Paul's family. Was Paul really a third-generation Pharisee? Just how many Pharisees were in his family, and how feasible is it that multiple Pharisees belonged to a single family living outside of the land of Israel?[1] With the singular, readers may simply assume that Paul was pointing to his father and avoid the difficulty of accounting for multiple Pharisees in a single family living in the Diaspora. In light of the strong external evidence and the arguably more difficult task of accounting for the plural *Pharisaiōn*, it would seem probable that the singular "son of a Pharisee" was a later rendering and that the original text read "son of Pharisees."

If it was in fact the case that the plural *Pharisaiōn* was original, what exactly was Paul's point? Was he asserting that he was the physical descendent of a long line of Pharisees? It would seem more likely that Paul was reminding his audience that he was trained under the tutelage and guidance of a number of prominent Pharisees, many of whom may have even been present at the very hearing in which he made this assertion! As Ben Witherington explains, "Paul's claim to be a son of Pharisees might mean that he was a product of Pharisaic instruction, for it was not uncommon for disciples to call their teachers things like 'father' or rabbi."[2] This type of language would certainly not be unusual for Paul. In fact, he uses similar language in his epistles, referring to individuals such as Timothy, Titus, and Onesimus as his "son" (see Phil. 2:22; 1 Tim. 1:2, 18; 2 Tim. 1:2; 2:1; Titus 1:4).

In light of the fact that terms of endearment such as "father" and "son" were often used to describe one's teacher or student, it is not too difficult to imagine Paul using similar language in this particular context. It would certainly seem to be the case that Paul spent considerable time interacting with various members

---

1. As Martin Hengel helpfully explains, "Before the destruction of the temple, [Jerusalem] was the only proper place for strict Jews—and Paul came from a strict Jewish family and was himself one—to study the Torah" (Martin Hengel, *The Pre-Christian Paul* [London: SCM Press, 1991], 27).

2. Ben Witherington III, *The Acts of the Apostles: A Socio-Rhetorical Commentary* (Grand Rapids: Eerdmans, 1998), 691. See also, Craig S. Keener, *Acts: An Exegetical Commentary Volume 3: 15:1–23:35* (Grand Rapids: Baker Academic, 2014), 3288–91.

of the Pharisees during his formative years in Jerusalem. Thus, Paul may be emphasizing his close relationship with a number of the members of the Sanhedrin during his address, or at least associating himself with many of the prominent religious authorities in the city. He was not merely sympathetic or supportive of the Pharisees, he was, at least in a figurative sense, their "son"! If this reading is adopted, the text of Acts 23:6 would not include a direct reference to a member of Paul's immediate family but would provide insight regarding his close ties to Jerusalem. While the likelihood that Paul's father was a Pharisee remains in doubt, we may at least infer that his father and the members of his family would have been supportive and proud of his accomplishments, the training he received, and his zeal for the law and Jewish traditions. After all, Paul did not find Judaism on his own. According to his own testimony he was "circumcised on the eighth day, of the people of Israel, of the tribe of Benjamin, a Hebrew of Hebrews" (Phil. 3:5).

Paul's Sister and Nephew

Although the identity of those referred to in Acts 23:6 remains a matter of dispute, there is an unambiguous reference to two of Paul's family members in Acts 23:16–22. Luke records that shortly after Paul's defense before the Sanhedrin, a well-orchestrated plot to take his life was discovered by the son of his sister. In response, this unnamed nephew reported the information to Paul, who then made arrangements for him to relay the information to the tribune (*chiliarchos*).[3] Given the number of those involved and their intent to kill Paul, the courage of Paul's nephew to deliver the news to the soldiers may have very well saved his life. Evidently, Paul's nephew had maintained communication with him and was concerned about his well-being. It is not clear if he was a Christian convert or if his concern was simply prompted by their familial ties. The fact that he learned of the plot, however, might suggest that he or his mother were connected to certain Jewish circles and were therefore not believers. We also cannot be certain whether Paul's nephew was living in Jerusalem or if he had simply traveled to the city to celebrate Pentecost or for some other reason.

Sergius Paulus

Acts 13:7 includes a reference to the first recorded convert of Paul and Barnabas on the island of Cyprus after they set out on their first missionary journey. The convert was no ordinary citizen, Luke reveals, but the provincial

---

3. No action of Paul's sister is recorded in the text, so it is not clear whether she played an active role in bringing her son to Paul or even if she was still living at this time. The reference to the officer taking Paul's nephew by the hand (v. 19) may suggest that his nephew was young, raising the likelihood that Paul's sister was alive and that she played a role in making the arrangements for her son to visit Paul.

proconsul (governor). While Luke does not hint at a familial relationship between Sergius Paulus and Paul, the fact that the two individuals share the same Roman *cognomen* (*Paulus*, sometimes spelled *Paullus*) has drawn attention. All male Roman citizens possessed at least three names, the *tria nomina*, which together indicated something about the individual's social status, background, and reputation. This would include the *praenomen*, what might be described as a personal name that was only used by family members and close friends, the *nomen*, the name of one's larger Roman clan, and, finally, the *cognomen*, a more specific name that identified a particular family within a larger clan. The *cognomen* is the name that is typically recorded in the New Testament for various Romans (e.g., Felix, Festus, and Gallio). Contrary to what might be assumed by modern readers, the English "Paul" is not a translation of what might be regarded as his first name but was instead closer to a modern family name. Unfortunately, there is no record of Paul's *praenomen* or *nomen*, though we can be confident that he possessed these names from birth since he was born a Roman citizen.[4] Because Paul and Sergius Paulus apparently shared the same *cognomen*, might it be possible that they were distant relatives? It is difficult to dismiss this possibility entirely, but this is probably unlikely given Paul's Jewish ancestry and the fact that Luke does not mention any family connection between the two. If the two men were related, this relationship would have been quite distant. Another possibility is that Paul's family was adopted into the wider Paulus line when they received citizenship. If this were the case, there would not have been a blood relationship between Sergius Paulus and Paul and it is unlikely that the two had met before this occasion.

Paul's Wife

Whether Paul may have been married at some point of his life has long been a matter of speculation. Marriage was certainly the normal practice and expectation of men living in Jewish society, particularly those who were respected religious figures. Curiously, however, certain passages in Paul's correspondence to the Corinthians indicate that he was not married, at least not at the time that 1 Corinthians was composed (see, e.g., 1 Cor. 7:7–8; 9:5). There are also no explicit references to a wife of Paul in Acts or his extant epistles. Although it is recognized that Paul was unlikely to have been married during much or all of his Christian life, it is sometimes speculated that he was married as a young man or even that he was married at some point in his ministry, but that he simply chose not to travel with his wife.

---

4. Contrary to what is often assumed, Paul did not receive a new name at conversion. "Saul" was his Hebrew name, a name which he appears to have used in Jewish settings such as Jerusalem. "Paul," on the other hand, was part of the Roman name he received at birth. This was the name he used when his ministry began to focus on Gentile areas.

A few passages from Paul's writings are sometimes thought to support the notion that he was previously married. Those who hold this position often suggest that his wife may have passed away early in their marriage or that she abandoned him when he became a Christian. Support for this position is thought to be found in Paul's instruction to those who were unmarried and widows in Corinth. He directs them, for example, "to remain single, as I am" (1 Cor. 7:8). The word translated as "remain" (*menō*) might be understood to imply that Paul was previously married and later chose to remain unmarried. In this same verse, Paul uses the term *agamos*, typically translated as "unmarried" in English translations. On some occasions, this word was used to refer not to single people in general, but more specifically to those who were previously married. In fact, this appears to be precisely how Paul uses the term just a few verses later in verse 11. If the term *agamos* is used in a similar manner in verse 8, it might be concluded that Paul was advising those who were previously married to "remain" in a state of singleness just as he had determined to do after his wife had either passed away or left him.

An additional passage that is sometimes suspected to refer to Paul's wife is Philippians 4:3. After appealing to Euodia and Syntyche "to agree in the Lord" (4:2), Paul makes a request of an individual he refers to simply as his "true companion." It has been noted that the term *suzugos*, translated by several English translations as "companion," was occasionally used in reference to one's spouse. This was indeed the case, though it was not the sole use of the term. In addition to a spouse, the word was also used in Greek literature in reference to fellow soldiers, close friends, coworkers, etc.[5] Because of the wide semantic range of the term and the absence of additional information in the text, it is simply not possible to know the specific individual that Paul was referring to on this occasion, though the Philippians would have certainly understood the reference.

Despite the imprecise nature of this reference, a number of scholars over the centuries have suggested that this passage makes a possible reference to Paul's wife. Even during the early centuries of the Christian era, this view appears to have been accepted by a handful of prominent figures including Clement of Alexandria and his student Origen. Clement claimed on one occasion that Paul was married but that he did not travel with his wife because it would have been impractical.[6] Taking a similar position, Origen explains that

---

5. This word appears occasionally in older Greek works such as Euripides's *Iphigenia in Tauris* 250 (c. 410–415 BCE) and Aristophanes's *Plutus* 945 (c. 388 BCE) where it refers to one's companion or friend. Euripides also uses the term in reference to a spouse in *Alcestis* 314 (c. 438 BCE). Polybius also uses the cognate verb συζυγέω in reference to soldiers joining together in formation in his *Histories* (*Polyb.* 10.23.7). See TDNT 7:748–50 for additional uses of the term in ancient literature.

6. Clement of Alexandria, *Miscellanies* 3.6.53. Eusebius also refers to Clement's position in *Ecclesiastical History* 3.30.

Paul, "if certain traditions are true, was called while in possession of a wife, concerning whom he speaks when writing to the Philippians. . . . Since he had become free by mutual consent with her, he calls himself a slave of Christ."[7] Interestingly, Clement and Origen raise the possibility not only that Paul was married at some point of time, but that he was married during his apostolic ministry. Understood in this light, Paul's reference in 1 Corinthians 9:5 to his willingness to travel without the company of a believing wife would not demand that he was single or widowed, but merely that he did not assert his right to travel with his wife.

While the viewpoint that Paul was married earlier in life or even after he was called as an apostle cannot be dismissed entirely, many scholars find it unlikely that Paul was previously married. At no point in Acts or in Paul's extant epistles do we find explicit reference to a wife of Paul. With regard to the suggestion that Paul was married earlier in life, we might note his assertion in 1 Corinthians 7:7 that each individual has been granted a unique gift (*charisma*) by God. Paul recognized that God has given some the desire to marry but that he has given others the ability to live in singleness without the desire or need for marriage. Paul clearly places himself in the latter category but understands that others were constituted much differently. We need not assume that the "gift" referred to by Paul is something he came to possess only at the time of his conversion. If Paul was not inclined to marry throughout his many years as a Christian, it might likewise be assumed that this was also the case when he was a younger man.

Summary

This chapter has analyzed a number of passages from Acts as well as Paul's own writings for possible insight relating to his family background. While the descriptions about his upbringing suggest that he grew up in a devout Jewish home, little is known about the specific members of his immediate family. None of his family members are referred to by name, and we can only speculate about the nature of Paul's relationship to them, especially after his encounter with Christ. Aside from the brief reference to his sister and nephew in Acts 23:16–22, only a small number of possible references to members of Paul's family may be found in the New Testament. It has been suggested that the reference in Acts 23:6 to Paul's background does not refer to his father, that the common name shared between Paul and the Roman proconsul Sergius Paulus was probably coincidental, and that Paul was most likely never married.

---

7. Origen of Alexandria, *Commentary on Romans* 1.1.3. Translation from Thomas Scheck, trans. *Origen: Commentary on the Epistle to the Romans, Books 1–5.* The Fathers of the Church: A New Translation (Washington DC: The Catholic University of America Press, 2001).

REFLECTION QUESTIONS

1. What are the major ways that Paul's description of himself as a "son" of Pharisees might be understood?

2. What factor(s) may suggest that Paul was or was not a distant relative of Sergius Paulus?

3. Aside from a possible reference to Paul's father, which family members of Paul are referenced in the book of Acts? What do we learn about them?

4. What are the most compelling arguments or factors that might suggest that Paul was married, at least at one point in his life?

5. What are some of the reasons that many scholars have been reluctant to conclude that Paul had ever been married?

What Do We Know About Paul's Education?

Despite the fact that Paul's writings were intended primarily for general audiences rather than scholars and those of the upper classes, they bear evidence that he had acquired a considerable knowledge of both Greco-Roman and Jewish culture and that he possessed a range of literary skills. The design and structure of his writings, the literary devices and rhetorical features he employs, and the manner in which he addresses a host of subjects demonstrate that Paul was an effective communicator who was able to address a wide range of subjects in a persuasive manner.

For some, Paul was something of an intellectual giant—a rare figure who could hold his own among the most advanced Roman and Greek thinkers of his day and who possessed an extensive knowledge of the Hebrew Scriptures and Jewish traditions. His unique background is often thought to have allowed him the ability to respond skillfully and effectively to the concerns of both Jewish and Gentile believers and to articulate the gospel message in a compelling manner in a variety of contexts. Others would suggest that Paul received sufficient or adequate training for the work to which he was entrusted, but that it would be overstated to portray him as an intellectual giant.

Although Paul would have benefited from valuable training in his early years in Tarsus and later in Jerusalem, it is difficult to determine precisely how extensive his education may have been, how it was administered, or how it might compare to that of the great thinkers and writers of his day. He does not provide specific information in his writings about the training he received during his pre-Christian life and merely emphasizes that he was a strict observer of Jewish laws and traditions, that he came from a Jewish family, and that he sought to excel in all facets of his faith. It is only in Acts that we find any indication that he was formally associated with any particular rabbinic school or Jewish sect. As might be expected, those who are cautious of the historical accuracy of Acts tend to be more reluctant to recognize Paul's impressive intellectual background, particularly his place in Judaism. So, what might we conclude about Paul's education and prior training? Is there reasonable evidence that his education was extensive and that he received advanced training and instruction in both Greco-Roman and Jewish settings, or would it be more appropriate to conclude that the training he received was more in line with what might be expected of those who grew up in a typical Jewish family living in the Diaspora? To answer these questions, we must consider what type of education someone like Paul likely received in Tarsus and Jerusalem, and, while often overlooked, how his knowledge and literary skills may have continued to develop and advance after his conversion.[1]

Paul's Early Training in Tarsus

In order to ascertain the nature of the education Paul obtained in his formative years, we must first consider what may be known of life in first-century Tarsus, specifically the type of education that would have been available to those raised in this city. As noted in Question 1, one of our most important historical sources of information about the ancient city of Tarsus is the Greek historian Strabo's famous *Geographica*. It will be helpful to begin our study of Paul's education by considering a significant portion of Strabo's description of Tarsus:

> The people at Tarsus have devoted themselves so eagerly, not only to philosophy, but also to the whole round of education in general, that they have surpassed Athens, Alexandria, or any other place that can be named where there have been schools and lectures of philosophers. But it is so different from other cities that there the men who are fond of learning are all natives, and foreigners are not inclined to sojourn there; neither do these natives stay there, but they complete their education abroad; and when they have completed it they are pleased to live abroad, and but few go back home. But the opposite is the case with the other cities which I have just

---

1. For further treatment of the subjects addressed in this chapter, see Stanley E. Porter and Andrew W. Pitts, "Paul's Bible, His Education, and His Access to the Scriptures," *JGRChJ* 5 (2008): 9–40; Stanley E. Porter and Bryan Dyer, eds., *Paul and Ancient Rhetoric: Theory and Practice in the Hellenistic Context* (Cambridge: Cambridge University Press, 2016); W. C. van Unnik, *Tarsus or Jerusalem: The City of Paul's Youth*, trans. George Ogg (London: Epworth Press, 1962); Martin Hengel, *The Pre-Christian Paul* (London: SCM Press, 1991), 18–62; E. P. Sanders, *Paul: The Apostle's Life, Letters, and Thoughts* (Minneapolis: Fortress, 2015), 70–76; and Jerome Murphy-O'Connor, *Paul: His Story* (New York: Oxford University Press, 2004), 4–12.

mentioned except Alexandria; for many resort to them and pass time there with pleasure, but you would not see many of the natives either resorting to places outside their country through love of learning or eager about pursuing learning at home. With the Alexandrians, however, both things take place, for they admit many foreigners and also send not a few of their own citizens abroad. Further, the city of Tarsus has all kinds of schools of rhetoric; and in general it not only has a flourishing population but also is most powerful, thus keeping up the reputation of the mother-city.[2]

From this account we learn that Tarsus was more than a mere regional center of culture and learning. Although Tarsus does not appear to have drawn as many from distant locations as some other cities, it nevertheless enjoyed a solid reputation as a premier place of learning, surpassing even notable cities such as Athens and Alexandria. Following this general description of the reputation of Tarsus, Strabo precedes to refer by name to a large number of philosophers and other intellects who were associated with the city, many of whom were noted Stoics.

The large number of philosophers and writers linked to the city would have certainly contributed to a stimulating intellectual environment and provided ample opportunities for those eager to expand their knowledge of various disciplines. It is not possible to determine if Paul studied under a particular philosopher or if he was enrolled in a particular school. It is clear, however, that the environment of Tarsus would have provided an ideal setting for a young man such as Paul who was intellectually gifted and eager to learn. Growing up in Tarsus, he would have had opportunities to become familiar with the basic viewpoints of various philosophers, to expand his knowledge of Greek rhetoric, and to become well-acquainted with the conventional structure and basic features of epistolary literature. The extent of this exposure, of course, would have depended largely on whether his parents limited his education to Jewish settings and how old he was when he departed for Jerusalem. However, even without formal instruction from a particular philosopher or formal training in a particular school, Paul would have had opportunities to become steeped in Greco-Roman culture. It was common in cities such as Tarsus for the works of famous teachers and writers to be read in public settings, for example, a practice that would have offered numerous opportunities for individuals such as Paul to engage in dialogue with members of the various philosophical traditions and to become familiar with their works. In addition to his exposure to Greco-Roman culture and learning, we might also assume that Paul became familiar with the Greek Septuagint at a young age.

---

2.   Strabo, *Geography* 14.5.13 (Jones, LCL 223).

Greek was not only the primary language spoken in Tarsus—and likely of his own family—it was also the primary language in which the majority of the Jewish population read the ancient scriptures. As might be suspected of a writer who grew up in this context, numerous quotations and allusions to the Greek Septuagint permeate Paul's writings.

Paul's Training in Jerusalem

Although Paul occasionally emphasizes his Jewish roots in his writings, he nowhere elaborates on his experiences in Jerusalem prior to his conversion. In none of his extant letters does he reveal that he studied under the tutelage of a particular rabbi or elaborate on the degree of training he received during his formative years. He does reveal that he was "as to the law, a Pharisee" (Phil. 3:5), but this reference provides little insight about his actual training and education.[3] As a result of the lack of references to the specific training he received, critical scholars such as Jürgen Becker often conclude that "by all appearances Paul was not instructed in the Pharisaic interpretation of the law as a regular student of a rabbi, in order later to assume the occupation of a rabbi himself" and that he was merely "educated in the Pharisaic spirit for his view of life."[4]

For insight relating to Paul's experience in the city, we must look to Acts, but even here the references are few in number and offer only limited insight.[5] As discussed in the previous chapter, Paul makes the claim that he was "brought up in this city, educated at the feet of Gamaliel according to the strict manner of the law of our fathers, being zealous for God as all of you are this day" (Acts 22:3). This is our most detailed reference to his more formal ties in Jerusalem. Gamaliel, as it is widely known, was a distinguished rabbi in the first century who was widely respected among members of various religious sects. He came from a prominent family, his grandfather was apparently the famous rabbi Hillel, and his opinions about the interpretation of the law were highly respected. For Paul to have studied under such a revered figure would have been no small honor and would have given him a unique opportunity not only to learn from an expert in the law but to build relationships with a number of prominent religious figures in Jerusalem.

---

3. Some have argued that Paul does not explicitly refer to himself as a Pharisee in Philippians 3:5 and that he was merely suggesting that he followed the law with the same fervor or with the same perspective as that of the Pharisees.

4. Jürgen Becker, *Paul: Apostle to the Gentiles* (Louisville: Westminster John Knox, 1999), 37.

5. Some contemporary scholars find Acts to be of less historical value to the study of Paul's background than Paul's "undisputed" epistles. It is often alleged that while the information contained in Acts is generally reliable, the work should be understood as an apologetic effort to legitimize the Christian faith and that some historical details may not have a solid basis. For a study of Luke's reliability as a historian, see I. Howard Marshall, *Luke: Historian & Theologian* (Downers Grove, IL: InterVarsity Press, 1998); Osvaldo Padilla, *The Acts of the Apostles: Interpretation, History and Theology* (Downers Grove, IL: InterVarsity Press, 2016).

A key historical consideration of relevance to our understanding of Paul's education is his precise age when he relocated to Jerusalem. One's position on this question is often related to whether one places more emphasis on his Greco-Roman or Jewish background and training. Those who emphasize Paul's Jewish background might be inclined to assume that he moved to Jerusalem very early, perhaps as a young teenager, while those who place more emphasis on the Hellenistic character of his writings might find it more likely that he remained in Tarsus for a longer period before moving to Jerusalem. A definite conclusion is difficult to maintain. Based on the language of Acts 22:3, however, it would seem that Paul relocated to Jerusalem fairly early and that he remained in the city for a number of years. The fact that he was "brought up" (*anatrephō*) in Jerusalem would suggest that he spent a considerable amount of his formative years in the city learning from Gamaliel and other religious authorities.

Paul's Post-Conversion Learning

If we are to conclude that Paul moved to Jerusalem as a young man, how might we explain his keen familiarity with the Hellenistic world? Among other things, his writings reveal a solid command of the Greek language and rhetoric, knowledge of the language and ideas associated with the various philosophical schools of thought (especially the Stoics), and the text of the Septuagint. How did Paul become so familiar with Greek culture, one might ask, if he was "brought up" in Jerusalem? Are we to suppose that his knowledge of the Greek world derived entirely from his childhood in Tarsus?

Aside from the fact that Greek culture was much more widespread and pervasive than is sometimes recognized,[6] the fact that Paul spent a considerable number of years ministering in Tarsus *after* his conversion should not be overlooked (see Acts 9:30; 11:25; Gal. 1:21). As will be discussed in Question 5, Paul appears to have spent roughly a decade ministering in and around Tarsus prior to his transition to Antioch at the invitation of Barnabas. As a result, he may have relocated to Jerusalem at a young age and still benefited from a considerable number of years in Tarsus after his conversion, at which time we can assume that he continued to develop many of the intellectual skills that later became apparent in his writings.

Although Paul would have likely profited from the intellectual environment of Tarsus during his childhood, we should not limit his learning and training to the early period of his life. There is often a tacit assumption that Paul's education was limited to the period of his life before he encountered Christ on the road to Damascus, an assumption that may stem from the rather stark separation that is often made in contemporary thought between

---

6. For insight relating to the advancement of Hellenization in the land of Israel, see Martin Hengel, *The 'Hellenization' of Judaea in the First Century after Christ* (London: SCM, 1989).

an individual's education and career. Because of the influence of this perspective, it is natural to make the assumption that Paul took the education he had received at the time of his calling as an apostle—the education he would have received growing up in Tarsus and the more specialized religious training he later received in Jerusalem—and used it to its maximum potential during the second half of his life.

If we are to limit our understanding of education to the more formal sense of the word in which a student is engaged in a prescribed study of a particular subject over a set period of time, then a plausible case could be made that Paul's education was largely, if not entirely, limited to his pre-Christian years. Not to be overlooked, however, is the likelihood that Paul's education and training involved much more than the formal studies he received as a youth. In fact, a persuasive argument could be made that much of Paul's literary abilities and his knowledge of the Greco-Roman world was developed not so much through his formal study as a young student in Tarsus or Jerusalem, but from his interaction with various individuals and cultures throughout his years of apostolic ministry. Much of his learning may have stemmed from unsuspecting places such as his interaction with his companions as he traveled from one location to another or from his study of the various cultures he encountered during his many years of ministry.

Paul seems to have been rather inquisitive, observant, and curious by nature, traits that would have served him well as he traveled throughout the Mediterranean world proclaiming Jesus as the Messiah and ministering among diverse audiences. From the descriptions of his travels in Acts and the content of his writings, it is clear that Paul was a keen observer of culture and that he possessed more than a passing interest in learning what he could about the religious beliefs and cultural practices of the people he sought to reach with the gospel. When in Athens, for example, Paul is said to have carefully observed (*anatheōreō*) the various altars and objects of religious worship (Acts 17:23) and to have engaged with various Epicurean and Stoic philosophers, something average travelers would not find themselves doing. Throughout his writings, we also find Paul reflecting upon the specific beliefs and cultural distinctives of those in several communities.

Summary

Raised in Tarsus by a presumably Greek-speaking family that carefully observed Jewish law and traditions, Paul then spent a number of years in the city of Jerusalem where he received more specialized training and became well-connected to the religious leadership of the city. His education and familiarity with various cultures does not appear to have developed strictly during his more formative years, however. Following his conversion, Paul spent a number of years ministering in his hometown of Tarsus and in other notable cities throughout the Greco-Roman world such as Antioch, Ephesus, and Corinth. Throughout his many years of missionary activity, he continued to expand his knowledge of various cultures and to refine many of the skills that enabled him to effectively communicate the gospel message in a variety of contexts.

REFLECTION QUESTIONS

1. What do we know about the reputation of Tarsus?

2. What unique information about Paul's training is revealed in Acts but absent from his own writings?

3. What are some possible arguments that Paul likely relocated from Tarsus to Jerusalem at an early age?

4. What are some possible arguments that Paul likely relocated from Tarsus to Jerusalem later than is sometimes assumed?

5. In addition to his formal studies, what are some of the ways that Paul may have continued to refine his skills and increase his knowledge of various cultures?

Why Was Paul Trying to Destroy the Church?

A study of the life and ministry of Paul would be incomplete without a consideration of his relentless effort to suppress the Christian movement prior to his life-altering encounter with the risen Christ. Before he was the tireless apostle to the Gentiles, Paul was the persecutor of the church and a passionate defender of the law and Jewish traditions. From the reflections in his own writings, and from the various accounts preserved in Acts, it is evident that Paul was far from indifferent about religious matters prior to this encounter. To the contrary, he built a solid reputation as a zealous defender of the Jewish faith as he actively sought to advance its influence in all spheres of society. As a young and devoted member of the Pharisees, Paul aspired to see the law serve a central role in Jewish life and the people devoting themselves to the ancient traditions as they awaited the fulfillment of God's promises. From his perspective, the Christian movement was a significant obstacle to this vision that could not be left uncontested. To his dismay, many of his countrymen were being drawn away to what he regarded as a dangerous deviation from Judaism that worshiped a false messiah and often placed less emphasis on the role of the law. Before considering in greater detail what Paul found so troubling about the Christian movement and why he found it necessary to suppress its advancement, we will examine our two primary sources of information about Paul's pre-Christian life—Acts and his own writings—for insight relating to his treatment of Christians prior to his conversion.

The New Testament Accounts of Paul's Persecution of the Church

We are introduced in the canonical writings to the apostle Paul in Luke's account of the martyrdom of Stephen (Acts 7). In this account we learn that Paul began to persecute believers fairly soon after Stephen was buried and that his opposition to the church was carefully planned and marked by brutal force and aggression. Luke records that "Saul [Paul] was ravaging the church, and entering house after house," and that "he dragged off men and women and committed them to prison" (Acts 8:3). Not content to simply harass and intimidate the believers in Jerusalem, Paul determined to pursue those who had resettled in Damascus. He was "still breathing threats and murder against the disciples of the Lord," Luke writes, and "went to the high priest and asked him for letters to the synagogues at Damascus, so that if he found any belonging to the Way, men or women, he might bring them bound to Jerusalem" (Acts 9:1–2).

According to Luke's record, the initial followers of Jesus faced strong opposition in Jerusalem with many of the apostles and other prominent figures beaten, imprisoned, publicly rebuked, and continuously threatened by the Jewish authorities. Paul seems to have escalated matters to an even higher degree. Rather than simply supporting measures to limit the spread and growth of the movement in Jerusalem, Paul organized an effort to seek out Christians who had fled Jerusalem and settled elsewhere. The decision to actively suppress the advancement of Christianity in distant locations does not appear to have been shared by all of his contemporaries. His own teacher Gamaliel, for example, famously encouraged his fellow members of the Sanhedrin to abstain from active persecution of the church's leadership. "If this plan or this undertaking is of man," he reasoned "it will fail; but if it is of God, you will not be able to overthrow them" (Acts 5:38–39).

It does not appear that Paul was seeking to apprehend every believer in every city. His mission, rather, seems to have been more targeted in nature. In fact, Luke's account would suggest that much of the persecution that took place shortly after the birth of the church was aimed primarily at those who were Hellenists. Although the persecution of the believers in Jerusalem was clearly intense and widespread, Hellenists such as Stephen appear to have bore the brunt of the oppression. This might explain why the disciples who were from the Hebraic wing of the church were able to continue ministering in Jerusalem after a number of believers from a Hellenistic background were quickly forced out of the city (Acts 8:1). Paul's mission to Damascus, therefore, does not appear to have been designed to actively search for and apprehend anyone who may have been associated with Christianity, but rather to detain Hellenistic believers who had recently relocated from Jerusalem to Damascus to establish a community there. As F. F. Bruce explains:

> It appears there was already in Damascus a community of followers of the Way, with whom the fugitives from Judaea could hope to find refuge. These Damascene disciples were not the subjects of the extradition papers which Paul carried; he may not even have been aware of their presence there. It was the refugees whom he had come to apprehend, no doubt

> hoping that if he could accomplish this purpose satisfactorily
> in Damascus, he could repeat the procedure in foreign cities.[1]

In addition to his brief account of Paul's persecution of the church, Luke also includes several of Paul's speeches, some of which allude to his treatment of the church prior to his conversion. Addressing the crowds in Jerusalem after he was targeted by an angry mob in the temple, Paul recounted that he "persecuted this Way to the death, binding and delivering to prison both men and women," that "the high priest and the whole council of elders can bear me witness," and that it was from these religious authorities that he "received letters . . . [and] journeyed toward Damascus to take those also who were there and bring them in bonds to Jerusalem to be punished" (Acts 22:4–5). Later before Agrippa II, Paul writes that he did "many things in opposing the name of Jesus of Nazareth" (Acts 26:9). This included the imprisonment of believers, an action that had the full backing of the chief priest, and even his support of the death sentence for those found to be associated with the Christian movement (Acts 26:10). Some apparently fled the city to avoid Paul's "raging fury," which led him "even to foreign cities" (Acts 26:11). This final description would seem to comport with the suggestion offered above that Paul was actively engaged in eradicating communities of Hellenistic Christians who had relocated from Jerusalem or elsewhere.

Paul's allusions to his pre-Christian life corresponds well with the brief references found in Acts. Referring to his "former life in Judaism," for example, Paul writes that he "persecuted the church of God violently and tried to destroy it" (Gal. 1:13). Similar language is found in Galatians 1:23 and Acts 9:41, where allusion is made to the reputation of Paul among early communities of believers. In each of these three passages, the verb *portheō* is used, a term that underscores the force used by Paul to suppress the Christian movement. In his epistle to the Philippians, Paul attributes his effort to persecute the church to religious zeal (Phil. 3:6). He was clearly not one who was opposed to religion in general. To the contrary, his religious passion and convictions incited him to oppose those he understood to be a threat. Finally, Paul makes reference to his former life as a persecutor of the church in 1 Timothy 1:13. In this passage, he describes himself as one who "was a blasphemer, persecutor, and insolent opponent." It might be thought somewhat odd that he would describe himself in these ways. In what sense could he be described as a blasphemer considering that he worshiped only the God of Abraham, Isaac, and Jacob? Paul seems to have applied these descriptions not because he worshiped a false God, but because he was hostile to the work of the very God he

---

1. F. F. Bruce, *Paul: Apostle of the Heart Set Free* (Grand Rapids: Eerdmans, 2000), 72–73. Martin Hegel likewise observes that it was Christian Hellenists who were targeted by Paul. See Martin Hegel, *The Pre-Christian Paul* (London: SCM Press, 1991), 72–79, 85–86.

claimed to worship and represent. He was a blasphemer in the sense that he had set himself up in opposition to God's people, and hence God's mission and work on the earth.

Motivating Factors in Paul's Persecution of the Church

The freedom to worship as one pleases is regarded as a fundamental element of a free society, with those who suppress religious freedom often regarded as oppressive or even associated with totalitarian rule. Consequently, making sense of Paul's decision to thwart the spread of Christianity with violent aggression can be a challenge for modern readers. We might admire his religious devotion, but few today would applaud his effort to eradicate another religious movement. It may also seem like a gross contradiction for someone like Paul who was deeply devoted to the law to violently oppose those who did not share his viewpoints. How could his treatment of early Christians not be regarded as a violation of the foundational principle in the law to love one's neighbor (Lev. 19:18)?

In addition to various political and cultural sensibilities that might make it difficult for contemporary readers to make sense of Paul's determination to eliminate the Christian faith, some may find it perplexing why he would have been so opposed to Christianity in the first place. Obviously, Paul rejected the notion that Jesus was the promised Messiah or the Son of God, but would it not have also been the case that he shared several foundational beliefs and practices with early Christians? Christianity was clearly not a faith at variance with Judaism on several fundamental theological matters. In fact, many of the early believers continued to worship in synagogues and to regard their faith in Jesus as compatible, even consistent, with their Jewish beliefs and practices. If he were to persecute any individuals for their faith, why not focus on those promoting pagan beliefs and practices?

Although Paul would have recognized these shared beliefs, he clearly did not regard Christianity as simply one of many Jewish sects or as an innocuous movement known for some eclectic beliefs and practices. To the contrary, he came to regard it more like a cancer or poison capable of causing great harm to the Jewish people. If left unconfronted, Paul was convinced that Christianity would continue to advance and draw many away from the observance of the law and all that he held dear. The Jewish people regarded themselves as God's covenantal people who worshiped the one true God in a prescribed manner while they anticipated the fulfillment of God's covenantal promises. For Paul, each of these central components of Judaism—belief in one God, adherence to the law, and the emphasis on the promises of the covenants—were all directly threatened by Christianity. Aside from the foolishness and blasphemy of worshiping a man like Jesus as a god, such worship, Paul was convinced, would inevitably result in a diminished role of the law and confusion about the fulfillment of God's promises. In sum, all that Paul cherished and all that seemed to be at the heart of his faith were challenged by a fledgling movement that worshiped Jesus and regarded him as the conduit of God's covenantal blessings.

But how could someone like Paul, we might ask, fail to recognize that there was something truly different about Jesus? How could he deny that Jesus was sent from God and that he was no ordinary prophet or rabbi? Paul's fellow Pharisee Nicodemus certainly struggled to reconcile his understanding of Jesus with what he knew about his ministry. Meeting Jesus at night, Nicodemus stated, "Rabbi, we know that you are a teacher come from God, for no one can do these signs that you do unless God is with him" (John 3:2). How could Paul deny what he had heard about Jesus and possibly even observed with his own eyes?[2] What we find in the Gospels is not a denial of Jesus's supernatural miracles. The power and public nature of his mighty works made their reality undeniable. What we find instead is that some of Jesus's opponents attributed them to the power of Satan (see, for example, Matt. 12:24). We cannot be sure if Paul reasoned in this precise way, but he would have undoubtedly been aware of Jesus's reputation as a miracle worker and found the appeal and popularity of Jesus to be alarming.

Despite Jesus's miraculous acts and powerful teaching, the fact that he died upon a Roman cross would have convinced Paul that the basic beliefs of the early Christians were untenable. Such an ignominious death could only lead to two important conclusions about Jesus: that he was cursed by God and that he was not the promised messiah. It was widely anticipated that the coming messiah would successfully establish God's rule and dominion on the earth and defeat Israel's enemies and that the Spirit of the Lord would rest upon him in a unique and undeniable way (see, for example, Isa. 11:1–4 and Dan. 7:13–14). Paul would not have been alone in his perspective that the suffering Jesus experienced at the hands of God's enemies serves as convincing evidence that he was not truly from God. There simply was no room in their thinking for a defeated messiah. As one scholar puts it: "To claim that a man who had died on a cross was the one divinely accredited to lead the nation to salvation would seem to be an intolerable offence to someone who combined nationalist aspirations with zeal for God and his law."[3]

Further, Deuteronomy 21:22–23 contains instruction regarding the removal of a corpse after execution. If a criminal has been put to death, Moses writes, "his body shall not remain all night on the tree." He should be buried that same day because "a hanged man is cursed by God." As Eckhard Schnabel explains, "Saul would have regarded the proclamation of a crucified Messiah

---

2. For a study of the possibility that Paul had observed Jesus's teaching and witnessed certain events in the life of Christ, see Stanley E. Porter, *When Paul Met Jesus: How an Idea Got Lost in History* (Cambridge: Cambridge University Press, 2016).

3. Justin Taylor, "Why Did Paul Persecute the Church?" in *Tolerance and Intolerance in Early Judaism and Christianity*, eds. Graham N. Stanton and Guy G. Stroumsa (Cambridge: Cambridge University Press, 2010), 112.

as utterly despicable, indeed blasphemous. . . . He was convinced that Jesus was under God's curse."[4] Paul notably alludes to this passage in Galatians 3:13, emphasizing that Christ became a curse for his people. For Paul, the idea that Christ was cursed did not change even after his conversion. What he came to understand, of course, is what theologians refer to as the substitutionary atonement, the understanding that Christ bore the curse of sinners upon himself. For Paul, the curse that Christ bore was no longer to be regarded as evidence that Jesus was not from God, but instead as an integral part of his redemptive work, whereby he made salvation possible for his people.

Summary

The New Testament reveals that Paul persecuted the church prior to his encounter with Christ on the road to Damascus. He was especially proactive and deliberate in his attempt to stamp out communities with a high concentration of Christians. Rather than dismissing Christianity as little more than a unique Jewish sect that is best ignored, Paul determined that it posed a serious threat to the Jewish people and was in need of direct confrontation. As one who deeply cherished the law and desired for it to play a central role in Jewish society, Paul became convinced that Christianity leads individuals away from adherence to the law and Jewish traditions to a false hope in one who was cursed by God.

REFLECTION QUESTIONS

1. What does Paul reveal in his writings about his former persecution of Christians?

2. How did Paul's response to the growing threat of Christians differ from that of other Jewish leaders such as Gamaliel?

3. How did some of Jesus's opponents account for his miracles?

4. How did the persecution of the church play a role in its early advancement?

5. What were some of the specific reasons that Paul may have been reluctant to recognize Jesus as the promised Messiah?

---

4. Eckhard J. Schnabel, *Acts*, ZECNT 5 (Grand Rapids: Zondervan, 2012), 395.

Paul's Christian Life

What Do We Know About Paul's Early Years of Ministry?

A significant challenge in the study of Paul's life and ministry is establishing his whereabouts, movements, and activities during the years immediately following his encounter with Christ on the road to Damascus. What exactly was Paul doing during this time? Did he go into relative seclusion for a period as the Lord prepared him for his future work, or did he quickly become active in sharing his new faith in local communities? Unfortunately, we have only limited historical sources that offer relevant information about Paul's early years of ministry. Aside from brief references in his writings to a few events that took place during this period, we are left with only short descriptions in Acts of his activities from the time of his conversion to his missionary journey with Barnabas, a span of roughly fifteen years. As limited as our information may be about the first several years of Paul's Christian life, it is possible to sketch the primary locations in which he served during these early years and some of the major events that transpired. Our brief survey of this evidence will examine the key passages in Acts and the Pauline Epistles and attempt to draw some basic conclusions about Paul's life and ministry in the years following his conversion.[1]

References to Paul's Early Christian Years in the Book of Acts

References to Paul's activities between his conversion and later missionary journey with Barnabas may be found in three locations in Luke's

---

1. Readers interested in exploring the subjects discussed in this chapter in greater depth are encouraged to consult the following studies: Martin Hengel and Anna Maria Schwemer, *Paul between Damascus and Antioch: The Unknown Years* (Louisville: Westminster John Knox Press, 1997); Rainer Riesner, *Paul's Early Period: Chronology, Mission Strategy, Theology* (Grand Rapids: Eerdmans, 1998); Robert Jewett, *A Chronology of Paul's Life* (Philadelphia: Fortress, 1979).

narrative. This includes Acts 9:19b–30, what is by far the most detailed account of the early years of Paul's Christian life, as well as brief references in 11:25–30 and 12:25. Although these accounts provide valuable information regarding Paul's missionary activities, it is difficult to establish a precise chronological framework of the events they describe given that Luke offers few historical references that allow us to date specific events with certainty. As will be seen later in this chapter, the precise manner in which Luke's testimony corresponds to references in the Pauline writings is also a matter of dispute.

Following his account of Paul's conversion (Acts 9:1–19a), Luke makes brief reference to some of Paul's ensuing activities in the cities of Damascus and Jerusalem (9:19b–30). He observes that "for some days" (9:19) Paul was in Damascus where "he proclaimed Jesus in the synagogues" (9:20) and "confounded the Jews" (9:22). After "many days" (9:23), he then became aware of a plot to take his life and escaped the city by being lowered in a basket (9:24–25). Luke then records a journey of Paul to Jerusalem where "he attempted to join the disciples" but encountered resistance (9:26). After Barnabas assuaged the concerns of local believers who were understandably concerned about Paul's intentions, Paul is said to have boldly proclaimed Christ and to have engaged in disputes with local Hellenists (9:27–29). His time in Jerusalem would come to an end when some of the locals sought to take his life (9:29), at which point he departed from the city and returned to his hometown of Tarsus (9:30).

After turning his attention to several events that involved the apostle Peter, Luke provides a few additional references to Paul's early activities in 11:25–30. He records that Barnabas, who at this time was a prominent figure in the church of Antioch, personally traveled to Tarsus to invite Paul to serve with him in Antioch. Paul agreed, and the two served together "for a whole year" (11:26). In addition to Paul's ministry to those in Antioch, Luke reveals that he and Barnabas were part of a delegation sent to Jerusalem to care for impoverished believers who were suffering from a severe famine (11:27–30). Luke situates this journey in the "days of Claudius" (11:28), a reference of limited insight given that the reign of Claudius spanned nearly fourteen years. Finally, Luke refers to the completion of this mission in 12:25, noting that John Mark relocated to Antioch at this time from Jerusalem, presumably to work alongside Paul and Barnabas.

References to Paul's Early Christian Years in the Pauline Epistles

References in Paul's writings to the early years of his Christian life are few in number and appear only in contexts in which Paul sensed a need to defend his apostolic calling and authority. We have nothing that resembles an autobiographical account, only brief allusions to his early years of ministry that are designed to emphasize the fact that he was commissioned directly by Christ to serve as an apostle and that his authority was not conferred upon him by other Christian leaders. There are two passages of particular relevance to our study of Paul's early years: Galatians 1:11–2:14 and 2 Corinthians 11:32–33.

The Galatians passage is of unique importance as Paul provides something of a timeline of several of the events that took place in the years following his conversion. In seeking to defend his apostolic authority from his Jewish opponents, Paul briefly refers to some of his early travels and activities. On the one hand, his account is designed to separate himself from the other apostles. He does so by demonstrating that his interaction with them was sporadic, limited, and that he related to them as equals, not as one of their disciples or assistants. On the other hand, he sought to clarify that he was not a maverick apostle whose teaching was inconsistent from that of the Twelve. In other words, Paul sought to establish that his apostolic authority derived from Christ alone but that he proclaimed the same gospel message as that of his fellow apostles. For the sake of brevity, we may briefly sketch the key events described by Paul in this passage as follows:

- A journey to "Arabia" and a return to Damascus in the period shortly after his conversion (1:17).
- A journey to Jerusalem "after three years" in which he visited Peter and James, the brother of Jesus, over a period of fifteen days (1:18–19).
- Ministry in "the regions of Syria and Cilicia" over an unspecified period of time (1:21).
- A subsequent journey to Jerusalem that took place "after fourteen years" in which he was joined by Barnabas and Titus (2:1). This journey resulted in a favorable reception among the apostles (2:9) who encouraged them to "remember the poor" (2:10).
- An occasion in Antioch in which he confronted Peter over his treatment of Gentile believers (2:11–14).

Several difficult questions relate to the details in this passage. What was he doing in "Arabia" and where was this location? How are the references to the spans of three years and fourteen years to be understood? Just how many trips did Paul make to Jerusalem? Finally, does the journey to Jerusalem described in Galatians 2:1–10 correspond to a specific journey described in Acts? We will briefly explore these types of questions below. Before we do so, however, we must note one additional passage in the Pauline corpus that refers to Paul's early activities.

In 2 Corinthians 11:32–33 Paul refers to an occasion in which he was forced to flee Damascus in order to escape from King Aretas, who was, as Paul recounts, "guarding the city . . . in order to seize me" (11:32).[2] The ruler named

---

2. A recent historical novel attempts to reconstruct what may be known of Paul's ministry in Arabia. See Ben Witherington III and Jason A. Myers, *Paul of Arabia: The Hidden Years of*

Aretas is not especially well-known today, but he played a consequential role in several of the political developments of this time. Aretas IV Philopatris was a Nabataean king from around 9 BCE until his death at some point around 39 or 40 CE. Around 36 or 37 CE, he occupied Damascus and other nearby areas, a provocative act of aggression that served in large part as retaliation for Herod Antipas's divorce from his daughter Phasaelis.[3] It will be recalled that Antipas divorced Phasaelis in order to marry Herodias, the sister of Agrippa I and niece of Philip I (also known as Herod II), a marriage that was famously denounced by John the Baptist (see Matt. 14:1–12; Mark 6:14–29).

Paul found himself in a precarious situation in Damascus and was fortunate enough to have escaped from the city (Acts 9:23–25 and 2 Cor. 11:32–33). When Paul's account is read alongside of Luke's narrative, we find that he was the target of a number of Jews and of Aretas during his brief time in the city. The reference to the event in 2 Corinthians helpfully provides us with a chronological reference point for when his second visit Damascus must have taken place, while also indicating that Paul was well-known to the Nabataean king. Paul does not appear to have been just one of many Jews who found himself caught in a tense political situation. We find, rather, that Aretas had actually targeted Paul and sought to apprehend him. This would suggest that Paul had been in the area of Nabataea at some point and that his presence in Damascus had become known. By this time, Paul had established a reputation among the Jews and the Nabataeans for his bold proclamation of the gospel. As will be suggested below, his ministry to the Nabataeans likely took place during Paul's time in "Arabia" (Gal. 1:17).

A Provisional Chronology of Paul's Early Travels and Ministry

Now that we have briefly surveyed the relevant passages in the New Testament that offer insight related to Paul's activities and travels during the early years of his Christian life, we may attempt to harmonize these passages and establish a basic chronological framework. While several conclusions related to the background of Paul's early Christian years cannot be made with full certainty and remain a matter of scholarly debate, we will attempt to sketch what may be known of the period of Paul's life from his conversion to his first major missionary journey with Barnabas during the late 40s.

- *Conversion of Paul (33/34 CE)*—This date assumes that Paul's conversion took place soon (i.e., within roughly a year) after Jesus's

---

the *Apostle to the Gentiles* (Eugene, OR: Cascade Books, 2020). For additional treatment of this period, see the resources in the preceding footnote as well as the following articles: Martin Hengel, "Paul in Arabia," *BBR* 12 (2002): 47–66; Jerome Murphy-O'Connor, "Paul in Arabia," *CBQ* 55 (1993): 732–37.

3.   Josephus provides the relevant background of this event in *Antiquities* 18.5.1–3 (Feldman, LCL 433).

resurrection when the church was still largely confined to Jerusalem and in its infancy. It is also based upon the likelihood that the death and resurrection of Jesus took place in the spring of 33 CE, a conclusion that is arguably most consistent with the New Testament evidence.

- *Initial Visit to Damascus (33/34 CE)*—The events recorded in Acts 9:19b–22 appear to have occurred shortly after Paul's conversion. During his visit, Paul passionately proclaimed the gospel in Damascus to what appears to have been a primarily Jewish audience.

- *Ministry in Arabia (33/34–36/37 CE)*—Following his conversion and early proclamation of the gospel in Damascus, Paul indicates that he spent around three years in Arabia (Gal. 1:17–18).[4] "Arabia" was not a specific nation or city, but a broad territory to the east of the land of Israel. During Paul's lifetime, much of this region was controlled by the Nabataean kingdom, a kingdom which ruled a significant portion of the territory located in modern Syria, Jordan, and Saudi Arabia. It would seem, therefore, that Paul visited this region for a significant period of time after his conversion and that he managed to irritate the local authorities in the process. This would explain his need to escape from Damascus after Aretas had taken control of the city. Contrary to the frequent claim made in popular literature, Paul does not indicate that his time in Arabia was focused on meditation and training for future ministry as he lived in relative isolation. It would seem, rather, that he was quite active in proclaiming Christ as the risen messiah in the years immediately following his conversion.

- *Subsequent Visit to Damascus (37 CE)*—Based on the historical background discussed above, Paul appears to have returned to Damascus around the time of Aretas's excursion into the city that took place around 37 CE. Because reference is made to Paul being lowered in a basket in both Acts 9:23–25 and 2 Corinthians 11:32–33, it would appear that both passages refer to the same event. Luke therefore seems to juxtapose two separate visits to Damascus in Acts 9:19b–25, the first taking place shortly after his conversion, and the second taking place "after many days had passed" (9:23). It is suggested here that the "many days" covered a span of roughly three or four years, a period that would have included his time in Arabia.

---

4. Scholars differ as to how the reference to "three years" in Galatians 1:18 should be interpreted. Should this be understood as three years from the time he returned from Arabia, or three years from his initial conversion and ministry in the city of Damascus? The most natural reading is arguably that the three years initiated with the events outlined in vv. 15–16, that is, his conversion.

- *Initial Visit to Jerusalem (37 CE)*—Following his ministry in Arabia/ Nabataea and his subsequent escape from Damascus, Paul journeyed to Jerusalem where he met with Peter and James, the brother of Jesus, over a span of fifteen days (Gal. 1:18–20). It is likely that this visit coincides with the visit Luke recounts in Acts 9:26–30 and which Paul alludes to in his address to the crowds in Jerusalem years later (Acts 22:17–21).
- *Ministry in Cilicia and Syria (37–48/49 CE)*—After Paul was forced to flee Jerusalem (Acts 9:26–30), he spent several years ministering in his hometown of Tarsus in the province of Cilicia (Acts 9:30; Gal. 1:21) before relocating to the province of Syria where he ministered primarily in Antioch. This is corroborated by Luke's reference to Barnabas traveling to Tarsus to recruit Paul (Acts 11:25) and their subsequent ministry together "for a whole year" in Antioch (Acts 11:26). Paul thus seems to have spend a bit more than a decade ministering primarily in Tarsus following his escape from Damascus and brief journey to Jerusalem around 37 CE.
- *Relief Offering to Jerusalem (47/48 CE)*—Paul observes that he made a subsequent trip to Jerusalem "after fourteen years" (Gal. 2:1). How these years are to be measured is a matter of dispute, but, like the reference to the "three years" in Galatians 1:18, it would appear likely that the reference point is to be understood as Paul's conversion and that roughly fourteen years transpired between this event, which we have provisionally dated to around 33 or 34 CE, and a subsequent journey to Jerusalem that would have taken place around 47 or 48 CE, a bit before he set out on his first major missionary journey with Barnabas. We may further infer that this journey to Jerusalem took place at some point during the year in which Paul was serving with Barnabas in Antioch (Acts 11:26).

Many scholars argue that the journey described in Galatians 2:1–10 is best understood as a reference to the Jerusalem Council, an event described in some detail by Luke (Acts 15:1–35). This is certainly possible, though the details in Paul's account seem to better correspond to the journey described in Acts 11:27–30, the journey in which Paul and Barnabas were sent by the church in Antioch to Jerusalem to "send relief to the brothers living in Judea" (Acts 11:29). Paul's reference to the admonishment he received to "remember the poor" is certainly consistent with this interpretation, as is the encouragement he was given to preach among the Gentiles. Among other things, we might also note that the visits recorded in Galatians 2 and Acts 11 were both preceded by some type of revelation (Gal. 2:2; Acts 11:27–28). It would also seem less likely that the apostles would have felt compelled to encourage Paul to "go to the Gentiles" after the first missionary journey.

Summary

This chapter has analyzed passages in the book of Acts and the Pauline Epistles that make reference to Paul's activities and whereabouts during the years following his conversion. The biblical accounts suggest that Paul quickly engaged in evangelistic activities after his conversion and that he had faithfully ministered in a number of locations by the time he arrived in Antioch just prior to his missionary journey with Barnabas. Neither Acts nor the Pauline Epistles provide comprehensive information about the first several years of Paul's Christian life, but they correspond well to one another and provide enough detail to construct a basic picture of Paul's activities during this time.

REFLECTION QUESTIONS

1. What are some of the challenges of reconciling Paul's accounts of his early ministry with the accounts recorded in Acts?

2. In your view, how plausible is the common assumption that Paul spent the first several years after his conversion in relative isolation as God prepared him for future ministry?

3. To what degree do you find the nature of Paul's ministry in the early years of his Christian life to be similar to that of his ministry in later years?

4. From your perspective, is Paul's journey to Jerusalem described in Galatians 2:1–10 more likely to correspond to the Jerusalem Council (Acts 15:1–35) or to the previous visit in which he delivered a relief offering collected by those in Antioch (Acts 11:27–30)?

5. How might we describe Paul's relationship to the apostles and key figures in Jerusalem in the years following his conversion?

What Major Events and Developments Are Associated with Paul's First Missionary Journey?

The previous chapter explored what may be known of the early years of Paul's ministry, the period stretching from his conversion around 33 CE to his arrival in Antioch in the late 40s. Although our knowledge of Paul's whereabouts and ministry during this time is limited, the brief allusions in his writings and in Acts to his activities during these years reveal that he had been engaged in missionary work for several years prior to being sent out with Barnabas by the church of Antioch. By the time of this journey, Paul had been a follower of Christ for roughly fifteen years and had considerable experience ministering to both Jews and Gentiles and in a variety of locations such as Arabia (Gal. 1:17), Cilicia (Acts 11:25; Gal. 1:21), and Syria (Acts 11:25; Gal. 1:17).

In this chapter, we will continue to trace Paul's missionary activities, focusing on the so-called "first missionary journey," a journey described in considerable detail by Luke; as well as his involvement in the Jerusalem Council, a notable event that took place soon after his return to Antioch. It should be understood, of course, that we only refer to this particular missionary excursion as the "first" journey because it is the first of three major journeys described in detail by Luke. Most of what is known of Paul's activities during this period derives from Luke's accounts in Acts 13–15, though occasional allusions to certain events and activities from this time also appear in Paul's writings.[1] As a result, this chapter will focus primarily on Luke's account.

---

1. For the sake of brevity, only a cursory summary of Paul's three major missionary journeys is offered in this volume. More thorough overviews may be found in the large number of introductory works to Paul's writings, commentaries on the book of Acts, Bible atlases, and general introductions to the New Testament. In addition to these types of resources,

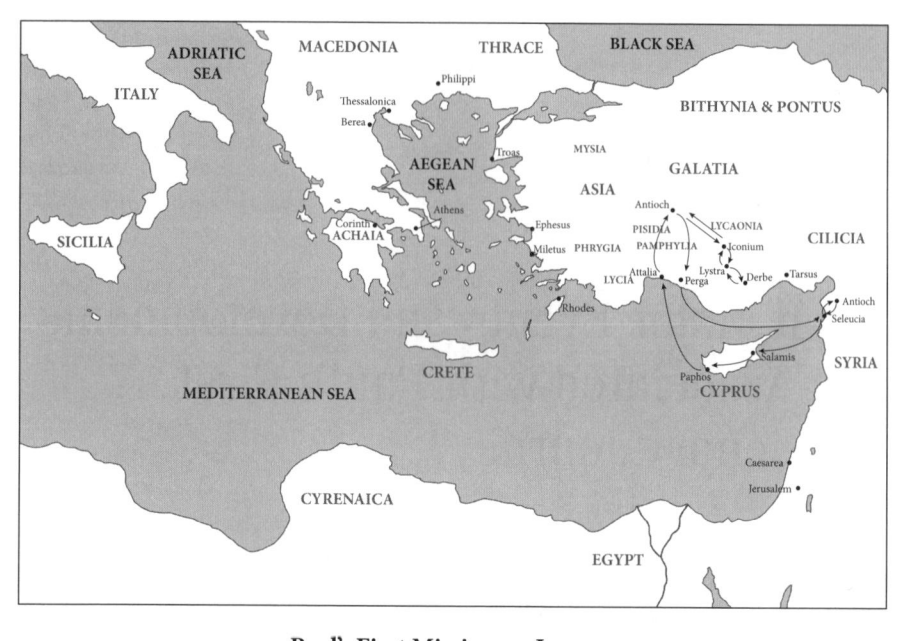

Paul's First Missionary Journey

The First Missionary Journey (c. 48–49 CE)

By the time Paul departed on this journey, he had been active in the churches of Antioch serving alongside of Barnabas for, as Luke records, "a whole year" (Acts 11:26). He appears to have been very active during this time and had even built a reputation among one of the city's "prophets and teachers" (Acts 13:1). Luke also reveals that both Paul and Barnabas represented the church of Antioch when they traveled to Jerusalem to deliver a relief offering that the church had collected for the impoverished "brothers living in Judea" (Acts 11:29–30; 12:25). Based on these brief descriptions, it is evident that Paul served in various capacities during this time and that he had become a well-known figure among Christians in Antioch.

Having already sent a delegation to Judea to minister to those suffering from a famine (Acts 11:27–30), the leadership in Antioch was prompted by the Spirit to send out Paul and Barnabas to proclaim the good news in regions outside of Syria (Acts 13:2–4). Soon thereafter, the two departed with

the following volumes offer helpful background information relating to Paul's missionary journeys: Charles L. Quarles, *Illustrated Life of Paul* (Nashville: B&H, 2014); Peter Walker, *In the Steps of Saint Paul: An Illustrated Guide to Paul's Journeys* (Oxford: Lion Hudson, 2011); William M. Ramsay, *St. Paul The Traveler and Roman Citizen*, ed. Mark Wilson (Grand Rapids: Kregel, 2001); David Bomar, ed., *Journeys of the Apostle Paul* (Bellingham, WA: Lexham, 2019); Alan S. Bandy, *An Illustrated Guide to the Apostle Paul: His Life, Ministry, and Missionary Journeys* (Grand Rapids: Baker, 2021).

John Mark (Acts 13:5), a cousin of Barnabas (Col. 4:10) who had likely left a favorable impression on Paul during their journey to Jerusalem (Acts 12:25). Barnabas, of course, played an important role in Paul's early missionary career by introducing him to the apostles (Acts 9:26–27) and believers in various locations before making a personal appeal for him to relocate to Antioch. The two had already traveled together, not only from Tarsus to Antioch, but from Antioch to Jerusalem and back.

It is unclear exactly how much planning for the journey took place prior to their departure, though it would seem that they had developed a basic idea of the general areas they intended to visit. Traveling was not as convenient during the first century as it is today, making it necessary to have a basic sense of where one intended to travel, how this was to be accomplished, and when it was to take place (sailing during the winter months was not advised!). Luke records that Paul and Barnabas first traveled to Cyprus (Acts 13:4–12), the native land of Barnabas (Acts 4:36), before traveling to the southern regions of Asia Minor. Cyprus, a large island in the eastern Mediterranean, was home to a sizable Jewish population and had been a Roman province for many years by this time. The island is unlikely to have been Paul's primary focal point of this journey as it was a relatively short distance from Antioch by sea and could therefore be evangelized fairly easily from there. The fact that there are no further records of Paul visiting the island after this journey would support the conclusion that this area was not the primary focus of his mission journey with Barnabas. He likely visited the island simply because it was conveniently located on the way to Asia Minor and perhaps because of Barnabas's personal connection to the region.

The small missionary team first ministered in the synagogues of the eastern port city of Salamis before traversing the entire island by foot and arriving at the western city of Paphos (Acts 13:4–12). It was here that they were challenged by a false prophet named Bar-Jesus who sought to undermine their work. The false prophet was strongly rebuked by Paul and was stricken blind, a somewhat ironic development considering the events surrounding Paul's personal conversion. Despite this opposition, the proconsul Sergius Paulus embraced the message Paul and Barnabas proclaimed and became a believer. Luke is known to place an emphasis in his writings on the conversion of a number of those in society who were oppressed, marginalized, or came from humble backgrounds. The conversion of the proconsul, however, reminds the reader that the gospel message is for all members of society and that the kingdom of God is continually advancing despite the spiritual opposition that God's people may encounter.

Following their excursion through Cyprus, Paul and his companions made their way to the southern regions of Asia Minor, home to several cities that had not previously been the focus of an organized effort to advance the gospel. This portion of the journey certainly did not begin well. After sailing from Paphos and arriving at Perga, a town a short distance from the port of Attalia (modern Antalya), John Mark abandoned the mission and returned to Jerusalem (Acts 13:13). Luke does not indicate what may have led to Mark's departure, but there is nothing to indicate that he experienced some type of spiritual crisis. A short time later we find that he was intent on rejoining his companions on a subsequent journey (Acts 15:37), hardly a sign that he had permanently abandoned his faith or lost interest in missionary service altogether. It is possible that Mark was simply fatigued—perhaps spiritually and physically—and that he did not believe he was prepared for the arduous journey to the north. We might suspect he had good intentions and that he joined his cousin Barnabas and Paul with a sincere desire to take part in the work but later became convinced that he was not up to the rigorous nature of the mission. By this point he had already journeyed through the island of Cyprus and would have understandably been weary. Consequently, he may have simply come to the decision at Perga that it would be unwise for him to continue. This would have been his last convenient opportunity to return to Jerusalem before making the long journey north to Antioch of Pisidia, a trip of well over 150 miles on the common routes used at this time.

Undeterred by Mark's decision to abandon the mission, Paul and Barnabas traveled north to minister in several of the prominent cities located in south central Asia Minor (Acts 13:13–14:28). Notable events that took place during this period included an address in the synagogue of Pisidian Antioch which resulted in the conversion of several Jews as well as strong opposition from those who rejected his message (Acts 13:13–52). Paul's address shares a number of similarities with the address of Stephen recorded in Acts 7. Both addresses refer to events from Israel's history and encourage listeners to recognize Jesus as the source of God's blessings to his people. Through Jesus, Paul proclaimed, "everyone who believes is freed from everything from which you could not be freed by the law of Moses" (Acts 13:39). This was quite an assertion from a Pharisee who had devoted himself from an early age to following the law!

As a result of the strong reaction his address provoked among many of the local Jews, Paul and Barnabas determined to begin focusing much of their efforts on Gentile audiences (Acts 13:46). Paul continued to minister to Jewish audiences for many years to come, of course, but not exclusively. His typical practice from this point was to proclaim Christ in Jewish settings and then turn his attention to the Gentiles once the message was rejected. Their displeasure in the response of the Jews was graphically demonstrated by their shaking the dust off their feet (Acts 13:51), a symbolic gesture that is also referred to in the Synoptic Gospels (see Matt. 10:14; Mark 6:11; and Luke 9:5). The Jewish people would often shake the dust from their feet when leaving Gentile territory and entering the land of Israel. In the Gospels and Acts, we find the Twelve and Paul shaking the dust off their feet not as a picture of derision for the Gentile world, but in response to the rejection of the gospel.

Angered by the preaching of Paul and Barnabas, many of the Jewish people forced them out of the city, at which point the two journeyed to the cities to the southeast. Luke records their proclamation of the gospel in the cities of Iconium (Acts 14:1–7), Lystra (Acts 14:8–20), and Derbe (Acts 14:20–21). A similar sequence of events took place in Iconium that had previously occurred in Antioch with Paul and Barnabas proclaiming Christ in the local synagogue and receiving a mixed response. While some believed, opposition became violent, once again forcing Paul and Barnabas to leave the area. Luke then describes the harsh treatment the two experienced after arriving in Lystra. After Paul had miraculously healed a disabled man who had never walked, the two were confused by the local population for the Greek gods Hermes and Zeus. Legends and myths about various gods appearing in human form were not unusual in the Greek world, and this was apparently the case in the region of Lycaonia. This mistaken response, however, was short-lived as their Jewish opponents arrived and once again incited the people to turn against them. The opposition to Paul had only intensified by this point and Paul was even stoned by his opponents and presumed dead. Luke then records that Paul was revived after "the disciples gathered around him" (Acts 14:20) and that he departed the next day with Barnabas for the city of Derbe where they continued the mission.

Following the tumultuous events that took place in this region, Paul and Barnabas decided to retrace their steps and return to the cities in Asia Minor where they had previously visited, "strengthening the souls of the disciples," and "encouraging them to continue in the faith" (Acts 14:22). Luke further notes that Paul and Barnabas appointed elders in each city during their return visits, an action designed to ensure the long-term stability of the newly established churches. The journey then concluded with a return to Antioch of Syria where they reported to the local believers "all that God had done with them, and how he had opened a door of faith to the Gentiles" (Acts 14:27). Years after these events took place, Paul wrote the following to Timothy, a native of Lystra: "You, however, have followed my teaching, my conduct, my aim in life, my faith, my patience, my love, my steadfastness, my persecutions and sufferings that happened to me at Antioch, at Iconium, and at Lystra—which persecutions I endured; yet from them all the Lord rescued me" (2 Tim. 3:10–11). He also reflected in his earlier epistle to the Galatians on how he proclaimed the gospel during this time despite suffering some type of physical ailment (Gal. 4:13). Paul never forgot the intense opposition he faced in these regions or the many trials he endured. Even more importantly, he did not forget the Lord's provision for him as he proclaimed the good news in very difficult environments.

Paul's Involvement in the Jerusalem Council

Luke records that a major controversy enveloped the church after Paul and Barnabas concluded their first missionary journey and had made their way back to Antioch (Acts 15:1–35). Essentially, a number of Jewish believers were adamant that Gentile converts were obliged to be circumcised and to follow the law of Moses. The fact that such a viewpoint was a matter of controversy may seem difficult for many to understand today. So widely recognized in post-Reformation Christianity is the understanding that salvation is by faith alone that it can be difficult for modern Christians to understand how or why the controversy over the relationship between Gentile converts and the law had become so controversial. For many centuries, however, the relationship between God's people and the law was perceived to be inexorably connected. It was widely understood that the covenants belong to Abraham's descendants (see Rom. 9:3–5) and that the law served as the means by which one's membership in the covenantal community was maintained and demonstrated. Gentiles could certainly become part of the covenantal community, but assimilation into Judaism was expected. This is why there was often a strong emphasis on circumcision. One did not become a Jew simply through personal faith, of course. One had to first receive the rite of circumcision, after which there was the expectation to live according to the law.

As might be expected, serious conflict ensued between those who viewed the role of the law in this traditional sense, and those like Paul who insisted that "Christ is the end of the law for righteousness to everyone who believes" (Rom. 10:4).[2] This controversy led to Paul and Barnabas's involvement after they had returned from the first missionary journey in what has come to be known as the Jerusalem Council.[3] Luke recounts that Paul traveled with Barnabas and several others from Antioch to Jerusalem where they met with the apostles and elders to "consider this matter" (Acts 15:6). After extensive discussion and hearing the reports of large numbers of Gentiles who had come to the faith, those in attendance voiced their agreement that God's promise of Gentiles becoming part of his people was being fulfilled (Acts 15:12–18). It was during this time that James, the brother of the Lord and a key leader of the church in Jerusalem, addressed those present and expressed his agreement that "we should not trouble those of the Gentiles who turn to God" (Acts 15:19). Luke then records that a letter was composed by the council that was to circulate among the Gentile believers in various communities in Syria and Cilicia. Contemporary readers may be somewhat puzzled by the request to abstain from the four practices that are referred to in the letter. Quite notably, none of the more culturally unique practices associated with the law

---

2. For additional treatment on Paul's perspective of the law, see Question 30 and Thomas R. Schreiner, *40 Questions about the Christian and the Law* (Grand Rapids: Kregel, 2010), 35–39.
3. It would also seem that the false teaching that led to this journey was not limited to the cities of Syria. As will be discussed more fully in Question 12, Paul appears to have written his first canonical work, the Epistle to the Galatians, shortly after he returned from ministering to the churches in Asia Minor.

are mentioned (e.g., Sabbath observance, circumcision, the observance of ko-sher, etc.). Gentile believers are simply encouraged to abstain from specific practices that would have needlessly offended Jewish sensibilities. It is likely significant that each of the stipulations were associated either with paganism in general (sexual immorality, most notably) or more specifically to pagan worship. It has also been observed that each of the stipulations correspond to instruction in the law that relates to Gentiles living in the land of God's people (see Lev. 17–18).

Summary

This chapter has surveyed the first major missionary journey of Paul re-corded in the book of Acts and key developments that took place upon his return. Paul was joined on this journey by Barnabas, and the two were sent out by the church of Antioch to proclaim the gospel and establish churches in Cyprus and several cities in Asia Minor. The opposition they experienced during this time was intense, yet they consistently modeled faithfulness and a reliance upon God's provision. After returning to Antioch, Paul and Barnabas participated in the Jerusalem Council, a landmark event that addressed the question of whether Gentile converts were obliged to follow the law of Moses. After much discussion, it was evident to all who were present that Gentile believers are not to be burdened with the expectation to follow the Jewish law.

REFLECTION QUESTIONS

1. In your view, does Paul's relationship with the church in Antioch provide a model for the relationship between missionaries and the local church?

2. What do you think best accounts for Mark's decision to abandon Paul and Barnabas on the first missionary journey?

3. What might we learn about Paul's missionary strategy from his ministry in Cyprus and Asia Minor?

4. What was the major controversy that led to the Jerusalem Council?

5. What do you believe is the best explanation for the specific prohibitions placed on Gentiles by the Jerusalem Council?

What Major Events and Developments Are Associated with Paul's Second and Third Missionary Journeys?

Following their meeting with the apostles and elders in Jerusalem, Paul sensed a need to revisit the believers in the cities he and Barnabas had visited during their recent journey to Asia Minor (Acts 15:36). After the recent controversy over the relationship between Gentile believers and the law, Paul was understandably concerned that many of the recent Gentile converts were in need of further instruction, guidance, and encouragement. Although Paul and Barnabas shared the desire to revisit the cities of Asia Minor, they were hampered by a heated disagreement over whether it was in their best interest for John Mark to rejoin them. Luke records that Barnabas was keen on Mark taking part on their second journey, while Paul was adamantly opposed to the idea (Acts 15:36–41). Barnabas, we might infer, was convinced that Mark was regretful for his premature departure to Jerusalem and that he was now fully committed to the mission. Paul, on the other hand, was much more cautious and appears to have been opposed to the prospect of partnering with someone of questionable commitment or reliability. As a consequence of this disagreement, the two determined to go their different ways and lead separate missions. We find that Barnabas and Mark set off at this time to Cyprus and perhaps elsewhere, and that Paul was joined by Silas, an individual briefly introduced by Luke as a prophet and early leader of the church in Jerusalem (Acts 15:22, 32). Luke's narrative then traces the journeys of Paul and Silas, while Barnabas no longer appears in his account.[1]

---

1. Paul refers to Barnabas in 1 Corinthians (1 Cor. 9:6), a letter that would have been written after the division recorded in Acts 15 took place. However, it is unlikely that this reference indicates that Barnabas was serving alongside of Paul at this time. Paul most likely made

The Second Missionary Journey (c. 50–52/53; Acts 15:36–18:22)

Traveling by land instead of by sea as he did in the first journey, Paul set out with Silas from Antioch through Cilicia, presumably through Paul's hometown of Tarsus, and then on to the communities such as Derbe, Lystra, Iconium, and Antioch of Pisidia where Paul had previously visited. In Lystra he was joined by a young believer named Timothy who would serve with him for many years (Acts 16:1–5). At this point we learn from Luke that the Spirit directed Paul and his companions to make their way to the northwestern regions of modern Turkey rather than directly west through the province of Asia to Ephesus where Paul was intent on ministering (16:6). There was also an attempt during this time to travel to Bithynia, a region to the north of the cities where he previously ministered. The Spirit rejected this effort as well, Luke records, and continued to direct their movements in ways they did not previously anticipate (16:7). Seeking the Lord's direction in the coastal city of Troas, Paul received a vision that set the course of his travels for the next several years. In his vision, Paul encountered a man from Macedonia, a province in the northern regions of modern Greece, who was imploring Paul to "Come over to Macedonia and help us" (16:9). Recognizing the vision as a divine directive, Paul, Silas, and Timothy journeyed west into Macedonia where they continued the mission.

Traveling from city to city on the Via Egnatia, Paul and his companions ministered in the cities of Neapolis, Philippi, Thessalonica, and Berea, with Luke focusing the majority of his attention on the events that transpired in Philippi and Thessalonica. In Philippi, a local church was formed after Paul encountered a small number of Jewish women praying outside of the city. One of those who was converted was Lydia, a woman of some means who invited Paul and his companions to lodge in her home (Acts 16:11–15). Despite some initial success, Paul and Silas were treated harshly by the city's leaders after Paul exorcised "a spirit of divination" (16:16) from a slave girl who made a profit for her master by fortune-telling. This resulted in Paul and Silas being publicly beaten and incarcerated in a Philippian jail. Luke then writes that they were miraculously delivered from their imprisonment by a divinely orchestrated earthquake, an event that led to the conversion of the jailer (16:16–40). As a bit of a surprise to readers, Luke recounts that it was only after this miraculous event that Paul and Silas revealed their Roman citizenship to the authorities, a status which came with certain protections that had been violated. After the authorities quietly sought to distance themselves from the events that had taken place, Paul demanded that he and his companions be publicly escorted out of the city, a gesture that would have only been a reasonable accommodation after the public humiliation and mistreatment they had recently endured. Paul's ultimate concern, it should be understood, was not ultimately personal honor,

---

reference to Barnabas on this occasion simply because he, like Paul, had a reputation for working with his own hands to cover his expenses.

but the advancement of the gospel, a concern that is evident in his later epistle to those in this city. Many of the locals would have been inclined to view the gospel message in an unfavorable light given the ways that Paul and Silas were publicly mocked and humiliated. Paul's demand for a public escort out of the city was largely motivated, it would seem, by the desire to publicly restore the credibility of the message they proclaimed.

After departing Philippi, opposition continued in Thessalonica where Paul and Silas proclaimed the gospel in a synagogue for three consecutive Sabbaths (Acts 17:1–9). In addition to a number of Jews, the converts in Thessalonica included "a great many of the devout Greeks and not a few of the leading women" (17:4). This led to fierce opposition from the local Jews who stirred up the crowds and formed a mob. Local believers such as Jason were charged with sedition, a very serious charge, and found themselves in a precarious situation. Out of concern for their safety, Paul and his companions were encouraged to leave by night. Although the opposition they experienced in Thessalonica was intense, the message Paul and Silas proclaimed had taken root and another new community of believers was established.

Following his brief visit in Berea (Acts 17:10–15), Paul traveled alone to the city of Athens where he delivered his famous address on Mars Hill before a gathering of Epicurean and Stoic philosophers (17:16–34). He used the occasion to introduce those in attendance to the one creator God and to encourage them to repent and turn to him before the day of judgment. Reaction to his message was mixed. A number of those present embraced the message, some seemed inquisitive but ultimately indecisive, while others rejected his message as foolishness (17:32–34). The resistance he experienced in Athens certainly did not take the violent form that it did in Macedonia, though some mocked his message—his claim in the resurrection in particular—and belittled his learning, dismissing him as one who babbles about matters he does not fully understand (17:18).

From Athens, Paul journeyed westward to the famous city of Corinth where he spent eighteen months ministering and establishing the church (Acts 18:1–17). The challenges associated with evangelizing unbelievers and training those who came out of a pagan background were substantial, but Paul understood the value of establishing a vibrant church in a city of such great commercial, cultural, and religious importance as Corinth. During his time in the city, Paul penned the two Thessalonian epistles, worked alongside believers such as Aquila and Priscilla, witnessed the conversion of prominent individuals such as Crispus, the synagogue ruler (18:8), and continued to preach the gospel despite facing continual resistance from his Jewish opponents. The Jews even made an attempt to have the proconsul Gallio convict him of a crime, an attempt that was unsuccessful. Following his lengthy ministry in Corinth, Paul returned once again to Antioch, where Luke simply records that he spent "some time" (18:23).

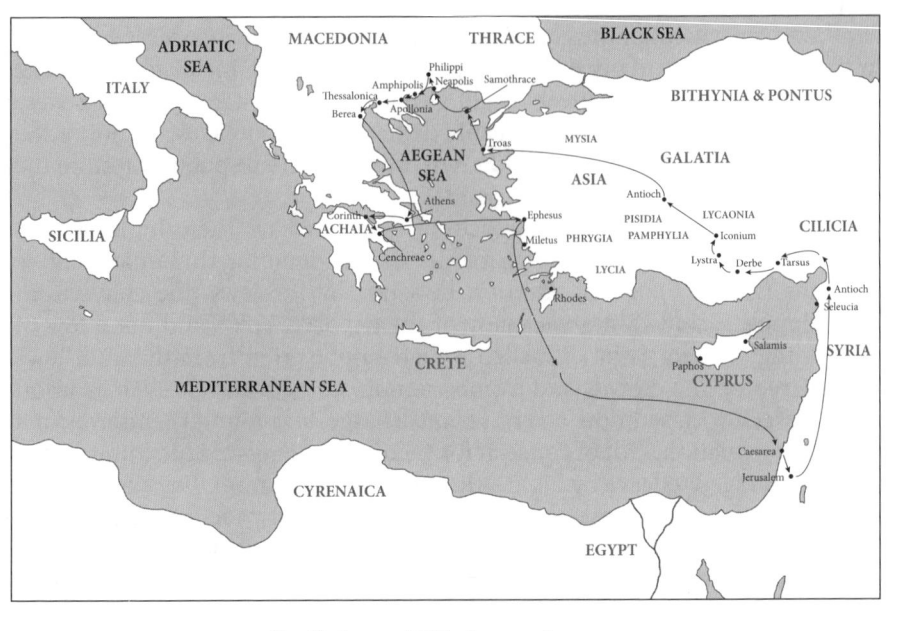

Paul's Second Missionary Journey

The Third Missionary Journey (c. 52/53–57/58; Acts 18:23–21:16)

What is now known as Paul's third missionary journey was the longest of the three major journeys recorded by Luke. This journey provided an opportunity for Paul to revisit many of the locations he had previously visited in Asia Minor, Macedonia, and Achaia. A high point of this period of Paul's life was his ministry in Ephesus. Unlike the second journey in which the Spirit did not permit Paul to spend extensive time in this important city, he was able to spend more than two full years ministering here during this period. Prior to this occasion, he had only made a brief stop in Ephesus on his way back to Antioch at the end of the second journey (Acts 18:19–21). His time in Ephesus, the well-known home of the Artemision, included three months of teaching in a Jewish synagogue, instruction in public settings, and intense periods of spiritual warfare. He was later forced to abruptly leave the city when a local association (*collegium*) of silversmiths incited a riot against the local Christians. As Luke makes clear, the silversmiths regarded the Christian movement as a threat to their livelihood (19:24–27).

To understand Paul's movements and activities after departing Ephesus, it is helpful to be aware of his relationship with the Corinthian church. When Luke's account is read alongside of Paul's reflections in 2 Corinthians, we find that Paul was greatly concerned about the situation in Corinth during his lengthy period of ministry in Ephesus. As noted above, the challenges of ministry in Corinth were great, as many of the believers came out of a life of paganism and found it difficult to conform to the expectations of their new faith or even to understand many of its central doctrines. Having already dispatched at least two letters to those in Corinth by the time he completed his ministry in Ephesus—the second of which is the canonical work of 1 Corinthians—Paul began to journey to Corinth by way of Troas and Macedonia. It was his hope to find Titus, one of his companions whom he previously dispatched to Corinth, making the return trip to Ephesus. Distressed about his whereabouts and the situation in Corinth, Paul was relieved to find Titus as he traveled through Macedonia (2 Cor. 2:13; 7:6–14). The epistle of 2 Corinthians was written at this time and Paul traveled soon thereafter to Achaia for a three-month period, which he presumably spent in the city of Corinth (Acts 20:1–3). It was during this stay in Corinth that Paul wrote the Epistle to the Romans and prepared for the long journey back to Jerusalem where he had planned to deliver a relief offering that he had organized for the impoverished Jewish believers.

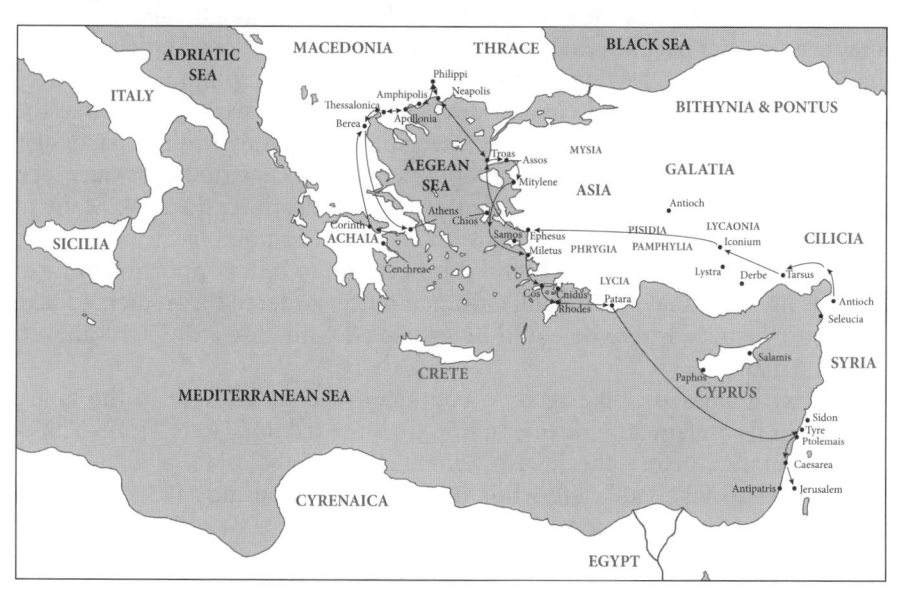

Paul's Third Missionary Journey

After the discovery of a plot to take his life during his sea voyage to Jerusalem, Paul determined to take the much longer route through Macedonia and Asia, a decision that prohibited him from making it to Jerusalem by Passover. Paul had wanted to reach Jerusalem by this time as it would have provided an ideal occasion to present the relief offering that he had collected among the Gentile churches. On his journey to Jerusalem, Paul and his party made a brief stop in the port city of Caesarea where he stayed at the home of Philip the Evangelist. It was from here that the prophet Agabus is said to have prophesied that Paul would be bound and handed over to the Gentiles (21:10–14), a prophecy that provides the reader with a clear expectation of what to expect in the following scenes. Paul and his companions eventually made their way to Jerusalem where they were received by James and the elders, with whom they shared many of the things the Lord had done among the Gentiles (21:17–20).

Paul's Arrest in Jerusalem and His Caesarean Imprisonment

Following his arrival in Jerusalem, Paul was at the center of a heated dispute at the temple. Luke records that Jews from Asia "stirred up the whole crowd and laid hands on him" (Acts 21:27). It might be assumed that some of these Jews were from Ephesus, where Paul had recently ministered. Seeing him in the temple, they accused him of turning the people against the law and of defiling the temple by bringing Trophimus, a Gentile from Ephesus, into the area that was forbidden to Gentiles (21:28–30). Though this accusation may seem rather harmless to modern readers, it was a very serious charge that had the potential of placing the life of both Paul and Trophimus in jeopardy. The Romans permitted the Jewish people jurisdiction over the affairs of the temple, and accusations such as this were not taken lightly. On this particular occasion, we find that Paul's Jewish opponents were eager to bypass any type of formal trial and were intent on putting him to death on the spot. Many of these individuals had likely sparred with Paul at some point in the past, either in Ephesus or elsewhere, and found this occasion to be an opportune time to end his life. Fortunately for Paul, a Roman officer ordered his soldiers to take him into custody where he could be protected while the authorities looked into the matter.

In what follows, Luke records Paul's courageous address to the angry crowds in Jerusalem and his interaction with the tribune (Acts 21:37–22:29), his appearance before the Jewish Sanhedrin (22:30–23:11), a further plot of the Jews to take Paul's life while he remained in custody (23:12–22), his hearings in Caesarea before the proconsuls Felix (23:23–24:27) and Festus (25:1–12), Agrippa II, a great-grandson of Herod the Great, and Agrippa's sister Bernice (25:13–26:32). Luke then provides a lengthy account of Paul's eventful voyage and arrival in Rome (Acts 27–28).

Luke recounts that the trials in Caesarea proved inconclusive. Felix, a freedman appointed as proconsul by Claudius, prolonged Paul's trial, conversing with him on occasion over a two-year period. Despite the weak charges against Paul, Felix was reluctant to free him out of concern for his reputation among the Jewish people and because he was hopeful that Paul would offer him a bribe (Acts 24:26–27). Festus, the proconsul who succeeded Felix around the year 59 or 60 CE, also struggled to find a meaningful accusation against Paul but was likewise concerned about his public image among the Jewish people. After Festus entertained the idea of Paul returning to Jerusalem to face the charges of his opponents directly, Paul determined to exercise his right as a Roman citizen to have his case heard before Caesar's court in Rome. Festus was certainly not happy to hear this request but had little choice but to honor his wishes and make the necessary arrangements. Luke then relates that Paul appeared before Agrippa II, the last of the Herodians and brother of Drusilla, Felix's wife (25:13–26:32). Though not under Agrippa's jurisdiction, Felix was hopeful that he might assist him in laying out reasonable charges that would justify Paul's arrest and subsequent trial in Rome (25:25–27).

Luke's account of Paul's mistreatment by the Jews in Jerusalem, his subsequent trials, and his lengthy voyage to Rome provide several striking parallels to the final chapters of his gospel. Both Jesus and Paul show determination to go to Jerusalem where they are met with fallacious accusations and endure a series of trials. The key difference between the two accounts, of course, is that Luke records the death of Jesus in his gospel, while Paul's death is not mentioned in Acts. The story of Paul comes to an abrupt end in Acts 28 with Paul in house arrest in Rome where he continued to proclaim the good news. By ending his account in this fashion, Luke may be making a subtle point to readers that the work of Christ continues and that any attempt to suppress its advancement will ultimately prove futile.

Summary

This chapter has briefly surveyed the second and third major missionary journeys of Paul recorded in the book of Acts and the events that transpired soon thereafter. Following the Jerusalem Council and his dispute with Barnabas, Paul took part in his second and third missionary journeys with Silas. These journeys brought Paul to some familiar locations as well as to new places of ministry in the provinces of Asia, Macedonia, and Achaia where he had not previously proclaimed the gospel message. The two journeys took place over a relatively brief period of Paul's post-Christian life, yet it was one of the most productive and consequential times in his apostolic career. Following his return to Jerusalem at the end of the third journey, Paul was apprehended when a riot formed at the temple. Taken to Caesarea, Paul testified before notable figures such as Felix, Festus, and Agrippa II, faithfully proclaiming the good news of Jesus Christ before being transported to Rome where his fate would be decided.

REFLECTION QUESTIONS

1. What is your perspective on the dispute between Paul and Barnabas? Do you sympathize more with the position of one individual over the other? Why?

2. What do we know about Paul's companions during the major missionary movements described in Acts?

3. What are the general areas where Paul traveled during the second and third missionary journeys?

4. What are some of the ways in which Paul's proclamation of the gospel in Jewish settings differed from his proclamation in Gentile areas such as Athens?

5. Paul appears to have made some decisions that were contrary to the advice of his companions (e.g., his determination to visit Jerusalem). What might we learn from Paul's life regarding the tension missionaries often face between personal safety and commitment to the Great Commission?

What Do We Know About the Final Years of Paul's Life?

Despite the preservation of a substantial collection of his writings and a significant portion of Acts that is devoted to his travels and missionary endeavors, ascertaining Paul's whereabouts and activities during the final years of his life remains a significant challenge. The book of Acts abruptly ends with Paul in house arrest in Rome with no mention of his subsequent trial, possible travels, or martyrdom. His extant writings provide only limited information as well. Most of his works are believed to have been composed before or during his house arrest in Rome in the late 50s or early 60s of the first century. This leaves the Pastoral Epistles as the only canonical works that are traditionally understood to have been composed by Paul during his final years. While there is much that simply cannot be determined about Paul's activities and circumstances during the final years of his life, passing references in the Pastoral Epistles and traditions preserved in early Christian literature provide the grounds for making some basic conclusions about a number of locations he may have visited and events that may have transpired after he initially arrived in Rome.[1]

Evidence from the Pastoral Epistles

A fundamental issue relating to the study of the final years of Paul's life is the authenticity of the Pastoral Epistles. Because Acts records Paul's activities only through his initial arrival in Rome, we must look elsewhere for information related to his final years. As noted above, the Pastoral Epistles are the only

---

1. In addition to the many scholarly works which survey Paul's life and letters, those interested in further exploration of the final years of his life will find the following collection of essays to be of interest: Armand Puid i Tàrrech, John Barclay, and Jörg Frey, eds., *The Last Years of Paul*, WUNT 1/352 (Tübingen: Mohr Siebeck, 2015).

works attributed to Paul that were likely written after the events recorded in Acts. Many scholars, however, regard these writings as inauthentic works that were composed by an unknown devotee of Paul subsequent to the apostle's martyrdom. As such, they are often considered to be of limited historical value in tracing Paul's activities during the final years of his life. The subject of their authenticity will be taken up in greater detail later in Questions 18 and 19. For the present, we will assume Pauline authorship and evaluate what these writings may reveal about the final years of Paul's life, recognizing that some of our conclusions will differ from those who regard the Pastorals as pseudonymous.

An initial observation that can be made from these epistles, 2 Timothy in particular, is that the description of Paul's circumstances is difficult to relate to any of the situations he describes in his other writings or even to the circumstances described in Acts 28. Luke refers to Paul living in a rented dwelling place (Acts 28:23) in Rome and enjoying the freedom to host visitors (Acts 28:30). Although Luke's account is brief and provides only limited details, there does not appear to be a sense that Paul's life was in peril or that he was living his final days. At the time of Paul's initial visit to Rome, Christians appear to have still been largely ignored by the Roman authorities. We would certainly not expect for Paul to have appealed to Caesar if the Romans were actively persecuting the church. Luke also describes Paul as living in a rented house during this "imprisonment" rather than in a Roman prison. Further, the writings traditionally dated to this time such as Philippians and Philemon seem to indicate that Paul was optimistic that he would soon be released (see, for example, Phil. 1:25; 2:24; Philem. 22).[2]

This generally positive portrayal of Paul's circumstances in Acts and several of his epistles may be contrasted with the decidedly more dismal outlook that permeates 2 Timothy. In the latter writing, Paul offers several admonitions to Timothy that are presented as final words to a beloved colleague. He also takes the opportunity to charge his companion to faithfully continue the work. He describes himself as "already being poured out as a drink offering," and states plainly that "the time of [his] departure has come" and that he has "finished the race" (2 Tim. 4:6–7). While Paul uses similar language in Philippians (see Phil. 2:7), he does not appear in this epistle to be resigned to the fact that he faced imminent death. He certainly presents death as a possible outcome in his correspondence with the Philippians but appears to be fairly confident that he would soon be released. How might the noticeably more negative outlook in 2 Timothy be explained? For those who deny the authenticity of this writing, the differences may simply be due to the fact that

---

2. As will be discussed in Question 12, there is a lack of universal consensus on the dating or provenance of these epistles. While some have suggested that they were written earlier, the traditional viewpoint is that they were written from Rome in the late 50s or early 60s.

2 Timothy was written by a later unknown writer who was aware of Paul's martyrdom. This writer could have presented Paul's imminent death in much more certain terms than we might expect of someone who could only speculate about how the circumstances might unfold. It is also possible, of course, that Paul's situation become more serious and dire with each passing month during his imprisonment in Rome. He may have enjoyed a degree of freedom for some time before his situation began to deteriorate and his prospect of being released became increasingly less likely.

While it is certainly the case that a prisoner's situation can quickly change, a more plausible theory that goes back to the early church is that Paul was imprisoned in Rome on two separate occasions, the first of which was the house arrest recorded in Acts 28, and the second being a later imprisonment that ended with his martyrdom. According to this perspective, Acts 28 records an initial imprisonment Paul experienced when he arrived in Rome after making his appeal to have his case heard in Rome. In Luke's account, Paul seems to have been fairly well cared for after he arrived in Rome and was confined to a rented house. It is during this time that many believe he wrote the four so-called Prison Epistles of Ephesians, Philippians, Colossians, and Philemon, the authenticity, dating, and provenance of which will be discussed in more detail in future chapters.

According to the two-imprisonments theory, Paul was eventually released from the initial Roman imprisonment recorded in Acts 28 and engaged in further missionary activity, some even suggesting that he made his way to Spain. After traveling throughout the Roman world for a number of years, Paul was then apprehended and taken back to Rome, where he faced a significantly harsher imprisonment that culminated in his martyrdom. It is understood that the two Roman imprisonments were prompted by different circumstances. His first imprisonment took place only because he made the decision to appeal to Caesar following a two-year imprisonment in Caesarea (Acts 25:10–12). The second imprisonment, on the other hand, appears to have been the result of Rome's attempt to suppress the Christian movement, an effort that intensified rather quickly after the fire that burned much of Rome in 64 CE.

Not all scholars find the viewpoint that Paul was eventually released from the house arrest described in Luke's account to be convincing. Some have objected that his release from Roman imprisonment would have surely been noted by Luke had this taken place and that it is difficult to accommodate Paul's supposed travels in areas around the Aegean Sea after his release with a possible voyage to Spain, a distant location where he clearly desired to go (Rom. 15:24, 28). In response, we might first note that Paul's plans frequently changed and that he was known to travel to areas well out of the way before traveling elsewhere. Even in Romans we find Paul explaining that his desire was to minister to those in Rome in person but that he found it necessary to first travel east to Jerusalem. We might also note the weak basis for the argument that Luke would have surely recorded Paul's release. If it was indeed the case that Paul was not released and that his house arrest in Rome culminated in his martyrdom, why did Luke not mention something about the circumstances surrounding his death? Aside from Jesus, Luke briefly records the death of John the Baptist (Luke 9:7–9) and the apostle James (Acts 12:1–3). Why would he not likewise offer at least a brief account of the death of such a notable figure as Paul? Either one must conclude that Luke chose not to record important events such as the trial and martyrdom of Paul or that the composition of Acts took place during the time in which Paul remained in house arrest.

If the two-imprisonments theory is recognized—a theory common among those who affirm an earlier date of composition of Acts and the authenticity of the canonical works attributed to Paul—we may look to the Pastorals for possible insight related to Paul's journeys and activities after his release from house arrest in Rome. Among those who recognize their authenticity, 1 Timothy and Titus are often understood to have been written between the two Roman imprisonments, that is, during a period of additional missionary activity, while 2 Timothy is thought to have been written from Rome shortly before Paul faced martyrdom.

In 1 Timothy Paul instructs his companion to "remain at Ephesus" (1 Tim. 1:2), noting that he had initially directed him to do so when "going to Macedonia." This would suggest that Paul met Timothy in the city of Ephesus or at least in the local area shortly before he made his way to the Roman province of Macedonia. Although Paul journeyed through Macedonia during his second missionary journey (Acts 16:6–17:15) and after his abrupt departure from Ephesus during the third missionary journey (Acts 20:1), Luke specifically states that Timothy was one of two individuals Paul sent into Macedonia prior to his own departure (Acts 19:22). It is thus best to understand Paul's instruction as taking place during a later period when Timothy was charged with carrying out the mission in Ephesus.

In Titus, an epistle often thought to have been written between the two writings to Timothy, we find possible evidence that Paul had been ministering in Crete for a time (Titus 1:5). Paul observes that he "left" Titus on this Mediterranean island. This may suggest that Paul played a role in the initial establishment of the church in Crete after his first Roman imprisonment and that he had entrusted Titus with continuing the mission there. Finally, Paul expresses his intention to spend the winter in Nicopolis, a port city on the western coast of Greece founded by Augustus to commemorate his victory over his opponents at the Battle of Actium (Titus 3:12). It is unclear if Paul made it to this location prior to his later arrest, but it is evident that this was at least one of Paul's intended destinations during this time.

Finally, references to Paul's travels are made in his final extant epistle, the second canonical writing addressed to Timothy. We find evidence that Paul had recently visited Troas, where he left several items behind (2 Tim. 4:13), as well as Miletus, where his companion Trophimus was left to recover from a sickness (2 Tim. 4:20). The reference to Erastus in 2 Timothy 4:10 may also suggest that he visited for a brief time in Corinth, though this is not entirely clear. With regard to his reference to Troas, it may be possible that Paul was apprehended here and taken to Rome where he endured his second imprisonment in the city. His request for his cloak and various writing materials may imply that he was not able to retrieve certain items and that his departure took place with little warning.

Evidence from Early Christian Writers

The theory that Paul was released from the house arrest recorded in Acts 28 before resuming his travels and ministry throughout several regions in the Mediterranean world is not a modern invention. In fact, a number of extant writings from the early centuries of the Christian era make this assumption, with some even stating that Paul eventually made his way to Spain during this time. This viewpoint is most clearly and fully spelled out by Eusebius, who records the following:

> Nero sent Festus as [Felix's] successor, and Paul was tried before him and brought as prisoner to Rome. Aristarchus went with him, whom he called his fellow prisoner in his epistles [Col. 4:10]. And at this point Luke, who wrote the Acts of the Apostles, finished his story with the statement that Paul spent two full years in Rome in free custody, preaching without hindrance. After defending himself [successfully], the apostle is said to have set out again on the ministry of preaching and, coming a second time to the same city, found fulfillment in martyrdom. During this imprisonment he composed the second epistle to Timothy, mentioning both his earlier defense as well as his impending fulfillment. . . . Therefore Luke probably wrote the Acts of the Apostles at that time, having recorded events throughout the time he was with Paul. I have said this to show that Paul's martyrdom did not take place during the stay in Rome that Luke describes. Since Nero's disposition was at first milder, it was likely easier for Paul's defense of the faith to be accepted, but when Nero preceded to commit reckless crimes, the apostles were attacked along with the others.[3]

---

3. *Ecclesiastical History* 2.22. Translation from Paul Maier, *Eusebius: The Church History* (Grand Rapids: Kregel, 2007), 69–70.

Eusebius was not the only ancient writer to record similar details. While not as specific as Eusebius, the late-first-century writer Clement of Rome observes that after Paul "had preached in the east and in the west, he won the genuine glory for his faith, having taught righteousness to the whole world and having reached the farthest limits of the west."[4] The reference to the "farthest limits to the West" is often understood as a reference to Spain, and more specifically to the Strait of Gibraltar. This understanding of Clement's account is consistent with the acceptance of the two-imprisonments theory, given the difficulty of placing a voyage of Paul to Spain prior to the imprisonment recorded in Acts 28. A similar reference is made in the Muratorian Fragment, an early introduction to the works of the New Testament traditionally dated to the latter half of the second century. In this writing, the author refers to "the departure of Paul from the city [of Rome] when he journeyed to Spain."[5] Later writers such as Chrysostom,[6] Jerome,[7] and Cyril of Jerusalem[8] made statements that share the same basic details about the final years of Paul's life. Although we cannot be certain as to whether Paul did in fact make his way to Spain during this period, the tradition for this conclusion is quite early and widely attested and should therefore not be quickly dismissed. At the very least, Paul's own testimony in the Pastorals would suggest that he spent a considerable amount of time strengthening Christian communities surrounding the Aegean Sea and other locations such as Crete before facing arrest and being taken back to Rome.

Summary

This chapter has explored a variety of evidence from Acts, the Pastoral Epistles, and early Christian writings for possible evidence relating to Paul's activities and whereabouts during the last several years of his life. It was observed that many of the locations where the Pastorals indicate Paul may have traveled are difficult to place within the context of the three major missionaries recorded in Acts. While many contemporary scholars regard the Pastorals as inauthentic and of little value for reconstructing the final years of Paul's life, a compelling argument could be made that they offer reliable, though limited, insight related to Paul's ministry during the years between the composition of Acts and his martyrdom. A plausible tradition that originated in the early centuries of the Christian era is that Paul was imprisoned twice in Rome: the first of which was the house arrest recorded by Luke in

---

4. *First Clement* 1.5.6–7. Cited from Michael W. Holmes, ed., *The Apostolic Fathers: Greek Texts and English Translations*, 3rd ed. (Grand Rapids: Baker, 2007), 53.
5. Translation from Bruce M. Metzger, *The Canon of the New Testament: Its Origin, Development, and Significance* (New York: Clarendon, 1987), 306.
6. Chrysostom, *Homilies on the Second Epistle of St. Paul the Apostle to Timothy* 10.
7. Jerome, *Lives of Illustrious Men* 5.
8. Cyril of Jerusalem, *Catechetical Lecture* 17.26.

Acts 28, while the second was a subsequent imprisonment that ended in Paul's martyrdom. Between these imprisonments, Paul appears to have traveled and ministered for several years in a number of locations throughout the Mediterranean world, possibly making it as far as Spain.

REFLECTION QUESTIONS

1. What are some of the major challenges related to the study of the historical context of the Pastoral Epistles?

2. From your observations, how does Paul's imprisonment described in Acts 28 compare to the circumstances he faced at the time he composed 2 Timothy?

3. What are some possible objections to the two-imprisonments theory?

4. If the two-imprisonments theory is rejected, how might we account for the references to Paul's travels in the Pastoral Epistles?

5. What can we observe about the responsibilities of Paul's associates during his final years of ministry?

What Do We Know About Paul's Death?

A s discussed in the previous chapter, there is an ancient tradition that the apostle Paul experienced two separate Roman imprisonments: the imprisonment recorded in Acts 28 that was originally prompted by the Jewish opposition he faced in Jerusalem, and a second imprisonment that was the result of Roman opposition. The two-imprisonments tradition has long been regarded as a plausible explanation for the noticeably different portrayals of Paul's situation found in Acts 28 and 2 Timothy and helps explain how Paul may have visited certain areas during his final years. Many questions still remain, however, about the circumstances relating to his death. Because of the fact that his martyrdom is not recorded in the New Testament, we must look outside the pages of Scripture for information about the circumstances that led to his execution. Our objective in this chapter, therefore, is to survey the earliest extant testimony related to the apostle Paul for possible insight relating to his death and burial.[1]

Early Christian Testimony Related to the Martyrdom of the Apostle Paul

In this section, we will briefly survey several of the earliest traditions related to the death of Paul that may be observed in early Christian literature.[2]

---

1. For further treatment of the sources and subjects discussed in this section, see David L. Eastman, *The Ancient Martyrdom Accounts of Peter and Paul*, WGRW 39 (Atlanta: SBL Press, 2015); Eastman, *Paul the Martyr: The Cult of the Apostle in the Latin West*, WAWSup 4 (Leiden: Brill, 2011); Eastman, *The Many Deaths of Peter and Paul*, OECS (New York: Oxford University Press, 2019); Bryan Litfin, *After Acts: Exploring the Lives and Legends of the Apostles* (Chicago: Moody Publishers, 2015), 161–84; Sean McDowell, *The Fate of the Apostles: Examining the Martyrdom Accounts of the Closest Followers of Jesus* (New York: Routledge, 2008), 93–114; Harry W. Tajra, *The Martyrdom of St. Paul: Historical and Judicial Context, Traditions, and Legends* (Eugene, OR: Wipf & Stock, 2010); F. J. Foakes Jackson, "Evidence for the Martyrdom of Peter and Paul in Rome," *JBL* 46 (1927): 74–78; Arthur Barnes, *The Martyrdom of St. Peter and St. Paul* (New York: Oxford University Press, 1933).

2. In addition to the primary historical witnesses to the martyrdom of Paul discussed in this section, reference or allusion to his martyrdom is also made in Ignatius, *Epistle to the*

1 Clement 5:5–7

Writing near the end of the first century, Clement of Rome writes the following:

> Because of jealousy and strife Paul showed the way to the prize for patient endurance. After he had been seven times in chains, had been driven into exile, had been stoned, and had preached in the east and in the west, he won the genuine glory for his faith, having taught righteousness to the whole world and having reached the farthest limits of the west. Finally, when he had given his testimony before the rulers, he thus departed from the world and went to the holy place, having become an outstanding example of patient endurance.[3]

Much of Clement's account praises Paul's faithfulness over many years of service. His faithfulness was most clearly demonstrated, Clement emphasizes, by his death, at which time he "departed from the world and went to the holy place." Although Clement does not offer specific details related to the circumstances of Paul's death, his reference to winning "the genuine glory for his faith," going on "to the holy place," and serving as "an outstanding example of patient endurance" all imply that Paul gave his life for Christ and that this was well-known to his readers. We may also note Clement's reference to Paul's "testimony before the rulers." Although he does not elaborate on the nature of this testimony or the identity of the rulers, the implication is that Paul faithfully testified before the Roman authorities during a pivotal event—perhaps his trial in Rome—and that his death took place shortly thereafter.

The Acts of Paul

The apocryphal work known as *The Acts of Paul* was an early Christian writing that appears to have been a compilation of various traditions and sources such as an alleged correspondence between Paul and the Corinthian church, a narrative relating to an early female devotee of Paul referred to as *The Acts of Paul and Thecla*, and a legendary account of Paul's martyrdom. These accounts were not widely regarded as authentic in the early church, as indicated by Eusebius's classification of *The Acts of Paul* as a spurious writing (*Ecclesiastical History* 3.25.4). Among the many claims made in the martyrdom account is that Paul lived in a rented barn outside of Rome and that a number of individuals from the city made

---

Ephesians 12.2; Polycarp, *Epistle to the Philippians* 9; Irenaeus, *Against Heresies* 3.1.1. These works do not offer details about Paul's death but do suggest that he died as a martyr.

3. Cited from Michael W. Holmes, ed., *The Apostolic Fathers: Greek Texts and English Translations*, 3rd ed. (Grand Rapids, Baker, 2007), 51–53.

the trip to hear him teach.[4] The text then states that Nero's cupbearer, Patroclus, fell out of a high window to his death as Paul taught. Those familiar with Acts will quickly note the parallel to the incident in which Paul raised Eutychus from the dead after he fell from a window in Troas (Acts 20:7–12). In the case of Patroclus, word got back to Nero that his cupbearer had died. Patroclus then unexpectedly appeared alive before Nero and revealed to him that he was raised from the dead by Christ. This incited Nero to respond harshly and to order the execution of many Christians, including Paul. Condemned to death, Paul asserted to Nero that he would soon appear before him after his execution. After appealing to certain soldiers to believe in the living God, Paul was beheaded. As anticipated, Paul appeared alive before the bewildered Nero and gave praise to God for raising him from the dead. While many of the details in this account are clearly fictitious and lack historical viability, the core elements of the story are consistent with other early witnesses to Paul's martyrdom which likewise claim that he was beheaded by Nero in Rome and that he died as a faithful witness to Christ.

Eusebius's Ecclesiastical History *2.25.5–8*

Eusebius's famous fourth-century history of the church provides additional details related to Paul's death:

> So it happened that this man, the first to be announced publicly as a fighter against God, was led on to slaughter the apostles. It is related that in his reign Paul was beheaded in Rome itself and that Peter was also crucified, and the cemeteries there still called by the names of Peter and Paul confirmed the record.[5]

Eusebius places his account of Peter and Paul's martyrdom in the context of the reign of Nero, an emperor who "plunged into nefarious vices and took up arms against the God of the universe." Among the many victims of Nero's offensive against the church, Eusebius records, were the apostles Paul and Peter. Eusebius writes that Paul was beheaded, a common form of execution of Roman citizens, while Peter was crucified. Eusebius further notes that the site of their graves could be found in Rome, apparently in different locations.

Following his brief description of Paul's death, Eusebius shares a few additional traditions that had been passed down from earlier writers. Gaius of Rome, a well-known critic of the Montanists, is said to relay the following: "I can point out the trophies of the apostles. If you will go to the Vatican or the

---

4. The basic storyline of the martyrdom account seems to serve as the basis for several future renditions of Paul's martyrdom in later Christian literature.

5. All quotations from Eusebius in this section derive from Paul Maier, *Eusebius: The Church History* (Grand Rapids: Kregel, 2007), 75.

Ostian Way, you will find the trophies of those who founded this church." The testimony of Gaius is of interest as it provides a few unique details related to the location of Peter and Paul's tombs. In fact, this is one of the earliest traditions that Peter was buried at the site known today as the Vatican and that Paul was buried along the Ostian Way (*Via Ostiensis*) which connected Rome to Ostia, a port city just under twenty miles to the southwest where the Tiber flows into the Tyrrhenian Sea. It was along this road, Gaius claimed, that Paul was buried. Marking this location was a "trophy," that is, some type of memorial or monument. Eusebius also shares the testimony of a bishop named Dionysius of Corinth who wrote in one of his letters that Peter and Paul were martyred together. Dionysius's claim that the two were executed on the same occasion seems unlikely, though it does appear to be the case that they were both put to death in Rome during the reign of Nero.

Jerome, *Lives of Illustrious Men* 5

Writing at the end of the fourth century, Jerome's account of the life and ministry of the apostle Paul includes a brief reference to his martyrdom. After recounting Paul's words in 2 Timothy, Jerome records the following: "He then, in the fourteenth year of Nero on the same day as Peter, was beheaded at Rome for Christ's sake and was buried in the Ostian Way, the thirty-seventh year after our Lord's passion."[6]

We once again observe a close link between the martyrdoms of Peter and Paul. In this case, Jerome places their executions not only in the same city, but, like Dionysius, on the same day. While this timing seems doubtful, Jerome's account provides important details that may be corroborated by other early testimony. Most notably, he states that Paul was beheaded and that he was buried on the Ostian Way, just as Eusebius had previously written. In addition, Jerome provides specific details about the year of Paul's death. Having begun his reign in October of 54 CE following the death of Claudius, the fourteenth year of Nero's reign might be calculated to around 67 or 68 CE. Further, thirty-seven years after Christ's passion would land somewhere in this same range, depending, of course, on the precise year of Jesus's death and how these years were intended to be measured.

Sulpicius Severus, *Chronicle* 2.29

Sulpicius Severus offered a brief description of the death of Paul in his notable early-fifth-century work which surveys the history of the world. Like his predecessor Eusebius, Severus places Paul's death in the context of Nero's persecution of the church. Following the large fire in Rome, an event typically dated to 64 CE, Nero is said to have blamed the Christians for the catastrophe

---

6.   Translation from Thomas P. Halton, *The Fathers of the Church* (Washington, DC: Catholic University of America Press, 1999), 13.

and to have begun aggressively marking them out for persecution. As Severus explains, "the most cruel tortures were accordingly inflicted upon the innocent," some of which he describes in morbid detail. Like Eusebius, Severus notes that both "Paul and Peter were condemned to death, the former being beheaded with a sword, while Peter suffered crucifixion."[7]

Possible Sites Linked to Paul's Final Imprisonment, Martyrdom, and Burial

Christians visiting Rome today might visit a site known as the Mamertine Prison. It was here, according to later tradition, that both Peter and Paul were held before their executions. We know very little about the use of this prison during the first century, though it is clear that it was in use long before this time. Although the site became known as the prison where Peter and Paul were detained in their final days, this tradition cannot be corroborated by early sources. Consequently, we simply cannot be certain if the two apostles were imprisoned here or at another location in the city.

While mention of the specific location of Paul's final imprisonment is absent from early Christian writings, there are several traditions that relate to the location in which he was executed or where his remains were buried. As the testimony of Eusebius and Jerome reveals, there was an early tradition that Paul's body was originally laid to rest at some point along the Ostian Way after he was beheaded during the final years of Nero's reign. Incidentally, there are several locations and churches in Rome that are purported to have been the site of Paul's martyrdom or burial at some point in church history.[8] According to some traditions, Paul was put to death at the present location of a church referred to as the Church of Saint Paul at the Three Fountains (*San Paolo alle Tre Fontane*). The church adopts its name from the legend that Paul's head bounced three times on the ground at the time of his execution, with fountains of water springing up from the ground in each spot! It is possible that this may have been the same location in which the marker described by Gaius was located, that is, the site of Paul's initial burial. Ultimately, however, it is difficult to establish with certainty that this site was the precise location of Paul's execution or burial as the traditions associated with it are not particularly early.

In addition to this site, some traditions indicate that the remains of Peter and Paul later rested in the catacombs where the Basilica of Saint Sebastian Outside the Walls (*San Sebastiano fuori le mura*) was later constructed. Paul's body was then believed to have been finally relocated a short distance away to the Basilica of Saint Paul Outside the Walls (*San Paolo fuori le mura*). This church, like many

---

7. Sulpicius Severus, *Chronicle* 2.29 (*NPNF* 2.11).
8. For a more complete discussion of these early sites, see Henry Chadwick, "St. Peter and St. Paul in Rome: The Problem of the Memoria Apostolorum Ad Catabumbas," *JTS* 8 (1957): 31–52.

ancient churches in Rome, has a very complex and fascinating history. It was originally constructed during the reign of Theodosius at the site of a shrine built earlier by Constantine. The building was then largely destroyed by fire in 1823 and subsequently rebuilt. In 2006, the Vatican revealed that a sarcophagus from the late fourth century had been located underneath the basilica's altar—an altar that was constructed by Pope Clement VI more than four hundred years ago. The discovery of this piece was not altogether surprising to many of those familiar with the site, however, since a Latin inscription was discovered at the location that contains the words "Apostle Paul, Martyr." Shortly after the discovery, the Vatican further announced that carbon dating of the bone fragments within the coffin confirm that the remains belong to a first-century figure, leading many to speculate that they are in fact the remains of Paul.

Summary

It is difficult to make certain conclusions regarding the precise circumstances that led to Paul's martyrdom or many of the details related to his death. We cannot be certain precisely where he was apprehended prior to being taken to Rome (assuming that he was imprisoned in Rome on two occasions), how long he was detained, what type of trial or hearing he may have been given, to whom he may have testified, the precise date or even year of his martyrdom, or the location of his original burial or present remains. Despite these uncertainties, there appears to have been a widespread consensus in the early church that Paul was put to death at some time between the great fire of Rome in 64 CE and Nero's death in 68 CE. His faithful and courageous testimony in the period leading up to his death was clearly a source of inspiration for many believers.

REFLECTION QUESTIONS

1. How did the early church portray Paul's witness during his final days?

2. In your estimation, do the early accounts relating to Paul's martyrdom best fit with the theory that Paul was imprisoned once or twice in Rome?

3. What are the core elements of Paul's martyrdom that appear to have been known to early Christians?

4. What specific locations in Rome are traditionally linked either to Paul's execution or burial?

5. In your view, might there be value in visiting sites alleged to have been associated with the martyrdom or burial of early Christian leaders such as Peter or Paul?

What Was Paul's Missionary Strategy?

Although the apostle Paul is known today primarily as the author of a large collection of biblical writings, he was known during his lifetime primarily as a missionary who was entrusted with the task of proclaiming the gospel throughout the Roman world. Each of the activities he took part in throughout his Christian life—his travels, writing, teaching, evangelism, and even the trials he endured—were all motivated by a passion to bring unbelievers into a saving relationship with Christ. As he wrote to Timothy in the years leading up to his death in Rome, "I endure everything for the sake of the elect, that they also may obtain the salvation that is in Christ Jesus with eternal glory" (2 Tim. 2:10). Paul was certainly not one who struggled to find meaning in life or to discern God's purpose for him. As far as he was concerned, he was nothing more than a slave of Christ who had been entrusted to "the ministry of the gospel of Christ" (Rom. 15:19). For a little more than three decades, he tirelessly and faithfully proclaimed that Jesus was God's anointed Son who has made salvation possible for all sinners, both Jew and Gentile. But what made him effective as a missionary? Was the success he experienced ultimately the result of his tenacity, his faithfulness, his ingenuity, or perhaps his unique abilities?

Our purpose in this chapter is to consider what may be determined about the missionary strategy that Paul utilized over the lengthy course of his ministry. Several aspects of Paul's ministry could be discussed—much more, in fact, than what can be addressed here.[1] For the sake of brevity, our discussion

---

1. For further treatment on Paul's missionary methods and strategies, see Eckhard J. Schnabel, *Paul the Missionary: Realities, Strategies and Methods* (Downers Grove, IL: InterVarsity Press, 2008); Paul Barnett, *Paul, Missionary of Jesus*, After Jesus 2 (Grand Rapids: Eerdmans, 2008); Ronald Allen, *Missionary Methods: St. Paul's and Ours? A Study of the Church in the Four Provinces* (Grand Rapids: Eerdmans, 1983); Robert L. Plummer and John Mark Terry, eds., *Paul's Missionary Methods: In His Time and Ours* (Downers Grove, IL: InterVarsity Press, 2012); Peter Bold and Mark Thompson, eds., *The Gospel to*

will center around four distinguishing characteristics of Paul's missionary strategy that may be observed in his writings and in Luke's narrative: (1) his focus on unreached urban areas, (2) his integrated lifestyle, (3) his contextualization of the gospel message, and (4) his concern for the long-term growth and stability of local churches.

Paul's Ministry to Large Unreached Urban Centers

The Roman Empire covered a vast territory during the first century, stretching from modern Spain to as far east as modern Turkey and Syria. While Paul made his way to an impressive number of cities and regions during his many years of missionary activity, there were many locations he simply could not visit. This begs the question of how Paul may have determined where to travel and minister. He was clearly purposeful and selective in where he chose to focus his time and energy, but how did he make these decisions? As we examine the relevant biblical narratives, we find that there does not appear to have been a single determining factor. On some occasions he simply traveled to a specific city or region to carry out a specific task (e.g., delivering a relief offering in Jerusalem), while on other occasions he determined to return to locations in which he had previously ministered in order to encourage believers and to provide them with additional instruction and guidance (see, e.g., Acts 14:21–23; 15:36). There were also times in which Paul believed God was directing him either to or away from a particular location. During the second missionary journey, for example, Luke recounts that the Spirit did not allow Paul to minister either in Ephesus or Bithynia and that he was eventually led to Macedonia (Acts 16:6–10).

Although a number of factors appear to have played a role in determining where Paul traveled and ministered, it would seem to be the case that he generally favored large urban centers where there was not already an established church. This may explain why he so eagerly sought to minister in cities such as Ephesus, Thessalonica, Corinth, and Athens. He did not bypass smaller cities entirely, but his ministry in smaller cities tended to be fairly brief and to take place as he traveled to or from one of the larger cities. Paul certainly appears to have understood the practical benefits of establishing strong and vibrant churches in the major urban centers of the Roman world. In addition to the opportunity it provided him to share the gospel with unbelievers who were unfamiliar with Christian teaching, the larger cities maintained a significant influence. Travelers were constantly coming to and from the larger urban areas. Because of this, a strong network of churches in these locations

---

the Nations: Perspectives on Paul's Mission (Downers Grove, IL: InterVarsity Press, 2000); Trevor J. Burke and Brian S. Rosner, eds., *Paul as Missionary: Identity, Activity, Theology, and Practice*, LNTS 420 (London: T&T Clark, 2011).

would have a significant influence not only in the local area but in the greater Roman world.

If a focus on large urban centers was a central focus of Paul's missionary activities, it might be asked why he does not appear to have visited certain cities such as Alexandria or Carthage, cities that had large populations and were known throughout the greater Roman world. There may have been various reasons for this. Perhaps he had a desire to reach these cites, but circumstances were simply prohibitive. More likely, perhaps, is that Paul sought to minister not only in large cities, but in areas where there was not already a strong Christian presence. As he explained to the Romans, "I make it my ambition to preach the gospel, not where Christ has already been named, lest I build on someone else's foundation" (Rom. 15:20). Rome was of course the largest and most important city of the empire. Yet, Paul's motivation for ministering there was not simply because it was a large city. In addition to his desire to minister in Rome where he could strengthen the local believers (Rom. 1:8–15), he was hopeful for an opportunity to partner with the local believers in his effort to preach the gospel in areas where Christ had yet to be preached (Rom. 15:24). With regard to the large cities in Northern Africa, Paul may have simply determined that these cities already benefited from a Christian presence or that they were not as strategic for future expansion.

Paul's Integrated Lifestyle

Often overlooked is the lifestyle that Paul frequently assumed when he ministered throughout the Mediterranean world. We obviously cannot know precisely where he may have lived during each phase of his life or the exact living and working conditions he experienced in each location. From passing references in his letters and in Luke's narrative of his missionary activities, however, it is possible to make some general observations. Most importantly, we find that Paul closely integrated himself into the communities where he ministered. From what may be observed in the New Testament writings, Paul seems to have lived, worked, and ministered alongside of the members of each community he visited. It would appear to have been his practice, for example, to reside in the homes of local believers and to support himself by working his trade. During his initial stay in Philippi, he and his companions lodged in the home of Lydia (Acts 16:15). While in Corinth, Paul lodged in the home of Priscilla and Aquilla, a couple who shared his occupation (Acts 18:1–3), and later in the home of Gaius (Rom. 16:23), possibly one of his converts (1 Cor. 1:14). We also find Paul instructing Philemon to prepare a room for him in the event that he would be able to make the journey to Colossae (Philem. 22).

Working his trade in public areas in cities such as Corinth would have provided Paul with many opportunities to interact with those in the local community without becoming a financial burden on local believers (Acts 20:34). We get a glimpse of his lifestyle in his address to the Ephesian elders on his journey to Jerusalem. He reminded them that he ministered "in public and from house to house" (Acts 20:20), that he served them night and day (Acts 20:32), and that he labored with his own hands to provide for his needs (Acts 20:34–35).[2] By his own admission, his speech and personal appearance were less than impressive (2 Cor. 10:10). Despite his personal limitations, the particular lifestyle Paul assumed provided him with frequent and natural opportunities to build personal relationships with those in local communities and to equip and train local believers.

Paul's Contextualization of Gospel Proclamation

Many of the locations where Paul ministered were much more diverse than is often realized, requiring him to become familiar with various cultures and people groups. As Luke's account of Paul's journeys makes clear, his ministry did not focus exclusively on Jewish or Gentile populations. In reality, there was a significant Jewish presence throughout the Greco-Roman world and Paul seems to have interacted quite frequently with Jewish audiences even when ministering in predominantly Gentile areas such as Asia Minor, Macedonia, and Achaia. We find, for example, that a common and well-known practice of Paul was to participate in gatherings at local synagogues. These occasions provided him the opportunity to engage in dialogue with fellow Jews and to proclaim Jesus as the fulfillment and focal point of the Jewish law.[3] In Pisidian Antioch, for instance, Paul offered a "word of encouragement" (Acts 13:15) to those gathered in the synagogue in which he contended that "by him everyone who believes is freed from everything from which you could not be freed by the law of Moses" (Acts 13:39).

Although Paul was persuaded that there is only one gospel that is "the power of God for salvation to everyone who believes" (Rom. 1:16), he often found it necessary to adopt different approaches when communicating the message of salvation. When proclaiming Christ to Gentile audiences, there was often little foundation upon which to build. As a result, it was often necessary for him to reveal to his listeners that there was a single God of the universe who is holy, all-wise, and the creator of all things, that this God has made himself known to mankind, and that sinners may be reconciled to him through the redemptive work of Jesus Christ. When addressing Jewish audiences, on the other hand, Paul tended to focus much more intently on matters such as the role that Christ played in fulfilling various institutions and

---

2. For additional treatment of the manner in which Paul lived and ministered among and developed close ties with those in local communities, see Robert J. Banks, *Paul's Idea of Community: The Early House Churches in Their Cultural Setting* (Grand Rapids: Baker Academic, 1994).

3. For further insight relating to Paul's engagement with Jewish audiences, see Michael F. Bird, *An Anomalous Jew: Paul among Jews, Greeks, and Romans* (Grand Rapids: Eerdmans, 2016), 69–107.

promises associated with the Old Testament writings. The differences in these two points of emphasis made be observed, for example, in Paul's address to the Jews in Antioch (Acts 13:13–52) and his address to pagan philosophers in Athens (Acts 17:16–34). This contextualization was not related merely to Paul's teaching, however. As he explains in his first epistle to the Corinthians:

> For though I am free from all, I have made myself a servant to all, that I might win more of them. To the Jews I became as a Jew, in order to win Jews. To those under the law I became as one under the law (though not being myself under the law) that I might win those under the law. To those outside the law I became as one outside the law (not being outside the law of God but under the law of Christ) that I might win those outside the law. To the weak I became weak, that I might win the weak. I have become all things to all people, that by all means I might save some. I do it all for the sake of the gospel, that I may share with them in its blessings. (1 Cor. 9:19–23)

Throughout his many years of missionary activity, Paul was careful to conduct himself in a manner that avoided needless offense of those with particular sensibilities, but he did so without compromising his personal beliefs or the message he proclaimed. When ministering to Jewish audiences, for example, he chose not to flaunt his freedom in Christ, living instead "as one under the law." Although he persistently pointed to Christ as the means of salvation and as the basis of a right relationship with God, he often found it necessary to live in a particular manner in order to "win those under the law." Conversely, Paul found it necessary to avoid living according to the law when ministering to Gentile audiences. He understood that his observance of Jewish traditions and customs might lead some to erroneously conclude that the law serves as the basis for one's relationship with God or that one must become Jewish in order to become part of God's people.

Paul's Concern for the Well-Being of Local Churches

Luke's account of Paul's missionary activities and his instruction in the Pastoral Epistles indicate that Paul was deeply concerned about the long-term stability, spiritual condition, and growth of the churches in which he served. Although Paul was certainly passionate about proclaiming Christ in new regions, he also recognized that his apostolic calling served an eschatological purpose that was to be carried out through the local church. From his perspective, he was charged not only with the proclamation of Christ, but with encouraging the spiritual growth and maturity of believers. To the Colossians, for example, Paul writes, "Him we proclaim, warning everyone and teaching everyone with all wisdom, that we may present everyone mature in Christ"

(Col. 1:28). When encouraging the Philippians to live in a praiseworthy manner, he expresses his desire to "be proud that I did not run in vain or labor in vain" on "the day of Christ" (Phil. 2:16). As his explanation makes clear, he recognized a correlation between the spiritual progress of the believers in Philippi and the fulfillment of his apostolic calling. From his perspective, he was tasked not simply with taking part in certain activities such as teaching and preaching, but in leading believers to spiritual maturity.

That Paul was devoted to the spiritual growth of his readers and the state of the churches throughout the Roman world is clear, but how did he encourage and promote the long-term growth and stability of Christians living in so many areas? There were clearly many ways Paul ministered to local churches, though we might observe three major elements of his apostolic ministry that were designed to encourage their long-term growth. First, we find that Paul maintained an active writing ministry that enabled him to help equip and edify believers in distant locations. Throughout his writings we find numerous admonitions, instructions, and words of encouragement that are aimed at fostering spiritual growth. Second, we find Paul traveling great distances in order to encourage and strengthen believers in local regions. On many occasions, he traveled to areas where he had previously ministered in order to provide further instruction and encouragement to those who belonged to existing local churches. Finally, we find that Paul worked closely with a number of colleagues throughout his years of service as an apostle.[4] On several occasions, he dispatched his companions to travel to areas that were in need of further instruction, encouragement, or where there may have been a controversy that needed to be addressed. His correspondence with Timothy and Titus would also indicate that some of his associates were tasked with important duties such as the appointment of elders and deacons in local churches (1 Tim. 3:1–13; Titus 1:5–9), an important step in ensuring their spiritual growth and long-term stability.[5]

Summary

For more than thirty years, the apostle Paul tirelessly proclaimed the gospel message and helped establish numerous local churches throughout the Roman world. While his ministry in each location was unique and had its own particular challenges, several characteristics of his missionary strategy may be observed. Among other things, Paul understood the importance of establishing strong and vibrant churches in large urban centers that could

---

4. For a brief study of the large network of individuals who worked with Paul, see F. F. Bruce, *The Pauline Circle* (Eugene, OR: Wipf and Stock, 2006).
5. For additional insight related to Paul's effort to establish healthy leadership in local churches, see John McRay, *Paul: His Life and Teaching* (Grand Rapids: Baker Academic, 2003), 372–90.

support further missionary activity in the local region and broader world, of living and working among the people he served, of presenting the gospel message in a manner that is appropriate to one's target audience, and of focusing on the long-term stability and well-being of local churches.

REFLECTION QUESTIONS

1. Are there particular elements of Paul's missionary methods that have not been widely implemented by contemporary missionaries? What might be some of the reasons for this?

2. How effective has the modern church been in reaching urban centers with the gospel?

3. What are your thoughts about pastors working outside of the local church? What might be some possible advantages and disadvantages of this?

4. What might be some potential risks of becoming "all things to all people"?

5. What might Paul's missionary activities suggest about the importance of establishing strong local churches on the mission field?

Who Were Paul's Primary Opponents?

Paul was certainly no stranger to controversy. That he faced frequent opposition throughout his many years of service as an apostle is clear from the testimony in Acts and the content of his own writings, but who exactly were his opponents and what motivated such strong resistance to his teaching? While we cannot account for every conflict in which Paul was involved, we may briefly consider four broad forms of opposition he frequently encountered as he proclaimed the gospel throughout the Roman world: (1) Jewish opposition, (2) Greek and Roman opposition, (3) opposition from other Christians, and (4) spiritual opposition.[1]

Paul's Jewish Opponents

In a stark reversal, Paul, the once zealous defender of Jewish traditions and an ardent persecutor of the church, came to recognize Jesus as the long-awaited messiah and suddenly found himself in conflict with his fellow Jews throughout the Roman world. Over the course of his Christian life, he was strongly opposed, often violently, by many Jews who viewed the Christian movement as a significant and intolerable threat. Soon after his conversion we find that "the Jews plotted to kill him" (Acts 9:23) during a visit in Damascus. Luke then records that Paul was vehemently opposed by many Jews throughout the provinces in Asia Minor and Greece during his major missionary journeys. We read, for example, of Jewish opposition to his teaching in cities such as Antioch of Pisidia (13:50), Iconium (14:2), Lystra (14:19), Thessalonica (17:5–9), Berea (17:13), Corinth (18:6), and Ephesus (19:8–9; 20:19), and that some plotted to take his life during his voyage to Jerusalem at the end of the third missionary

---

1. For a treatment of several specific conflicts involving Paul, see the various essays contained in Stanley E. Porter, ed., *Paul and His Opponents*, PAST 2 (Leiden: Brill, 2005). Another helpful survey is located in Luke Timothy Johnson, *Constructing Paul: The Canonical Paul 1* (Grand Rapids: Eerdmans, 2020), 105–18.

journey (Acts 20:3). During his final stay in Jerusalem, he was nearly killed by a mob of his Jewish opponents, an incident that led to his subsequent detainment in Caesarea; his hearing before various dignitaries such as Festus, Felix, and Agrippa; and his voyage to Rome (see Acts 21–28).

Luke's description of the opposition Paul encountered from the Jewish people is very much consistent with Paul's personal reflections in his writings. In recounting the many trials he endured as an apostle, Paul observed that "five times I received at the hands of the Jews the forty lashes less one" (2 Cor. 11:24), that he was beaten and stoned, presumably once again from Jewish opponents (11:25), and that he often faced "danger from my own people" (11:26). For Paul, the tragedy in all of this was not so much that he faced personal hardships and suffering, but that his own people, a people for whom he had great affection (see Rom. 9:1–5), had rejected the promised Messiah. Christ is the "end of the law" (Rom. 10:4), Paul asserted, and "the power of God for salvation to everyone who believes, to the Jew first and also to the Greek" (Rom. 1:16). Rather than treating the Jews as an adversary, he greatly desired to see his people embrace the gospel message, often placing himself in dangerous situations and accepting mistreatment simply for the opportunity to proclaim the good news of salvation to them.

Paul's Greek and Roman Opponents

The opposition Paul encountered was not limited to the Jewish people, of course. We also find that many of the Greeks and Romans often opposed his work, many of whom were local government officials and businessmen. Their opposition to Paul seems to have taken place not so much because of their objection to his message—a message which they often did not fully understand or care to investigate—but because of a variety of practical concerns. Government officials were often alarmed at the civil unrest that took place between local Christians and their Jewish opponents. Examples of this may be found in Luke's account of Paul's ministry in Philippi (Acts 16:19–24), Thessalonica (17:1–9), and Ephesus (19:23–41). Soon after arriving in Philippi on his second missionary journey, Paul was opposed by owners of a slave girl after he exercised a "spirit of divination" from her (16:16). He and Silas soon found themselves before the city's authorities, who ordered that they be beaten and detained in prison (16:20–24). In Thessalonica, local Jews are said to have formed a mob and to have "set the city in an uproar" (17:5). They then charged the local Christians with sedition, a charge that the local authorities naturally found disturbing (17:8). These developments forced Paul to abruptly depart the city (17:10). Finally, Paul and local Christians faced spirited opposition in Ephesus when members of what appears to have been a local trade association of silversmiths became threatened by the growth of the Christian movement. These businessmen stirred up the crowds and a riot quickly ensued.

Throughout most of Paul's missionary career, the opposition he encountered from Greeks and Romans tended to be localized and to have taken place primarily when citizens came to regard Christianity as a threat to the local economy or when the peace of the city seemed threatened. In most cases, Greeks and Romans seem to have regarded Christianity as little more than a unique intra-Jewish movement or as a harmless superstition that was attractive to those of the lower classes.[2] We find a helpful example of Roman perceptions about Christianity in Acts 18:12–17 where Luke records Paul's hearing before the Roman proconsul Gallio in Corinth. Charged with "persuading people to worship God contrary to the law" (Acts 18:13), Paul was brought before the *bema* seat to offer a defense. Before he could even speak, however, Gallio abruptly dismissed the case, describing the dispute as little more than a religious conflict over the finer points of the Jewish law. From this brief account it would appear that Gallio, like many from his time, regarded Christianity simply as a particular Jewish movement with some unique beliefs and practices that were not embraced by all Jews. He thus reasoned that any religious disputes between Paul and his opponents were beyond his purview.

Gallio's perspective appears to have been consistent with the prevailing attitudes of many non-Christians during the first thirty years or so of Christianity's existence. During these initial decades, Christians were largely ignored by the Roman authorities and were not typically viewed as a significant threat to society. As long as Christianity was regarded as a Jewish movement, Christians experienced only occasional conflict with Roman authorities. There was nothing that resembled a systematic or widespread effort to eradicate the movement during the initial decades of the church's existence. This general posture began to change, however, during the final years of Nero's reign. By this time Christianity was becoming increasingly recognized as an independent movement and regarded less favorably by the Roman authorities. A key turning point in the relationship between Christians and the Roman authorities took place in 64 CE when large portions of Rome were consumed by fire. According to ancient accounts, Nero blamed the Christians for the catastrophe and a period of intense persecution promptly followed.[3] As was discussed in Question 9, early Christian writers seem to have situated the martyrdoms of both Peter and Paul to this time.

Paul's Christian Opponents

One might naturally assume that the opposition Paul encountered derived strictly from non-Christians such as the Roman authorities or from the Jewish

---

2. For insight related to the manner in which ancient Greeks and Romans understood Christianity, see Robert Louis Wilken, *The Christians as the Romans Saw Them* (New Haven, CT: Yale University Press, 2003); Larry W. Hurtado, *Destroyer of the Gods: Early Christian Distinctiveness in the Roman World* (Waco, TX: Baylor University Press, 2016).

3. The fire in Rome and Nero's treatment of the Christians is recorded by historians such as Tacitus (*Annals* 15.38–44 [Jackson, LCL 322]), Suetonius (*Nero* 16 [Rolfe, LCL 38]), Dio Cassius (*Roman History* 62.16–18 [Cary and Foster, LCL 176]), and Sulpicius Severus (*Chronicle* 2.29).

people. He died, after all, as a martyr and was a deeply beloved apostle with great influence. What we find in Paul's epistles, however, is that he was often opposed by members of local churches who sought prominence and public recognition. We find in the Corinthian epistles, for example, that his work was undermined by a number of prominent figures whom he pejoratively described as "super-apostles" (2 Cor. 11:5). We do not know the identity of these individuals, but it appears from Paul's rebuke of their behavior that they had challenged his authority, questioned his reputation and motivations, and sought to undermine his teachings. In his epistle to the Philippians, we find similar allusions to those who preached the gospel "out of selfish ambition" (Phil. 1:17).

The opposition Paul encountered from self-described Christians was not limited to detractors who sought notoriety for themselves or who resented the success that Paul achieved. In addition to those who were threatened by Paul's influence and sought positions of prominence in Christian communities, Paul also faced opposition from those who were resistant to core elements of his teaching. His epistle to the Galatians, for example, was written in part to correct a "different gospel" (Gal. 1:6) that had advanced throughout the region, while Colossians appears to have been written largely to address the advancement of some type of syncretic form of Christianity that incorporated various Jewish, Christian, and ascetic practices and teachings.

Paul's Spiritual Opposition

In addition to the personal and often violent opposition Paul experienced from those who opposed his teaching, we also find that he encountered significant opposition in the spiritual realm. In fact, Paul appears to have regarded this form of opposition as his main threat. From his perspective, the human opposition he experienced was little more than a tangible manifestation of the spiritual warfare that is taking place throughout the world, warfare that will ultimately culminate with Christ's victory over his enemies.

Paul clearly affirmed that those who reject the gospel message are culpable for their willful rejection of the truth, yet he also understood that sinners suffer from spiritual blindness. Regeneration occurs, therefore, not merely when one understands a key intellectual concept or affirms the reality of a particular historical event, but as a result of the Spirit's work in the life of the individual. From his perspective, all of humanity falls into one of two major camps: those who have experienced spiritual rebirth, and those who exist in a state of spiritual deception and ignorance and live according to the flesh.[4] Note Paul's descrip-

---

4. This is not to suggest, of course, that salvation entails a complete and instantaneous transformation of the mind. In fact, Paul encourages believers to proactively renew their minds (Rom. 12:2). For a recent study on Paul's understanding of the spiritual transformation of the human mind, see Craig S. Keener, *The Mind of the Spirit: Paul's Approach to Transformed Thinking* (Grand Rapids: Eerdmans, 2016).

tion in Ephesians of believers prior to their conversion: "And you were dead in the trespasses and sins in which you once walked, following the course of this world, following the prince of the power of the air, the spirit that is now at work in the sons of disobedience—among whom we all once lived in the passions of our flesh, carrying out the desires of the body and the mind, and were by nature children of wrath, like the rest of mankind" (Eph. 2:1–3). To the Corinthians, Paul explained that "The natural person does not accept the things of the Spirit of God, for they are folly to him, and he is not able to understand them because they are spiritually discerned" (1 Cor. 2:14). In keeping with this reality, Paul emphasizes that the primary conflict in which God's people find themselves engaged is spiritual in nature. "We do not wrestle against flesh and blood," he explains to the Ephesians, "but against the rulers, against the authorities, against the cosmic powers over this present darkness, against the spiritual forces of evil in the heavenly places" (Eph. 6:12).

One of the more striking observations that might be made from these passages is the close connection Paul makes between the spiritual warfare taking place in the world and his work as an apostle. He understood that he was engaged in a spiritual battle, a battle that would result in fierce opposition from God's enemies but would ultimately end in victory. From his perspective, those who have not experienced spiritual rebirth are held captive to Satan and live enslaved to their sinful human nature. Christ will ultimately defeat Satan and all who follow him (Rom. 16:20). In the meantime, however, the mission of the church stands in direct opposition to "the prince of the power of the air." Paul recognized that he stood in direct opposition to the work of Satan whenever he proclaimed Christ and that this results in significant resistance. He was also aware that this opposition might be enacted through various human agents, while on other occasions Satan would actively attempt to thwart his efforts to advance the gospel by directly impacting his immediate circumstances. In 1 Thessalonians 2:18, for example, Paul assures his readers that he and his companions desired to visit them but that "Satan hindered us."

Interestingly, Paul also relates the enigmatic "thorn in the flesh" to the work of Satan (2 Cor. 12:7). While offering few details, he observes that this "thorn" served as a "messenger of Satan to harass me" in order to keep him from being conceited. This explanation may seem unexpected given that Satan would have surely had few objections to Paul exhibiting pride. Why would Satan seek to make Paul dependent on God's grace? We find in the verses that follow, of course, that Paul looked to the Lord to relieve him of this source of agony. This would suggest that God allowed the "thorn" in Paul's life, and that Satan used it as a means of harassing him. What this thorn may have been is difficult to discern. Some have identified it as certain temptations he may have experienced throughout his Christian life, to some type of physical ailment or injury that diminished his quality of life (e.g., an eye injury), to depression or some type of psychological distress, or simply as a general description of the opposition and hostility he consistently encountered. Without additional details, we can only speculate about the specific nature of the affliction that he alludes to here. What is clear, however, is that he recognized a spiritual dimension to the pain he experienced.[5]

Summary

Several New Testament writings indicate that the apostle Paul faced significant opposition over the course of his many years of missionary activity and that efforts to suppress his teaching and ministry often took many forms. As he journeyed throughout the Roman world proclaiming Jesus as the promised Messiah and taking part in the establishment of local churches, he often faced opposition from Jewish opponents who were convinced that his teaching was misguided and that it posed a significant threat. On other occasions he was opposed by Greeks and Romans who were concerned that he was the cause of civil unrest or that his movement was having a deleterious impact on the local economy. Opposition to Paul did not derive solely from non-Christians, however. As noted in his writings, he was often challenged by various Christian teachers and leaders who viewed him more as a competitor than as a companion. Despite the intensity of the opposition he encountered, Paul understood that his main form of opposition was spiritual in nature and that it was therefore necessary for him to remain faithful to the calling he received from the Lord and to view his struggles and hardships with an eternal perspective.

REFLECTION QUESTIONS

1. What appears to have been the main causes for the Jewish opposition Paul frequently experienced?

2. Generally speaking, how did the Romans' perception of Christianity evolve during Paul's lifetime?

3. What are some of the ways that Paul's awareness of spiritual warfare may have influenced the manner in which he responded to opposition?

4. In your own experience, have you faced more conflict with those inside or outside of the church?

5. What are some of the similarities between the manner in which Paul and Jesus responded to the opposition and mistreatment they encountered?

---

5. For a recent study of this subject, see Kenneth Berding, *Paul's Thorn in the Flesh: New Clues for an Old Problem* (Bellingham, WA: Lexham, 2023).

PART 2

Questions About Paul's Writings

SECTION A

The Writing of Paul's Letters

When and Where Did Paul Write His Letters?

In addition to the difficulty of accounting for Paul's background and tracing his activities and movements, interpreters are faced with the challenge of ascertaining when and where each of his canonical writings were composed. This is no simple task. The book of Acts does not make mention of Paul's writing ministry, and references in Paul's letters to his immediate circumstances are often limited. Further complicating matters, there are only a limited number of historical events recorded in his writings that provide a chronological reference point. In what follows, we will consider the available evidence relating to the background of Paul's writings and seek to establish the probable provenance of each of the canonical writings attributed to Paul and when they may have been composed. Our treatment will follow the assumed chronological order in which the writings were composed, an order that begins with Galatians and ends with 2 Timothy.[1]

Galatians (c. 48–49 CE)

A number of subjects relating to the background of Galatians remain widely disputed. One of the more foundational subjects that interpreters have debated is Paul's intended audience, a subject that has implications for how other aspects of the epistle's background are understood. Prior to the mid-twentieth century, the majority of scholars held to the so-called North Galatian theory,

---

1. For further discussion of the dating and provenance of Paul's writings, readers will benefit from graduate-level introductions to the New Testament as well as biblical commentaries and dictionary articles (see, for example, the helpful entries in *DPL*). Two recent monographs that offer fresh and alternative perspectives on the dating and background of the Pauline letters include Douglas A. Campbell, *Framing Paul: An Epistolary Biography* (Grand Rapids: Eerdmans, 2014); Jonathan Bernier, *Rethinking the Dates of the New Testament: The Evidence for Early Composition* (Grand Rapids: Baker Academic, 2022).

a theory which holds that Paul wrote the epistle to those in the northern regions of the Roman province of Galatia who were a distinct ethnic people of Celtic background known variously as the Gallograecians (Gallo-Greeks), or simply as Gauls or Galatians. This people group had migrated to Asia Minor from Macedonia and the surrounding areas roughly three centuries before the birth of Christ. The area which they inhabited during the first century is not as well known to those familiar with Paul's missionary journeys, in large part because of the fact that Acts makes no mention of Paul ministering in this area. Those who hold to the North Galatian theory tend to argue that Paul wrote Galatians after the Jerusalem Council (c. 49 CE). If Paul did write his epistle to this particular people, it is unlikely that he did so until at least the second major missionary journey recorded in Acts given that Luke's account of the first journey does not allow for a visit to this region, an important factor considering that Paul was clearly writing to a body of Christians with whom he was familiar. Because proponents of this theory argue for a date of composition at some point after the Jerusalem Council, they tend to identify the journey to Jerusalem described in Galatians 2:1–10 as Paul's description of this event.

Since the mid-twentieth century, a number of scholars have defended the alternative South Galatian theory. Proponents of this theory argue that the "Galatians" to whom Paul addressed were part of a more eclectic group of individuals living throughout the southern regions of the area loosely referred to as Galatia. This might include those living in cities where he had previously ministered such as Antioch of Pisidia, Iconium, Lystra, and Derbe (see Acts 13–14). According to this theory, Paul likely wrote Galatians after returning from the first major journey when he received the troubling news that many of those from this area had fallen sway to false teaching. Because it is clear from Acts that Paul visited these cities during the first missionary journey, it might be supposed that Paul wrote Galatians at some time after returning to Antioch at the conclusion of the journey, that is, around 48 or 49 CE, with many assuming a date of composition just before to the Jerusalem Council. The provenance would be a bit difficult to determine given that Paul traveled from Antioch to Jerusalem for the Jerusalem Council during this time. He may have written the epistle from Antioch, a nearby city such as Damascus, or another location as he traveled to and from Jerusalem. Because of the fact that Antioch was a hub of early Christian activity and that Paul and Barnabas "remained no little time with the disciples" (Acts 14:28) there after the first journey, it is perhaps most likely that Galatians was written from this location, that is, if the South Galatian theory is affirmed.

While compelling arguments have been presented for both major theories relating to the background of Galatians, the balance of evidence appears to favor the South Galatian theory. As Luke's narrative reveals, much of Paul's missionary activity was centered in the southern regions of Galatia and there is no direct evidence that he was engaged in missionary activity in the northern regions. The concerns that are addressed in Galatians would also seem to have been of greater consequence prior to the Jerusalem Council than in the years that followed. Although we should not assume that the Jerusalem Council resulted in a decisive end to the controversy over the relationship between Gentile believers and the Mosaic law, it would certainly seem likely that the teaching of Paul's opponents would have garnered less influence after this time.

1 and 2 Thessalonians (c. 50–52 CE)

On the basis of Luke's account of Paul's ministry in Thessalonica and his subsequent travels, it may be inferred that Paul wrote both epistles to the new converts in Thessalonica shortly after he was forced to flee Macedonia during the second missionary journey. Luke records that Paul first traveled to Berea (Acts 17:10–15), before traveling alone to Achaia where he ministered for a short time in Athens (Acts 17:16–34) before moving on to Corinth (Acts 18:1–18), where he was joined by Silas and Timothy (Acts 18:5). Because the names of his companions are placed in the greeting of the Thessalonian epistles, it may be reasonably assumed that Paul wrote both epistles from Corinth during his visit to the city.

While several clues within Acts and the Thessalonians epistles provide a basic sense of the period of Paul's ministry in which these epistles were written, it is an archaeological discovery that has enabled scholars to ascertain the most likely of composition. From Acts we learn that Paul spent eighteen months in Corinth (Acts 18:11) and that his time in the city overlapped with the tenure of the proconsul Gallio (18:12–17). In the early twentieth century, an inscription was located at the site of the famous Temple of Apollo in the city of Delphi. Notably, the inscription contains a greeting from the emperor Claudius to the local citizens and refers to the proconsul Gallio by name. Because the inscription refers to the year of Claudius's reign and makes reference to Gallio, we may infer that Gallio served in this capacity from approximately the summer of 51 to the summer of 52 CE. With these factors taken into consideration, it may be concluded that Paul wrote 1 and 2 Thessalonians after arriving in Corinth, perhaps as early as 50 CE but certainly not later than 52 CE.[2] In light of Paul's urgent tone throughout the epistles, it would seem more likely that he penned these writings closer to the time of his arrival in Corinth than to the time of his departure.

1 Corinthians (c. 53–56 CE)

The Corinthian epistles appear to have been written during Paul's third missionary journey, during a period in which he remained concerned about

---

2. While some have suggested that 2 Thessalonians may have actually been written first, most scholars have concluded that the canonical order is likely consistent with the order of composition.

the spiritual progress of those in Corinth. With regard to 1 Corinthians, a few clues appear in the final chapter that provide insight about the writing's provenance. In 1 Corinthians 16:8, Paul writes of his intention to "stay in Ephesus until Pentecost." Later in the chapter he sends greetings from "the churches of Asia" (1 Cor. 16:19). Ephesus, of course, was the capital city of the province of Asia and where Paul spent a considerable amount of his time during the third missionary journey. Based on this reference, we may conclude that Paul likely wrote 1 Corinthians during his lengthy stay in Ephesus, perhaps somewhere between 53 to 56 CE. Dating the Corinthian epistles with precision is difficult because it is not exactly clear how long Paul stayed in Antioch prior to the start of the third missionary journey or how long he ministered in the various cities of Asia Minor before arriving in Ephesus. The dating of 1 Corinthians is also complicated by the difficulty of determining how long Paul had been in Ephesus by the time the writing was composed.

2 Corinthians (c. 55–57 CE)

Second Corinthians appears to have been written shortly after Paul was forced to abruptly leave the city of Ephesus, an event described in Acts 19:21–20:1. In addition to Luke's account of the circumstances that led to his departure from Ephesus, Paul alludes in 2 Corinthians to his journey through Macedonia on his way to Corinth after he left Ephesus. We learn from Paul's reflections that Titus had been previously dispatched to Corinth to minister to the believers there, presumably to provide them with further instruction and to assess the situation before returning with a report for Paul. This plan was hindered, however, by Paul's untimely exit from Ephesus. Because Titus had yet to return to Ephesus by the time he left the city, Paul sought to intercept him as he returned to Ephesus. Failing to find his companion in Troas (2 Cor. 2:12–13), Paul sailed to Macedonia, where he eventually located Titus who brought with him encouraging news about the Corinthians' reaction to Paul's instruction (2 Cor. 7:5–16). In response to this report, Paul wrote to the Corinthians once again, expressing joy for their progress and their reception of his instruction. It is unclear precisely where Paul composed and dispatched what is now known as 2 Corinthians. Possibilities include cities he had previously visited such as Philippi, Thessalonica, and Berea. Like 1 Corinthians, it is difficult to be confident in a precise date of composition of 2 Corinthians, though a date in mid-50s is most likely.

Romans (c. 56–57 CE)

Paul's celebrated epistle to the Roman believers appears to have been written from Corinth near the end of his third missionary journey, just before he departed to Jerusalem to deliver the relief offering that he had organized among the Gentile churches. Acts records that Paul visited Greece for a three-month period after he had traveled through Macedonia (Acts

20:2–3), a period that would have been an ideal occasion for him to write the epistle before making the eastward journey. Although Luke does not identify the particular areas where Paul was located during this three-month period, references in the text of Romans strongly suggest that he was in Corinth when he penned this writing. Given his concern for the situation in Corinth throughout the third missionary journey, it is highly likely that he made his way to Corinth during this time. The large number of individuals referred to by name in Romans who appear to have been linked to the city of Corinth also suggest a Corinthian provenance. He refers by name, for example, to his host Gaius, possibly one of his earlier converts (1 Cor. 1:14), and a city treasurer (*oikonomos*) named Erastus (Rom. 16:23). Remarkably, an inscription with the name of an individual named Erastus has been located in Corinth. It is possible that this was the same individual referred to by name in Romans. Paul also commends an individual named Phoebe who is said to be on her way to Rome, presumably as part of the delegation delivering the epistle. Paul notes that she was from "the church at Cenchreae" (Rom. 16:1), a port city just a few miles to the east of Corinth. Because the writing was composed near the end of Paul's third major missionary journey, a date of composition around 56 or 57 CE is plausible.

The Prison Epistles (c. 59–62 CE)

The epistles of Ephesians, Philippians, Colossians, and Philemon, writings commonly referred to as the Prison Epistles, have been traditionally understood to have been written during the Roman imprisonment recorded in Acts 28:17–31, a two-year event that is often thought to have begun sometime between the years of 58 to 60 CE. Although alternative theories have been proposed, many scholars who affirm the authenticity of these works remain convinced that they were written by Paul from Rome. In both Colossians and Philemon, Paul describes himself as a prisoner (Col. 4:18; Philem. 9) and refers to several of the same individuals, suggesting that they were likely written on the same occasion. The large number of individuals who had apparently been with Paul would also seem consistent with the theory that the epistles were written during his first Roman imprisonment. As Luke records, Paul "welcomed all who came to him" (Acts 28:30) during this time. Conversely, Paul reveals in 2 Timothy that he was joined only by Luke (2 Tim. 4:11). Also of interest is the similar content contained in Colossians and Ephesians, parallels that may suggest that the two epistles were written around the same period of time. We might thus conclude from the internal evidence that Ephesians, Colossians, and Philemon were likely written within a fairly short time of one another and from the same location, Rome being the most likely.

Although the text of Philippians does not provide direct parallels or links to the epistles of Colossians, Ephesians, or Philemon, the references to the "whole imperial guard" (*praitōrion*) and to "those of Caesar's household"

(Phil. 4:22) have traditionally been understood as evidence for a Roman provenance. It is certainly the case that the term *praitōrion* was used on occasion to refer to the headquarters of a Roman procurator in one of the provinces or simply to the soldiers who were assigned to protect the emperor, though a Roman provenance would seem to provide the most natural explanation for these references. In sum, a Roman provenance for the four "Prison Epistles" is not demanded by the evidence, though it is consistent with early Christian tradition and provides what is arguably the most plausible explanation for the parallels between these writings and the unique language they contain.

The Pastoral Epistles (c. 62–67 CE)

Assuming the authenticity of the Pastoral Epistles and the plausibility of the two-imprisonments theory, we may now consider when Paul wrote these epistles in relation to the two imprisonments. While not universally recognized, it would seem most likely that Paul wrote all three of the Pastorals after the first Roman imprisonment.[3] As previously discussed, the Pastorals include references to Paul's activities that cannot be easily placed within the narrative of Paul's missionary journeys recorded in Acts. This would suggest that 1 Timothy and Titus were likely written after Paul was released from house arrest in Rome, perhaps between 62 and 65 CE, and that he composed 2 Timothy during his second imprisonment somewhere around 65 to 67 CE.

The text of 1 Timothy 1:3 implies that Paul was somewhere in Macedonia when he wrote to Timothy, his trusted companion who was continuing the work that Paul had previously begun in Ephesus. More difficult is the task of ascertaining Paul's location at the time in which he wrote Titus. While it would seem likely that he also wrote this epistle between the two Roman imprisonments, the provenance of the writing simply cannot be determined on the basis of internal evidence. The content of 2 Timothy, however, implies that it was written by Paul as he faced imminent martyrdom. Unlike the hints of optimism that may be observed in the Prison Epistles, Paul seems resigned to the reality that he would soon give his life for his Lord (2 Tim. 4:6–8).

Summary

Determining when and where Paul composed each of his writings is a difficult task. In the case of some of the letters, the specific occasion in which he wrote can be determined with reasonable confidence and dated to a fairly specific window of time. On other occasions, however, we must be satisfied with

---

3. A date of composition prior to Paul's Roman imprisonment is advocated by John A. T. Robinson, *Redating the New Testament* (London: SCM, 1976), 67–85. Robinson finds the two-imprisonment theory to be unconvincing and thus places the composition of the Pastorals to an earlier period of Paul's ministry. Similar conclusions are also defended in Bo Reicke, *Re-examining Paul's Letters: The History of the Pauline Correspondence*, eds. David P. Moessner and Ingalisa Reicke (Harrisburg, PA: Trinity Press International, 2001).

more tentative and less precise conclusions. Although various aspects of the background of the epistles remain a matter of debate, the evidence suggests that Paul's writings were composed over a period of nearly twenty years and written from a variety of locations, which are summarized with the following chart.

Paul's Writings		
Letter	**Date**	**Provenance**
Galatians	c. 48–49	Antioch or another location in Syria or Judea
1–2 Thessalonians	c. 50–52	Corinth
1 Corinthians	c. 53–56	Ephesus
2 Corinthians	c. 55–57	Macedonia
Romans	c. 56–57	Corinth
Prison Epistles	c. 59–62	Rome (traditional site)
1 Timothy	c. 62–65	Macedonia
Titus	c. 62–65	Unknown location
2 Timothy	c. 65–67	Rome

REFLECTION QUESTIONS

1. How might the question of the original recipients of Galatians relate to our understanding of other aspects of the letter's background?

2. How does the archaeological discovery of an obscure inscription at Delphi provide evidence for the dating of the Thessalonian epistles?

3. In your view, how compelling is the evidence for a Roman provenance of the Prison Epistles?

4. Do the close parallels between the text of Ephesians and Colossians lead you to the conclusion that they were likely written from the same location and around the same time? Why or why not?

5. From your perspective, how feasible is to place one or more of the Pastoral Epistles into the period of Paul's ministry that is recorded in Acts?

How Did Paul's Companions Assist in the Composition and Distribution of His Letters?

When thinking about the composition of Paul's letters, our natural inclination is to assume that the process would have been somewhat similar to that of modern letter writing, but obviously with more primitive technology. Rather than typing out a letter on a computer and sending it either electronically or through the postal service, it is recognized that different tools would have been used and that the delivery of the letter would have been much less convenient and taken much more time. It is certainly helpful to be familiar with the various materials and writing instruments that were commonly used by ancient authors such as Paul and John when they determined to "write with pen and ink" (3 John 13). What is often overlooked, however, is the basic process involved in the composition and dispatch of writings in the Greco-Roman world. When an author such as Paul determined to write a letter to a community of Christians in a distant location such as Corinth or Rome, how would he have gone about doing so? Would it have been as simple as acquiring unused sheets of papyri, mixing the necessary ingredients to produce the ink, possibly reviewing material recorded on a *tabula* (wax tablet), and finding a quiet place to gather one's thoughts and produce the work? In reality, the differences between ancient and modern letter writing are not limited to the tools, materials, and technology available to authors. Often overlooked is the collaborative nature of ancient writing. Rather than a private activity, writing for ancient authors such as Paul often involved collaboration with a number of individuals. In this chapter we will consider some of the more common ways that Paul's trusted associates would have likely assisted him in the writing and distributions of his letters.[1]

Paul's Sources of Information

Paul's letters are often described as occasional in nature. By this it is understood that he did not simply craft theological treatises on matters of personal interest or address issues of general interest to readers across the Roman world, but that he used his letters to respond to actual events and circumstances that were of relevance to Christians living in particular communities. In light of this, it might be asked how Paul came to learn about the circumstances facing his readers in the first place. He lived, of course, during a time in which information was much more difficult to obtain and when news traveled much more slowly. Given these challenges, how would he have learned about the troubling developments in Galatia, for example, or the various matters that needed to be addressed in Corinth?

It is helpful to keep in mind that communication between Paul and the churches to which he ministered often took place in both directions. In order for Paul to address specific matters of relevance to those in a particular community, he first needed to acquire information about the circumstances they faced and the matters that needed to be addressed. This type of information would have come to Paul through two basic types of individuals: those who were part of the communities he sought to address, and members of his apostolic circle. Several examples could be cited. With regard to the former, we find that Epaphroditus, a member of the church in Philippi, was sent to minister to Paul while he was imprisoned (Phil. 2:25–30). Much of Paul's understanding of the situation in Philippi would have derived from the report he received from Epaphroditus before Philippians was composed. Also of interest is Paul's remark in 1 Corinthians 1:11. "For it has been reported to me by Chloe's people," Paul writes, "that there is quarreling among you, my brothers." It might be possible that these "people" were Christian slaves who were familiar with the situation in Corinth and that they relayed information to Paul. They may have been a part of the Corinthian church and brought news to him when they were in Ephesus completing business on behalf of Chloe. Another possibility, of course, is that Chloe lived in Ephesus and that members of her household brought news to Paul about the situation in Corinth after they had recently traveled there. Paul also refers to the arrival of individuals from Corinth such as Stephanas, Fortunatus, and Achaicus (1 Cor. 16:15–17). These are just a few of the individuals who may have provided Paul with information related to the situation in the city.

---

1. The subjects explored in this chapter are taken up in greater detail in Benjamin P. Laird, *Creating the Canon: Composition, Controversy, and the Authority of the New Testament* (Downers Grove, IL: InterVarsity Press, 2023).

In addition to a number of individuals from churches throughout the Roman world who brought news to Paul about the circumstances facing Christians in various communities, we know from his letters and the various accounts in Acts that he often sent his coworkers to distant locations in order to minister in local Christian communities. Upon their return, they would have naturally provided him with updates related to the recent developments that had taken place and offered their perspective on urgent matters that needed to be addressed either in person or through written instruction. Luke records, for example, that Timothy and Silas stayed behind in Macedonia after Paul was forced to leave the region (Acts 17:14) and that they later joined him in Corinth (Acts 18:5). We may assume that they provided him with news about the recent developments that had taken place in Macedonia after they met him Corinth. This information would have certainly proven useful to Paul as he composed his letters to the Thessalonians. We find direct evidence of the importance of their reports in 1 Thessalonians 3:6–7: "But now that Timothy has come to us from you, and has brought us the good news of your faith and love and reported that you always remember us kindly and long to see us, as we long to see you—for this reason, brothers, in all our distress and affliction we have been comforted about you through your faith." We also learn that Paul dispatched Timothy to Macedonia during his time in Ephesus (Acts 19:22; 1 Cor. 4:17; 16:10), and that Titus was sent out by Paul on important assignments (see, e.g., 2 Cor. 8:16–18). These are just a few of the many examples we find in Scripture of Paul dispatching his associates to various locations.

Paul's Secretaries

We find direct evidence in Paul's writings that his common practice was to enlist the services of a secretary, also referred to as an amanuensis or scribe.[2] At the end of his epistle to the Romans, Paul's secretary interjects with the words "I Tertius, who wrote this letter, greet you in the Lord" (Rom. 16:22). Rather than composing Romans by hand as he worked in solitude, this greeting reveals that Paul worked directly with Tertius, presumably a local believer in Corinth. This would suggest that Paul's custom, like many ancient authors, was to dictate the content of his writings to a secretary who was tasked with the actual composition. Some may find it difficult to understand why secretaries would have been commonly used by ancient authors in

---

2. For additional background relating to Paul's use of secretaries, see E. Randolph Richards, *Paul and First-Century Letter Writing: Secretaries, Composition and Collection* (Downers Grove, IL: InterVarsity Press, 2004); Richard N. Longenecker, "Ancient Amanuenses and the Pauline Epistles," in *New Dimensions in New Testament Study*, eds. Richard N. Longenecker and Merrill C. Tenney (Grand Rapids: Zondervan, 1974), 281–97; Hans-Josef Klauck, *Ancient Letters and the New Testament: A Guide to Context and Exegesis* (Waco, TX: Baylor University Press, 2006), 55–60; Jerome Murphy-O'Connor, *Paul the Letter Writer* (Collegeville, MN: Liturgical Press, 1995), 1–41.

the first place. Why would educated individuals like Paul find it necessary to enlist the services of a secretary? To answer this question, it must first be recognized that reading and writing were regarded as two separate tasks in the Greco-Roman world. In contrast to reading, writing was regarded as a technical skill that required specialized training and expertise. Even those who were well educated would often work with a secretary when composing letters and other pieces of literature. Secretaries typically maintained all the needed writing materials, could write in a style that was more efficient and attractive to the eye, and could provide the author with advice and recommendations regarding the wording and structure of a writing. While those who were illiterate often hired a secretary to write a letter simply out of necessity, members of the upper classes were known to train or purchase slaves to serve as their personal secretary. Cicero, for example, is known to have collaborated with his slave Tiro when composing his writings.

The degree to which authors relied upon their secretary would have differed considerably. One with little literary abilities who needed to write a letter might visit the shop or home of a secretary and simply share the basic information that he or she wished to communicate. When traveling on business in a city such as Corinth, for example, an individual might hire a secretary to compose a letter for his wife back home in Athens. In such cases, he might simply share the basic information that he wished to convey, and the secretary would then put together the letter for his client. Others preferred to dictate the text directly to their secretary and to exert more control over the precise language that was used. This was likely the case with the apostle Paul. His letters were considerably longer than the average letter of antiquity, were written for public rather than private consumption, and address a number of theological matters that could not be articulated in just any way by any secretary. Each of these factors would suggest that Paul would have been very particular in how his letters were composed. Instructing a secretary to pass along news about one's intended travel or recent business dealings is one thing; instructing a secretary on how to address complex theological matters is quite another.

Regardless of the degree to which secretaries may have been responsible for the content of a writing, it appears that it was a common practice for them to read the completed letter to their client or for them to offer them the opportunity to read the finished work before it was dispatched. Once it was approved by the author, he or she would then sign his or her name at the end of the manuscript. This would often include a short personal greeting. As might be expected, this personal greeting would often result in a noticeable change of handwriting where the transition was made from the hand of the secretary to the hand of his client.[3] Many of Paul's writings, of course, conclude with

---

3. For background related to this practice, see Steve Reece, *Paul's Large Letters: Paul's Autographic Subscriptions in the Light of Ancient Epistolary Conventions*, LNTS 561

a short greeting in which he draws attention to the fact that it was written in his hand (see 1 Cor. 16:21; Gal. 6:11; Col. 4:18; 2 Thess. 3:17; Philem. 19). His final words in Galatians even draw attention to what would have been a noticeable change of handwriting in the original manuscript. "See with what large letters I am writing to you with my own hand" (Gal. 6:11), Paul writes. In addition to providing a personal touch, the signature and personal greeting served as a means of authentication. In many cases, it would be difficult for the recipients to assess the authenticity of a letter apart from the signature and greeting at the end of the work. This would have especially been the case if the letter was delivered by someone who was unknown to the recipients.

Paul's Letter Carriers

Now that we have briefly considered some of the primary ways that Paul's companions may have assisted him with the composition and production of his letters, it will be helpful to address how they likely assisted him with the delivery of his works.[4] Because there was no postal system in the Roman world available to the general public, it was necessary for authors such as Paul to make arrangements for the delivery of their writings. The least expensive method, though certainly not the most dependable, was to send a letter off with the care of a stranger who was traveling near the letter's intended destination. Travelers would often carry letters from one town to another, leaving the letters at a known location where they could then be collected by the recipients or picked up by those who were heading even closer to those addressed in the letter. There was nothing, of course, that could guarantee the ultimate arrival of a letter or that its contents would not be tampered with. As a result, this method was typically reserved for communication that was rather mundane or when the sender did not have the means for a more reliable manner of delivery. In Paul's case, we may assume that his letters were not typically dispatched in this way. Because of the importance of his writings and the significant amount of time and energy that would have been invested in their production, it is doubtful that he would leave the delivery of the writings

---

(London: T&T Clark, 2017). Reece provides several examples of extant writings from antiquity in which this change in handwriting may be observed.

4. For further treatment on role of letter carriers, see Richards, *Paul and First-Century Letter Writing,* 171–209; M. Luther Stirewalt, *Paul, the Letter Writer* (Grand Rapids: Eerdmans, 2003), 9–19; Margaret M. Mitchell, "The New Testament Envoys in the Context of Greco-Roman Diplomatic and Epistolary Conventions: the Example of Timothy and Titus," *JBL* 111 (1992): 641–62; Klauck, *Ancient Letters,* 43–66; Peter M. Head, "Letter Carriers in the Ancient Jewish Epistolary Material," in *Jewish and Christian Scripture as Artifact and Canon,* eds. Craig A. Evans and H. D. Zacharias, SSEJC 13 (London: T&T Clark, 2009), 203–19; Head, "Named Letter-Carriers Among the Oxyrhynchus Papyri," *JSNT* 31 (2009): 279–99; Matthew S. Harmon, "Letter Carriers and Paul's Use of Scripture," *JSPL* 4 (2014): 129–48; Stephen Llewelyn, "Sending Letters in the Ancient World: Paul and the Philippians," *TynBul* 46 (1995): 337–56.

to chance. It is thus much more likely that his practice was to entrust the delivery of his letters to his associates or those from local churches who were available to travel. In fact, several possible references to those who served as Paul's letter carriers may be found throughout his writings:

Letter	Possible Letter Carrier(s)	Reference
Romans	Phoebe	Rom. 16:1–2
1 Corinthians	Timothy or Stephanas, Fortunatus, and Achaicus	1 Cor. 4:17; 16:10–11 1 Cor. 16:17–18
2 Corinthians	Titus	2 Cor. 8:16–22; 9:3–5
Ephesians	Tychicus	Eph. 6:21–22
Philippians	Timothy or Epaphroditus	Phil. 2:19–23 Phil. 2:25–30
Colossians and Philemon	Tychicus	Col. 4:7–9; Philem. 12
2 Timothy	Tychicus	2 Tim. 4:12
Titus	Artemas or Tychicus or Zenas and Apollos	Titus 3:12 Titus 3:13

In addition to their main responsibility of delivering letters to their intended readers, letter carriers were known to have fulfilled additional roles as well. In the case of Paul's correspondence, his letter carriers may have been responsible not simply for delivering his writings, but with providing the recipients with clarification regarding its content. This was a known responsibility of ancient letter writers, and one which we may assume was shared by those who were dispatched by Paul. In a practical sense, a letter carrier represented the author. As Peter Head observes, "the letter-carrier can have an important role in the communication process, in supplementing verbally material that appears in written form in the letter, continuing or extending the conversation of the letter. This can involve further discussion and the return of the letter-carrier."[5]

---

5. Head, "Named Letter-Carriers, 288–89.

In addition to providing readers with clarity and additional insight, letter carriers could also bring back a report to the author of the situation facing the readers and how they responded. As Margaret Mitchell explains, letter carriers were expected to "bring return messages and personal attestation of what they had witnessed."[6] We may infer that Paul often relied on those who delivered his writings to inform him of the state of affairs in the various churches where he maintained ties. On certain occasions, these updates may have prompted him to write additional follow-up letters.

Summary

Paul's writing ministry was much more collaborative in nature than is often realized. In many cases, he relied upon those who had recently visited a particular community to provide him with relevant information about the circumstances the community was facing and the issues that needed to be addressed. This collaboration also extended to the composition and distribution of his writings. In keeping with common practice at the time, there is evidence that Paul worked closely with a secretary when composing his letters and that he relied upon trusted companions to deliver the completed letters to their intended destination.

REFLECTION QUESTIONS

1. If Paul's writings were occasional in nature and written for specific individuals and communities, why are they regarded as relevant for the entire church?

2. Does the prospect that Paul commonly used a secretary seem unsettling to you? Why or why not?

3. Do you think it is possible that Paul's secretaries influenced the wording or content of his writings in any way? If they did, would this be problematic?

4. Do you think it is reasonable to assume that Paul relied upon trusted companions to deliver his letters?

5. Aside from delivering a letter, what are some of the ways that Paul's letter carriers may have contributed to his ministry?

---

6. Mitchell, "New Testament Envoys," 653–54.

Did Paul's Letters Resemble the Style and Structure of Contemporary Letters?

Paul's Jewish heritage, his use of the Old Testament in his writings, and the ways in which he related the work of Christ to the various Old Testament covenants, prophecies, and institutions have received considerable scholarly attention, while his reputation as a passionate Jewish follower of Jesus remains widely recognized. What is not as widely understood or appreciated, however, are the ways in which his writings demonstrate a familiarity with the Greco-Roman world. As discussed in the first three chapters of this volume, Paul was born into a Jewish family that lived in a city permeated by Greek culture. Although he was "a Hebrew of Hebrews" (Phil. 3:5), he was very much at home in Hellenized settings. In fact, we may safely assume that Paul grew up speaking Greek and that he was acutely familiar with the culture and customs of the Greco-Roman world. In addition to the content of his writings, Paul's acquaintance with the Hellenized world may be observed in both the structure and style of his letters. In light of this, it is helpful for students of Paul's writings to become familiar not only with his Jewish background, but the Greco-Roman world in which he lived and ministered. This chapter will offer a concise summary of the typical components of Paul's letters, the ways in which he typically arranged and presented his content, and some of the stylistic features of his writings that were common in the Greco-Roman world at the time.

Over the last century and a half, a large body of Greek letters and other writings from the early centuries of the Roman era have been discovered throughout the Mediterranean world. Perhaps most famously, thousands of ancient manuscripts, most of which were written in Greek, were discovered in the Egyptian city of Oxyrhynchus at the end of the nineteenth century and into the twentieth century by teams led by British scholars Bernard P. Grenfell and Arthur S. Hunt. So numerous were the manuscripts discovered during these years that only a small portion of the writings have been transcribed and published. Most of the manuscripts are commercial or legal in nature (e.g., receipts, bills, tax statements, business records, and personal wills), though a number of personal letters and literary works were discovered, including some biblical writings.[1]

As a result of the large number of Greek letters that have been discovered in Oxyrhynchus and elsewhere, scholars are now more familiar with the standard components and features of letters written during the New Testament era.[2] As might be assumed, letters from the Greco-Roman world were written for a variety of occasions and purposes and for different types of audiences. Some writings were designed to be read privately (e.g., a letter from a husband to a wife), while others were intended for a wider audience and tended to be more formal in nature (e.g., the letters of Cicero or Seneca).[3] Despite these differences, a number of common features may be observed in the letters from this time. As we compare Paul's writings to other ancient letters from the Greco-Roman world, we find that his writings were similar in style and structure to that of his contemporaries but that he often added a unique personal touch and made some interesting modifications. In what follows, we will outline the basic parts of Greek letters and make several observations relating to the way in which they tended to function in Paul's writings.[4]

---

1. This includes a large portion of the New Testament papyri that have been catalogued. For background on the Christian texts discovered at this site, see Lincoln H. Blumell and Thomas A. Wayment, eds., *Christian Oxyrhynchus: Texts, Documents, and Sources* (Waco, TX: Baylor University Press, 2015). For accounts related to the discovery of several of the notable biblical manuscripts discovered in Egypt, see Brent Nongbri, *God's Library: The Archaeology of the Earliest Christian Manuscripts* (New Haven, CT: Yale University Press, 2018).

2. For further treatment of the various types and features of ancient letters in the Greco-Roman world, see Hans-Josef Klauck, *Ancient Letters and the New Testament: A Guide to Context and Exegesis* (Waco, TX: Baylor University Press, 2006); Stanley K. Stowers, *Letter Writing in Greco-Roman Antiquity*, LEC 5 (Philadelphia: Westminster, 1986); David E. Aune, *The New Testament in Its Literary Environment*, LEC 8 (Philadelphia: Westminster, 1987).

3. Nearly a century ago, Adolf Deissmann observed a difference between public and private Hellenistic letters. Private letters were typically shorter and less formal, Deissmann explained, while letters designed for public use tended to be much longer and formal in nature. Deissmann referred to the former as "letters" and the latter as "epistles." In this volume, the terms "letters" and "epistles" are used interchangeably, though it is helpful for readers to be aware that a distinction is often made in more technical studies. See Adolf Deissmann, *Light from the Ancient East: The New Testament Illustrated by Recently Discovered Texts of the Graeco-Roman World*, trans. Lionel Strachan (New York: George H. Doran Co., 1927).

4. For additional treatment of the structure and style of Paul's letters, see Jeffrey A. D. Weima, *Paul the Ancient Letter Writer: An Introduction to Epistolary Analysis* (Grand Rapids: Baker

The Opening

It was customary for Greek letters to begin with an opening that identifies the author (placed in the nominative case) and the recipients (placed in the dative case) followed by a brief greeting. In some writings, the greeting was placed at the very beginning of letter, but even in these cases the author was commonly placed before the recipient. The common "greeting" that appeared in Greek letters was the word *chairein*, the present active infinitive of the Greek verb *chairo*, though alternative spellings may be found in ancient literature. We find examples of this type of opening throughout the New Testament:

- "The brothers, both the apostles and the elders, to the brothers who are of the Gentiles in Antioch and Syria and Cilicia, greetings (*chairein*)" (Acts 15:23).
- "Claudius Lysias, to his Excellency the governor Felix, greetings (*chairein*)" (Acts 23:26).
- "James, a servant of God and of the Lord Jesus Christ, To the twelve tribes in the Dispersion: Greetings (*chairein*)" (James 1:1).

This type of greeting was also common in private letters from the early centuries of the Christian era. A few examples from the discoveries at Oxyrhynchus will suffice:[5]

- "Sarapas to her sister Diogensis, greeting (*chairein*)."
- "Eudaemonis to my lord Ptolemaeus, greeting (*chairein*)."
- "Didymus to his father Chaeremon, very many greetings (*chairein*)."
- "Aristandrus to his son Apion, greeting (*chairein*)."

As the greetings in Paul's writings are compared to that of his contemporaries, two unique characteristics of his writings stand out. First, as can be seen from

Academic, 2016); M. Luther Stirewalt, *Paul, the Letter Writer* (Grand Rapids: Eerdmans, 2003); Jerome Murphy-O'Connor, *Paul the Letter Writer* (Collegeville, MN: Liturgical Press, 1995); William Doty, *Letters in Primitive Christianity* (Minneapolis: Fortress, 1973); Stanley E. Porter, *Paul the Apostle: His Life, Thought, and Letters* (Grand Rapids: Eerdmans, 2016), 136–55; Stanley E. Porter and Sean A. Adams, eds., *Paul and the Ancient Letter Form*, PAST 6 (Leiden: Brill, 2010); Detlev Dormeyer, "The Hellenistic Letter-Formula and the Pauline Letter-Scheme," in *The Pauline Canon*, ed. Stanley E. Porter, PAST 1 (Leiden: Brill, 2004), 59–94; Ben Witherington III, *The Paul Quest: The Renewed Search for the Jew of Tarsus* (Downers Grove, IL: InterVarsity Press, 1988), 103–15; Timothy A. Brookins, *Ancient Rhetoric and the Style of Paul's Letters: A Reference Book* (Eugene, OR: Cascade Books, 2022).

5. The examples in this chapter from Oxyrhynchus letters derive from Bernard P. Grenfell and Arthur S. Hunt, *The Oxyrhynchus Papyri*, vol. 9 (London: Egypt Exploration Fund, 1898), 259–63.

these examples, the opening of Greek letters tended to be very succinct. The author would simply cite his or her name, the name of his recipient(s), and offer a brief word of greeting. In contrast, Paul was often quite expressive in this section, including much more detailed descriptions of his background and apostolic role while offering various reflections and insights about his readers. A good example of this comes from his greeting to the Roman church. Rather than simply refer to himself as Paul, he includes a series of descriptions, each of which provide further insight relating to his background and apostolic calling. This information would have been useful in this context given that many of his readers had not met him in person by the time he wrote the letter. It is quite re-markable that the first six verses of the epistle is nothing more than an expansion of the name "Paul!" The other letters of Paul do not contain such lengthy personal identifications, but they still tend to be longer than typical greetings from this time. Only the Thessalonian letters lack any additional information about Paul's background or self-understanding and simply cite his name.

Another interesting observation regarding Paul's letters is that he does not use the typical Greek word to greet readers, opting instead to use a similar sounding word that offers a unique Christian flavor. As noted above, letters commonly included the word *chairein* in the greeting. Paul, on the other hand, commonly used the noun *charis*, a word typically translated into English as "grace." In fact, each of the thirteen writings attributed to Paul begin with the words *charis hymin*, "grace to you" and end with similar language (e.g., "The grace of the Lord Jesus be with you" in 1 Cor. 16:23).

The Thanksgiving or Blessing

The greeting was often followed by an expression of gratitude or blessing upon the reader(s), a section that is sometimes referred to as the "thanksgiving." In the majority of cases, this is placed after the author greets his reader(s) near the beginning of the letter, though it was occasionally placed near the end of the work. Some scholars regard this portion of the letter as an extension or part of the greeting, while others view it as a separate unit. Because it was not always placed in a specific location, it might be best to view it as a discrete section, though compelling arguments have been offered for the alternative perspective.

Examples of a "thanksgiving" may be observed throughout the extant literature. In many cases, the author simply includes a brief word of gratitude for his reader(s) or express his or her desire for their well-being, often making reference to his prayer to the gods. Note the following examples from the same sources cited above (listed in the same order):

- "I pray always to all the gods for you . . ."
- "I am again writing you this my letter, first sending you salutations, and secondly praying to all the gods that you may receive them in health and prosperity along with all our friends. . . . I pray for your health."

- "I pray for your health."
- "I pray for your perpetual health and prosperity, my son."

In the first two examples, the thanksgiving is offered after the initial greeting, an arrangement that differs in the final two examples, in which cases the thanksgiving is placed near the end of the letter. While the location of the thanksgiving was not the same in each letter, it is clear from even these few examples that they typically include some type of prayer or wish for the well-being of the reader(s).

Paul's writings also include a thanksgiving or blessing, though they typically refer to spiritual realities rather than physical health and prosperity, the more common items appearing in literature from the time. For Paul, the thanksgiving sections were not included as a mere formality but as an opportunity to expound upon profound theological realities. To cite but a few examples, Paul expresses his gratitude to God for his readers' faith in Romans 1:8 and elaborates on the "grace of God that was given you in Christ Jesus" in this letter to the Corinthians (1 Cor. 1:4–9). Perhaps the most developed thanksgiving section in all of Paul's writings is found in Ephesians 1:3–23. Throughout these verses, Paul describes the rich spiritual transformation that his readers have experienced through the work of Christ. Many additional examples could be offered, though it is clear even from these few examples that it was Paul's practice to use the thanksgiving section of his writings to remind his readers of the rich spiritual blessings that belong to God's people through the work of Christ.

The Body

The body of Greek letters served as the heart of the author's message. It was here that the author would provide news and information deemed useful or of interest to his or her readers, instruction about particular matters, explanations about various subjects, appeals to complete certain tasks, and so on. A solider writing home, for example, might use this portion of the letter to provide his family with news about his recent activities, to instruct his wife about a particular business deal, or to encourage his children to remain diligent in their studies and daily responsibilities. This section of the letter was typically the longest and tended to vary the most widely from letter to letter.

While the content of each letter was unique, scholars have noted several specific types of phrases, expressions, and statements, "formulas" as they are often called, that were commonly used in the body of ancient letters. Paul's letters are known to make frequent use of several of these formulas. He will often include, for example, specific formulas to make a transition to a new section (e.g., the formula *peri de* "now about"[6]) or to introduce certain material (e.g.,

---

6. The formula *peri de* appears in 1 Corinthians 7:1, 25; 8:1; 12:1; 16:1, 12; 1 Thessalonians 4:9; 5:1. These formulas are often used to introduce subjects. Paul, for example, writes in 1 Corinthians 8:1, "Now concerning food offered to idols. . .".

appeal[7] or disclosure formulas[8]). His writings are especially diverse in the types of material they include and often transition quickly from one form (e.g., an appeal of some kind) to another (e.g., a prayer or doxology). Consequently, the more familiar the interpreter becomes with the conventional formulas that were used in Greek letters, the better equipped he or she will be in recognizing the various literary units in Paul's writings, how he intended certain portions of his writings to be understood, what he sought to emphasize, how certain portions of his writings were designed to function, and how the various portions of his writings were meant to relate to one another.

Scholars have identified a large portion of the material in the body of Paul's writings as *paraenesis*, material that might be described as moral instruction or exhortation. These types of appeals are common in Greek letters and are not found in religious writings alone. A father might write his son, for example, and admonish him to live a life of virtue, to honor his family, to devote himself to his responsibilities, etc. As might be expected, Paul's writings are replete with various exhortations, what many today might refer loosely describe as "application." In many cases the *paraenetic* material in Paul's writings builds upon the didactic material placed earlier in the epistle, providing readers with clarification regarding the practical implication of what has been previously addressed. At times readers might be encouraged to maintain a particular perspective or attitude, to engage in a specific action, to behave in a particular manner, to flee a particular sin, etc. In his epistle to the Romans, for instance, Paul treats a number of theological subjects throughout the first eleven chapters of the epistle and then encourages his readers over the last several chapters to live and think in a way that is consistent with these theological realities.

The Closing

Like the opening, the closing of Greek letters tends to be concise and to contain some type of final blessing or wish for the good health of the reader(s) along with a final "goodbye." In more formal letters such as the Pauline Epistles, the closing might be used to reinforce key points the author made

---

7. Appeal formulas typically include the Greek verb *parakaleō* ("I appeal") and refer to the recipient. Examples of this abound in Paul's letters. Weima's study cites the following passages: Romans 12:1–2; 15:30–32; 16:17; 1 Corinthians 1:10; 4:16; 16:15–16; 2 Corinthians 10:1–2; Philippians 4:2; 1 Thessalonians 4:1, 10b–12; 5:12, 14; 2 Thessalonians 2:1–2; 1 Timothy 2:1; Philemon 9–10. Weima, *Paul the Ancient Letter Writer*, 93.

8. Disclosure formulas typically include a verb that relates to a state of knowledge such as *oida*, *ginōskō*, or *agnoeō* and are used to emphasize points that the author wishes his readers to understand. A good example is Philippians 1:12: "I want you to know, brothers." The point can also be made in the negative. In Romans 1:13, for example, Paul writes "I do not want you to be unaware, brothers . . .". Additional examples include 2 Corinthians 1:8; Galatians 1:11; 1 Thessalonians 2:1. See Weima, *Paul the Ancient Letter Writer*, 93–100.

in the body of the letter or simply to offer a final word of encouragement or exhortation. Scholars have noted several reoccurring elements in the closing of Paul's writings. Jeffrey Weima, for example, observes that there were five common elements in Paul's closings: (1) a peace benediction; (2) a hortatory section which offers final instruction or exhortation; (3) a greeting, which in Paul's epistles often referred to those in his company and included instruction to greet specific individuals; (4) an autograph statement in which Paul took up the pen himself (rather than dictating to his scribe) to authenticate the work; and (5) a final grace benediction, which, unlike typical closings that charged the reader to "be strong" or to "prosper," appealed to the grace that derives from Christ.[9]

Summary

Over the course of many years, Paul used his letters to communicate with a number of Christian communities and to provide them with needed encouragement and instruction. Although Paul was one of the first Christian authors to use letter writing to instruct Christians in distant locations, the letter itself was widely used in the Greco-Roman world. Paul's letters typically contained each of the basic elements of letters from this time though he often made notable adaptations and modifications. Each portion of Paul's writings was carefully designed for a particular purpose and exhibited a distinctively Christian flavor.

REFLECTION QUESTIONS

1. In your view, what might be some possible advantages of becoming familiar with the various features and characteristics of letters from the Greco-Roman world?

2. What are some of the ways that Paul appears to have used the greetings of his writings to introduce himself or the subjects he sought to address?

3. What are some of the ways that Paul uses the "thanksgiving" or "blessing" elements in letters? Can you think of any specific examples?

4. What are some of the common features or characteristics of the bodies of Paul's writings?

5. What appears to have been the major purposes or functions of the closing element in Paul's writings?

---

9.   Weima, *Paul the Ancient Letter Writer*, 165–204.

When and How Were Paul's Writings First Collected and Published?

It is only natural to question how the letters of Paul originally came together to form a single collection. How might we explain how a large number of writings, each of which were composed in different places, at different times, and written to different readers, were collected and placed in a single collection of authoritative Scripture? There was clearly some type of deliberate effort in the early church to preserve Paul's writings, but what is the most plausible explanation for how several disparate writings initially came to form a single collection? To answer this fundamental question, it will be helpful to begin our discussion with a brief survey of some of the more common explanations that have been offered over the last century. We will then consider what is arguably the most plausible explanation for the formation of the Pauline corpus.[1]

Before we begin our study of this intriguing subject, it will be helpful to place this chapter in relation to those that immediately follow. As one might suspect, it is difficult to ascertain the process that led to the formation of the Pauline corpus without addressing questions related to its content. The process that took place naturally involved a selection of material. As a consequence, a number of questions are commonly asked about the rationale for the inclusion of certain works and the omission of others, topics that will be taken up in greater detail in the following chapters. After introducing the

---

1. For a more extensive overview of the formation of the Pauline corpus, see Benjamin P. Laird, *The Pauline Corpus in Early Christianity: Its Formation, Publication, and Circulation* (Peabody, MA: Hendrickson, 2022); Stanley E. Porter, ed., *The Pauline Canon*, PAST 1 (Leiden: Brill, 2001); David Trobisch, *Paul's Letter Collection: Tracing the Origins* (Minneapolis: Fortress, 1994); Leslie C. Mitton, *The Formation of the Pauline Corpus of Letters* (Eugene, OR: Wipf & Stock, 2009); L. Scott Kellum and Charles L. Quarles, *40 Questions About the Text and Canon of the New Testament* (Grand Rapids: Kregel, 2023).

basic process that likely resulted in the formation of the Pauline letter corpus in this chapter, we will consider the canonical connection between the Epistle to the Hebrews and the Pauline letter corpus (Question 16), the fate of the lost letters of Paul (Question 17), why many scholars have questioned the authenticity of some of the canonical works attributed to Paul (Question 18), and the possible basis for the authenticity of these writings (Question 19). In many ways, this chapter will serve as our starting point for the questions addressed in the next several chapters.

Scholarly Theories Pertaining to the Origin of the Pauline Letter Corpus

Before we consider the most likely set of circumstances that led to the initial formation of the collection of Paul's writings, it will be helpful to briefly describe some of the more influential theories that have been advanced at some point over the last century and a half of scholarship. During the twentieth century, American scholars such as Edgar Goodspeed (1871–1962), John Knox (1901–1990), and C. Leslie Mitton (1907–1998) suggested that Paul's writings were largely neglected until several years after their initial composition. According to this viewpoint, the Pauline writings went largely unnoticed for several years as the church dealt with a number of pressing concerns and controversies. It was not until other writings were produced around the end of the first century that the Pauline Epistles began to draw interest from broad audiences. It has been suggested that the composition of Acts near the end of the first century led many Christians to begin taking interest in the writings of Paul. As a result of the prominent role of Paul in the second half of Acts, the publication of Luke's narrative is thought to have led to greater interest in the works attributed to the "apostle to the Gentiles." Several writings then began to circulate that had previously been known only to those in local communities or were largely forgotten. As more writings became known, definitive collections containing multiple letters began to form. Some who hold to his theory would also place the composition of certain works such as the Pastoral Epistles to the period after Paul's death, concluding that the initial collections of Paul's writings contained a mere handful of authentic writings that were later combined with several recently composed pseudonymous writings.

A second major theory is that Paul's writings were highly valued in a number of Christian communities in the years following his martyrdom but that the process leading to the collection's formation was rather slow and gradual and that it took many years for all of the writings attributed to Paul to be composed and to achieve widespread recognition. Several of Paul's letters likely began to circulate shortly after his death, at least in certain regions, though it took a number of years for the larger collections to emerge. This could have taken place either through the exchange of letters between various Christian communities (e.g., the churches in Macedonia exchanging letters with the churches of Asia) or perhaps through the effort of one or more individuals who searched the Roman world for Paul's writings. Like the first theory discussed above, this theory is also compatible with the viewpoint of many scholars that a number of pseudonymous writings were composed in the years following Paul's death, some of which began to circulate as part of the collections that emerged during this time.

A third major theory, one that is related in certain ways to the viewpoints articulated above, is that the formation of the Pauline letter corpus was the work of one or more groups of individuals, "schools" as they are often described, which sought to enhance Paul's legacy and/or to combat heretical teaching. These groups are understood to have functioned as custodians of Paul's letters in the years following his martyrdom and to have played a role in their initial circulation. Some who hold to this basic understanding of the corpus's formation have also suggested that members of these groups may have been responsible for penning writings such as Ephesians, Colossians, and the Pastoral Epistles in the years following Paul's death. These individuals may have therefore played a role not only in collecting and preserving the letters of Paul, but in expanding and circulating the collection. The additional writings they produced would have been designed to preserve Paul's legacy and to address a number of contemporary concerns. Members of these schools may have included former associates and companions of Paul who sought to continue his mission, or simply a number of individuals who were devoted to his teaching but had no formal connection to him. As the church wrestled with various controversies and conflicts, it is often thought that one or more particular groups of Paul's devotees sought to use a collection of Paul's writings to direct and influence the greater Christian movement. In contrast to those who advocated a more Jewish-friendly form of Christianity, for example, members of these schools may have championed the law-free gospel of Paul and sought to use the writings to point the church in a direction that was more accommodating to Gentile converts. Others point to theological controversies such as Gnosticism as the primary concern of these individuals, and that works such as the Pastorals were composed largely to suppress and combat these types of movements.

Literary Conventions and the Emergence of the Pauline Letter Corpus

The three basic theories discussed above have drawn a number of adherents, in large part because of the common assumption that the Pauline letter corpus would have taken many years to develop, and, at least to a certain extent, because of their compatibility with the viewpoint that the New Testament canon contains several pseudonymous writings attributed to Paul. It is often assumed that the collection of such a diverse body of writings must have taken a considerable period of time to form, especially if there was not a significant demand for Paul's writings after they were first written and if several letters in the corpus were not even composed until several years after Paul's death. Recent advancements in our understanding of first-century literary conventions have made it clear, however, that a lengthy period of time to locate letters throughout the Roman world may not have been necessary.

As discussed in Question 13, Paul appears to have worked with various secretaries when composing his letters. This is a significant factor since secretaries were known to produce duplicate copies of the works they produced for their clients. This practice would have enabled writers to maintain a copy of their writings for future reference and to ensure their preservation. There were no guarantees, of course, that a letter would ultimately be delivered to its intended readers or that it would be preserved once it arrived. As Harry Gamble explains:

> Ancient writers often kept copies of their private letters even when no particular literary merit or topical importance was attached to them; and copies of instructional, administrative letters were all the more likely to be kept. In antiquity, collected editions of letters were nearly always produced by their author or at their author's behest, often from copies belonging to the author.[2]

As Gamble observes, the duplicate copies maintained by ancient authors were often used to form collections of their writings. In fact, an argument could be made that the collections of the epistolary literature of ancient authors such as Cicero, Seneca, Plutarch, Ignatius of Antioch, Pliny the Younger, and possibly Cyprian were formed not from individuals traveling through large areas in search of their writings, but from the duplicate copies maintained by the authors or their companions.[3] An author such as Paul would have found the practice of maintaining duplicate copies to be especially useful. As is often observed, his writings are not the everyday works of antiquity. They were significantly longer than the average letter, required careful thought and planning, and treated subjects that were of relevance to broad audiences. Preserving a copy of these works would have allowed him the opportunity to consult them after they were dispatched and help ensure that they would not be forever lost if they did not make it to the intended readers or if they were somehow lost or destroyed at some point after their arrival. It would indeed be difficult to

---

2. Harry Y. Gamble, *Books and Readers in the Early Church* (New Haven, CT: Yale University Press, 1995), 101.

3. For a treatment of early letter collections from the Roman period, see Bronwen Neil and Pauline Allen, eds., *Collecting Early Christian Letters: From the Apostle Paul to Late Antiquity* (Cambridge: Cambridge University Press, 2015); Cristiana Sogno, Bradley Storin, and Edward Watts, eds., *Late Antique Letter Collections: A Critical Introduction and Reference Guide* (Oakland: University of California Press, 2017).

imagine Paul dispatching the sole manuscript of an important work such as Romans without first taking the necessary precaution of having it duplicated.

In light of the strong probability that Paul's custom was to maintain copies of his writings, we may posit that the formation of the corpus is unlikely to have resulted from one or more individuals searching throughout the Roman world for his letters or even from a mutual exchange of writings between various communities. More probable is the prospect that someone within Paul's immediate circle simply took the works he maintained, selected the writings that were of relevance to wider audiences, and prepared them for circulation as a single collection. In addition to selecting material to be included in this work, it may also be possible that the initial editor(s) of the collection assigned the letter titles that have been preserved.[4] Some have even suggested that Paul may have taken part in selecting material for a collection of his writings in the period leading up to his martyrdom, though it is also possible that one or more of his trusted associated such as Luke completed this work at some point after Paul's death.

With regard to the content of the initial edition of Paul's letters that were formed from these duplicates, it is unlikely that less than ten epistles were included. While there is evidence that there were some early collections in circulation that did not include either the Pastoral Epistles or Hebrews, it is difficult to demonstrate that the collection ever circulated in a form that contained less than the ten canonical writings that Paul addressed to seven specific individual churches or communities (Philemon appears to have been closely linked to Colossians). Each of these writings commonly appear in early textual witnesses to the corpus and are treated as authoritative Scripture by several early Christian writers. As noted in Question 19, the Pastorals also appear to have been recognized as Scripture by early Christian writers, though they may not have been included in each of the earliest collections. For some, this observation is consistent with the viewpoint that these writings are later pseudonymous works. It should be kept in mind, however, that ancient authors are known to have occasionally expanded their letter collections over time. It may certainly be possible, therefore, that an initial collection of ten epistles was released at some point in the final decade or so of Paul's ministry and that expanded editions were subsequently produced that included writings composed during the final years of his lifetime.[5] In fact, we find reference to a body of Paul's works in 2 Peter 3:16. Assuming the authenticity of 2 Peter, this passage may suggest that many of Peter's readers were familiar with a

---

4. It is noteworthy that each of the titles are designed in a similar fashion (the preposition *pros* followed by the name of the recipients), suggesting that they were created by the same individual(s) at a very early period. Unlike many of the titles in the New Testament, each of the Pauline letter titles refer to the recipients rather than the name of the author.
5. This basic idea was suggested in Lewis Foster, "The Earliest Collection of Paul's Epistles," *BETS* 10 (1967): 44–55.

collection of Paul's writings during the 60s of the first century. Certainty regarding the circumstances leading to the initial formation of the corpus is difficult to achieve, though the prospect that the initial collection of letters was formed from the duplicate copies in Paul's possession is arguably the most plausible explanation for the emergence of the collection.

The Arrangement of Letters in the Pauline Corpus

Now that we have considered how the corpus of Paul's writings most likely formed, a brief word about the arrangement of the Pauline Epistles in modern English Bibles may be helpful. Some readers may be surprised to learn that the arrangement of writings they are accustomed to is noticeably different than the chronological order in which they appear to have been written. The reason for this is simply that early collections of the Pauline letters were arranged on the basis of length. When copying multiple works, scribes often found it convenient to begin with the longest writing and to leave the shortest writings to the end. If running short on writing space, a scribe would naturally prefer to find himself in the middle of a shorter letter such as Titus or Philemon than in the middle of a longer work such as Romans or 1 Corinthians.

The major difference between the standard arrangement in modern English Bibles and what may be observed in early Christian manuscripts is that Hebrews appears to have been originally placed near the beginning of the corpus. In the important manuscript $\mathfrak{P}^{46}$, for example, Hebrews is placed between Romans and the Corinthian Epistles. It then appears to have been commonly placed for a time between 2 Thessalonians and 1 Timothy. By the end of the fifth century, it became most frequently placed at the end of the collection after Philemon. The relocation of Hebrews was likely due to questions about its background and relationship to Paul.

Summary

This chapter has considered some of the common theories relating to the formation of an initial collection of Paul's writings and articulated a possible explanation for how the individual works were originally brought together. In contrast to theories which posit that the collection likely emerged after a lengthy period in which the writings were exchanged between churches or discovered by individuals traveling throughout the Roman world, it has been suggested that the initial collection of Paul's writings was likely formed from the duplicate copies in Paul's possession. Ancient authors such as Paul were known to maintain duplicate copies of their works in order to ensure their preservation and to provide them with access to their works after they were dispatched. It was also suggested that an initial collection of Paul's writings containing ten epistles was soon supplanted by larger collections that contained the Pastoral Epistles and Hebrews.

REFLECTION QUESTIONS

1. Of the major theories relating to the emergence of the Pauline corpus, which seems most convincing to you?

2. How likely do you believe it was that Paul maintained copies of his writings? How might this practice inform our understanding of the collection's formation?

3. What steps may have been involved in preparing an epistolary collection such as the Pauline corpus for its initial publication?

4. Assuming that the initial edition of Paul's writings included ten epistles, what do you believe is the best explanation for how the Pastoral Epistles and Hebrews were incorporated into the larger editions that soon followed?

5. In your view, is there possible hermeneutical significance to the manner in which the Pauline Epistles are arranged?

Did Paul Write the Letter to the Hebrews?

One of the most intriguing subjects relating to the study of the early collection of Paul's writings is the early reception of the letter to the Hebrews. Modern scholarship has decidedly rejected the possibility that Paul was the author of this writing, yet it is clear that it was closely linked to the apostle Paul in early Christianity. A casual reading of Hebrews will reveal that it is noticeably different than the thirteen canonical letters attributed to Paul. It reads more like an oral address than a typical letter, contains unique vocabulary and stylistic features, and addresses certain subjects that are not emphasized in Paul's writings (e.g., the priestly ministry of Christ). Despite these differences, many early Christians attributed the work to Paul and treated it as authoritative Scripture. So, what are we to make of this unique writing that circulated in early Christianity exclusively as part of the *corpus Paulinum*? How did it come to be closely connected to the apostle Paul and his writings, and is it possible that Paul was involved in some way in its composition? We will begin our discussion of these enthralling subjects by offering a brief overview of the reception of Hebrews in early Christianity and will then consider the possibility that Paul may have been responsible in some way for its content.[1]

The Reception of Hebrews in Early Christianity

It is widely assumed that the early church was deeply divided over the possibility that Hebrews was written by Paul and that its placement in the canon took several centuries to achieve. In fact, one might reach the conclusion from contemporary scholarship that a sizeable portion of the early

---

1. For further treatment of the canonical reception of Hebrews, see Benjamin P. Laird, *The Pauline Corpus in Early Christianity: Its Formation, Publication, and Circulation* (Peabody, MA: Hendrickson, 2022), 202–34.

church flatly rejected the possibility that Paul was the author of this writing and that it was not recognized as Scripture until many centuries after its composition. To be sure, there were certainly some who objected to the notion that the work was written by Paul. For the most part, however, the evidence would suggest that Hebrews was embraced very early as a Pauline writing and that its Pauline authorship was widely recognized. Even those who did not affirm direct Pauline authorship often assumed that it was written by someone in his immediate circle. This may be observed in the earliest textual witnesses to the collection of Paul's letters as well as the surviving testimony of early Christian writers.

Few manuscripts containing Paul's writings from the first few centuries of the Christian era have survived. What remains extant, however, indicates that Hebrews was incorporated into the Pauline letter collection remarkably early. One of the most important extant early manuscripts containing Paul's letters is 𝔓⁴⁶, an early Christian papyrus that contains the majority of the Pauline writings. Understood by many scholars to have been produced sometime around 200 CE, this manuscript includes the text of Hebrews and places it near the beginning of the Pauline corpus between Romans and 1 Corinthians.[2] Other early papyri also included Hebrews. This is the case in 𝔓¹³ and 𝔓¹²⁶, both of which contain only small fragments of the text of Hebrews in their extant condition but include pagination suggesting that Hebrews was placed near the beginning of a larger body of Paul's writings. Hebrews was also included in a number of well-known Greek majuscules produced during the fourth and fifth centuries. This would include Codex Sinaiticus (א 01), Codex Alexandrinus (A 02), Codex Vaticanus (B 03), Codex Ephraemi Rescriptus (C 04), and Codex Freerianus (I 016). Other notable manuscripts that contain Hebrews that were written a bit later include Codex Coislinianus (H 015), Codex Claromontanus (D 06), and Codex Vaticanus Graecus (048). Often overlooked is that Hebrews appears to have circulated exclusively as part of the Pauline letter corpus. We do not find examples of it circulating in other collections such as the Catholic Epistles (James–Jude).

The testimony of early Christian writers is also of importance for our understanding of the early reception of Hebrews.[3] As early as the late first century, we find evidence that it was regarded as authoritative Scripture. *First Clement*, one of the oldest extant Christian writings outside of the New Testament, quotes extensively from the first chapter of Hebrews. This is notable not only because this writing is thought by many to have been composed

---

2. As noted in Question 15, scribes commonly arranged the epistles according to length.
3. For further treatment of the early reception of Hebrews, see Laird, *The Pauline Corpus in Early Christianity*, 113–89; Andreas Lindemann, "Paul in the Writings of the Apostolic Fathers," in *Paul and the Legacies of Paul*, ed. William S. Babcock (Dallas: Southern Methodist University Press, 1990), 25–44; Jennifer R. Strawbridge, *The Pauline Effect: The Use of the Pauline Epistles by Early Christian Writers*, SBR 5 (Berlin: de Gruyter, 2015).

in the final decade of the first century, but because it is of western origin. Early reluctance to embrace the Pauline origin of Hebrews is known to have been more common among those living in the West, but this writing would indicate that there were some in the West who did in fact recognize the authoritative status of Hebrews from a very early period.

Establishing what writers from the next century or so may have understood about the background of Hebrews is a significant challenge, yet some interesting observations can be made about the epistle's early reception. We find that there are a lack of clear and unambiguous references to the text of Hebrews in the extant writings of some ancient Christian authors, making it difficult to determine whether they recognized the authority of the writing. This appears to be the case with notable writers such as Ignatius, Irenaeus, Athenagoras, and Theophilus of Antioch. In contrast, Pauline authorship appears to have been recognized by notable figures such as Clement of Alexandria, Adamantius, Epiphanius, Eusebius, Athanasius, Cyril, Gregory of Nyssa, Gregory of Nazianzus, Amphilochius, Didymus, Origen, and Chrysostom. In addition to these notable figures, Tertullian recognized Hebrews as authoritative Scripture but was of the persuasion that it derived from Paul's companion Barnabas. Jerome may have also regarded Hebrews as Pauline, though he observes in his writings that he is aware of differing opinions. Significantly, there is a lack of clear rejection of the Pauline authorship of Hebrews until around the late second or early third century. According to the later testimony of Eusebius, Gaius of Rome rejected the Pauline authorship of Hebrews,[4] a sentiment that may also be observed in the extant work of Victorinus of Pettau, a third-century writer who was convinced that the recognition of Pauline authorship is incompatible with the early tradition that Paul only wrote to seven churches.[5]

Paul's Possible Influence on the Composition of Hebrews

A common assumption of modern scholarship is that Hebrews was written by an unknown writer and that the work circulated independently for a period of time before it was incorporated into the collection of Paul's writings. The unique theological content of this writing and the notable linguistic differences with the undisputed Pauline Epistles are often thought to be too significant for it to have been composed by Paul.[6] In addition, the assertion made by the author in Hebrews 2:3 about the "great salvation" that he and his readers had come to know is widely regarded as contrary to Paul's

---

4. Eusebius, *Ecclesiastical History* 6.20.
5. Victorinus, *Commentary on the Apocalypse of the Blessed John* 1.16.
6. Not all would agree that the language and style of Hebrews precludes Pauline authorship. For an alternative viewpoint, see David Alan Black, *The Authorship of Hebrews: The Case for Paul* (Cantonment, FL: Energion Publications, 2013).

assertions elsewhere that he came to understand the gospel message after a direct encounter with Christ.[7] The challenge for many scholars, therefore, is accounting for its early association with Paul without embracing Pauline authorship. As David Allen explains: "New Testament scholarship has been reluctant to divorce the epistle to the Hebrews from Pauline influence, yet it has also been reluctant to identify the epistle as Paul's."[8] For some, there is a good possibility that the author was a close associate of Paul. As noted above, this seems to have been the viewpoint of Tertullian, the famed theologian of Carthage who held that the work was written by Paul's companion Barnabas. Allen holds a similar viewpoint, arguing that the work was composed by Paul's companion Luke. For many evangelical scholars, the viewpoint that Hebrews was composed by a companion of Paul such as Barnabas, Luke, Silas, or Apollos remains an especially attractive theory as it is thought to explain how the writing came to be closely associated with the Pauline letter collection apart from direct Pauline authorship.

Although it is difficult to make certain conclusions regarding the background of Hebrews, the possibility that its content may have derived from Paul should not be quickly dismissed. A connection to Paul would provide the most natural explanation for its early circulation as part of the Pauline letter collection. But what about its unique content and features? Would they not preclude Pauline authorship? Simply put, it is possible that many of the differences between Hebrews and the writings attributed to Paul may be attributed to is oral rather than epistolary style and to the fact that it was written to a primarily Jewish audience. The work lacks the traditional epistolary greeting and is presented more like an oral address than a written composition. In fact, the author (or speaker) refers to himself as speaking in several passages (cf. Heb. 2:5; 5:11; 6:9; 8:1; 9:5; 11:32). Curiously, the work reads like an oral address but ends like a typical epistle. Perhaps the best explanation for this is that the work represents some type of oral address that was later recorded, at which point it was dispatched to a particular audience and soon thereafter placed with the Pauline letter collection. One possibility is that the content of Hebrews originated as a speech that Paul made in a Jewish setting at some point in his career and that it was later recorded by one of his companions. This basic theory was advanced as early as Origen, who, according

---

7. Care should be made about reading too much into the text about the background of the author. It might be noted that the author makes frequent use of the inclusive "we" throughout the letter and that the specific verb used in this passage (Greek *bebaioō*) may not refer specifically to the act of passing something down from one person or group to another, but simply to the act of agreeing, establishing, or confirming something. Understood in this latter sense, the author may have simply been making the point that the gospel message he and his readers embraced was the same message that had been recognized by believers from the very beginning of Jesus's ministry.

8. David L. Allen, *Lukan Authorship of Hebrews*, NACSBT 6 (Nashville: B&H, 2010), 74.

to Eusebius, summarized his understanding of the background of Hebrews as follows:

> That the verbal style of the epistle entitled "To the Hebrews,"
> is not rude like the language of the apostle, who acknowl-
> edged himself "rude in speech," that is, in expression; but
> that its diction is purer Greek, anyone who has the power
> to discern differences of phraseology will acknowledge.
> Moreover, that the thoughts of the epistle are admirable, and
> not inferior to the acknowledged apostolic writings, anyone
> who carefully examines the apostolic text will admit. . . . If
> I gave my opinion, I should say that the thoughts are those
> of the apostle, but the diction and phraseology are those
> of someone who remembered the apostolic teachings, and
> wrote down at his leisure what had been said by his teacher.
> Therefore if any church holds that this epistle is by Paul, let
> it be commended for this. For not without reason have the
> ancients handed it down as Paul's. But who wrote the epistle,
> in truth, God knows. The statement of some who have gone
> before us is that Clement, bishop of the Romans, wrote the
> epistle, and of others that Luke, the author of the Gospel and
> the Acts, wrote it.[9]

Several important elements of Origen's testimony are of note. He readily acknowledges that the style of the writing differs from that of the Pauline Epistles and that its substance is weighty. He then makes an important distinction between the author of Hebrews and his secretary. This point is often overlooked or misunderstood. In many cases, Origen's exclamation, "But who wrote the epistle, in truth, God knows" is taken to suggest that he was uncertain about the subject of authorship and that he regarded the identity of the author to be unknowable. In reality, he seems to be suggesting that the content of the epistle derived from Paul, but that it is unclear who the individual may have been who served as the secretary. He suggests that it may have been someone like Clement of Rome or Paul's companion Luke, but he ultimately concludes that we cannot know who played this role.[10]

The recognition that Hebrews originated as an oral address of Paul that was later recorded by one of his companions accounts wells for the early placement of the work in the Pauline corpus, its widespread recognition in early Christianity as a Pauline epistle, as well as the many stylistic differences

---

9. Eusebius, *Ecclesiastical History* 6.25.11–14 (*NPNF* 2.1).
10. For further discussion, see Matthew Thomas, "Origen on Paul's Authorship of Hebrews," *NTS* 65 (2019): 598–609.

between this writing and the works attributed to Paul. We should certainly not expect a work that originated as an oral address to read like a typical letter, especially if the secretary had a significant influence on the language and style of the writing. If the work originated as a Pauline sermon or address, we might suspect that one of his colleagues took notes on the content of the oral address and, as Origen claimed, "wrote down at his leisure what had been said by his teacher." This type of procedure would not be as unusual as might be assumed. In fact, several early Christian writers indicate that Mark's gospel originated in this fashion. According to tradition, Peter shared his recollections pertaining to the ministry and teaching of Jesus in a series of oral addresses before he was martyred in Rome. During this time, Mark is said to have served as Peter's *hermēneutēs*, or "interpreter," carefully recording what he shared with those in attendance. Mark is not the only biblical author who is known to record oral addresses. As is widely known, Luke includes several speeches throughout his gospel as well as in Acts. Because of Luke's close connection to Paul, his demonstrated literary abilities, and his practice of recording speeches, he is an especially strong candidate to have served as the secretary responsible for composing the work that came to be known as Hebrews.[11]

Finally, if the theory that Hebrews originated as a Pauline speech that was later recorded by someone like Luke is accepted, we may further speculate that the epistolary postscript at the end of the writing may have served as Pauline authentication. As briefly noted in Question 13, writers would often review the work of a secretary before it was dispatched. In many cases, they would record a short greeting in their own hand to affirm to the original readers their approval of the content of the work. The Pauline features of the final verses of Hebrews have long been recognized. In addition to the update about Timothy (Heb. 13:23), the author closes with the word "Grace be with all of you" (Heb. 13:25), a common Pauline expression. As previously noted, each of the canonical epistles of Paul conclude with a similar greeting. So characteristically Pauline is the content of the final verses of the writing that these verses have been alleged by some scholars to have been written to deceive readers into thinking that the work was a genuine Pauline epistle.[12] Attributing the content of the writing to a speech of Paul, however, would eliminate the need for such conclusions. Not all scholars find the arguments in favor of an original Pauline sermon behind Hebrews to be convincing, though in the very least it

---

11. For further support of this conclusion, see Andrew W. Pitts and Joshua F. Walker, "The Authorship of Hebrews: A Further Development in the Luke-Paul Relationship," in *Paul and His Social Relations*, eds. Stanley E. Porter and Christopher D. Land (Leiden: Brill, 2013), 143–84. Pitts and Walker note several similarities between the language and style of Hebrews and Luke-Acts.

12. See, for example, Clare K. Rothschild, *Hebrews as Pseudepigraphon: The History and Significance of the Pauline Attribution of Hebrews*, WUNT 1/235 (Tübingen: Mohr Siebeck, 2009).

should be recognized that the arguments against Paul's possible relationship to the epistle are not as strong as typically assumed.

Summary

The background and reception of Hebrews are as unique as its content. Scholars often struggle to account for its early recognition as a Pauline writing while also accounting for the ways in which its style and content differ from that of the canonical works attributed to Paul. While no theory is free from speculation, it has been suggested in this chapter that a possible solution to these challenges is to attribute the content of the writing to an oral address originally delivered by Paul and the composition of the work to one of his companions.

REFLECTION QUESTIONS

1. What is your impression of the content of Hebrews? Do you get the sense that it could have derived from Paul?

2. What are some of the major objections to the Pauline authorship of Hebrews?

3. What might the final greeting of Hebrews reveal about its background?

4. What is your overall assessment of the possibility that someone like Luke may have recorded an oral address originally delivered by Paul or another figure?

5. If the possibility that Paul was responsible for the content of Hebrews is rejected, what might be the basis for its status as authoritative Scripture?

What Happened to the Lost Letters of Paul?

One of the most common questions raised in discussions about the composition of Paul's writings is the fate of his lost letters. Paul clearly wrote a number of letters that do not appear in the New Testament, leading to speculation about what may have happened to them after they were written. This is often followed up by the question of whether they should be included in the New Testament canon if they were miraculously discovered today. Many students are enthralled by these types of questions, perhaps because they address intriguing historical subjects that seem to have unclear theological implications. While there is much that we do not know about Paul's literary activities and the early circulation of his writings, a plausible theory related to the manner in which Paul's letters were originally collected and prepared for public circulation may provide a reasonable explanation for why certain writings were "lost." Following a brief survey of references in Paul's writings to works that are no longer extant, we will briefly consider some of the common explanations for why a number of Paul's letters were not included in the New Testament. We will then discuss how our understanding of the process leading to the formation of the Pauline letter corpus may help account for their omission.[1]

References to Lost Letters of Paul in Paul's Extant Writings

In light of the fact that Paul actively served as an apostle for more than three decades and that his work frequently required him to travel and communicate with a large number of communities and individuals, it might be reasonably assumed that he wrote far more letters than what has been

---

1. The issues discussed in this chapter are treated more fully in Benjamin P. Laird, *The Pauline Corpus in Early Christianity: Its Formation, Publication, and Circulation* (Peabody, MA: Hendrickson, 2022), 307–16.

preserved. In fact, we find evidence in the canonical writings for several letters of Paul that have not survived. In 1 Corinthians 5:9, Paul writes, "I wrote to you in my letter not to associate with sexually immoral people." Some might assume that Paul is referring in this passage to something he wrote earlier in the same writing. It is more likely, however, that he is alluding here to a separate letter that the Corinthians had previously received. In 2 Corinthians, we also find possible references to a nonextant writing, though this would seem less conclusive. Paul states, "For I wrote to you out of much affliction and anguish of heart and with many tears, not to cause you pain but to let you know the abundant love that I have for you" (2 Cor. 2:4). Later in the same epistle he writes, "For even if I made you grieve with my letter, I do not regret it—though I did regret it, for I see that that letter grieved you, though only for a while" (2 Cor. 7:8). It is certainly possible that this so-called "severe letter" was the first canonical letter addressed to the Corinthians. Most scholars would argue, however, that Paul was likely referring to a different epistle that has not been preserved. If it is in fact the case that both 1 and 2 Corinthians refer to nonextant works of Paul, we may conclude that Paul wrote no less than four letters to the Corinthians during his lifetime, though the actual number may have been even greater.

Another reference to a lost letter of Paul appears in Colossians 4:16. In this passage, Paul writes "And when this letter has been read among you, have it also read in the church of the Laodiceans; and see that you also read the letter from Laodicea." Various interpretations of this passage have been proposed since the early centuries of the church. The second-century theologian Marcion, for example, appears to have held that the passage refers to the epistle that came to be known as Ephesians. The most natural explanation, however, is that Paul is referring here to a letter he wrote for the church in Laodicea that has not been preserved. An additional reference to a lost letter appears in Ephesians. In Ephesians 3:3, Paul writes that he had "written briefly" about "how a mystery was made known to me by revelation." It is difficult to locate a reference to this mystery in the early portion of the epistle, making it possible that Paul was referring to a separate letter that he had previously sent to the Ephesians which no longer exists.

Outside of Paul's own writings, we find an early reference to one or more lost letters of Paul in Polycarp's second-century letter to the church in Philippi. He reminds his readers that "when he [Paul] was with you in the presence of the people of that time, he accurately and reliably taught the word concerning the truth. And when he was absent he wrote you *letters*."[2] Polycarp seems to have been aware that Paul composed several epistles for the church in Philippi. While this is sometimes explained by the theory that the canonical

---

2. *The Letter of Polycarp to the Philippians* 3:2. Cited from Michael W. Holmes, ed., *The Apostolic Fathers: Greek Texts and English Translations*, 3d ed. (Grand Rapids, Baker, 2007), 283–85.

epistle of Philippians is likely comprised of several smaller letters that were later brought together to form a single writing, it is more likely that Polycarp was referring to multiple writings that Paul sent over a period of time to those in Philippi, only one of which was preserved.

The Formation of the Pauline Corpus and the Lost Letters of Paul

Once it is recognized that Paul likely wrote several letters that have not been preserved, questions inevitable rise about their fate. Commentators have offered various explanations for how the letters may have possibly been lost. To mention just a few examples, it is sometimes suggested that a number of Paul's writings may have been lost as he traveled from location to location (e.g., in a shipwreck), that some may have disappeared as a result of the failure of the recipients to produce copies, that some may have been tragically destroyed in fire or in some other unfortunate event, or that some may have been confiscated or otherwise destroyed in the violent and turbulent years that followed Paul's death. Eventually the writings that survived were assembled and began to circulate as a literary collection. By this point, however, many of Paul's writings would have already been destroyed or lost and no longer in circulation.

To use an illustration, this understanding of the emergence of the Pauline letter corpus might be compared to the artwork of the seventeenth-century Dutch painter Carel Fabritius. While the works of Fabritius are highly prized, only about a dozen of his paintings have survived from what would have originally been a much larger collection. Had a large portion of his artwork not been destroyed in an explosion that rattled the city of Delft in the mid-seventeenth century—an explosion that also claimed his life—many more of his works would undoubtedly be displayed today in museums around the world. Similarly, many of Paul's writings are understood to have been destroyed in tragic circumstances, inadvertently lost, or simply neglected. As a consequence, the writings contained in the New Testament are simply assumed to be the sum of what has survived the many twists and turns of history. Understood in this manner, the loss of these writings was an unfortunate loss to the church, while the writings of Paul that have been preserved may simply be attributed to favorable settings, good luck, or God's providence. Just as Fabritius may have regarded some of the paintings that were claimed by the explosion to be of equal or even greater importance to the works that have survived to the present day, so too, some might infer, is it possible that Paul wrote several nonextant letters that he regarded to be of equal importance to the works in the canon. We have the writings that have been preserved not so much because they are the most valuable, it might be assumed, but simply because of the unpredictable ways that history unfolded.

This type of explanation may seem to be the only plausible explanation for how the corpus emerged and why certain letters were lost. An important point that was made in Question 15, however, is that scribes were known to produce copies of the works they composed for their clients. This practice is well attested in the ancient world, and it is clear that scribes often made duplicate copies not only of important business and legal documents, but of epistolary literature as well. Because this was a common scribal practice in the first century and the fact that Paul's writings were, to use the language of 2 Corinthians, "weighty and strong" (2 Cor. 10:10), it would be difficult to imagine that he sent his letters off without first ensuring that a copy was produced. There would have certainly been occasions in which he would have found it helpful to consult what he had previously written to a particular congregation or found it convenient to take a portion of a previously written letter and reuse a portion of it in his correspondence with other readers. Many of the issues that Paul addressed in his writings were of widespread relevance, of course. We may therefore assume that he occasionally found it helpful to place a portion of the content of one letter within another, or at least to base a portion of one letter off previously written material. However, even if Paul never found the need to consult a previously written work or to adopt portions of it in subsequent letters, it would have still been helpful for him to maintain copies of his letters simply to ensure that his work was preserved.

The idea that Paul or his associates maintained copies of his writings over several years may initially seem difficult to imagine. Are we to suppose that Paul carried a large bag with him from location to location that contained copies of all his works? Did he haul a cart that resembled something like an ancient bookmobile? Transporting a large body of his writings would have been inconvenient and often risky. What are the chances that Paul hauled a large stash of writings with him from location to location over many years and that they somehow survived all of his travels and the tumultuous events he encountered? It is perhaps more likely that he stored copies of his letters with trusted companions in cities where he frequently traveled. He may have had some copies of his works stored in the homes of fellow Christians in cities such as Antioch of Syria, Ephesus, and Corinth, for example. When needed, he could then make arrangements for one or more writings to be brought to him. In fact, we may find reference to this type of practice in 2 Timothy 4:13 where he instructs Timothy to bring not only the cloak that was left in Troas, but "also the books, and above all the parchments."

We might further suppose that there were many times in which Paul would have had access only to a small collection or his works—perhaps those that had been recently composed or that were stored in a particular area—but not to his entire collection. This may explain, for example, some of the parallels between 1 and 2 Thessalonians and Ephesians and Colossians. As discussed in Question 18, some scholars believe that the similar greeting in the two Thessalonian epistles serves as evidence that an unknown writer produced 2 Thessalonians at some time after Paul's death and that he simply patterned it after the features in 1 Thessalonians. A more natural explanation is that Paul simply patterned portions of his second work after his initial composition. A similar situation may have occurred with Ephesians and Colossians. There are debates regarding which of the two epistles were likely written first, but it is possible that Paul may have drawn upon and amended portions of one epistle when writing the other.

If it was indeed the case that Paul maintained copies of his previous letters, we may have a more plausible explanation for why some letters were "lost" and why other were preserved. Rather than an unintentional and unfortunate loss, the writings that were included in the Pauline letter corpus may have been intentionally selected from a larger body of works that was maintained by Paul and/or his companions. We may speculate that at some point in the final years of Paul's life or in the years that immediately followed his martyrdom, that he and/or his close companions carefully and thoughtfully selected specific letters from the large body of copies in their possession for inclusion in a single collection of his writings. We obviously cannot know how many copies of Paul's letters were available, but it is plausible that the works that now belong to the canon were intentionally selected for inclusion in the initial edition of the Pauline corpus from the copies maintained by Paul and his companions. The canonical writings were likely selected because of their perceived universal relevance, unique material, rich theological content, or for other considerations. Conversely, works that were determined to have been relevant only to a particular community, lacked meaningful theological content, or lacked unique material may have been passed over and eventually became "lost." On some occasions, Paul may have written a similar letter to multiple communities. In these cases, it would not have been unnecessary to include each writing in the collection. At other times he may have simply written a brief letter to inform one of his associates of his travel plans without delving into theological matters or offering instruction regarding the Christian life. We might imagine that these letters were omitted simply because they lacked relevant content for universal audiences. The fact that each of the canonical works attributed to Paul is of universal relevance and contains rich theological content and meaningful instruction strongly indicates that their preservation was not the result of mere happenstance or fortuitous developments.

A slightly different explanation has been offered by E. Randolph Richards. In his discussion of the lost letters to the Corinthians, Richards suggests, "It is easier to place the problem, not in Corinth, but with Paul. These letters are lost because copies were not made of them before they were dispatched. Thus, Paul's personal set of copies did not have them." He then makes the helpful reminder that "even though writers kept copies of their letters, they did not always make copies of every letter."[3] Richards makes a valid point that Paul is unlikely to have maintained a copy of every letter he ever wrote. Having said that, we would suggest that it was likely a fairly common practice of Paul to

3. E. Randolph Richards, *Paul and First-Century Letter Writing: Secretaries, Composition and Collection* (Downers Grove, IL: InterVarsity Press, 2004), 220–21.

maintain copies of his letters and that a selection of a larger body of works would have likely been necessary when it came time to begin preparing his writings for their initial circulation. In sum, we might conclude that the writings of Paul that have been preserved in the New Testament are not simply the works that happened to be copied by the initial recipients. Rather, the writings that are now part of the canon were carefully selected from what would have originally been a much larger body of material maintained by Paul and/ or his companions over the course of his missionary career.

Summary

Several references to nonextant works in Paul's writings reveal that Paul wrote more letters than what has been preserved in the New Testament, leading many to speculate what may have become of them. A common assumption is that a number of Paul's writings were simply lost, destroyed, or neglected and that their disappearance from history was an unfortunate loss to the church. In contrast to this common perspective, it has been suggested that the collection of Paul's writings likely derived from the copies in Paul's possession. According to this perspective, Paul's companions, and possibly even Paul himself, would have deliberately and thoughtfully selected specific works for inclusion in an initial collection of his writings from the larger body of works that Paul maintained throughout his career. Rather than include all the material they possessed, a relatively small body of works were selected. These works would have presumably been selected on the basis of their theological content, practical relevance, unique material, and universal significance.

REFLECTION QUESTIONS

1. What passages in Paul's writings appear to make reference to one of his lost letters?

2. What is the most common explanation for the lost letters of Paul?

3. How might our understanding of first-century literary practices offer possible insight into how the corpus of Paul's letters may have formed and why some of his letters were not included?

4. Having briefly considered the subject of the lost letters of Paul, what do you believe is the most likely explanation for why some of Paul's writings were lost?

5. In your view, is it possible to affirm God's providence in the shaping of the canon while also recognizing the role that various individuals may have played in the selection and preservation of material?

Why Do Some Scholars Question the Authenticity of Certain Canonical Letters Attributed to Paul?

Students taking introductory courses to the New Testament are often surprised to learn that many scholars reject the authenticity of several of the canonical writings attributed to the apostle Paul. How could one deny that Paul was the author of these writings, it might be asked, when his name clearly appears in the text? In this brief chapter we will discuss some of the major reasons why the authenticity of some of Paul's writings are regarded by many scholars as pseudonymous, that is, to have been produced after Paul's lifetime by unknown writers who deceitfully wrote in his name. Our objective in this chapter is not to critique these arguments or to defend the authenticity of each work attributed to Paul, but simply to offer an overview of the major factors that have led some scholars to reject the authenticity of several of the canonical letters. The following chapter will then offer an assessment of these arguments and consider the possible basis for recognizing the authenticity of each of the canonical writings attributed to Paul.

While there have been several disputes over the centuries relating to the interpretation of Paul's writings, it was not until around the beginning of the Enlightenment period that scholars began to seriously question whether Paul was indeed the true author of each of the canonical writings that are attributed to him. During the late seventeenth and eighteenth centuries, scholars such as John Locke (1632–1704), Richard Simon (1638–1712), John Toland (1669–1722), Johann August Ernesti (1707–1781), Johann David Michaelis (1717–1791), Johann Semler (1725–1791), and Johann Jakob Griesbach (1745–1812) began to place a much stronger emphasis on the importance of historical-critical approaches to the study of the Scriptures. No longer content to treat the writings of the Bible simply as divine works that are impervious to human analysis, scholars began to emphasize that the biblical writings are to be studied, investigated, and analyzed in a similar fashion as other ancient works. Many scholars during this time regarded the biblical writings to be inspired but were convinced of the value of utilizing various methodological approaches that were being used to study and analyze other ancient writings. For some, the application of fresh approaches to the study of the Scripture was regarded as a means by which scholars might reconcile some of the perceived discrepancies between the biblical accounts and the claims of scientists. Others were intent on separating the inherent spiritual truths of Scripture from the perceived corruptions and imperfections of the biblical compositions.

Biblical scholarship during this time rarely challenged the authenticity of the Pauline Epistles, though the adoption of these approaches was not without consequence. The emphasis that was placed on the historical and grammatical analysis of the biblical writings and the use of various approaches prepared the conditions for the more vigorous challenges to the authenticity of several of these writings that became more common during the nineteenth century. Rather than viewing the canonical writings as fully authoritative works that were composed by those who functioned as the human conduits of divine revelation, a growing number of scholars began to regard the biblical writings as human inventions that are useful merely for what they reveal about the religious perspectives of ancient writers. Others became persuaded that several of the traditional assumptions about the composition of the biblical writings are in need of further scrutiny.

With respect to the Pauline Epistles, one of the most influential scholars of this time was F. C. Baur (1792–1860), a German theologian and historian who spent much of his career in Tübingen. Baur became convinced that it is only Romans, 1 and 2 Corinthians, and Galatians—what he referred to as the *Hauptbriefe* ("primary letters")—that are to be recognized as authentic. The other writings, he argued, are later works that were falsely penned under Paul's name. Many of Baur's basic conclusions remain entrenched in the world of scholarship, though many scholars no longer affirm some of the specific conclusions he made about the composition of the Pauline writings. In contrast to Baur, scholars now generally recognize the authenticity of Philippians, 1 Thessalonians, and Philemon. This leaves six writings attributed to Paul that remain disputed: Ephesians, Colossians, 2 Thessalonians, and the three Pastoral Epistles. While these epistles are widely recognized as genuine by many evangelical and conservative scholars, critical scholars of a more liberal or moderate bent tend to deny the authenticity of these works, often referring to them as the "deutero-Paulines." In what follows, we will briefly discuss the most consequential factors that have led scholars to reject the authenticity of these six writings.[1]

---

1. For further treatment on the authorship of the disputed epistles in the Pauline corpus, readers are encouraged to consult graduate-level introductions to the New Testament and

Major Arguments Against the Authenticity of Ephesians

The authenticity of Ephesians has been widely questioned since the time of Baur, though there were lesser-known works published prior to this time that made similar assertions.[2] Baur himself was persuaded that Ephesians and other writings attributed to Paul such as Colossians include a number of words and expressions that are reflective of a later period when elements of Gnostic Christianity had taken deeper root. Not all would agree with this sentiment today, but it remains widely recognized that Ephesians contains a number of words that do not appear in Paul's other writings and that some words and phrases contained in Ephesians are used differently than they are in the undisputed writings. It has also been argued that the author of Ephesians often expresses himself using certain common grammatical conventions and parts of speech that was not customary for Paul. These factors are often thought to indicate that a later writer was responsible for the writing's composition.

In addition to arguments that relate to the language and style of the epistle, some scholars have observed that the author appears to have been familiar with a large body of Pauline writings, evidence, some conclude, of a later work. As suggested many years ago by Edgar Goodspeed, "Ephesians shows the unmistakable influence of every one of the nine genuine letters of Paul." In this case, Goodspeed was referring to each of the Pauline Epistles with the exception of the Pastorals. "The writer of Ephesians knows them all, and knows them well," Goodspeed contends. This led him to the conclusion that "Ephesians is, on the whole, a generalization of Paulinism much more like a later Paulinist than like Paul himself."[3] Goodspeed concludes, therefore, that Ephesians was likely written as a compilation of insights and material that was adopted from the previously written epistles and that the work served as a "summary of Pauline Christianity."[4]

Finally, it is often observed that Ephesians bears a considerably more impersonal tone than what is typically found in the undisputed writings. This is thought to be inconsistent with the more personal nature of Paul's writings and his practice of referring to specific individuals by name. Throughout his writings, Paul addresses specific concerns, questions, and controversies

---

exegetical commentaries on these writings. See also the various articles on the individual Pauline writings in *DPL*. Additional arguments against the authenticity of these writings are laid out in Raymond F. Collins, *Letters That Paul Did Not Write: The Epistle to the Hebrews and the Pauline Pseudepigrapha* (Eugene, OR: Wipf & Stock, 2005).

2. Edward Evanson, a controversial English scholar during the eighteenth century, is often thought to be the first modern scholar to challenge the authenticity of Ephesians and other Pauline writings such as the Pastorals.

3. Edgar J. Goodspeed, *The Key to Ephesians* (Chicago: The University of Chicago Press, 1956), vii.

4. Edgar J. Goodspeed, *The Meaning of Ephesians* (Chicago: The University of Chicago Press, 1933), 17.

that relate directly to his readers and refers to several individuals. In contrast, Ephesians contains no references to specific individuals, while the content of the letter seems to have been written for a more general audience. One could have easily addressed the same letter to Christians living in any city, one might argue, without having to make changes to its content. In fact, many believe that this is not so hypothetical, and that Ephesians was actually designed as a circular letter to various communities. It is often noted that several of the early Greek witnesses lack the words "in Ephesus" (*en Ephesō*) in Ephesians 1:1 and that the letter may not have been associated with the city of Ephesus until some time after its composition.[5] Some have even theorized that the original manuscript may have included a blank space that enabled those who produced later copies of the work to insert the name of whatever city was appropriate at the time! A compelling argument could be made, however, that the words were original and that one or more early scribes removed them in an effort to make the letter seem more universally relevant.

Major Arguments Against the Authenticity of Colossians

Colossians, while noticeably more personal in nature than Ephesians, also contains a number of words and expressions that are not found in Paul's undisputed writings. This has led many modern scholars to assume that the text was written by a later author who was clearly familiar with Paul's authentic writings, but who often expressed himself in a unique way. Others have charged that some of the foundational soteriological matters and other theological topics that are emphasized in Romans and Galatians receive little attention in Colossians and that the author emphasizes certain subjects that do not feature prominently in the authentic writings. The author's treatment of Christological themes in the first half of the epistle, for example, is sometimes alleged to differ from how these themes are presented in Paul's authentic writings.

Finally, it is often observed that much of the content in Colossians bears a significant resemblance to the content of Ephesians. Both epistles contain similar expressions and vocabulary and address several of the same subjects. As a result of the noticeable similarities between the two epistles, some have concluded that a literary relationship between the two is likely. If the author of Colossians drew upon Ephesians, it must be assumed that both writings are inauthentic, some would suggest. Others would argue, of course, that Colossians was written first and that the author of Ephesians later drew upon it. Either way, the parallels between the two writings are often thought to preclude the authenticity of at least one writing, if not both.

---

5. These words are lacking in 𝔓⁴⁶, the oldest textual witness to a majority of the Pauline corpus, and in notable codices such as Sinaiticus and Vaticanus. In both of these important codices, the words ἐν Ἐφέσῳ (*en Ephesō*) appear to have been added to the manuscript by a later scribe.

Major Arguments Against the Authenticity of 2 Thessalonians

Despite the fact that the authenticity of 1 Thessalonians is now generally recognized, many scholars remain reluctant to affirm 2 Thessalonians as a genuine Pauline letter.[6] There are several reasons for this. Like Ephesians and Colossians, it has been observed that the letter contains a number of words and phrases that do not appear in the undisputed Pauline epistles. In addition, it is often alleged that various elements of the writing appear to have been patterned after 1 Thessalonians and that the eschatological perspective of the two writings differ in key respects. To cite but one example, scholars have long noted the similarities between the opening greetings of 1 and 2 Thessalonians. This is sometimes thought to suggest that a later author sought to pattern his or her work after Paul's earlier epistle.

With regard to the theological orientation of the writings, scholars have observed that the author of 1 Thessalonians encourages his readers to take comfort in the promise that Christ will soon return and that this epochal event will take place at an unexpected time (1 Thess. 5:1–11). In 2 Thessalonians, however, the author emphasizes that certain events must take place before the second coming and that they will occur with little warning (2 Thess. 2:1–12), a contradiction, according to some scholars. It has also been alleged that the emphasis in 2 Thessalonians on the coming destruction of unbelievers (2 Thess. 1:5–12) is inconsistent with Paul's clear concern and affection for the lost, a further indication of pseudonymous authorship.

Major Arguments Against the Authenticity of the Pastoral Epistles

Several objections to the authenticity of the Pastoral Epistles have been made since the late eighteenth century when scholars such as Edward Evanson began to challenge their authenticity. Over the last several centuries, a number of scholars have regarded these writings as pseudonymous works that were written under Paul's name by a later writer.[7] By writing in Paul's name, the author could ensure that his work would be taken seriously and treated as authoritative Scripture. Some have objected that the purported situation in which the "Paul" of the Pastorals finds himself is historically implausible. The Pastorals, it will be recalled, allude to Paul's recent journeys to various locations that do not easily comport with the narrative of Paul's travels contained in Acts. The dire situation in which Paul finds himself in 2 Timothy is also thought to be inconsistent with Luke's portrayal of Paul's situation in Rome. As discussed previously, the recognition of the two-imprisonments theory is often regarded as a plausible solution to these issues. Not all scholars remain

---

6. For additional treatment of scholarly theories pertaining to the composition of these epistles, see Nijay Gupta, *1 & 2 Thessalonians*, ZCINT 13 (Grand Rapids: Zondervan, 2019).
7. Many who reject the authenticity of the Pastorals believe that a single writer was responsible for the composition of all three works.

convinced, however, concluding instead that the Pastorals represent a poor attempt to provide a historical setting for "Paul," the alleged author.

In addition to the charge that the purported *Sitz im Leben* of the Pastorals is incongruent with what is known of Paul's life and ministry, others have objected that the theology of the Pastorals—its ecclesiology in particular—is inconsistent with Paul's teaching or that it is too advanced to have been written during his lifetime. As James Aageson contends, "the new and seemingly more developed sense of church structure, authority, and leadership reflected in the Pastorals also appeared to confirm their dating after the death of Paul, perhaps as late as sometime in the second century."[8] In addition to a recognized hierarchy of church leadership with particular offices, each of which have specific responsibilities and qualifications for service, the Pastorals contain instruction regarding specific ministries that are to take place in the local church. The author also appears to be familiar with a widely recognized body of Christian doctrine, an indication to many scholars that the writings were produced after Paul's lifetime. Finally, the author's instruction to avoid "what is falsely called 'knowledge'" (*gnōsis*) in 1 Timothy 6:20 is sometimes thought to indicate that the text was written during a later period when Gnostic Christianity had become a significant threat.

While a number of scholars have objected to the authenticity of the Pastoral Epistles over the last few centuries, two studies in particular have proven to be especially influential. Heinrich Holtzmann (1832–1910), a German theologian who was known primarily for his scholarship on the Gospels, published a work that made a variety of linguistic arguments against the authenticity of the writings and contended that much of their content is indicative of a later date of composition.[9] The ideas that are presented in these writings are much too developed, he concluded, to have been written during Paul's lifetime. Another influential work was P. N. Harrison's *The Problem of the Pastoral Epistles*, a work that likewise challenged the authenticity of the Pastorals on the basis of several linguistic arguments.[10] While recognizing the possibility that much of the content in the writings may be indirectly linked to Paul, Harrison suggested that the text of the Pastorals is inconsistent with Paul's style and vocabulary. This detailed study was one of the first major works to employ statistical analysis of the writings. Since its publication, linguistic arguments have been at the forefront of the debate surrounding the authorship of the Pastorals.

---

8. James Aageson, *Paul, the Pastoral Epistles, and the Early Church* (Peabody, MA: Hendrickson, 2008), 5.

9. Heinrich Holtzmann, *Die Pastoralbriefe, kritisch und exegetisch behandelt* (Leipzig: Wilhelm Engelmann, 1880).

10. P. N. Harrison, *The Problem of the Pastoral Epistles* (London: Oxford University Press, 1921).

Summary

Although each of the thirteen canonical writings attributed to Paul were widely recognized as authentic throughout the majority of church history, a number of scholars in recent centuries have questioned the authenticity of several of these writings. Serious objections have been raised regarding the authenticity of Ephesians, Colossians, 2 Thessalonians, and the three Pastoral Epistles. It is often alleged that these writings were falsely written under Paul's name in the decades following his death in order to perpetuate his legacy or to invoke his authority while addressing the concerns of Christians in later periods. Scholars have offered a wide range of arguments in favor of the pseudonymity of these writings. For many scholars, the "deutero-Paulines" contain content and language that is thought to be implausible or inconsistent with the material contained in the undisputed epistles.

REFLECTION QUESTIONS

1. What are some of the major developments that took place after the Protestant Reformation that helped prepare the way for challenges to the authenticity of several biblical writings?

2. What are some of the primary arguments made against the authenticity of Ephesians and Colossians?

3. What are some of the primary arguments made against the authenticity of 2 Thessalonians?

4. What are some of the primary arguments made against the authenticity of the Pastoral Epistles?

5. Are there any arguments against the authenticity of one or more of the Pauline Epistles that you find particularly compelling or difficult to refute?

What Is the Basis for Affirming the Authenticity of the Disputed Pauline Letters?

The previous chapter offered a brief survey of the major factors that have led many scholars to question the authenticity of Ephesians, Colossians, 2 Thessalonians, and the three Pastoral Epistles. Having identified some of the major arguments that are often made against the authenticity of these writings, we will now consider the possible basis for affirming their Pauline authorship. Our treatment will begin with a brief discussion of the early reception of these writings and will then assess the major arguments that are often made by those who reject their authenticity.

The Reception of the Disputed Pauline Writings in Early Christianity

Perhaps the best way to begin our discussion of the authenticity of the disputed writings is to reiterate some of the key conclusions that were made in our treatment of the formation of the Pauline letter corpus (Question 15). We are not, after all, attempting to account for the origin of recently discovered works that were unknown in the early church, but for writings that were widely recognized as authentic by early Christians. Any theory that holds to the pseudonymity of these writings must provide a plausible explanation for their early incorporation into the Pauline letter corpus and the role that they played in early Christian teaching and worship.

The conclusion that the New Testament canon contains pseudonymous works that are falsely attributed to Paul cannot be made without affirming that early Christians were unconcerned about the subject of authorship or that they made mistaken judgments about the authenticity of the writings. However, the assumption that early readers of Scripture were unconcerned about the subject of authorship is plainly contradicted by the evidence. What is known of the reception of the New Testament writings strongly suggests that it was only the works that were understood to have derived from the apostles or their close associates that were recognized as authoritative Scripture. As the historian J. N. D. Kelly explains:

> Unless a book could be shown to come from the pen of an apostle, or at least to have the authority of an apostle behind it, it was peremptorily rejected, however edifying or popular with the faithful it might be. Secondly, there were certain books which hovered for long on the fringe of the canon, but in the end failed to secure admission to it, usually because they lacked this indispensable stamp.[1]

It is significant that there are no known examples of works that were recognized as authoritative Scripture apart from a widespread recognition of their apostolic status.[2] Conversely, we do not find any works outside of the canon that were widely recognized as apostolic in origin. Even critical scholars such as Bart Ehrman have acknowledged that the majority of early Christians only recognized the authority of works understood to be of apostolic origin. As he concedes, early Christians viewed the practice of pseudepigraphy, that is, of falsely attributing one's work to another author, as "a form of lying" and as "a culturally despised activity."[3]

In contrast to those who suggest that the practice of pseudepigraphy was an accepted practice, or that early Christian were ambivalent about the relevance of authorship, the reception of early Christian literature would suggest that the subject of authorship was a leading factor in whether it was recognized as authoritative Scripture. It is also apparent from the early reception of Paul's writings that each of the six disputed letters in the Pauline letter collection were widely understood to have been written by Paul.[4] Apart from the widespread conviction that they were composed by Paul and bore apostolic testimony, early readers would simply have not recognized the authority or canonical status of these works.

Because of the importance that was placed on apostolic authorship, it would seem difficult to establish a plausible scenario in which the disputed writings first circulated decades after Paul's lifetime when his companions and original readers were no longer living. To the contrary, each of these writings are likely to have been widely read in the years following Paul's death, and, in some cases,

---

1. J. N. D. Kelly, *Early Christian Doctrines* (Peabody, MA: Prince Press, 2004), 60.
2. One might object that Hebrews serves as a possible example, but this work is anonymous.
3. Bart D. Ehrman, *Forgery and Counterforgery: The Use of Literary Deceit in Early Christian Polemics* (New York: Oxford University Press, 2013), 43, 132.
4. For further treatment of the subject of pseudepigraphy and how it pertains to the study of the Pauline Epistles, see Stanley E. Porter and Gregory P. Fewster, eds., *Paul and Pseudepigraphy*, PAST 8 (Leiden: Brill, 2013).

even during his lifetime when many of his companions and his original readers could attest to their authenticity. For a writing such as Ephesians to be deemed inauthentic, one would have to conclude that it was unknown to Christians until decades after Paul's death or that it was recognized as a Pauline writing despite being unknown to Paul's companions. It would certainly seem difficult to imagine a scenario in which a writing such as Ephesians began to circulate as part of the Pauline letter corpus if it was unknown to early readers in Ephesus or those who worked closely with Paul. While it is indeed the case that the canonical reception of these works does not alone prove their authenticity, its reception is nonetheless an important factor that must not be overlooked. Because of the difficulty of establishing a plausible scenario in which inauthentic works were later embraced as genuine Pauline writings, we would suggest that the onus is on those who reject their authenticity to provide compelling evidence that they are later pseudonymous works.

In addition to what may be observed about the importance of apostolic authority in the early church, it will be helpful to make a few observations about early witnesses to the disputed writings. While there is not a large number of early witnesses to the collection of Paul's writings, the evidence that has survived would suggest that there was considerable agreement regarding the scope of the writings that were attributed to Paul. The earliest Greek witnesses to the Pauline letter corpus demonstrate that the writings of Ephesians, Colossians, and 2 Thessalonians were recognized as authentic works remarkably early and that this recognition was never seriously questioned. Even the three Pastoral Epistles appear to have been widely regarded as authentic letters from a remarkably early period. We find, for example, possible allusions or references to the Pastoral Epistles in early Christian writers such as Clement or Rome (*1 Clement* 1:3; 2:7), Ignatius (*Letter to the Ephesians* 14:1; 20:1; *Letter to the Magnesians* 8:1), and Polycarp (*The Letter to the Philippians* 4:1). Reference to these writings may also be found in the early canonical list known as the Muratorian Fragment and in important biblical manuscripts such as Codex Sinaiticus, Codex Alexandrinus, and Codex Ephreimi Rescriptus. Although it appears to be unlikely that the Pastorals were included in every early collection of the Pauline corpus—some collections, as noted in Question 15, appear to have contained only ten epistles—their authenticity does not appear to have been seriously questioned. Some may have been unaware of these writings, but it is difficult to demonstrate that they were rejected. Now that we have made some observations about the early reception of the disputed writings attributed to Paul, we may turn our attention to some of the major arguments against their authenticity that were introduced in the previous chapter.

An Assessment of Common Linguistic Arguments

Perhaps the most common type of argument made by those who reject the authenticity of one or more of the canonical writings attributed to Paul are those that relate to the vocabulary and style of the writings. As is frequently emphasized, the six disputed letters contain a number of words that do not appear elsewhere in the undisputed Pauline writings and often use certain words in ways that differ from their conventional usage in the undisputed Paulines. Because linguistic analysis is often thought to be an objective and reliable method of analysis, arguments for pseudonymity that relate to matters of language and style tend to have considerable appeal. There is little room for debate, after all, about how many unique words appear in a particular writing, the particular ways in which certain words are used, the use of certain grammatical features, etc. Despite the seemingly straightforward and objective nature of these studies, it is important to consider the nature and significance of linguistic analysis in assessing the authenticity of ancient works such as those attributed to Paul. Assessing the various features and nuances of a given writing is one thing, while ascertaining its implications is quite another.

It might first be observed that a variety of factors may influence the specific vocabulary and literary style of a given writing and that differences in language between one writing and another may not always point to different authors. An author's language may be shaped by their intended audience, the particular literary genre of their work, or simply the subject matter that is addressed. As is widely recognized, each of Paul's writings address different subjects, were written under a variety of circumstances, and were addressed to different audiences, each of whom were facing unique circumstances. There is reason to question, therefore, the expectation that each of the Pauline writings contain language that is largely confined to an established base of words or even that individual words be used in a consistent manner.[5] A degree of variability is certainly to be expected between the works of a single author, especially an author such as Paul whose circumstances were constantly changing and whose writings address a wide spectrum of subjects and were written for different audiences. It should also be recognized that it is not in the disputed epistles alone that we find unique language. In fact, there are a number of words and expressions that are limited to works such as 2 Corinthians and Galatians. If the unique linguistic features that appear in writings such as the Pastoral Epistles are determined to preclude their authenticity, it might be asked why the authenticity of works such as 2 Corinthians and Galatians is not likewise challenged![6]

---

5.   Despite the length of Romans and the Corinthian letters, many linguists would argue that the sample size of an author's work needs to be considerably longer than what has been preserved of Paul's writings in order to make definitive judgments about their literary style.
6.   For a recent study of the linguistic similarities between the Pastoral Epistles and the other Pauline writings, see Jermo van Nes, *Pauline Language and the Pastoral Epistles: A Study of Linguistic Variation in the Corpus Paulinum*, LBS 16 (Leiden: Brill, 2018).

Second, it should be recognized that individual authors are often capable of writing in a range of styles and that it is possible for an author's style to evolve over time. Several examples could be cited of modern authors who exhibit the ability to write in a variety of styles, even within a single literary genre. We might point to examples such as Mark Twain, Ernest Hemingway, and more recently, Ray Bradbury, each of whom wrote several novels that display differing styles and a wide range of literary features. The ability to vary one's style is not a recent development, however. As Luke Timothy Johnson observes, ancient authors were known to adjust the style of their writings to fit their immediate circumstances. "Style was a matter of being rhetorically appropriate to circumstances and followed definite conventions," he explains. "In Paul's time, style was less a matter of personal expressiveness and more a matter of social presence and rhetorical craft."[7]

Third, with regard to judgments that are sometimes made about the authorship of certain writings on the basis of their language, structure, and content, we might observe that scholars often use contrasting arguments to reach the same conclusions. Those who question the authenticity of 2 Thessalonians, for example, often point to the similarities between the form and features of this writing and that of 1 Thessalonians. These similarities, it is sometimes thought, may indicate that the unknown author of 2 Thessalonians intentionally patterned his work after 1 Thessalonians. One must question the rationality of such an argument. If a work is determined to contain unique language or to address subjects not contained in the undisputed writings, its authenticity is often questioned. In such cases, the differences are thought to indicate that the work was produced by a later unknown author. On the other hand, if it is concluded that a writing contains similar features and language as another recognized writing, scholars often theorize that another author attempted to pattern his work after it. One wonders how a work could ever be regarded as authentic if its authenticity is to be questioned if it contains language or content that is either similar or dissimilar to that of other writings!

An Assessment of Common Historical and Theological Arguments

It is sometimes suggested that the content of the disputed writings provide clues that they were written long after Paul's death. The Pastorals, for example, are often alleged to have been written at a later time in which the church was more established. It not until several years after Paul's passing, some have argued, that a well-organized system of church leadership first developed. The detailed instructions in the Pastorals that relate to various activities in the church and the qualifications of those serving in specific offices are thought to reflect a period of church history that was far removed from the primitive

---

7. Luke Timothy Johnson, *The First and Second Letters to Timothy*, AB 35A (New York: Doubleday, 2001), 60.

days of the early church. In response, it should be noted that Philippians, a work thought to have been written by Paul no later than the early 60s, refers in its opening greeting to "the overseers and deacons" (Phil. 1:1), a clear indication that particular offices were recognized by this time. It would indeed be difficult to imagine that it was not until the end of the first century or even the second century that local churches first began to establish a system of church government or began to appoint individuals to provide spiritual oversight or to serve in particular ways. As we find in Acts 6, the church's leadership began appointing individuals for service as soon as there were practical needs.

As discussed in the previous chapter, it has also been alleged that some of the works attributed to Paul reflect a date of composition well after Paul's martyrdom when a core body of Christian doctrine was more widely recognized or when the church was embroiled in controversies that took place in later periods. It has been suggested, for example, that the warning about false knowledge (*gnōsis*) in 1 Timothy 6:20 may serve as evidence that the letter of 1 Timothy was penned several decades after Paul's lifetime when Gnosticism was a significant concern. In response, it might be noted that there is nothing particularly unique about the language used in this verse. The term *gnōsis* appears twenty-nine times in the New Testament, all but six of which appear in the Pauline Epistles. It would be difficult to explain how the use of the term *gnōsis* in 1 Timothy 6:20 provides evidence for a later date of composition when the same term appears frequently in undisputed writings such as Romans and the Corinthian Epistles.

We may also note the difficulties associated with the charge that the Pastorals were written during a later period of church history when there was widespread recognition of an established and well-developed body of Christian doctrine, what the author of the Pastorals refers to simply as "the faith." This type of argument is predicated upon the assumption that Christianity was in a largely unsettled state during Paul's lifetime and that it took many years for a core body of teachings to become widely recognized. A problem for this viewpoint, of course, is the remarkable theological consistency that may be observed in the New Testament writings and among early Christian writers. Although various theological matters have been debated since the inception of Christianity, we need not assume that it took until the second century before a core body of Christian doctrine was first recognized. The Pastorals certainly include specific instructions about a number of ecclesiastical matters that are not addressed in the other writings, but it would be unwarranted to suggest that the subjects they address are too advanced to have been written during Paul's lifetime or that it was not until several decades after his death that Christians first began to affirm a core body of central doctrines.[8]

---

8.   For further discussion of the degree to which early Christianity was characterized by theological diversity, see Andreas J. Köstenberger and Michael J. Kruger, *The Heresy of*

Summary

Although the authenticity of Ephesians, Colossians, 2 Thessalonians, and the Pastoral Epistles are regarded by many contemporary scholars as later pseudonymous works, they were widely recognized in early Christianity to have been composed by the apostle Paul. Each of these letters circulated in the early centuries of the Christian era as part of the Pauline corpus and there is a lack of historical evidence that their authenticity was seriously questioned. Despite the fact that a number of scholars continue to hold that these writings were composed by unknown writers under Paul's name, it has been suggested in this chapter that there is nothing related to the content or language of these writings that precludes Pauline authorship.

REFLECTION QUESTIONS

1. In your estimation, how important is the subject of authorship? Is the authority of the New Testament writings tied in any way to the human authors?

2. What are some of the factors that may account for the differences in style and language among the Pauline Epistles?

3. How persuasive do you find the linguistic arguments often used to demonstrate that certain writings are inauthentic?

4. In your view, how significant is the fact that the early church widely recognized the authenticity of each of the canonical works attributed to Paul?

5. From your perspective, what are some possible benefits of becoming familiar with the common arguments that are used to challenge the authenticity of certain writings?

Orthodoxy: How Contemporary Culture's Fascination with Diversity Has Reshaped Our Understanding of Early Christianity (Wheaton, IL: Crossway, 2010).

The Authority of Paul's Letters

Did Paul Think His Letters Were Authoritative Scripture?

Paul wrote letters to churches throughout the Roman Empire, thirteen of which made their way into the New Testament canon.[1] Most of his writings address issues relating to specific churches.[2] Regardless of occasion, each of Paul's letters make doctrinal or ethical demands on his readers. Paul's authority for making such demands came from the fact that he had seen the Lord (1 Cor. 9:1), who had called him to be an apostle (Gal. 1:1). Paul therefore ministered with apostolic authority, just like James, Peter, and John (Gal. 1:17, 2:1–10; 2 Cor. 11:5).[3] His awareness of his apostolic status is what emboldens him to call the Galatians "foolish" for considering works of the law (Gal. 3:1) and what rouses him to exhort the Corinthians to "be united in the same mind and the same judgment" (1 Cor. 1:10).

We could argue that Paul's self-conscience apostolic authority meant he assumed his letters were authoritative Scripture. Peter certainly considered Paul's letters to be Scripture, arguing that "some things in them are hard to understand, which the ignorant and unstable twist to their own destruction, as they do the other Scriptures" (2 Peter 3:16). But can we really affirm that Paul was conscience that his letters were authoritative Scripture?

To answer this question, we must first determine what Paul himself considered Scripture. This will give us the standard by which we may measure

---

1. Some also include Hebrews in the Pauline corpus. See Question 16 on whether Paul may have been involved in the some way with composition of this writing.
2. As discussed in Question 18, it is possible that Ephesians was a general (or circular) letter. Important witnesses like 𝔓⁴⁶ and the uncorrected versions of Sinaiticus (א 01) and Vaticanus (B 03) exclude the words ἐν Ἐφέσῳ (*en Ephesō*) in Ephesians 1:1, which eliminate a specific audience for the letter.
3. See the helpful discussion in D. A. Carson and Douglas J. Moo, *An Introduction to the New Testament*, 2nd ed. (Grand Rapids: Zondervan, 2005), 370.

his writings. Then, we will determine whether Paul was aware that his writings carried the same authoritative status as what he considered Scripture. Our investigation will not address whether Paul believed his letters were part of a New Testament canon. We have no clear evidence that first-century Christians were aware of such a collection. What we seek to determine, therefore, is whether Paul understood his writings to be authoritative Scripture, a question that we will discuss apart from the subject of the canon's formation. As we have mentioned, Paul's letters testify that he wrote with a sense of apostolic authority. Whether he thought his own letters were authoritative Scripture requires further investigation.

Paul's Scripture

Paul clearly recognized the Old Testament writings as authoritative Scripture.[4] We see this in his frequent interaction with these writings. One example is found in 1 Corinthians 1:18–25, where Paul corrects his readers' understanding of wisdom and folly. Although some argue that the gospel is foolishness, Paul declares it "the power . . . and the wisdom of God" (1 Cor. 1:24). In making this claim, Paul asserts that the gospel, which the world considers foolishness, is actually true wisdom. In the midst of his instruction, he cites Isaiah 29:14: "I will destroy the wisdom of the wise, and the discernment of the discerning I will thwart" (1 Cor. 1:19). His citation of this passage adds authority to his correction of the Corinthians.

Another example is found in Romans 2:17–29 where Paul rebukes hypocritical Jewish teachers, who themselves transgress the law. In the midst of his argument, Paul cites Isaiah 52:5: "The name of God is blasphemed among the Gentiles because of you" (Rom. 2:24). The citation lends weight to his criticism of Jewish teachers. These examples show how Paul often used the binding authority of the Old Testament to instruct or correct his readers, expecting them to conform to its expectations.

We must mention, however, that Paul never defines which Jewish writings he considered authoritative Scripture. Would he have considered books like *Tobit*, *Judith*, and *Sirach*, writings which some Bibles like the RSV and the NRSV include as apocrypha? While such deuterocanonical writings are found alongside more recognized Old Testament books in fourth-century codices like Sinaiticus and Vaticanus, we have no evidence that Paul ever cites

---

4. In Question 22, we discuss Paul's use of Hebrew and Greek Old Testament Scriptures. For now, we will not distinguish between these writings but simply use the designation Old Testament in reference to Israel's canonical writings. We should note, however, that Paul would not have recognized Israel's Scriptures as "old." The Old Testament is a later Christian designation for Israel's sacred writings. Other acceptable terms are Elder Testament or Hebrew Bible.

such writings to support his arguments.[5] In Romans 4:13, for instance, he could have cited *Sirach* 44 or *4 Ezra* 7 to support his cosmic understanding of the inheritance. Yet, he appeals to Genesis to contend that the innumerable offspring of Abraham will inherit the world (Rom. 4:13, 17). Roger Beckwith, examining an impressive amount of Jewish and Christian evidence, convincingly argues that the matter of the Jewish canon was settled about 164 BC, when Judas Maccabaeus "collected together the scattered Scriptures after the Antiochene persecution; and the fixed list of books on which he worked was found to be the same content as the present Hebrew Bible."[6] The contents of such canonical writings, what first-century Christians like Paul recognized as Scripture, would have been in line with Jesus's words in the gospel of Luke: "everything written about me in the Law of Moses and the Prophets and the Psalms must be fulfilled" (24:44). While this description can still lend itself to a degree of fluidity, it points to a structured threefold division in Israel's Scriptures, one which Paul himself would have recognized.

When we consider Paul's use of Israel's Scripture, the canonical boundaries for which would likely have been settled by the first century, we have warrant to conclude that Paul's authoritative Scriptures would have closely resembled the Old Testament in modern Protestant Bibles. We witness the authoritative sense of these writings in the way that he interacts with them and in his frequent appeals to their authority. Having established the scope of writings Paul deemed as Scripture, we may now consider whether he believed his letters bore the same authoritative weight as canonical writings in the Old Testament.

Paul's Writings

Although Peter thought Paul's letters were authoritative (2 Peter 3:16), we have no such confirmation from Paul himself. We could make an argument from silence that Paul assumed his letters carry the same authority as the Old Testament. But that would leave too much to the imagination. A better approach would be to compare Paul's words to another authoritative source on which he draws in his writings, one to which he attributes as much weight as the Old Testament and to which he assumes his writings have the same status. We can make such a comparison in 1 Corinthians, where he employs the teachings of Jesus, also known as the Jesus tradition, alongside his own.

In 1 Corinthians 7:10–16, Paul instructs his readers about matters related to divorce. He first appeals to the teachings of Jesus: "To the married I

---

5. Bruce K. Waltke, *An Old Testament Theology: An Exegetical, Canonical, and Thematic Approach* (Grand Rapids: Zondervan, 2007), 37.
6. Roger T. Beckwith, *The Old Testament Canon of the New Testament Church and Its Background in Early Judaism* (repr., Eugene, OR: Wipf & Stock, 2008), 436. Possible evidence for the early recognition of the three major units of the Hebrew Bible (Law, Prophets, and Writings) may be observed in Josephus's *Against Apion* 1.8; *2 Maccabees* 2:13, and the prologue of *Sirach* (*Ecclesiasticus*).

give this charge (not I, but the Lord): the wife should not separate from her husband . . . and the husband should not divorce his wife" (1 Cor. 7:10–11). Here, Paul derives authority for such a charge from the words of Jesus. This is akin to the way he draws on Old Testament passages like Isaiah 29:14 and 52:5 in 1 Corinthians and Romans, respectively. For Paul, then, Jesus's words carry just as much authority for instructing his readers as those of the Old Testament Scriptures.

After appealing to the teachings of Jesus, Paul turns to another charge: "To the rest I say (I, not the Lord) that if any brother has a wife who is an unbeliever, and she consents to live with him, he should not divorce her" (1 Cor. 7:12). Paul expects the same from a woman married to an unbelieving husband (1 Cor. 7:13–16). In 1 Corinthians 7:12–16, Paul's parenthetical note ("I, not the Lord") serves to distinguish his own authoritative instructions from those of the Lord in the prior verses. By comparing his instructions to those of Jesus, Paul reveals his conviction that his written words carry an authority equal to that of the Jesus tradition. He makes the same assumption in 1 Corinthians 14:37, where he affirms that "the things I am writing to you are a command of the Lord." Paul goes so far as to say that those who do not "recognize" the authority of his instructions are themselves "not recognized" (1 Cor. 14:38).

The evidence in 1 Corinthians leads us to believe that Paul likely held that his words carried an authority equal to that of the Lord Jesus. We see this in the way he appeals to his own authority when admonishing his readers. In his instruction to the Corinthians, Paul draws on the weight of Jesus's words in a manner similar to the way he employs the Old Testament writings. While the evidence points to this conclusion, our understanding of Paul's self-awareness would be stronger had he established a more frequent pattern of relying on Jesus's teachings, especially in letters universally deemed authentic, like Romans, Galatians, and Philippians.

Summary

Paul's letters reveal that he was conscious of his own apostolic authority to instruct and make demands of his readers (e.g., Gal. 1:11). Yet, this point alone does not permit us to conclude that Paul assumes his letters are authoritative Scripture. Paul certainly recognized the Old Testament writings as Scripture, freely using them to add weight to his arguments. But nowhere does he explicitly claim that his own writings carry the same authority. Nor does he compare the authority of his own words to those of the Old Testament.

We must look primarily to how Paul appeals to Jesus's teachings in 1 Corinthians, in which he draws on Jesus's authoritative words to instruct his readers (1 Cor. 7:10–12). What we find is that he follows a similar approach to the way he appeals to the Old Testament to instruct readers in letters such as Romans. We may infer, therefore, that Paul believed Jesus's words carried the same authority as those of the Old Testament Scriptures. So, when he appeals to his own authority after appealing to Jesus, we have reason to conclude that Paul believed his written instructions to be authoritative—just like those of Jesus and the writings of the Old Testament. Our conclusion would be stronger if we had more evidence on which to draw. The most reasonable conclusion we can muster is that Paul *likely* believed his letters to be authoritative Scripture. We may certainly go beyond our tentative conclusion, assuming that the evidence in 1 Corinthians is enough to confirm that Paul believed his letters were authoritative Scripture. But we should do so with caution, knowing that only one Pauline letter reveals how Paul compares his own writings with another authoritative source of instruction.

A definitive answer to our question does not change the fact that Paul's writings are included in the canon of Scripture. What matters is not Paul's self-consciousness of the authoritative status of his writings—but his authority as an apostle who was directly commissioned by Christ, an authority that has been recognized by countless Christian communities throughout church history.

REFLECTION QUESTIONS

1. Is it safe to conclude that Paul would have understood his writings as authoritative Scripture simply because of his apostolic status?

2. What writings did Paul likely regard as authoritative Scripture?

3. If Paul never compared his own writings to what he deemed as Scripture, how can we be certain that he viewed his own writings as authoritative Scripture?

4. What would allow us to make a stronger conclusion about whether Paul believed his letters to be authoritative Scripture?

5. Why does the church's recognition of Paul's writings confirm their authoritative status?

Why Did Peter Say Some of Paul's Writings Are "Hard to Understand"?

Peter notably ascribes scriptural status to Paul's letters (2 Peter 3:16). Yet, in the same context he makes a sobering assertion: "There are some things in them [Paul's letters] that are hard to understand" (2 Peter 3:16). Does Peter suggest that Paul's writings are incoherent or illogical? Some scholars would answer yes, arguing that Paul's letters are torturous pieces of writing or that they are indiscernible to the average reader. Early-twentieth-century scholar William Wrede, for instance, contends that "[Paul's] thought wavers and alters with heedless freedom from one letter to another, even from chapter to chapter, without the slightest regard for logical consistency in details."[1] More recently, E. P. Sanders argued that Paul, when addressing his Jewish kin, could not "contain all his convictions at once . . . without both anguish and finally a lack of logic."[2] Sanders contends that Paul's lack of coherence was due in large part to the anguish he felt over his ethnic brethren (see, e.g., Romans 7 and 9–11).

Regardless of our take on the difficulty of Paul's writings, we must concede that it was never his intention to be incoherent or illogical.[3] Paul took great care to ensure that his audiences understood his arguments, even anticipating counter arguments and objections (e.g., Rom. 3:1; 9:20). We also witness his desire for clarity in the way he usually explains Old Testament Scripture shortly after quoting it, not leaving it to his audiences to discern the meaning for themselves. A clear example is found in Galatians 3:16, where he follows the citation of the phrase "and to your offspring" from Genesis 13:15;

---

1. William Wrede, *Paul* (repr. Lexington: American Theological Library Association, 1962), 77.
2. E. P. Sanders, *Paul, the Law, and the Jewish People* (Philadelphia: Fortress, 1983), 199.
3. In this paragraph, we follow the argument of Victor Paul Furnish, "On Putting Paul in His Place," *JBL* 113 (1994), 15.

17:8 and 24:7 with the explanatory clause "who is Christ." If examples like this are not convincing enough, Paul puts into words his desire for lucid communication, asserting that "we are not writing to you anything other than what you read and understand and I hope you will fully understand" (2 Cor. 1:13).[4] If Paul is incoherent, then, it is not for lack of trying.

All this brings us back to the question at hand: Why did Peter say that some of the things in Paul's letters "are hard to understand"? We can respond in one of two ways: (1) we can blame Paul for writing incoherent or confusing epistles, or (2) we can place the blame on Paul's readers (perhaps a select group) for distorting his words.

The Incoherent Paul

We have noted that some scholars argue that 2 Peter 3:16 speaks to the incoherence of Paul's writings. While an atomistic reading may yield this interpretation, the wider context of the verse reveals that Peter is not speaking of "all" of Paul's writings. Peter speaks of "some things" with which he and his readers would have been familiar.[5] He could have in mind any number of difficult passages, such as the broken grammatical construction in Romans 5:12;[6] the notoriously difficult context of Romans 7:11–25, where Paul may be using the pronoun "I" in reference to his pre-converted self, his converted self, or to personify the entire human race; the Sarah and Hagar allegory in Galatians 4:21–31; the "Christ-rock" that followed the Israelites in the wilderness in 1 Corinthians 6:9–10; or the self-emptying of Christ, also known as the *kenosis*, in Philippians 2:5–11. We could speculate about any number of difficult Pauline passages—none of which would provide warrant for finding fault with Paul as a letter writer.

Many of us can testify to the difficulty of interpreting Paul's arguments in texts such as Galatians 4:21–31 and Philippians 2:5–11. The sheer volume of monographs and articles on these passages attests to the difficulty in interpreting such texts. Moreover, the growing list of commentaries and books on Paul's letters and the number of scholarly articles on interpretive conundrums like *pistis Christou* ("faith in Christ" or "Christ's faithfulness"?) attest to the ongoing quest to understand the apostle Paul—who, granted, is at times "hard

---

4. Furnish cites this passage ("Putting Paul in His Place," 15).
5. Peter does not identify the Pauline letters with which he was acquainted, nor does he provide any evidence for identifying such letters. Identifying the exact number of Paul's writings takes us into the bottomless rabbit hole of speculation. Thomas R. Schreiner argues: "We would be overreading the text to deduce from 'all his letters' that . . . Peter was personally familiar with all of Paul's letters. How many letters are in view is impossible to say, but it is obvious that Peter knew a number of Pauline letters" (*1–2 Peter and Jude*, Christian Standard Commentary, eds. E. Ray Clendenen and Brandon D. Smith [Nashville: Holman Reference, 2020], 474).
6. Peter H. Davids, *The Letters of 2 Peter and Jude*, PNTC (Grand Rapids: Eerdmans, 2006), 304.

to understand." But that does not mean we should blame Paul for our interpretive struggles. Before we accuse Paul of being inconsistent, incoherent, or arcane, we should first examine our own interpretive practices. Could it be that we are too removed from the historical circumstances of Paul's first-century audiences or that we have not spent enough time discerning Paul's grammatical constructions, causing us to overlook important details of his argument? Could it be that Paul does not quite fit into our social or political persuasions, making his letters "hard" or "difficult"? Whatever the reason for finding difficulty with Paul's letters, simply placing the blame on Paul is taking the easy way out.

Moreover, we should observe that Peter does not assign blame to Paul. The initial portion of 2 Peter 3:16 simply says, as we have noted, that "some things" in Paul's writings are "hard to understand" (*dysnoēta*). The adjective *dysnoētos*, which the ESV renders "hard to understand," is rare in contemporary Greek literature. Lucian (*Alexander* 54), for instance, uses the adjective in reference to "incomprehensible oracles" and Diogenes Laertius (*Vitae Philosophorum* 9.13) in reference to a treatise which is "difficult to understand."[7] As in 2 Peter 3:16, the sense of *dysnoētos* does not assign interpretive blame to the author. The word merely conveys that something is "hard to understand." As we would with other Greek texts, like those of Lucian and Diogenes, it is only right that we read within the wider context of Peter's argument. Only then will we discover who is to blame for the things in Paul's letters that are "hard to understand." Maybe Paul is at fault—or maybe certain readers have distorted his teachings.

The Distorted Paul

After claiming that "some things in Paul's letters are hard to understand," Peter adds the following clause: "which the ignorant and unstable twist to their own destruction, as they do the other Scriptures." The "ignorant" are the false teachers of whom Peter warns his readers (2:1–3:7). The "unstable" are the ones who have no firm ground for what they believe, making them particularly vulnerable to the false teachers' heresies.[8] The "ignorant" and "unstable" distort elements of Paul's letters, likely those relevant to Peter's argument, such as his teachings on sexual morality (1 Cor. 6:12–17) and the second coming of the Lord Jesus (2 Thess. 2:2–3; 2 Tim. 2:17–18; cf. 2 Peter 3:1–10). Although they deny that they will stand accountable for their actions, Peter adds that their purposeful misreading of Paul's letters, as they are in the habit of doing with other Scriptures, places them in danger of eternal judgment. The seriousness with which Peter speaks of those who distort Paul's

---

7. See the discussion in BDAG, 265; J. N. D. Kelly, *The Epistles of Peter and Jude*, BNTC (Peabody, MA: Hendrickson, 1969), 373.

8. Gene L. Green, *Jude & 2 Peter*, BECNT (Grand Rapids: Baker Academic, 2008), 340.

teaching would have served as a warning for those even remotely interested in following the interpretive practices of the "ignorant" and "unstable."

What the larger context of 2 Peter 3:16 reveals is that interpretive blame for misinterpreting Paul's writings lies with false teachers and those who succumb to their doctrines. This does not negate that "some things" in Paul's letters are "hard to understand." Yet, such difficulties are no reason for describing Paul's letters as incoherent or illogical. After all, Peter clearly assigns blame for misreading Paul on those who purposely twist the meaning of his letters. The problem is not that they are unable to understand Paul's letters. Rather, the issue is that they distort the meaning of his writings in order to continue living in immorality, assuming that Christ will never return to judge their wickedness.

Summary

That some things in Paul's letters are "hard to understand" does not mean that Paul's letters are illogical, incoherent, or incomprehensible. Such conclusions would be reading too much into Peter's statement. While Peter does acknowledge the difficulty of interpreting some of Paul's arguments, he blames those who malign Paul's teachings for their own selfish purposes. This is a dangerous habit that places them, and any who follow their practices, in danger of God's judgment. But Peter's words are not only for his historical audiences—they are also for us. We, too, must be careful to avoid the interpretive practices of the "ignorant" and "unstable," who twist the meaning of Scripture to support their selfish agendas. Failure to do so would also place ourselves under the threat of God's judgment.

REFLECTION QUESTIONS

1. Does Peter insinuate that "some things" in Paul's writings are incoherent or illogical?

2. If Paul's writings are not incoherent or illogical, then what factors tend to make his instruction "hard to understand"? What might be a motivation for distorting Paul's teachings on matters related to sexual morality and eschatology?

3. What are some dangers in distorting the clear teaching of Scripture?

4. If 2 Peter 3:16 also applies to us, how should we approach Pauline passages that are difficult to interpret?

5. Should difficult Pauline passages, which result in contested interpretations, be relegated to secondary and tertiary differences among believers?

What Sources Did Paul Use?

Paul was undoubtedly influenced by a variety of sources. He may have been acquainted, for instance, with Aristotle's analysis of emotions and moral habits in *Nicomachean Ethics*, which influenced his friendly tone in Philippians and his emphasis on the importance of fellowship in 1 Corinthians.[1] In addition, Paul's view of rivalry and envy as harmful for friendship in Philippians may have been influenced by Aristotle's *Rhetoric* (1387B).[2] It is also possible that Paul's household code instructions in Ephesians and Colossians may have been influenced by Stoic philosophers.[3] But influence is not the same as dependence—it is one thing to argue that Paul was influenced by certain sources; it is quite another to argue that he used particular sources in his writings. A quest for Paul's literary influences relies mainly on discerning similarities with other ancient authors,[4] whereas a search for Paul's sources relies on textual evidence of quotations and allusions in his writings. While a quest for the influences on the apostle Paul is a worthwhile pursuit, we will limit our investigation to the sources which Paul employs in his writings—ones to which his letters give evidence: the Septuagint, the Hebrew Scriptures, the Jesus tradition, and Greek poets.[5]

---

1. Luke Timothy Johnson, *Constructing Paul*, The Canonical Paul 1 (Grand Rapids: Eerdmans, 2020), 183.
2. Johnson, *Constructing Paul*, 183.
3. E.g., Aristotle, *Politics* 1.2.1 (Rackham, LCL 21).
4. For a study that follows Paul's thought in view of Stoicism, see Troels Engberg-Pedersen, *Paul and the Stoics* (Louisville: Westminster John Knox, 2000). For essays that compare Paul with contemporary philosophers, see Joseph R. Dodson and David R. Briones, eds., *Paul and the Giants of Philosophy: Reading the Apostle in Greco-Roman Context* (Downers Grove, IL: InterVarsity Press, 2019).
5. We are only attempting a brief overview of such sources. For a more complete list of reference in Paul's writings to the Septuagint and Hebrew text, see Moisés Silva, "Old Testament in Paul," *DPL*, 631. For more thorough analyses of Paul's use of Jesus traditions, see Craig L. Blomberg, "Quotations, Allusions, and Echoes of Jesus in Paul," in *Studies in the Pauline*

Septuagint (LXX)

The Septuagint (LXX) is the Greek translation of the Hebrew Scriptures. As a first-century Jew, Paul would have been thoroughly at home in this version of Israel's Scriptures. In fact, the Septuagint is the version Paul most frequently employs in his writings. Paul, however, did not rely on a homogeneous Septuagint text, for there was no single, authorized version of the Greek Scriptures. Over the course of two to three centuries, beginning in the third century BCE, a number of scholars translated or revised the books of the Hebrew Scriptures. Some translations were more wooden, while some were more dynamic or paraphrased. To complicate matters, there were multiple translations and recensions of individual books.[6] The book of Daniel, for instance, exists in at least two versions, the Old Greek and the Theodotion translation.[7] Accordingly, then, we use the term Septuagint as representative of various Greek translations of the Hebrew Scriptures.

When Paul uses the Septuagint, he mainly appeals to the Pentateuch, Psalms, and Isaiah. In Romans 3:4, for instance, he quotes the words *hopōs an dikaiōthēs en tois logois sou kai nikēseis en tō krinesthai se* ("that you might be justified in your words, and prevail when you are judged") from Psalm 50:6. In Galatians 3:6, he cites the words *kai elogisthē autō eis dikaiosunēn* ("and it was counted to him as righteousness") from Genesis 15:6. And in Romans 10:16, Paul quotes *kyrie, tis episteusen tē akoē hēmōn* ("Lord, who has believed what he has heard from us?") from Isaiah 53:1. In Question 23, we will go into more detail about how Paul quotes and alludes to the Greek Scriptures. For now, the aforementioned verses serve as examples of how the Septuagint was the primary source from which Paul drew.

We may wonder why Paul did not primarily draw from the Hebrew versions of the Old Testament. After all, Paul was a trained as a rabbi, which would have made him well versed in Hebrew texts (Acts 22:3). The answer is fairly straightforward: Since Paul's writings were directed at Greek speaking audiences, it was more effective for him to quote or allude to the Septuagint.[8]

Epistles: Essays in Honor of Douglas J. Moo, eds. Matthew S. Harmon and Jay E. Smith (Grand Rapids: Zondervan, 2014), 129–43; Seyoon Kim, "Sayings of Jesus," *DPL*, 474–92.

6. Karen H. Jobes and Moisés Silva, *Invitation to the Septuagint*, 2nd ed. (Grand Rapids: Baker Academic, 2015), 11–110; Timothy M. Law, *When God Spoke Greek: The Septuagint and the Making of the Christian Bible* (New York: Oxford University Press, 2013); Natalio Fernández Marcos, *The Septuagint in Context: Introduction to the Greek Version of the Bible*, trans. Wilfred G. E. Watson (Atlanta: Society of Biblical Literature: Atlanta, 2000), 35–103; Gregory R. Lanier and William A. Ross, *The Septuagint: What It Is and Why It Matters* (Wheaton, IL: Crossway, 2021), 25–98.

7. See the text of Daniel in Alfred Rahlfs, ed., *Septuaginta*, Id est Vetus Testamentum graece iuxta LXX interpretes (Stuttgart: Deutsche Bibelgesellschaft, 2006).

8. Jobes and Silva, *Invitation to the Septuagint*, 23. Richard Hays observes: "It appears that Paul, whose missionary activity concentrated on predominantly Gentile congregations in Asia Minor and Greece, normally read and cited Scripture in Greek, which was the

This is akin to how English works cite other English texts with which readers would be familiar or the way Anglophone preachers cite English Bible translations in their sermons.[9] Thus, it made sense for Paul to make frequent use of the Greek Old Testament in his writings.

Hebrew Scriptures

Paul's letters also show evidence of his use of the Hebrew Scriptures, though less often than the Septuagint.[10] In such cases, scholars dispute whether Paul actually employs the Hebrew Scriptures or a version the Septuagint, or a combination of both. Some scholars are so inclined to see the Septuagint as the main source of New Testament writings that, in cases of dependence on the Hebrew Scriptures, they argue authors may be employing a version of the Greek Old Testament that is no longer extant.[11] We will therefore proceed in our discussion with caution, noting that some scholars question whether Paul even relied on these writings.

One example of Paul's possible use of a Hebrew text is his quotation of Habakkuk 2:4 in Galatians 3:11: "The righteous shall live by *faith*" (*ho dikaios ek pisteōs zēsetai*). The Septuagint version of Habakkuk 2:4 reads, "The righteous will live from *my faithfulness* (*ho de dikaios ek pisteōs mou zēsetai*), which places the onus on "God's faithfulness."[12] If we claim that Paul follows the Septuagint, we must consider why Paul drops the possessive pronoun *mou* ("my"), an omission which nullifies the emphasis on "God's faithfulness." The Hebrew version, on the other hand, reads, "The righteous will live by his faith" (*waṣaddîq beĕmūnātōw yiḥyeh*), which stresses the righteous person's "faith." Much depends on whether we believe Paul emphasizes "God's faithfulness," as reflected in the Septuagint, or the believer's "faith," as reflected in the Hebrew version of Habakkuk.[13] Consequently, our theological persuasion is a major factor in determining whether we believe Paul follows the Septuagint or the Hebrew Scriptures.[14] Nevertheless, Galatians 3:11 is a possible example of Paul's use of the Hebrew Scriptures.

Another example is Paul's use of Deuteronomy 32:35 in Romans 12:19: "'Vengeance is mine, I will repay,' says the Lord" (*emoi ekdikēsis, egō*

---

common language of the eastern empire at the time" (*Echoes of Scripture in the Letters of Paul* [New Haven, CT: Yale University Press, 1989], xi).

9. See Marcos, *The Septuagint in Context*, 324.

10. We use the term Hebrew Scriptures, rather than Hebrew Bible, to reflect the complexity of the manuscript tradition. Paul may have been familiar with a version in line with, or very similar to, the Masoretic Text (MT) but we cannot say for certain.

11. See Marcos, *The Septuagint in Context*, 223–32, 265; Hays, *Echoes*, x–xi.

12. This is our own translation of Habakkuk 2:4 LXX.

13. The Hebrew version of Habakkuk 2:4 may also be translated as "The righteous (one) will live by his faithfulness."

14. See the excellent discussion of this problem in Moisés Silva, *Interpreting Galatians: Explorations in Exegetical Method* (Grand Rapids: Eerdmans, 2001), 159–67.

antapodōsō, legei kyrios). The Septuagint version of Deuteronomy 32:35 reads: "In the day of vengeance, I will repay" (*en hēmera ekdikēseōs antapodōsō*).[15] Although the general sense is close to how it is used by Paul, the main similarity with Romans 11:35 is the verb *antapodōsō* ("I will repay"). The Hebrew version of Deuteronomy 32:35 is closer to Paul's wording: "Vengeance is mine, and recompense" (*lî nāqām wəšillêm*). Paul seems to directly render the words *lî nāqām* with *emoi ekdikēsis*, both of which may be rendered "vengeance is mine," and captures the sense of judgment associated with *antapodōsō* ("I will repay") with the prepositional phrase *en hēmera ekdikēseōs* ("in the day of judgment"). While we can argue that Paul follows the Hebrew version more closely, one can just as well argue that, in Romans 11:35, Paul relies on both the Hebrew and Septuagint versions, once more displaying the contested nature of Paul's use of the Hebrew Scriptures.[16]

The Jesus Tradition

Paul also appeals to the Jesus tradition—teachings sourced in the historical Jesus, also known as Jesus sayings, which may have circulated in oral or written form, or both. Early Christian communities would have likely considered them authoritative for ecclesial instruction. The following are examples in which Paul may have appealed to the Jesus tradition.

In 1 Corinthians 7:10–11, Paul exhorts husbands and wives not to divorce one another—a "charge" which Paul credits to the Lord Jesus ("not I, but the Lord," 7:10). Here, Paul grounds his instruction in Jesus's teaching, which is also preserved in Mark 10:10–12 and Matthew 5:32, emphasizing God's intended permanency for marriage, despite the more permissive instructions of Moses (e.g., Deut. 21:10–14; 24:3). Paul's appeal to the Jesus tradition recontextualizes Moses's teaching on divorce, stressing the institution's permanency.[17] Since 1 Corinthians was likely composed before Mark and Matthew, it is unlikely that Paul relies on either of these Gospels. It is, perhaps, more probable that he draws from authoritative Jesus sayings to which the evangelists were also privy.[18]

---

15. This is our own translation of Deuteronomy 32:35 LXX.
16. See also 1 Kings 19:18 in Romans 11:4, Job 41:11 in Romans 11:35, and Numbers 16:5 in 2 Timothy 2:19.
17. There is too much ambiguity in dating Paul's letters in relationship to the Synoptic Gospels to argue that Paul draws from Matthew, Mark, or Luke. For discussion related to the dating of NT books, see Andreas J. Köstenberger, L. Scott Kellum, Charles L. Quarles, *The Cradle, the Cross, and the Crown: An Introduction to the New Testament*, 2nd ed. (Nashville: B&H Academic, 2016); Jonathan Bernier, *Rethinking the Dates of the New Testament: The Evidence for Early Composition* (Grand Rapids: Baker Academic, 2022).
18. Kim notes how Paul's knowledge of Jesus's saying on divorce is grounded in the traditions behind the Synoptic Gospels ("Sayings of Jesus," 475).

First Corinthians provides several other important examples. In 1 Corinthians 11:17–35, Paul corrects his readers practice of the Lord's Supper. Within this context, he argues that he received the supper tradition "from the Lord" and passed it on to the Corinthians (1 Cor. 11:23). Paul is not saying that he received the teaching directly from Jesus—but that the tradition itself is sourced in his teaching. His recitation of the tradition is similar to what is recorded in texts such as Mark 14:22–24 and Luke 22:19. In 1 Corinthians 15:1–11, Paul reminds his readers of the gospel he "preached" to them, which he himself "received," and which centers on the death and resurrection of Jesus, and his appearances to the apostles. The collective witness of the Synoptics and John, which were written after Paul penned 1 Corinthians, also testifies to the gospel tradition upon which Paul draws.[19]

One final example is found in Romans 14:14, where Paul says that he "is persuaded in the Lord Jesus that nothing is unclean in itself." Jesus's instruction is preserved in Matthew 15:11 and Mark 7:15, passages in which he affirms that it is not "what goes into a person" that defiles them, but "what comes out of them."[20] Jesus's position on clean and unclean foods would have recontextualized the way he thought about food laws in the Torah, which regarded certain foods as unclean (Lev. 11; Deut. 14). As in 1 Corinthians, Paul likely appeals in this passage to the Jesus tradition on the Lord's Supper to which gospel authors would also have had access.

Greek Poets

On occasion, Paul quotes Greek poets. In 1 Corinthians 15:33, for instance, he quotes the poet Menander, likely from his comedy *Thais*: "Bad company corrupts good morals."[21] In Titus 1:12, he cites Epimenides, possibly from the ode *Concerning Oracles*: "Cretans: always liars, evil beasts, lazy gluttons."[22] Paul uses clichés or common sayings that would have resonated with his original readers, so as to give his arguments a rhetorical punch. These are sources from his audiences' own contexts which would have condemned their sinful behavior.

---

19. Another possible Jesus saying in 1 Corinthians is found in verse 9:4, where Paul refers to the Lord's command "that preachers of the gospel should get their living from the gospel" (see Luke 10:7).

20. See also Romans 12:14–21; Galatians 5:14; 1 Thessalonians 5:1–7.

21. The ultimate source of Paul's quotation is likely Menander, *Thais* 218. Anthony C. Thiselton points out that in Paul's day the quotation had become a "popular maxim" that he may have heard recited on more than one occasion (*The First Epistle to the Corinthians*, NIGTC [Grand Rapids: Eerdmans, 2000], 1254).

22. William D. Mounce argues that "the saying of Epimenides is known only through the citations" of authors such as "Clement of Alexandria (*Strom.* 1.59.2) and Callimachus (*Hymn to Zeus* 8)." See his discussion in *Pastoral Epistles*, WBC 46 (Nashville: Thomas Nelson, 2000), 397–400. See also Donald Guthrie, *Pastoral Epistles: An Introduction and Commentary*, TNTC 14 (Downers Grove, IL: InterVarsity Press, 1990), 210.

Summary

The apostle Paul employs a variety of sources in his letters. While the quest for Paul's literary influences is important, we have focused on the sources which he most likely employed in his writings: the Septuagint, the Hebrew Scriptures, the Jesus tradition, and Greek poets. Of these sources, Paul mainly relies upon the Septuagint, the version of the Old Testament with which his Greek-speaking audiences would have been most familiar. His letters also show that he may have relied on the Hebrew Scriptures, though not as often as the Septuagint. He also draws on the Jesus tradition and, on occasion, Greek poets. Paul often weaves such sources into his writings to support his respective arguments.

REFLECTION QUESTIONS

1. Why does Paul commonly refer to the text of the Septuagint when interacting with Old Testament writings?

2. What are some of the passages in which Paul may have relied on the Hebrew Scriptures?

3. What are some examples of Paul's use of the Jesus tradition?

4. Why does Paul occasionally cite Greek poets?

5. Can you think of other types of sources that Paul may have used in his writings?

How Does Paul Use the Old Testament?

Paul's use of the Old Testament is the subject of numerous books and mono-graphs.[1] Some argue that his use of the Old Testament is akin to midrash, that is, that it represents the exegetical methods of pharisaic Judaism.[2] Others contend that Paul is merely proof-texting to support his arguments. Still others insist that Paul uses the Old Testament as a way of conveying his new existence in Christ through an outmoded text.[3] While such views often convey (at least) a kernel of truth—for example, Paul's hermeneutic may indeed be similar to what was common in Pharisaic Judaism—they do little beyond explaining the basic characteristics of Paul's use of the Old Testament. We should seek a model that highlights the exegetical implications of Paul's use of Israel's Scriptures.

Richard Hays's *Echoes of Scripture in the Letters of Paul* proposes one of the most helpful approaches to Paul's use of the Old Testament.[4] Hays ana-lyzes Paul's use of Scripture through the concept of intertextuality, which is

---

1. The discussion of Paul's use of the Old Testament is too extensive to cover in this short chapter. For a more thorough discussion, see Steve Moyise, *Paul and Scripture: Studying the New Testament Use of the Old Testament* (Grand Rapids: Baker Academic, 2010); Richard B. Hays, *The Conversion of the Imagination: Paul as Interpreter of Israel's Scripture* (Grand Rapids: Eerdmans, 2005); E. Earl Ellis, *Paul's Use of the Old Testament* (Edinburgh: Oliver and Boyd, 1957); Stanley E. Porter, ed., *Hearing the Old Testament in the New Testament* (Grand Rapids: Eerdmans, 2006).

2. See Richard Longenecker, *Biblical Exegesis in the Apostolic Period* (Grand Rapids: Eerdmans, 1999), 88–116.

3. Rudolf Bultmann, *Theology of the New Testament*, trans. Kendrick Grobel (repr. Waco, TX: Baylor, 2007), 1:187–352.

4. Some scholars eschew the application of intertextuality to the study of the Old Testament in the New Testament because it allows for allusions or echoes for which the author may not have been conscience. For a helpful article on this matter, see Russell Meek, "Intertextuality, Inner-Biblical Exegesis, and Inner-Biblical Allusion," *Biblica* 95 (2014): 280–91.

"the embedding of fragments of an earlier text within a later one."[5] He draws on the field of literary studies to elucidate the well-established tradition in ancient Israel, in which "the voice of Scripture, regarded as authoritative in one way or another, continues to speak in and through later texts that both depend on and transform the earlier."[6] We see this when the Chronicler imports the promise of a Davidic King from 2 Samuel 7 into the context of 1 Chronicles 17 to reassure the Israelites of a ruler who will deliver them from exile. We also see this when the author of Nehemiah draws on the exodus tradition to remind readers that the pillar of fire and cloud were visible manifestations of God's Spirit leading his people through the wilderness (Neh. 9). Since Paul was trained in Israel's Scriptures, he would have been at home in this interpretive tradition—the main difference being that his encounter with the resurrected Jesus opened his eyes to the one who fulfills Israel's Scriptures.

The two main categories associated with intertextuality are quotations and allusions.[7] We will now examine examples of quotations and allusions in the Pauline epistles to determine how Paul uses the Old Testament.

Quotations

Paul "quotes" several Old Testament passages verbatim or alters them slightly.[8] He frequently introduces quotations using introductory formulas, such as "it is written" (Rom. 3:4; Gal. 3:10; 4:27) or "it says" (Eph. 4:8). On some occasions, he uses no introductory formula. In such instances, his quotations are so close, if not exactly parallel, to Old Testament passages that one can rather easily discern the source of his citation (Gal. 3:6; Eph. 6:2–3). The

---

5.   Richard Hays, *Echoes of Scripture in the Letters of Paul* (New Haven, CT: Yale University Press, 1989), 14. Some of the works that influence Hays's approach are Erich Auerbach, *Mimesis: The Representation of Reality in Western Literature*, trans., William R. Trask (Princeton, NJ: Princeton University Press, 2003); Michael Fishbane, *Biblical Interpretation in Ancient Israel* (Oxford: Clarendon, 1988).

6.   Hays, *Echoes*, 14.

7.   Some also argue for "echoes," which is even more difficult to discern than allusions. Hays provides a helpful explanation of his perspective on the relationship between quotations, allusions, and echoes: "Quotation, allusion, and echo may be seen as points along a spectrum of intertextual reference, moving from the explicit to the subliminal. As we move farther away from overt citation, the source recedes into the discursive distance, the intertextual relations become less determinate, and the demand on the reader's listening power grows greater" (*Echoes*, 23). Some also argue that the difference between allusion and echoes is artificial. Thus, the only real distinguishing categories are quotations and allusions. We will follow this basic distinction in this chapter. While one can make an argument for echoes, our definition of allusions will be broad enough to include any resonance to an Old Testament text outside of a quotation.

8.   G. K. Beale argues that a "quotation is a direct citation of an OT passage that is easily recognizable by its clear and unique verbal parallelism" (*Handbook on the New Testament Use of the Old Testament: Exegesis and Interpretation* [Grand Rapids: Baker Academic, 2012], 29). Moisés Silva provides a helpful chart of Old Testament citations in Paul's epistles ("Old Testament in Paul," in *DPL*, 631).

wider context of quotations provides the interpretive framework for Paul's use of the Old Testament.

In 1 Corinthians 10, Paul recalls that the wilderness generation was "overthrown" because of their rebellion against God (10:5). Paul links the Corinthians' plight to that of Israel's wilderness generation, calling them "our fathers" (1 Cor. 10:1). For Paul, the events that happened in the wilderness serve as "examples" for the Corinthians, Paul's allusion to these events is designed to dissuade them from desiring the same evils that led to the destruction of their spiritual ancestors (1 Cor. 10:6). Within this context, Paul quotes verbatim the Septuagint version of Exodus 32:6: "Do not be idolaters as some of them where; as it is written: 'The people sat down to eat and drink and rose up to play'" (*ekathisen ho laos phagein kai pein kai anestēsan paizein*, 1 Cor. 10:7). The quotation brings into view the context of the golden calf incident—an instance in which Israel's idolatry brought the Lord's wrath and judgment (Exod. 32:35).[9] Consequently, the Corinthians' ethical dilemma about whether to eat meat offered to idols (1 Cor. 10:28) is linked to the idolatry and consequent judgment of their Israelite ancestors in the wilderness.[10] If the Corinthians desire to escape the current wilderness of sin and death (the present evil age), they should avoid the sin of idolatry that beset their Israelite ancestors. It is only then that will they have hope of dwelling in the land for which God's people have truly longed (see Rom. 4:13).

In the household code of Ephesians 6, Paul exhorts children to "obey their parents in the Lord" (6:1). Then, without using an introductory formula, he quotes from the Old Testament: "Honor your father and mother (which is a commandment of great importance[11] with a promise) that it may go well with you and you might live a long life in the land" (*tima ton patera sou kai tēn mētera hētis entolē protē en epangelia hina eu soi genētai kai esē makrochronios epi tēs gēs*, Eph. 6:2–3). Paul either quotes from the Septuagint version of Exodus 20:12 or Deuteronomy 5:16.[12] We compare below these verses to Ephesians 6:2–3.[13]

Ephesians 6:2–3: "Honor your father and mother (which is a commandment of great importance with a promise) so that

---

9. See Roy E. Ciampa and Brian S. Rosner, *The First Letter to the Corinthians*, PNTC (Grand Rapids: Eerdmans, 2010), 456; Hays, *Echoes*, 92.

10. Hays, *Echoes*, 92.

11. The ESV renders πρῶτος (*prōtos*) as "first," causing confusion as to which command Paul actually refers to. More likely, the adjective should be rendered as "of great importance" (BDAG, 893).

12. Harold W. Hoehner, *Ephesians: An Exegetical Commentary* (Grand Rapids: Baker Academic, 2002), 788.

13. Translations of quotes and allusions to the Old Testament are from Albert Pietersma and Benjamin G. Wright, eds., *A New English Translation of the Septuagint: A New Translation of the Greek into Contemporary English—An Essential Resource for Biblical Studies* (Oxford: Oxford University, 2007).

it might go well with you and you might live a long life in the land" (*tima ton patera sou kai tēn mētera hētis entolē protē en epangelia hina eu soi genētai kai esē makrochronios epi tēs gēs*).

Exodus 20:12: "Honor your father and mother so that it may be well with you and so that you may be long-lived on the good land that the Lord your God is giving you" (*tima ton patera sou kai tēn mētera, hina eu soi genētai, kai hina makrochronios genē epi tēs gēs tēs agathēs, hēs kyrios ho theos sou didōsin soi*).[14]

Deuteronomy 5:16: "Honor your father and your mother, as the Lord your God commanded you, so that it may be well with you and that you may be long-lived in the land that the Lord your God is giving you" (*tima ton patera sou kai tēn mētera sou, hon tropon eneteilato soi kyrios ho theos sou, hina eu soi genētai, kai hina makrochronios genē epi tēs gēs hēs kyrios ho theos sou didōsin soi*).[15]

Although Exodus 20:12 and Deuteronomy 5:16 are very similar, even in the use of the subjunctive verb *genē* ("you may be"), which Paul exchanges for the future indicative *esē* (lit., "you will be"), the following reasons give priority to Deuteronomy 5:16. (1) Exodus 20:12 includes the words *tēs agathēs* ("the good"), whereas Deuteronomy 5:16 omits them, as does Paul. Ephesians 6:2 is therefore closer to the Septuagint version of Deuteronomy 5:16. (2) Although some argue that Paul interrupts his citation with a parenthetical note ("which is a commandment of great importance with a promise"), it is more likely he has in mind the parenthetical note from Deuteronomy 5:16 ("as the Lord commanded to you"). While the wording is not identical, Ephesians 6 shares enough of the emphasis on the "command" to children in Deuteronomy 5:16 that we could argue that most of Paul's quotation in Ephesians 6:2–3 comes from this context. We argue that Paul's use of the phrase "which is a commandment of great importance with a promise" is intended to clarify that the "command" mentioned in Deuteronomy 5:16 is of "great importance" for children.[16] Children who obey their parents show that they are true followers of God who have hope of dwelling in the land prophets like Isaiah expanded to include the entire renewed earth (Isa. 65–66).[17]

---

14. Translation is from Larry J. Perkins, "Exodus," in *A New English Translation of the Septuagint*, 65.
15. Translation is from Melvin K. H. Peters, "Deuteronomion," in *A New English Translation of the Septuagint*, 151.
16. See Francis Foulkes, *Ephesians: An Introduction and Commentary*, TNTC (Downers Grove, IL: InterVarsity Press, 1989), 168.
17. See Miguel G. Echevarría, *The Future Inheritance of Land in the Pauline Epistles* (Eugene, OR: Pickwick, 2019), 57–72.

Allusions

Paul also "alludes" to several Old Testament passages in his writings. His use of allusions is distinguishable from his use of quotations, as it shares enough of a prior scriptural passage without directly citing it.[18] This may include the embedding of several words or concepts from a prior context into a new one. Since we are not dealing with verbatim quotations, our level of involvement for discerning an Old Testament allusion is greater than what is required for a quotation.[19]

Our first example of an allusion is found in Paul's letter to the Philippians, which contains far more allusions to the Old Testament than explicit citations.[20] One well-attested allusion is found in Philippians 2:10–11, where Paul states the reason for the exaltation of Jesus: "so that at the name of Jesus every knee should bow, in heaven and on earth and under the earth, and every tongue confess that Jesus Christ is Lord, to the glory of God the Father" (*hina en tō onomati Iēsou pan gony kampsē epouraniōn kai epigeiōn kai katachthoniōn kai pasa glōssa exomologēsētai hoti kyrios Iēsous Christos eis doxan theou patros*). Paul reproduces enough of the Septuagintal version of Isaiah 45:23 to discern an allusion to this passage: "to me every knee shall bow and every tongue shall acknowledge God" (*emoi kampsei pan gony kai exomologēsetai pasa glōssa tō theō*). The similarity of the words "every knee should bow" (*pan gony kampsē*) and "every tongue confess" (*pasa glōssa exomologēsētai*) in Philippians 2 to "to me every knee shall bow" (*emoi kampsei pan gony*) and "every tongue shall acknowledge God" (*exomologēsetai pasa glōssa tō theō*) in Isaiah 45 strongly suggests that Paul evokes this prior context, where God calls his people to turn to him for salvation. The effect is that Paul applies Isaiah's promise of salvation to Jesus Christ. Thus, those who swear allegiance to Jesus, Israel's God, will be the beneficiaries of the salvation which the faithful have anticipated for centuries.

In 2 Thessalonians 2, Paul assures his readers that Jesus has not yet returned. So, there is no reason to be alarmed (2 Thess. 2:2). They can be sure of this because "the man of lawlessness" has not yet been "revealed, the son of destruction, who opposes and exalts himself against every so-called god (*hyperairomenos epi*

---

18. See discussions in Hays, *Echoes*, 29–32; Beale, *New Testament Use of the Old*, 31–37.

19. Hays proposes seven criteria for discerning proposed allusions: (1) availability (the echo's availability to the original author and audience), (2) volume (mainly repetition of words and syntactical patterns), (3) recurrence (the frequency of Paul's use of the same scriptural passage elsewhere), (4) thematic coherence (the echo's fit into Paul's argument), (5) historical plausibility (determining whether Paul's readers would have understood the echo), (6) history of interpretation (determine whether other interpreters have heard such echoes), and (7) satisfaction (appeases competent readers) (*Echoes*, 31–32). For a similar summary of these categories, see Echevarría, *Future Inheritance of Land*, 25–26 n. 22.

20. Some argue that there are no quotations of the Old Testament in Philippians. One example of an explicit quotation is found in Philippians 1:19: "this will lead to deliverance for me." The Greek (τοῦτό μοι ἀποβήσεται εἰς σωτηρίαν) is a verbatim citation of Job 13:16 LXX. Most commentaries on Philippians miss this quotation, failing to discuss its significance. See Silva, "Old Testament in Paul," 634.

panta legomenon theon) or object of worship" (2 Thess. 2:4). The words "exalts himself against every so-called god" (*hyperairomenos epi panta legomenon theon*) sound remarkably similar to Daniel 11:36, which speaks of a ruler who "will be exalted over every god" (*hypsōthēsetai epi panta theon*). The larger context of the allusion notes that this figure is exalted even above God himself, seducing those who violate the covenant. Yet, the people of God stand firm (Dan. 11:30, 32). Even though Paul does not reproduce the exact wording of Daniel 11:36, his admonishment shares enough of this passage to discern his allusion to the end-time figure of whom Daniel prophesies. When he appears, drawing away worship from the true God, Jesus will return and condemn those who have been deceived into venerating him (2 Thess. 2: 8–12; cf. Dan. 11:30, 32). Since Jesus has yet to return, believers can reassure themselves of the future day of the Lord and be on guard for the long-anticipated man of lawlessness.

Summary

While there are many perspectives on Paul's use of the Old Testament, Hays's intertextual approach provides what many others lack: an exegetical payoff for understanding the apostle's letters. When we see how Paul embeds fragments of Old Testament texts into the contexts of his writings, either through quotations or allusions, we are able to read beyond mere surface statements, envisioning the broader interpretive framework for respective passages. Paul, however, was not inventing a new method for reading the Scriptures. He was following the traditions of Old Testament authors like the Chronicler and the author of Nehemiah, who employed earlier texts to convey fresh significance for later readers. Paul uses the Old Testament similarly, generating new meanings of Israel's Scripture for new covenant audiences.

REFLECTION QUESTIONS

1. How might one describe the phenomenon of intertextuality?

2. What are the two primary ways to describe Paul's intertextual use of the Old Testament?

3. What might be some possible benefits of an intertextual understanding of Paul's letters?

4. What might be some possible disadvantages of not recognizing Paul's use of the Old Testament in his letters?

5. Is it legitimate for readers to discern citations or allusions to Old Testament texts that Paul may not have intended?

PART 3

Questions About
Paul's Theology

SECTION A

General Questions

Is There a "Center" to Paul's Theology?

It is a significant challenge to interpret just one Pauline epistle. Much more challenging is the task of synthesizing the arguments of thirteen diverse letters to discern a "center" to Paul's theology—one that functions as "a web that binds Paul's various theological points together"[1] or as a "foundation" upon which other elements of his theology depend.[2] While discerning a center is a worthwhile pursuit, we should be aware of some of the dangers. Among them is the risk of overshadowing the arguments of his individual writings, making other themes appear less significant, or imposing a central theme that the apostle Paul would not have recognized. But none of these should deter us from identifying a central theme in Paul's letters. We should simply keep the risks in mind as we pursue a center to his theology. Nor should we hold too tightly to a central theme, for our interpretive horizons influence the themes we prefer over others. This is why there are almost as many proposed centers as there are Pauline interpreters. Bearing all this in mind, we should seek to discern a center of Paul's thought with epistemological humility.

With these necessary precautions, we will now evaluate several of the more prominent proposals for a possible center to Paul's theology. Then, we will argue for a theme that is robust enough to hold together a number of subordinate topics. Even though we will identify a center to Paul's thought, we concede up front the value of reading the text through the lens of different theological themes. We agree with Schreiner: "having several different centers is useful, as NT theology can be studied from a number of different perspectives . . . examining the NT from a number of different angles allows new light

---

1. Douglas J. Moo, *A Theology of Paul and His Letters: The Gift of the New Realm in Christ*, BTNT (Grand Rapids: Zondervan, 2021), 349.
2. Thomas R. Schreiner, *Paul, Apostle of God's Glory in Christ: A Pauline Theology*, 2nd ed. (Downers Grove, IL: InterVarsity Press, 2020), 5–8. We are following Schreiner's illustration of a "house."

to be shed upon the text."[3] This chapter, then, will argue for a central theme, while not devaluing the benefit of reading Paul through other themes that may helpfully illuminate other aspects of Paul's letters.

Proposed Centers

Our overview of the proposed centers to Paul's theology begins in the nineteenth century and concludes in the twenty-first. We will briefly survey ten of the most prominent proposals.

1. **The Spirit (Baur):** The nineteenth-century New Testament scholar F. C. Baur argued for a central theological focus from the only Pauline letters he considered authentic: Romans, Galatians, and 1 and 2 Corinthians. He contended that the "spirit," which he interpreted through a Hegelian framework as the Christian's "consciousness,"[4] accomplishes a person's justification, union with Christ, and sonship.[5] As a result of the spirit's work, Paul believed he was free from the constraints of Jewish law.[6] For Baur, the spirit—as he understood "it"—was the key to unlocking other Pauline concepts.

2. **In Christ (Schweitzer):** Albert Schweitzer eschewed the common Pauline interpretive paradigm of his day espoused by scholars such as Baur: that Paul had departed from Judaism in favor of Hellenism. Situating Paul within a Jewish apocalyptic framework, Schweitzer argued that Paul's theology centers on the mystical doctrine of being "in Christ," which he called "Christ-mysticism."[7] The state of being "in Christ" signifies that believers experience a present manifestation of the future eschatological kingdom.[8] When a person is "in Christ," they are also justified. While Protestants are inclined to see justification as the center of Paul's thought, Schweitzer argued that being "in

---

3. Thomas R. Schreiner, *New Testament Theology: Magnifying God in Christ* (Grand Rapids: Baker Academic, 2008), 13.
4. G. W. F. Hegel was a nineteenth-century German philosopher whose influential dialectical method relied on contradicting "two sides," such as two "logical concepts" or "definitions of consciousness." Over time, as "two sides" oppose one another, a linear progression often takes place from "less sophisticated views to more sophisticated ones." See the substantive entry on "Hegel's Dialectics," in *Stanford Encyclopedia of Philosophy*, https://plato.stanford.edu/entries/hegel-dialectics. See also Bertrand Russell, *A History of Western Philosophy* (New York: Touchstone, 2007), 730–46.
5. F. C. Baur, *Paul the Apostle of Jesus Christ* (repr. Grand Rapids: Baker Academic, 2011), 2:135–68. See also discussion in N. T. Wright, *Paul and His Recent Interpreters: Some Contemporary Debates* (Minneapolis: Fortress, 2015), 14.
6. Baur, *Paul the Apostle*, 2:271.
7. Albert Schweitzer, *The Mysticism of the Apostle Paul* (New York: Henry Holt, 1931).
8. Schweitzer, *Mysticism of Paul*, 380.

Christ" is Paul's primary concern. He downplayed the former, calling it a "subsidiary crater" in Paul's thought.

3. **Anthropology (Bultmann):** Rudolf Bultmann famously argued that Paul departed from Judaism, preferring to read his writings in view of a Gnostic or even Stoic framework. In so doing, he contended for the centrality of "anthropology" in Paul's theology.[9] This does not mean that he believed God has no place in Pauline theology—quite the opposite! Bultmann held that the actions of God and human deeds are intimately related: "Every assertion about God is simultaneously an assertion about man."[10] He says the same of Christ, through whom God works salvation for the benefit of humankind: "every assertion about Christ is simultaneously an assertion about man and vice versa."[11] In all this, Bultmann places priority on "anthropology," organizing his theology of Paul under the categories "man prior to the revelation of faith" and "man under faith."[12]

4. **Righteousness of God (Käsemann):** Ernst Käsemann read Paul in view of Jewish apocalyptic tradition. Yet, he differs from Schweitzer, contending that "the righteousness of God" is "the central problem in Pauline theology."[13] For Käsemann, this phrase signifies that "God's power reaches out for the world, and the world's salvation lies in its being captured for the sovereignty of God. For this reason, it is the gift of God and also the salvation of the individual human being when we become obedient to divine righteousness."[14] Contemporary scholars such as Peter Stuhlmacher and Mark Seifrid also argue for the centrality of righteousness in Paul's theology.[15]

5. **Participation in Christ (Sanders):** Along similar lines as Schweitzer, E. P. Sanders appeals to the centrality of "participation in Christ" in

---

9. Rudolf Bultmann, *Theology of the New Testament*, trans. Kendrick Groebel (Waco, TX: Baylor University Press, 2007), 190–355.
10. Bultmann, *Theology of the New Testament*, 191.
11. Bultmann, *Theology of the New Testament*, 191.
12. Wright also highlights these themes (*Paul and the Faithfulness of God*, Christian Origins and the Question of God, vol. 4 [Minneapolis: Fortress, 2013], 778).
13. Ernst Käsemann, "The Righteousness of God in Paul," in *New Testament Questions of Today* (Philadelphia: Fortress, 1969), 169. See also the entire essay (pp. 168–182), and his "On the Subject of Christian Apocalyptic," in *New Testament Questions of Today*, 108–37; *Commentary on Romans*, trans. Geoffry W. Bromiley (Grand Rapids: Eerdmans, 1980).
14. Käsemann, "Righteousness of God," 182.
15. Peter Stuhlmacher, *Biblical Theology of the New Testament*, trans. Daniel P. Bailey (Grand Rapids: Eerdmans, 2018), 346–84, 371; Mark A. Seifrid, *Christ, Our Righteousness: Paul's Theology of Justification* (Downers Grove, IL : InterVarsity Press, 2000).

Paul's theology, whom he situates within Second Temple Judaism.[16] Sanders contends that the theme is witnessed in a variety of phrases, such as "being in the body of Christ, the short phrase 'in Christ', and the like."[17] No one phrase encapsulates the importance of participation in Paul's letters. According to Sanders, we witness its centrality in that "it is the theme, above all, both to which Paul appeals in parenesis and polemic."[18] What is more, "the diversity of the terminology helps to show how the general conception of participation permeated his thought."[19]

6. **Redemptive History (Ridderbos):** Herman Ridderbos argues that "redemptive history," also called "salvation history," is the controlling element in Paul's ministry.[20] For Paul, the death and resurrection of Jesus is the climax of history, fulfilling the promises to Israel, while also anticipating the consummation of all things at the second coming. According to Ridderbos: "It is this great redemptive-historical framework within which the whole of Paul's preaching must be understood and all of its subordinate parts receive their place and organically cohere."[21]

7. **Covenant (Wright):** While finding general agreement with Sanders's placement of Paul within Judaism, N. T. Wright departs from understanding "participation" as the center of Paul's thought. He argues, instead, that "covenant" is the theme in which the stories of the promises to Abraham, exile, restoration and the like are brought together.[22] According to Wright, Paul presupposes the theme of covenant, even where he does not explicitly mention the term. This is akin to the way Sanders argues that covenant is presupposed everywhere in rabbinic and other Palestinian Jewish texts. If covenant can be assumed as central in Jewish literature, then Wright believes we can also assume the centrality of covenant in Paul's letters.

---

16. E. P. Sanders, *Paul and Palestinian Judaism: A Comparison of Patterns of Religion*, 40th Anniversary ed. (Minneapolis: Fortress, 2017).
17. Sanders, *Paul and Palestinian Judaism*, 456.
18. Sanders, *Paul and Palestinian Judaism*, 456.
19. Sanders, *Paul and Palestinian Judaism*, 456.
20. Herman Ridderbos, *Paul: An Outline of His Theology*, trans. John Richard de Witt (Grand Rapids: Eerdmans, 1975).
21. Ridderbos, *Paul*, 39.
22. See N. T. Wright, *Paul and the Faithfulness of God*, Christian Origins and the Question of God, vol. 4 (Minneapolis: Fortress, 2013), 780–81. See also his *The Climax of the Covenant: Christ and the Law in Pauline Theology* (Minneapolis: Fortress, 1993).

8. **Glorification of God in Christ (Schreiner):** Thomas Schreiner argues that Paul's foundational theme is the "glorification of God in Jesus Christ."[23] According to Schreiner, God is magnified in sending Jesus to redeem sinners, fulfilling the promises to Abraham to bring blessing to the nations. Simply put, God receives all the glory through the person and work of Jesus, the one in whom salvation history finds its climax (Eph. 1:10).

9. **Cruciformity (Gorman):** Michael Gorman argues that "cruciformity"—conformity to the crucified Christ—is central to Pauline theology.[24] He describes the term as "a dynamic correspondence in daily life to the strange story of Christ crucified as the primary way of experiencing the love and grace of God."[25] The entirety of Paul's mission was intended to shape the lives of congregations through the narrative of the cross. We witness the centrality of "cruciformity" in Paul's thought in 1 Corinthians 2:2: "For I decided to know nothing among you except Jesus Christ and him crucified."[26]

10. **New Realm (Moo):** More recently, Douglas J. Moo claims that the "new realm" is what binds together a large body of Pauline themes.[27] Jesus Christ is the last Adam and descendant of Abraham, God's very Son and Messiah, who inaugurates the "new realm." What is more, Jesus's substitutionary death brings together Jews and Gentiles into one people who will enjoy all the blessings of the sphere to which they now belong, such as the reception of the Spirit, justification, adoption, and a new creation. Paul, according to Moo, calls believers to live holy lives in anticipation of the consummation of the "new realm" when God renews his creation.

We could discuss other proposed centers, like Ralph Martin's focus on "reconciliation" with God and others as the "single principle that runs through Paul's teaching,"[28] and J. Louis Martyn's thesis that Jesus's "apocalyptic" overthrow of

---

23. See Schreiner, *Paul, Apostle of God's Glory in Christ*. Schreiner also sees the centrality of this theme in the entire New Testament. See his *New Testament Theology: Magnifying God in Christ*.
24. Michael J. Gorman, *Cruciformity: Paul's Narrative Spirituality of the Cross*, 20th anniversary ed. (Grand Rapids: Eerdmans, 2021).
25. Gorman, *Cruciformity*, 5.
26. Gorman, *Cruciformity*, 7.
27. Moo, *Theology of Paul*.
28. Ralph P. Martin, *Reconciliation: A Study of Paul's Theology* (Eugene, OR: Wipf & Stock, 1997), 6, 224.

the world's powers is at the core of Paul's theology.[29] Nevertheless, the ones we have overviewed allow us to reflect on a discernable center to Paul's theology.

A Discernable Center

The search for a center to Paul's theology is a worthwhile pursuit. We have noted several of the more prominent proposals. Of these, the only one that does not address a legitimate theme is Baur's "spirit consciousness." Paul was no Hegelian. He did not believe that an impersonal spirit produces the blessings associated with salvation. He left that to the divine Spirit (Rom. 8:1–11; Gal. 3:1–5; 4:6–7; Eph. 1:13–14).

While each of the remaining proposals make legitimate claims for a center to Paul's thought, such as Sanders's argument for "participation" and Käsemann's for "righteousness," Gorman makes a compelling argument that "cruciformity" strikes at the heart of Paul's theology. For Paul, nothing was so central as the crucified Christ (Gal. 2:20; 1 Cor. 1:23–24; 2:2). In fact, the centrality of the crucifixion makes it a point of cohesion for other proposed themes in Paul's letters. We may observe this in the aim of God sending his son at the climax of "salvation history" was to "redeem those under the law, so that we might receive adoption as sons and daughters" (Gal. 4:4–5). The redemption from the law's curse, according to Paul, was made possible through the crucifixion of Jesus (Gal. 3:13–14). Also, Christ's blood shed on the cross "reconciles" people to God (1 Cor. 15:3; 2 Cor. 5:18–20; Col. 1:18–20) and brings Jews and Gentiles into one family, making them beneficiaries of the "covenantal" promises to Abraham (Eph. 2:11–16; Gal. 3:13–14, 15–18, 25–29; 4:6–7). Additionally, Christ's crucifixion makes believers "righteous" (Rom. 3:24; 8:3; 2 Cor. 5:21) and causes them to be found "in Christ" (Eph. 2:13; Phil. 3:9).[30] Believers also "participate" in the death of Christ, resulting in benefits such as deliverance from the power of sin (Rom. 6:6) and the present evil age (Gal. 1:3) and being indwelt with his presence (Gal. 2:20). Lastly, all Christ makes possible through his crucifixion brings "glory" to God.

While Gorman's proposal is arguably more satisfactory than others, we would like to offer our own qualification: Paul binds the benefits of Christ's death along with those of his resurrection.[31] Thus, the death and resurrection of Jesus are like two sides of the same coin. We see this in Romans 6:5–11:

---

29. J. Louis Martyn, *Galatians: A New Translation with Introduction and Commentary*, AB 33A (New York: Doubleday, 1997); Martyn, *Theological Issues in the Letters of Paul* (Nashville: Abingdon, 1997).

30. Another possible way to read Philippians 3:9 (*dia pisteōs Christou*) is as a subjective genitive: "through the faithfulness of Christ." Thus, it is through "Christ's faithfulness" to redeem his people that Paul has the hope of being found "in him."

31. We are not arguing that Gorman deemphasizes the resurrection, merely that his main focus is on the transformation associated with the crucifixion.

> For if we have been united with him in a death like his, we shall certainly be united with him in a resurrection like his. (v. 6)

> Now if we have died with Christ, we believe that we will also live with him. (v. 8)

> For the death he died he died to sin, once for all, but the life he lives he lives to God. So you also must consider yourselves dead to sin and alive to God in Christ Jesus. (vv. 10–11)

These verses demonstrate how Paul considers the centrality of both the crucifixion and resurrection of Christ—the former gives believers confidence of being delivered from sin and the latter gives them hope of being raised from the grave.

We also see how Paul associates Christ's death and resurrection in 1 Corinthians 15. In verses 2–3, he affirms the centrality of Christ's death and resurrection "in accordance with the Scriptures" (vv. 3–4). Since the Corinthians struggled with the notion of a physical resurrection, Paul emphasizes that Christ's resurrection makes possible our own resurrection from the dead (vv. 15, 20–22). Paul preached the importance of the resurrection of Christ, without which we have no hope of life beyond the grave (vv. 16–19). In this passage, we see how closely Paul ties the significance of resurrection to the death of Christ, so much so that forsaking its significance risks losing the very message of the Pauline gospel, that which he considered to be of "first importance" (vv. 1–3).[32] What we see in Romans 6 and 1 Corinthians 15, then, is that crucifixion and resurrection cohere into a central Pauline theme. In other passages, we also witness that the ethical transformation of sinners is the result of being both crucified (Gal. 2:20, 5:22–23) and also raised with Christ (Rom. 6:12–14), further strengthening the connection between crucifixion and resurrection in Paul's thought.

Summary

The "crucifixion and resurrection" of Christ coalesce into a central theme in Paul's theology. From this center flows doctrines such as forgiveness, righteousness, participation, and ethical transformation. Thus, we have warrant to read Paul through the lens of Christ's "death and resurrection," without which there is no redemption and in light of which we can imagine a world with limitless salvific possibilities. What is more, Christ's "death and resurrection" are not tied to the particularities of his letters nor does Paul's thinking ever change on these events. Rather, they are timeless events that merge into

---

32. See also Romans 8:33–34; Ephesians 2:4–6; Colossians 2:13–15.

the main theme through which Paul writes letters to churches. We understand, however, that our conclusion is born of our interpretive horizon, so we hold to this center loosely, knowing that others will see flaws we have not yet envisioned.

REFLECTION QUESTIONS

1. What are some risks to identifying a center to Paul's theology?

2. What are some benefits to discerning a central theme in Paul's letters?

3. What are some of the proposed centers to Paul's thought?

4. Of the proposed centers, including our own, which one do you find most convincing and why?

5. What are some possible centers to Paul's theology that were not addressed in this chapter?

What Is Paul's Christology?

Paul's gospel was centered around the person and work of Christ (Rom. 2:16; 16:25; 1 Cor. 15:1–11; 2 Tim. 2:8). He made it his aim to take his gospel to the Gentiles (Rom. 15:15–29; Gal. 2:7)—even to Spain, the westernmost edge of the Roman Empire (Rom. 15:24). Proclaiming Christ among the Gentiles was so important for Paul that he exchanged a privileged life in Judaism (Gal. 1:13–23) for one of persecution (Acts 9:15–16; 2 Cor. 4:8–12; 11:23–28; Gal. 5:11) and imprisonment (Acts 26:23; 28:13–15). But what exactly did Paul believe about the Christ for whom he risked everything? Simply put, what was Paul's Christology? In order to address this important question, we will consider the background of the main Christological titles that appear in his writings, how he treats the divine and human natures of Jesus, and what he anticipates about the return of Christ. Exploring these important subjects will enable us to develop a well-grounded understanding of Paul's Christology.[1]

Significant Christological Titles

Paul uses three significant Christological titles to highlight unique aspects of Jesus's identity. Son of Man" is the only Christological title Paul does not employ in his writings. This designation most commonly appears in the Gospels and was Jesus's preferred title.

---

1. Whether Paul's Christology was normative for the earliest Christians is beyond the scope of the present discussion. For helpful discussion on such matters, while not limiting the discussion to Paul, see Richard Bauckham, *Jesus and the God of Israel: God Crucified and Other Studies on the New Testament's Christology of Divine Identity* (Grand Rapids: Baker Academic, 2008), 127–232; Oscar Cullmann, *The Christology of the New Testament*, New Testament Library, trans. Shirley C. Guthrie and Charles A. M. Hall (Philadelphia: Westminster, 1963); Larry W. Hurtado, *Lord Jesus Christ: Devotion to Jesus in Earliest Christianity* (Grand Rapids: Eerdmans, 2003); Stanley E. Porter and Bryan R. Dyer, *Origins of New Testament Christology: An Introduction to the Traditions and Titles Applied to Jesus* (Grand Rapids: Baker Academic, 2023).

Christos ("Christ")

Paul most commonly uses the Greek term *Christos* to describe Jesus. He uses the term on its own or in a variety of combinations, such as "Jesus Christ," "Christ Jesus," "Lord Jesus Christ," and "Lord Jesus."[2] Significantly, *Christos* is often used in the Septuagint to translate the Hebrew *Mashiach*, a term which identifies Israel's "anointed ruler" or "Messiah" who shall have dominion over the earth (Ps. 2:2).[3] The eschatological nature of Messiah's reign is evidenced in texts such as Daniel 9:25–27. In Second Temple Judaism, messianic language is increasingly tied to Israel's hopes for an eschatological redeemer. *Fourth Ezra*, for instance, links Israel's messianic hopes to one who "will arise from the line of David" (12:32; cf. 7:28–29). The *Psalms of Solomon* makes a similar association, linking Israel's eschatological hopes for a Messiah to the figure of King David (17:21–46). The text even states that "their king shall be *christos kyrios*" (17.32), that is, "Christ the Lord." Messianic hope is also evident in the Dead Sea Scrolls.[4] Paul likely draws his understanding *Christos* from such Jewish texts to identify Jesus as Israel's promised "Messiah" or "anointed ruler" who will reign over the earth.

Despite the well-established use of the term, many argue that Paul's use of *Christos* implies that it had lost its titular significance, becoming essentially the same as a proper name for Jesus.[5] We should be surprised to learn that Paul forsook the way *Christos* is associated with messianic eschatological hopes in Jewish literature. As discussed in previous chapters, Paul was a Jew who was well-acquainted with Jewish literature. We therefore disagree that Paul disregarded the titular significance of *Christos*, for that would have been unconscionable for a Jew who was familiar with the messianic allusions tied to the term. This may be observed in texts such as Romans 9:3–5, where *Christos* is linked to the hopes of Israel's patriarchs,[6] and Galatians 3:16, where *Christos* is grounded in the promises to Abraham (also Rom. 1:3–4; 1 Cor. 15:23–28). Unless we have clear evidence to the contrary, then, we should assume that Paul uses *Christos* to associate Jesus with Israel's promised king who will rule over the cosmos. Those familiar with Jewish texts would have certainly picked up on these messianic overtones in Paul's letters.[7]

---

2. Douglas J. Moo, *A Theology of Paul and His Letters: The Gift of the New Realm in Christ*, BTNT (Grand Rapids: Zondervan, 2021), 363.
3. The information in this paragraph derives from Miguel G. Echevarría, *The Future Inheritance of Land in the Pauline Epistles* (Eugene, OR: Pickwick, 2019), 112.
4. See 4QDibHam [–4Q504] 3.4–7; 4Q246 2.1; 1QS 9.11 (1QS speaks of two Messiahs).
5. James D. G. Dunn, *The Theology of Paul the Apostle* (Grand Rapids: Eerdmans, 1998), 197. Ben Witherington III, "Christology," in *DPL*, 104. See also the discussion in Matthew V. Novenson, *Christ among the Messiahs: Christ Language in Paul and Messiah Language in Ancient Judaism* (Oxford: Oxford University Press, 2012), 64.
6. Dunn, *Theology of Paul*, 198.
7. See N. T. Wright, *The Climax of the Covenant: Christ and the Law in Pauline Theology* (Minneapolis: Fortress, 1993), 40–55.

Kyrios ("Lord")

Paul refers to Jesus as *Kyrios* almost as often as he refers to him as *Christos*. Paul testifies that Jesus received this title, translated "Lord," following his death on the cross:

> And being found in human form, he humbled himself by becoming obedient to the point of death, even death on a cross. Therefore God has highly exalted him and bestowed on him the name that is above every name, so that at the name of Jesus every knee should bow, in heaven and on earth and under the earth, and every tongue confess that Jesus Christ is Lord, to the glory of God the Father. (Phil. 2:8–11)[8]

When we see the exaltation of Jesus associated with his resurrection, we envision that Jesus was declared Lord at his resurrection. Other Pauline texts make an explicit connection between his lordship and resurrection, such as Romans 10:9, where confessing "Jesus is Lord" is associated with his resurrection, and Romans 14:9, where his lordship over the living and the dead is linked to his death and "living again" (also Rom. 8:34; 1 Cor. 15:23–25; Col. 3:1; cf. Acts 2:29–36).[9] Another important passage is Romans 14:9: "For to this end Christ died and lived again, that he might be Lord both of the dead and of the living."[10] Paul's affirmation of Jesus's lordship is likely grounded in Old Testament texts such as Psalm 110:1, where God's coregent, described as *Kyrios*, is given dominion over his enemies, something Jesus achieved following his resurrection from the grave.

The implication for believers is that they are called to live under the lordship of Jesus (Rom. 10:12; Col. 2:6). This means that they are accountable to him (1 Cor. 4:4; 5:3–4; 2 Cor. 8:21) and must submit themselves to his will (e.g., Eph: 5:10, 17; Col. 1:10).[11] Should they withhold obedience, Paul warns his readers of the "coming of the Lord" (e.g., 1 Thess. 2:19; 3:13; 4:15). The day he returns will be a day of reckoning for all the people of the earth (1 Cor. 1:8; 2 Cor. 14). No one will be able to escape the judgment of the Lord to whom all people will give an account.

Unlike the supposed divinity of other rulers, Paul argues that Jesus is the divine Lord, even ascribing to him equal status with the Father (1 Cor. 8:6; Phil. 2:6; Col 1:15). The divine status of Jesus is also seen in the use of the term *Kyrios* in the Septuagint where it frequently serves as the Greek translation for the name of God (*YHWH*, e.g., Ps. 110:1). This is likely why Paul applies soteriological significance

---

8. Dunn, *Theology of Paul*, 245–46.

9. Dunn, *Theology of Paul*, 245.

10. Simon Gathercole, "Paul's Christology," in *The Blackwell Companion to Paul*, ed. Stephen Westerholm (West Sussex: Wiley & Sons, 2014), 174.

11. Moo, *Paul*, 368.

to calling on the name of Jesus, who is one and the same with God (Rom. 10:13; 1 Cor. 1:2).[12] This would have had a profound effect on audiences who recognized the way Paul applies the Septuagint term *Kyrios* to Jesus.[13] All in all, Paul uses the term *Kyrios* to signify that Jesus is the divine Lord over all creation.

Son of God

The title Son of God is one of Paul's more infrequent titles for Jesus. When he does use the designation, the relationship between Jesus and the Father is in view. Paul argues that the Father sent the Son to earth (Gal. 4:4) at the pivotal moment in history in order to accomplish reconciliation and redemption (Rom. 5:10; 8:3; Gal. 2:20; 4:4–5). Dunn argues that the death of the "beloved son" in Paul's letters alludes to Abraham offering Isaac as a sacrifice in Genesis 22:1–19.[14] He points to the possible connection in Romans 8:32, where Paul's words ("he who did not spare his own Son") closely echo those of Genesis 22:16 ("[you] have not withheld your son").[15] If Dunn is right, then Paul applies Son of God terminology to Jesus to recall the powerful imagery of Abraham offering Isaac, which typifies the Father giving his own Son for the redemption of all people (Rom. 8:32).

Paul also declares that God's Son is the royal descendant of David, who was raised from the dead "in power" (Rom. 1:3). Romans 1:4 reveals that God's Son is one and the same with the *Christos* and *Kyrios* (Rom 1:4). While these terms do not exhaust Paul's Christology, they together reveal that Paul believes Jesus to be God's royal messianic Son, whose death and resurrection results in his lordship over, and his redemption of, all of creation.

Divine and Human Natures of Christ

We can conclude that the titles for Christ emphasize his divine and human natures. Take, for instance, the way Paul applies the terms *Christos* and *Kyrios* to Jesus, the former referring to a messianic figure and the later recalling the divine name of YHWH. Yet, Paul also makes explicit affirmations about the divinity and humanity of Jesus.

Divinity

The *Shema* ("Hear, O Israel: The Lord our God, the Lord is one") was central to Paul's understanding of God (Deut. 6:4; cf. 1 Cor. 8:6).[16] Paul was a Jewish monotheist, who would have only attributed divinity to the God who had chosen

---

12. Gathercole, "Pauline Christology," 174.
13. See Gordon D. Fee, *Pauline Christology: An Exegetical-Theological Study* (Peabody, MA: Hendrickson, 2007), 20–25.
14. Dunn, *Theology of Paul*, 224.
15. Dunn, *Theology of Paul*, 224.
16. On the importance of 1 Corinthians 8:6 and its Christological meaning, see Fee, *Pauline Christology*, 89–94; Wright, *The Climax of the Covenant*, 120–36.

and elected Israel.[17] Thus, in Romans 9:5 Paul speaks volumes when he assigns the status of God to Jesus Christ: "To them [Israel] belong the Patriarchs, and from their race, according to the flesh, is the Christ, who is God overall, blessed forever. Amen." The relative clause ("who is") clarifies that Jesus is "God overall" (cf. 2 Cor. 11:1). Paul also assigns divine status to Jesus in Titus 2:13: "waiting for our blessed hope, the appearing of our great God and Savior Jesus Christ." Grammatically, both "Great God" and "Savior" refer to Jesus Christ. Thus, both of these texts directly attribute divinity to Jesus Christ.[18]

Another important text is Philippians 2:6–7, which asserts that Jesus "was in the form (*morphē*) of God." While the passage is debated, we argue that Paul uses *morphē* to emphasize that "being in the form of God" is the same as being "equal with God."[19] Paul contrasts Jesus's preincarnate status with his state during the incarnation in which he "emptied himself" and took on humanity (Phil. 2:7). Paul is not suggesting that Jesus emptied himself of deity. Although Jesus has always been "equal to God," he willingly deprived himself of the advantages available to him and selflessly submitting himself in obedience to the Father "to the point of death, even death on the cross" (Phil. 2:8).

Other significant texts include 2 Corinthians 4:4 and Colossians 1:15, which affirm that Jesus is the "image (*eikōn*) of God." Paul's use of *eikōn* alludes to the Septuagint version of Genesis 1:26–27, which suggests that humanity is to represent the "divine likeness" of God. Paul's point is that only Jesus Christ perfectly bore the divine image of God, and it is he who now transforms humanity into the image bearers for which they were originally created.[20] Passages which call Christians to pray (1 Cor. 1:2; 2 Cor. 12:8) and worship Jesus (1 Cor. 12:3) serve to show that Paul understood Jesus to have the same divine status as the God to whom old covenant saints cried for salvation (Exod. 3:7–8; Judg. 10:10; Hos. 8:2). N. T. Wright correctly argues that Paul "believed that Israel's God was fully and personally present in and as Jesus the Messiah."[21]

Humanity

In addition to describing Jesus as the divine Son, Paul also emphasizes the humanity of Jesus. In Romans 1:2–3, for instance, he underscores that Jesus is the descendent of David "according to the flesh." In Galatians 4:4, he asserts that Jesus was "born of a woman." Rather than denying the preexistence of Jesus, this passage affirms that the eternal Son of God was born into the world like any other human being, through a woman. In Philippians 2:7–8, Paul claims that

---

17. See N. T. Wright's discussion on Jewish monotheism and Paul (*Paul and the Faithfulness of God*, Christian Origins and the Question of God, vol. 4 [Minneapolis: Fortress, 2013], 619–43).
18. See discussion of these passages in Murray J. Harris, *Jesus as God: The New Testament Use of Theos in Reference to Jesus* (Grand Rapids: Baker Academic, 1992), 143–85.
19. Moisés Silva, *Philippians*, BECNT (Grand Rapids: Baker Academic, 1992), 114–15.
20. Fee, *Pauline Christology*, 185.
21. Wright, *Paul and the Faithfulness of God*, 1073.

Jesus was born into the world and suffered as a human being. Paul affirms this point in Romans 8:3, arguing that Jesus condemned sin in his human flesh. In addition to these passages, we argue that Paul's affirmation of the gospel tradition in 1 Corinthians 15:1–11 is based on the fact that Jesus Christ suffered in the flesh, was raised physically from the grave, and appeared in glorified humanity to his followers. For Paul, then, Jesus is both divine and human, the one in whose likeness humanity will be raised (1 Cor. 15:12–58).

The Return of Christ

Paul's references and reflections on the first coming of Jesus Christ focus on his death and resurrection in order to establish his cosmic supremacy and redemption of creation (Rom. 1:3–4; Gal. 4:4–5; Phil. 2:1–11; Col. 2:15). According to Paul's testimony, the same Christ later ascended into heaven where he currently exercises his lordship over all things (Eph. 4:8–10). But Christ will not remain in the heavenlies. Paul fully expects that Jesus Christ will come again to consummate what he began at his first coming.

Paul's hope in the eschatological return of Christ is most prominent in 1 and 2 Thessalonians, where he encourages his readers "to wait for his Son [Jesus] from heaven, whom he raised from the dead" (1 Thess. 1:10). The Thessalonians are Paul's "hope or joy or crown of boasting before our Lord Jesus at his coming" (1 Thess. 2:19). Paul expresses his hope that the Thessalonians would increase in their love for one another so that they might be "blameless in holiness before our God and Father, at the coming of our Lord Jesus with all of his saints" (3:12–13). Paul assures the Thessalonians that when Jesus returns, he will raise the dead in Christ and those who remain alive (1 Thess. 4:13–18). He makes a similar point to the Corinthians, arguing that the Christ who rose from the dead will return to raise them as well (1 Cor. 15:20–22; 2 Cor. 4:14), and to the Philippians, whom Paul assures that Jesus will return from heaven in order to "transform our lowly body to be like his glorious body" (Phil. 3:20–21; cf. Col. 3:3–4). Paul's confidence in the return of Christ therefore is closely linked to his hope that believers will be resurrected in the likeness of Christ.

Whereas believers will be gloriously resurrected, Paul assures the Thessalonians that Christ's return will result in eternal judgment for their enemies (2 Thess. 1:7–10; cf. Gal. 6). In 1 Corinthians 4:4–5, Paul expands the nature of the judgment to include all people. We can synthesize these accounts to envision that Christ's return will result in punishment for unbelievers and eternal life for believers. Along with resurrection and judgment will be the consummation of the kingdom, when God will at last be "all in all," meaning that God's power over the cosmos will be reasserted (1 Cor. 15:23–28).[22] In

---

22. Roy E. Ciampa and Brian S. Rosner, *The First Letter to the Corinthians*, PNTC (Grand Rapids: Eerdmans, 2010), 776.

short, Paul foresees that Christ will consummate his work when he returns to resurrect the dead and enact the final judgment, resulting in the resurrection and restoration of the creation and God's reign over the earth.

Summary

Paul was determined to preach Jesus Christ to the Gentiles. What he proclaimed about Christ was grounded in what he believed about him, i.e., his Christology. We have seen that the titles which Paul applies to Jesus—*Christos, Kyrios,* and Son of God—suggest he recognized him to be God's royal messianic Son, whose death and resurrection result in his lordship and redemption of the creation. This fully divine and human Jesus died, rose from the grave, and will return to raise believers to life and condemn the wicked. When all this takes place, God's rule over the cosmos will be forever restored and unchallenged. A brief synthesis of relevant passages reveals that Paul was wholly convinced of each of these realities—convictions which compelled him to risk everything to proclaim the message of the divine king who will one day return to establish God's rule over creation.

REFLECTION QUESTIONS

1. What do Paul's use of the titles *Christos, Kyrios,* and Son of God suggest that he believed that about Jesus?

2. What are some texts which indicate that Paul understood Jesus as both divine and human in nature?

3. What are some of the central events associated with the eschatological return of Jesus that are emphasized by Paul?

4. How would you summarize Paul's Christology? What are some of its primary features?

5. How might Paul's Christology compel you to share the gospel with the nations?

What Is Paul's View of the Atonement?

The death of Christ is of central importance to Paul's theology. His teachings on subjects such as justification by faith and the reception of the Holy Spirit are grounded in Jesus Christ's death through which sinners are forgiven and reconciled to God.[1] Historically, Christians have referred to Christ's sacrifice as the "atonement."[2] In recent years, much of the discussion on this subject has centered around whether Paul displays a "substitutionary" or "representative" view of Jesus's death.[3]

Scholars who hold to "substitution" contend that Paul envisions Christ "dying in place of sinners." Martin Luther and Karl Barth provide helpful summaries of this perspective. Luther notes: "we are sinners and thieves, and therefore we are worthy of death and eternal damnation. But Christ took all our sins upon himself, and for them he died on the cross."[4] Barth observes: "In his doing this for us, in his taking to himself—to fulfill all righteousness—our

---

1. Richard Hays argues similarly: "his [Paul's] teaching about justification by faith presupposes and rests upon the story of the cosmic event whereby God reconciles the world to himself" (*The Faith of Jesus Christ: The Narrative Substructure of Galatians 3:1–4:11*, 2nd ed. [Grand Rapids: Eerdmans, 2002], 216.). By "cosmic event," Hays is speaking of the atonement.
2. Robert Yarbrough, "Atonement," in *NDBT*, eds. T. Desmond Alexander, Brian S. Rosner, D. A. Carson, and Graeme Goldsworthy (Downers Grove, IL: InterVarsity Press, 2000), 388. Kenneth Mulzac, "Atonement," in *Eerdmans Dictionary of the Bible*, ed. David Noel Freedman (Grand Rapids: Eerdmans, 2000), 127.
3. Space does not allow for an exhaustive review of all the positions (e.g., apocalyptic and interchange) on the atonement in Paul's letters. We will limit our discussion to the most popular position (representation) and the most contested one (substitution). See Simon Gathercole's discussion for a current state of the conversation on atonement in Paul and an evaluation of views not covered in this chapter (*Defending Substitution: An Essay on Atonement in Paul* [Grand Rapids: Baker Academic, 2015]). Gathercole's *Defending Substitution* has been influential in shaping our view of the atonement and provides a helpful treatment of some of the relevant literature, some of which is cited in this chapter.
4. Martin Luther, *Lectures on Galatians*, Luther's Works, vol. 26, ed. Jaroslav Pelikan (St. Louis: Concordia, 1963), 277.

accusation and condemnation and punishment, in his suffering in our place and for us, there came to pass our reconciliation to God."[5] Some even call substitution the *classic* view of the atonement.

A number of modern scholars, however, are unconvinced that substitution is the best way to describe Christ's death, preferring the "representation" view: that Christ represented sinners on the cross, making it possible for us to *participate* in his death and resurrection. According to this position, Jesus does not act "in our place," for we are *with him* in his suffering.

In what follows, we will examine how proponents of the "substitution" and "representation" viewpoints interpret key passages in Paul's epistles and offer an assessment of Paul's understanding of the atonement. As a word of caution, modern readers often systematize Paul's thought into singular categories. It may be that his teaching on the atonement is entirely consistent with a particular position. Or, it may be that his perspective is simply too robust to be limited to a single theory. We must therefore broaden our horizons to accept either possibility.

Substitution

That Christ died "in place of" sinners is at the core of substitution. But there is still more to grasp. According to Gathercole, Jesus "did something, underwent something, so that we did not and would never have to do so."[6] Gathercole underscores that substitution encompasses both what Jesus did and, as a result, what believers no longer have to endure. With this in mind, we may now consider several passages that appear to refer to the Christ event in this manner.

The traditional gospel formula in 1 Corinthians 15:3 is of central importance for Paul's view of the atonement. Paul argues that it is the gospel "by which you are being saved" (v. 2) and that it is "of first importance" (v. 3).[7] Of particular relevance is the phrase, "Christ died in place of (*hyper*) our sins according to the Scriptures" (v. 3).[8] Scholars frequently cite the preposition *hyper* in support of substitution, contending that it conveys the idea that Christ died "in place of" sins.[9] That New Testament authors use this preposition in passages where Jesus gives himself "on behalf of" or "in place of"

---

5. Karl Barth, *Church Dogmatics* IV/1, The Doctrine of Reconciliation (Edinburgh: T&T Clark, 1956), 223.
6. Gathercole, *Defending Substitution*, 15.
7. Richard Hays argues that Paul's gospel tradition can be traced to "the time surrounding Paul's own call and apostleship—in other words, back to within about three years from the time Jesus was crucified in Jerusalem" (*First Corinthians*, Interpretation [Louisville: Westminster John Knox, 1997], 255).
8. Translations of atonement-related prepositions often deviate from the ESV.
9. See Thomas R. Schreiner, *Galatians*, ZECNT (Grand Rapids: Zondervan, 2010), 76; A. Andrew Das, *Galatians*, ConcC (St. Louis: Concordia, 2014), 83.

others (e.g., Rom. 5:6) lends support to this position.[10] Some argue, however, that *hyper* may also carry a causal sense, underscoring that Jesus died "because of" or "for the sake of" our sins.[11] Does Paul, then, intend for *hyper* to mean "in place of" or "because of"?

Some contend that Paul would have used the preposition *anti* if he wanted to convey substitution, for it clearly denotes the sense of "in place of."[12] Dan Wallace, however, observes that there is overwhelming support in Greek literature for *hyper* "bearing a substitutionary force."[13] Paul's uses of *hyper* in other key passages are in line with this use of the preposition. For example, in Galatians 1:4 Paul says that Jesus died "in place of (*hyper*) our sins." In Galatians 2:20, he says that God's son "gave himself in place of (*hyper*) me." Later in Galatians 3:13, he argues that Jesus became a curse "on behalf of (*hyper*) us," suggesting that Jesus was accursed, so that we would not have to be.[14] These examples display that Paul's use of *hyper* in 1 Corinthians 15:3 is consistent with the sense in which substitution is depicted in other passages, showing that Jesus suffered "in our place." As a consequence of the atonement, we no longer have to endure the penalty for sins.

Further support for a substitutionary understanding of 1 Corinthians 15:3 may come from the "Scriptures" from which Paul's gospel tradition draws. The most likely source is Isaiah 53, which speaks of the Lord's servant offering his life for Israel's trespasses. Verse 6 is key in this chapter, as it affirms that the people's trespasses led to the Lord handing over the servant "for our sins" (cf. vv. 4, 12). The language here closely mirrors Romans 8:32, where Paul affirms that God "handed him [Jesus] over for us all." What we have in Isaiah 53, then, is the source of Paul's gospel, the servant who offered his life for the people's transgressions.[15] We can even argue that Paul's substitutionary theology in passages such as Galatians 1:4, 2:20, and 3:13 are drawn from Isaiah 53. In sum, the "substitution" perspective of the atonement in Paul's letters emphasizes that Jesus died "in place of" sinners, so that we would not have to endure the punishment for our iniquities.[16]

---

10. BDAG, 1031–32.
11. BDAG, 1030.
12. BDAG, 87–88. See the discussion in Ben Witherington III, *Grace in Galatia: A Commentary on Paul's Letter to the Galatians* (Grand Rapids: Eerdmans, 1998), 76.
13. Daniel B. Wallace, *Greek Grammar beyond the Basics* (Grand Rapids: Zondervan, 1996), 386. Wallace cites a lengthy list of Greek literature from the New Testament era in support of this conclusion.
14. A. T. Robertson, *Word Pictures in the New Testament: Epistles of Paul*, vol. 4 (Nashville: Broadman, 1931), 186–87.
15. See Gathercole for a compelling comparison of the structure of Isaiah 53 and 1 Corinthians 15 (*Defending Substitution*, 65).
16. See also substitution in Romans 3:25; 5:5; 11:24; 1 Corinthians 11:24; 2 Corinthians 5:19; Ephesians 5:2; 1 Timothy 2:16; Titus 2:14.

Representation

The representation view of the atonement contends that Jesus Christ *represented* sinners on the cross.[17] Believers are not spared the penalty for transgressions but instead *participate* in Jesus's suffering and death. According to James Dunn, "Paul's teaching is *not* that Christ dies 'in the place of' others so that they *escape* death (as the logic of substitution implies). It is rather that Christ sharing *their* death makes it possible for them to share *his* death."[18] This view may also be described as "participation," a "participatory event," or as "corporate solidarity."

One of the main ways in which proponents of the concepts of representation and substitution differ from one another is in how the various "in place of" phrases are understood. Robert Jewett argues that "the widely used formula of Christ dying on behalf of others should be understood 'in terms of representation and not in terms of substitution.'"[19] Daniel Powers prefers the language of "corporate solidarity." In examining 1 Corinthians 15:3, Powers contends that Paul has "close solidarity between Christ and the believers" in mind.[20] Since believers have been united to Christ, Powers argues that the death and resurrection of Christ have the positive benefit of removing believers from the state of being "in their sins" (cf. 1 Cor. 15:17).[21] Thus, Paul does not use the phrase "for our sins" to convey that Christ died "in place of" sinners. Instead, Christ's death has the effect of *uniting* his followers to himself, resulting in their forgiveness. Powers also takes Paul's "for our sins" phrase in Galatians 1:4 and the "for me" phrase in 2:20 in the sense of corporate solidarity, with no sense of substitution whatsoever.

Hartmut Gese takes a similar approach. In his essay on the atonement, he examines 1 Corinthians 15:3, arguing for the idea of "corporate union."[22] Through this union, believers' sins are atoned for, and they are reconciled to God. Powers grounds his interpretation in Israel's Day of Atonement, in which the nation *participated* in the death sentence on account of sin, when the priest laid his hands on the scapegoat (Lev. 16).[23] For Gese, when the priest *represents* the community by laying his hands on the animal, he establishes a symbolic connection between the animal and the priest who *represents* the

---

17. See Joel B. Green, "Death of Christ," in *DPL*, 207.
18. James D. G. Dunn, *The Theology of Paul the Apostle* (Grand Rapids: Eerdmans, 1998), 223. Dunn italicizes words for emphasis.
19. Robert Jewett, *Romans: A Commentary*, Hermeneia (Minneapolis: Fortress, 2006), 362. Jewett cites Daniel Powers, *Salvation through Participation: An Examination of the Notion of the Believer's Corporate Unity with Christ in Early Christian Soteriology* (Leuven: Peeters, 2001), 233.
20. Powers, *Salvation through Participation*, 52.
21. Powers, *Salvation through Participation*, 52.
22. Hartmut Gese, "The Atonement," in *Essays on Biblical Theology*, trans. Keith Crim (Augsburg: Minneapolis, 1981), 116.
23. Gese, "The Atonement," 100–15.

people, so that when the animal experiences death, so too does the community. The same principle applies to 1 Corinthians 15:3. For Paul, Christ is not depicted as a substitute for sinners who offers himself so that they do not likewise suffer death. Rather, believers are united to Christ in his suffering, sharing both in his death and resurrection. Gese also sees the sense of corporate solidarity in Galatians 1:4 and 2:20.

Galatians 3:13 is also read differently by those holding to the representative position. In the previous section on substitution, we observed that Christ becoming a curse "for us" means that he suffered and died in our place, so that we would not suffer this penalty. Dunn, however, argues that in Galatians 3:13 humanity's plight under sin and death is put in terms of "curse."[24] Paul's reference to a curse alludes to Deuteronomy 21:23 and 27:26 and falls on both Jew and Gentile, because they have both failed to obey the Mosaic law. As a result, the Jew is like the Gentile in that he is also outside the covenant. Dunn argues:

> The theological logic in Gal. 3:13, therefore, seems to be that the cursed Christ has been in effect put out of the covenant. In his death he identified with the sinning Jew and Gentile alike. Thus he brought the blessing of Abraham to the Gentiles and made it possible for all to receive the promised Spirit (3.14).[25]

This was good news for Paul, because those who identified with Christ's death and experienced his suffering are delivered from sin's power. In Dunn's representative reading of Galatians 3:13, death is still inescapable.

Another important text often used in support of the representation theory is 2 Corinthians 5:14, where Paul says, "one died *for all*, therefore all have died" (cf. Rom. 8:3).[26] In sharing Christ's death, Dunn contends that the power that sin and death had over us has been broken. This verse shows that, in *representing* believers on the cross, Christ makes it possible for them to *participate* in his death, freeing them from the powers that enslaved them.

Summary

Now that we have examined the concepts of "substitution" and "representation," we can now answer the question: "What is Paul's view of the atonement?" On the basis of passages such as those discussed above, we would suggest that both positions contribute to our understanding of the atonement. According to the substitution viewpoint, Christ died "in our place," as our *substitute*, delivering us from the penalty of death. What we escape is the *physical* punishment for not doing all the Mosaic law requires (Gal. 3:10, 13;

24. Dunn, *Theology of Paul*, 225.
25. Dunn, *Theology of Paul*, 227.
26. We are citing Dunn's translation (*Theology of Paul*, 210).

James 2:10; cf. Deut. 21:21; 27:26). According to the representation viewpoint, on the other hand, Christ died as our *representative*, permitting us to partake of the saving benefits of dying and rising with the Messiah. We partake of his death in a *spiritual* (or existential) manner, not a *physical* one. Thus, we ultimately need not be forced to choose either substitution or representation. We need to avoid an either/or false dichotomy that forces us to choose one position to the exclusion of the other. This does not mean that we must agree with every argument for substitution and representation. We can agree on the main thrust of each position, while disagreeing with certain interpretations of Paul's instruction. For example, we can argue for substitution in verses such as 1 Corinthians 15:3 and Galatians 3:13, disagreeing with the respective representative readings, while still seeing representation emphasized in verses such as 2 Corinthians 5:14.

What we witness in Paul's letters, then, is that Jesus dies "in place of" sinners, so that we would not have to endure the same *physical* penalty. Substitution readings of 1 Corinthians 15:3, and Galatians 1:4 and 2:20 demonstrate this point clearly. The preposition *hyper* denotes that Jesus died "in place of" or "instead of" our sins, a traditional formula grounded in the suffering servant of Isaiah 53. In addition to this important reality, Christ also *represents* sinners, uniting them *spiritually* to himself, so that they might *participate* in the saving benefits of his death and resurrection (2 Cor. 5:14; see also Rom. 6:5; 8:4; Gal. 2:19; Phil. 3:10; 1 Thess. 5:9–10). We can therefore think of "substitution" and "representation" as two streams running parallel in Paul's mind, both of which are essential for understanding his view of the atonement.

REFLECTION QUESTIONS

1. What is the substitution view of the atonement?

2. What is the representation view of the atonement?

3. What are some verses in Paul's letters that support the perspective that Paul understood the atonement in the sense of substitution?

4. What are some verses in Paul's letters that support the perspective that Paul understood the atonement in the sense of representation?

5. Do you agree that Paul has a both/and rather than either/or view of the atonement? If you disagree, which (singular) view do you prefer?

What Is Paul's View of Conversion?

Discussions on Paul's view of conversion are likely to recall his Damascus Road encounter with the risen Christ (Acts 9, 22, and 26). Some argue that this is when Paul "converts" or "turns" from Jewish legalism to righteousness in Christ.[1] Despite the popularity of this assumption, we have no convincing evidence that Paul's Damascus Road experience resulted in him turning away from his Jewish heritage. Nor do we have credible evidence to support the notion that first-century Judaism was overwhelmingly legalistic in nature.[2] We have more reason to assume that what happened on the Damascus Road led to Paul's clear understanding of "true Judaism": that Jesus is the promised Messiah (Gal. 3:16), whose crucifixion means the end of the old age of sin and death (Rom. 6:1–11; Col. 2:15) and whose resurrection initiates the new age of life (2 Cor. 5:17).[3] Paul's encounter with the risen Jesus therefore opened his eyes to the age that the prophets envisioned, which coincides with the Messiah reigning over a new creation (2 Sam. 7; Isa. 65–66; Ezek. 36–37). This realization results in Paul himself being transferred—or "converted"— from the "old age" to the "new age" (2 Cor. 5:17)—from being "in Adam" to being "in Christ" (Rom. 5:12–21). When we view Paul's Damascus Road experience this way, we envision that Paul's encounter with Jesus shapes his understanding of the change in realms that occurs when a person trusts in Jesus as the Messiah.

In this chapter we will flesh out Paul's understanding of the nature of conversion. We will address the divine and human roles in conversion and

---

1. For a discussion of possible interpretations, see Larry W. Hurtado, "Convert, Apostate or Apostle to the Nations: The 'Conversion' of Paul in Recent Scholarship," *SR* 22 (1993): 273–84.

2. See Question 33 for a further discussion of Judaism in relation to the New Perspective on Paul.

3. Craig G. Bartholomew and Michael W. Goheen, *The Drama of Scripture: Finding Our Place in the Biblical Story*, 2nd ed. (Grand Rapids: Baker Academic, 2014), 204–5.

examine the role of baptism in portraying the transfer of a person from the old age to the new. In the end, we hope to demonstrate that what happened to Paul on the road to Damascus is common for many believers who trust in God's saving work in Christ.

The Nature of Conversion

Some may be surprised to learn that Paul seldom uses the terms most closely linked to "turning" (*epistrephō*) or "converting" (*metanoia*). He only uses the verb *epistrephō* on three occasions (2 Cor. 3:16; Gal. 4:9; 1 Thess. 1:9). Second Corinthians 3:16 describes a person "turning" (*epistrepsē*) to the Lord, while in 1 Thessalonians 1:9 Paul refers to someone "turning" (*epestrepsate*) from idols to God. Finally, Galatians 4:9 expresses concern about a person "turning back" (*epistrephete*) to the weak and poor elements associated with the passing age. Paul's only use of *metanoia* is found in Romans 2:4. Although the ESV translates this term as "repentance," it can also carry the sense of "conversion."[4] The latter sense is more suitable for the context of Romans 2:4, which speaks of the Lord's kindness in leading a person to "conversion." Although he effectively uses *epistrephō* and *metanoia* with respect to conversion, Paul undoubtedly prefers other ways to communicate the transfer of a believer's allegiance from the old age to the new.[5]

Paul communicates the concept of conversion in several ways in Romans: "and, having been set free from sin, [you] have become slaves of righteousness" (6:18; similarly, 6:22); "you also have died to the law through the body of Christ, so that you may belong to another, to him who has been raised from the dead" (7:4); "you, however, are not in the flesh but in the Spirit" (8:9); "For you did not receive the spirit of slavery to fall back into fear, but you have received the Spirit of adoption . . . [who] bears witness with our spirit that we are children of God" (8:16–17). Paul also speaks of conversion in Ephesians: "even when we were dead in our trespasses, [God] made us alive together in Christ" (2:5); "for at one time you were in darkness, but now you are light in the Lord" (5:8). Similarly in Colossians: "and you, who were dead in your trespasses and the uncircumcision of your flesh, God made alive together with him" (2:13). Such texts allow us to envision that conversion from Paul's perspective takes place when one is transferred from the prior age associated with sin, death, fear, darkness, the flesh, and slavery to the new one associated with Christ, the Spirit, adoption, light, and life. No one is ever born into the new age. Rather, they must undergo a conversion from the old age to the new age in order to share in all of its benefits.

---

4. BDAG 640.
5. Paul never uses the verbal cognate *metanoeō*, which is common in the Gospels (e.g., Matt. 11:21; Luke 13:3), Acts (e.g., 8:22; 26:20), and Revelation (e.g., 2:5; 16:9).

The entrance into the new realm begins with the work of regeneration, which is the act of being made new. When we envision the cosmic nature of redemption in texts such as Romans 8:12–25, we see how a person's regeneration coincides with God delivering the entire creation from the curse of sin associated with the passing age. Paul envisions God commencing the process of forming a person into a new creation (2 Cor. 5:17) when he sends his Spirit to indwell them (Gal. 4:4–6; Titus 3:5). Many centuries prior, Ezekiel anticipated regeneration when he prophesied of the day when the Spirit would cleanse his people and give them new life (Questions 36–37). This spiritual reorientation empowers God's people to "put off" the sinful manner of life associated with the prior age and be "renewed" into new creations fit for a new age (Rom. 12:1–2; Eph. 4:22–23; Col. 3:9–10). The process begun by the work of regeneration will reach its goal when believers are resurrected from the dead along with the entire cosmos. This is the end result of what Paul envisions when he aspires to "attain the resurrection from the dead" (Phil. 3:11; cf. Eph. 1:14; Titus 3:7).[6] It will be at this time that believers experience the full benefits of being converted to the new realm.

God's Role in Conversion

We have already seen that the Spirit's role in regeneration is linked to conversion. Yet, Paul does not limit the work of conversion to any one member of the godhead. Sometimes Paul speaks of the work of the Father, whom he often calls God: "even when we were dead in our trespasses, [God] made us alive together with Christ" (Eph. 2:5); "He [the Father] has delivered us from the domain of darkness and transferred us to the kingdom of his beloved Son" (Col. 1:13). On other occasions he speaks of the work of Christ: "For freedom Christ has set us free; stand firm therefore, and do not submit again to a yoke of slavery" (Gal. 5:1); "In him also you were circumcised with a circumcision made without hands, by putting off the body of the flesh, by the circumcision of Christ" (Col. 2:11). Other times he emphasizes the work of the Spirit: "For you did not receive the spirit of slavery to fall back into fear, but you have received the Spirit of adoption" (Rom. 8:15); "Having begun by the Spirit, are you now being perfected by the flesh?" (Gal. 3:3). Still, in other contexts, Paul testifies to how more than one person of the godhead is involved in conversion, such as the Spirit and Christ (2 Cor. 3:3), the Father and Christ/the Son (1 Cor. 1:9), or the Father and the Spirit (1 Cor. 1:21–22). Paul even speaks of all three persons of the godhead involved in conversion (1 Thess. 1:4–6). From these passages, we conclude that Paul recognized that the Father, the Son, and the Spirit are all involved in transferring a person from one realm to another.

---

6. Moisés Silva, "γίνομαι," in *NIDNTTE* (Grand Rapids: Zondervan, 2014), 1:574.

Humanity's Responsibility in Conversion

While each member of the Trinity plays a role in conversion, Paul also emphasizes that humans have a responsibility in the process. He commonly uses the verb *pisteuō* and the noun *pistis* to convey people's "faith" or "belief" in the God who transfers them from the old age to the new.[7] In Romans 1:16, Paul contends that "the gospel is the power of God for salvation for everyone who believes (*pisteuonti*)." Here, the "gospel" depicts God's power to save sinners from the judgment associated with the evil age.[8] Everyone who "believes" in the God who accomplishes such salvation will experience deliverance. In light of Romans 3:23 and the use of "save" in 8:24, Moo argues that Romans 1:16 also has a positive connotation: "the restoration of the sinner to share the 'glory of God.'"[9] In Romans 1:17, we see that this restoration is in keeping with God's righteousness to save people who exhibit "faith" (*pistis* 2x).[10] Thus, Paul links faith to a person being delivered from the judgment of the old age to the glory of the new age.

Later in Romans 4, Paul also uses *pisteuō* and *pistis* on several occasions in reference to saving "faith." This context portrays Abraham as one who "believed" (*episteusen*) in the God who "gives life to the dead and calls into existence the things that do not exist" (v. 17). Abraham's "faith" (*episteusen* v. 17, *pistis* v. 18, etc.) resulted in his righteous status (Rom. 4:18–22). Paul goes on to argue that Abraham serves as a type of those who "believe (*tois pisteuousin*) in him who raised from the dead Jesus our Lord, who was delivered up for our trespasses and raised for our justification" (Rom. 4:24–25). Paul's argument suggests that our faith is in the same God in whom Abraham trusted, the very God who displayed what it means to give life to the dead in the resurrection of Jesus.

Like Abraham, faith in the powerful saving God results in our "righteousness," meaning that we are the people of God who will be saved from the

---

7. We will discuss Paul's use of "faith" language in Question 31. The words *pisteuō* and *pistis* have a semantic range that includes senses like "faith" and "belief," which suggest cognitive understanding, as well as "loyalty," which suggests obedience. Covenantal understandings of these terms in texts such as Galatians suggest translations such as "faithfulness," encompassing the "faith" and "obedience" expected of God's people. Our discussion is far too short to argue for any further nuance. For an excellent work on faith terminology in Paul's letters, see Nijay K. Gupta, *Paul and the Language of Faith* (Grand Rapids: Eerdmans, 2020).

8. See Brendan Byrne, *Paul and the Economy of Salvation: Reading from the Perspective of the Last Judgment* (Grand Rapids: Baker Academic, 2021), 73–76.

9. Douglas J. Moo, *The Letter to the Romans*, 2nd ed., NICNT (Grand Rapids: Eerdmans, 2018), 70.

10. We favor translating the notoriously difficult *ek pisteōs eis pistin* phrase as "by faith in the faithful one." Taking the first prepositional phrase with a sense of "means" and the second as the "object" of faith is consistent with Paul's emphasis on "faith" in the one who was "faithful" to deliver people from the present evil age.

present age and transferred into an age where we will be resurrected to reflect the glory of God (Rom. 4:24–25; 8:12–25). Paul makes a similar argument in 1 Corinthians 15, where the resurrection of Christ effects the transfer of believers from being "in Adam," who represents the old realm, to being "in Christ," who is the first-fruits of those who will raised to experience fullness of life in the new realm.

Galatians 3–4 is another prominent text where Paul uses *pisteuō* and *pistis* with regard to saving faith. Like Romans 4, in Galatians 3:6 Paul uses Abraham as an example of one who "believed (*episteusen*) God" and was declared a "righteous" recipient of the saving promises. Those who have faith (*hoi ek pisteōs*) in the same God become Abraham's children (Gal. 3:6) and receive the Abrahamic blessing of the Spirit (Gal. 3:14) and the hope of a cosmic inheritance (3:18, 22 [*tois pisteuousin*]; cf. Rom. 4:13). In Galatians 3:23–4:7, Paul argues that the arrival of Jesus initiates this new era of faith (*tēn pistin*, v. 23), which transfers believers from the era of slavery under the elementary principles of the old age to a new one of adoption as children of God. As partakers of the new age, believers possess the regenerating Spirit, who assures them of their status as sons and daughters who will ultimately inherit the fullness of the future age (Gal. 4:6–7).

Paul also uses the verbs *elpizō* and *peithō* in a similar fashion to the way he uses *pisteuō* to convey "faith" in the saving God.[11] Examples of *elpizō* may be found in 2 Corinthians 1:10: "He delivered us from such a deadly peril, and he will deliver us. On him we have set our hope (*elpikamen*) that he will deliver us again"; and in 1 Timothy 4:10: "we have set our hope (*elpikamen*) on the living God, who is the Savior of all people, especially those who believe." An example of Paul's use of *peithō* is found in 2 Corinthians 1:9: "Indeed, we felt that we had received the sentence of death. But that was to make us rely (*pepoithotes*) not on ourselves but on God who raises the dead." Paul's use of these terms emphasize that he links "faith," "belief," and "trust" in the God who raises the dead to conversion from this age to one far better.

Baptism

As will also be discussed in the following chapter, Paul recognizes a clear relationship between baptism and conversion. The two are so closely intertwined that he assumes all believers have been baptized.[12] In Ephesians 4:4–6, for instance, Paul presumes his readers have several realities in common, among which are "one Lord, one faith, one baptism" (v. 5). He makes a similar assumption in 1 Corinthians 12:13: "For in one Spirit we were all baptized into one body—Jews or Greeks, slaves or free." Here we see not only the

---

11. Douglas J. Moo, *A Theology of Paul and His Letters: The Gift of the New Realm in Christ*, BTNT (Grand Rapids: Zondervan, 2021), 526–27.
12. See also G. R. Beasley-Murray, "Baptism," in *DPL*, 60–66.

commonality of baptism, but also its association with the Spirit's immersion of believers into the new age of unity between believers of different ethnic and social standings.[13] This revolutionary new reality exemplified in baptism, where ethnic and social barriers linked to the old age are obsolete, is also evident in Galatians 3:27–28 and Colossians 3:9–11.

We see the transfer of ages associated with baptism more vividly in Romans 6:1–11. Here, Paul argues that believers are "buried" with Jesus "by baptism into death, in order that, just as Christ was raised from the dead by the glory of the Father, we too might walk in newness of life" (v. 4). The unity we have with Christ in baptism will ultimately result in a "resurrection like his" (v. 5). Because of this, believers are no longer "dead to sin" but "alive to God in Christ Jesus" (v. 11). Paul uses similar imagery in Colossians 2:12, arguing that believers have been "buried with him [Christ] in baptism, in which you were also raised with him through faith in the powerful working of God, who raised him from the dead." From these texts, we find that Paul links baptism to a person dying and rising to new life in Christ.

While the Spirit is responsible for a conversion, Paul also links faith and baptism in texts like Galatians 3:26–27 and Colossians 2:11–12.[14] Paul assumed, then, that a person with "faith" underwent the transfer of ages associated with baptism. Also, since he never distinguishes between Spirit baptism and water baptism, we should not assume that Paul would have distinguished between the two.[15] He would likely have seen a person's entrance into and rising from the waters as intertwined with the Spirit transferring them from the old age to the new.

Summary

Paul's encounter with Jesus on the road to Damascus reoriented his understanding of Judaism. The result was that he understood that God had worked through Jesus Christ to save people from the old age of death and deliver them to a new age of life. While the New Testament speaks of no other conversion experience, we can imagine that people have a similar experience when they trust in God's salvific work in Christ. Although they may not initially understand all the ramifications of their conversion, it is at the moment of faith that God transfers them from old age to the new, when the Spirit begins the work of regenerating them into new creations.

---

13. Richard B. Hays, *First Corinthians*, IBC (Louisville: Westminster John Knox, 2011), 214.

14. Robert H. Stein, "Baptism and Becoming a Christian in the New Testament," *SBJT* 2 (1998), 7.

15. Thomas R. Schreiner, "Baptism in the Epistles," in *Believer's Baptism: Sign of the New Covenant in Christ*, eds. Thomas R. Schreiner and Shawn D. Wright (Nashville: B&H, 2006), 74. See also, Stein, "Baptism and Becoming a Christian," 6–17.

REFLECTION QUESTIONS

1. How might you describe Paul's understanding of the nature of conversion?

2. What are some of the specific ways that God works in the life of the believer at the time of conversion?

3. What is the basis of conversion? Is there anything a sinner must do in order to be converted?

4. From Paul's perspective, what type of connection is there between conversion and regeneration?

5. From Paul's perspective, what type of connection is there between conversion and baptism?

What Is Paul's View of Baptism?

From the very inception of the Christian movement, believers have followed the pattern set forth by Christ who was baptized by John the Baptist (Matt. 4:13–17; Mark 1:9–11; Luke 3:21–22) and who later instructed his disciples to "make disciples of all nations, baptizing them in the name of the Father and of the Son and of the Holy Spirit" (Matt. 28:19).[1] For Paul and the early Christians, baptism serves as a powerful witness to a believer's new life in Christ and the work of the Spirit in transferring them into the new eschatological age, while also celebrating his or her new place within the spiritual community of believers, the church. Baptism has thus served as a public witness to profound soteriological, Christological, and ecclesiastical realities. In addition to offering a tangible picture of the spiritual work of regeneration in the life of a new believer, baptism demonstrates one's new relationship "in Christ," to use a common Pauline phrase, and, by extension, one's new relationship with Christ's body, the church.

Despite the widespread recognition of the importance of baptism, it was not long before disputes took place over several foundational matters related to its nature and purpose and the manner in which it is to be administered.[2]

---

1. The background and theological significance of baptism and the Lord's Supper (the latter of which is discussed in Question 29) are addressed in greater detail in John S. Hammett, *40 Questions about Baptism and the Lord's Supper* (Grand Rapids: Kregel, 2015). Other recent works that introduce or explore the subject of Christian baptism include the following: Thomas R. Schreiner and Shawn D. Wright, eds., *Believer's Baptism: Sign of the New Covenant in Christ* (Nashville: B&H, 2006); Paul E. Engle and John H. Armstrong, eds., *Understanding Four Views on Baptism* (Grand Rapids: Zondervan, 2007); David Wright, ed., *Baptism: Three Views* (Downers Grove, IL: InterVarsity Press, 2009); G. R. Beasley-Murray, *Baptism in the New Testament* (Eugene, OR: Wipf & Stock, 2006); Stanley E. Porter and Anthony R. Cross, eds., *Dimensions of Baptism: Biblical and Theological Studies*, JSNTSup 234 (London: Sheffield Academic Press, 2002).
2. For background on the practice of baptism in early Christianity, see Everett Ferguson, *Baptism in the Early Church: History Theology, and Liturgy in the First Five Centuries*

During the early centuries of the Christian era, we find that there were differences of opinion related to the appropriate age in which individuals should be baptized, what type of preparation or training was needed beforehand, who was permitted to perform baptisms, the precise manner in which baptism is to be administered, and even the significance and purpose of the event. While the relevant biblical texts reveal that baptism was originally performed by immersion and that the practice was reserved for those who confessed their loyalty to Christ as Lord, it was not long before some began baptizing young children and infants, practicing alternative forms of baptism such as pouring, and placing a greater emphasis on the perceived spiritual benefits that baptism offers to individuals and less emphasis on its ecclesial significance or the manner in which it serves as a public witness to one's faith.

Such controversies were not limited to the first several centuries of church history. During the Protestant Reformation, for example, many were condemned to death, the Anabaptists in particular, in part for holding viewpoints on baptism that conflicted with that of the Magisterial Reformers or the Catholic Church. As the study of church history reveals, the significance, purpose, and meaning of baptism has been variously understood and have often been the subject of significant conflict. Even today, the practice of baptism is understood and practiced in a variety of ways by Christians throughout the world. With so many different traditions and perspectives on the nature and purpose of baptism, it is clear that there is a need for a greater understanding of the biblical foundations of the practice and its significance in the Christian life and the local church. Consequently, our objective in this chapter will be to consider how Paul understood the nature, purpose, and practice of baptism and the role that it served in his apostolic ministry.[3]

The Language of Baptism in the Pauline Epistles
Paul makes several references to baptism in his writings, though most of these passages do not refer directly to the practice of water baptism. He refers, for example, to the ancient Hebrew people who "were baptized into Moses in the cloud and in the sea" (1 Cor. 10:2), to the spiritual work in which believers are baptized into Christ (Rom. 6:3–4; Gal. 3:27–28; Col. 2:12) and into one body (1 Cor. 12:13; Eph. 4:5), and to the spiritual work of regeneration (1 Cor. 6:11; Titus 3:5). Words such as the verb *baptizō* and the nouns *baptisma*

(Grand Rapids: Eerdmans, 2009); Maxwell E. Johnson, *The Rites of Christian Initiation: Their Evolution and Interpretation*, rev. and enl. ed. (Collegeville, MN: Liturgical Press, 2007); For a compilation of early Christian writings addressing the practice of baptism, see Steven A. McKinion, ed., *Life and Practice in the Early Church: A Documentary Reader* (New York: New York University Press, 2001), 5–41.

3. For additional treatment of Paul's understanding of the doctrine of baptism, see "Baptism," in *DPL* 60–66; Paul Deterding, "Baptist according to the Apostle Paul," *Concordia Journal* 6 (1980): 93–100.

(neuter form) and *baptismos* (masculine form) are often used in Paul's writings not in reference to the act of baptism or to some form of physical washing or purification ritual, but in reference to one's membership in something or participation with someone. For Paul, those who trust in Christ become fully and inseparably bonded together with him, and, as a natural consequence, with each other. Those who are "in Christ," to use Paul's language in Romans 6:3 and Galatians 3:27, belong to one spiritual family and participate together with him in profound ways. Most importantly, Paul emphasizes that those who belong to Christ, that is, those "who have been baptized into Christ" (Rom. 6:3; cf. Col. 2:12), participate in his death and resurrection. This experience includes both a spiritual and physical dimension. Spiritually, those who are in Christ have died to sin and enjoy spiritual life through the regenerating work of the Spirit, a work that is colorfully described in Titus 3:4–7. In addition to this spiritual reality, believers are given the hope that, like Christ, they will one day rise physically from the dead.

The Practice of Water Baptism in the Pauline Epistles

With regard to the practice of water baptism, Paul makes only two direct references in his writings, both of which appear in 1 Corinthians. Despite the limited number of references, we have every reason to assume that he regularly instructed new converts to publicly testify to their new relationship with Christ by means of baptism. In fact, Luke records several instances in which converts were baptized during Paul's missionary journeys. This includes Lydia and members of her household (Acts 16:15), the Philippian jailer and members of his household (Acts 16:33), and several converts in Corinth (Acts 18:8) and Ephesus (Acts 19:5). We also find that Paul was baptized at the time of his conversion (Acts 9:18), an event he later refers to in Acts 22:16.

As noted above, references to water baptism appear only in his first canonical epistle to the Corinthians. In 1 Corinthians 1:10–17, Paul addresses the ongoing problem of division in the church of Corinth and expresses concern about a number of factions that had recently formed. His discussion of the situation indicates that many of the Corinthians were divided, at least in part, on the basis of their allegiance to certain teachers (e.g., Paul, Apollos, Cephas, and Christ). In response to this development, Paul expresses relief that he baptized few of the Corinthians during his time among them. He mentions baptizing only two specific individuals, Crispus and Gaius, before recalling that he also baptized members of Stephanas's household. He then states that he was not certain as to whether he had baptized others before making the unexpected assertion, "Christ did not send me to baptize but to preach the gospel" (1 Cor. 1:17).

How might we understand Paul's seemingly indifferent attitude concerning baptism in this passage? His reflections make clear that he took part in baptizing new converts, at least on some occasions, but might be taken to suggest that he did not find the practice to be of great importance or that he did not relate it directly to the work of evangelism and missions. How important could the practice of baptism be to Paul if he had trouble recalling exactly who he had baptized and if he took part in baptizing new converts only on rare occasions? His rather modest description of the baptisms he performed may certainly seem unexpected in light of the call of the Great Commission to make disciples and baptize them in "the name of the Father and of the Son and of the Holy Spirit" (Matt. 28:19). Are not evangelism and baptism inescapably linked? If so, should we not expect that Paul, the most famous Christian missionary who ever lived, made it his personal ambition to baptize new disciples of all nations?

To make sense of Paul's assertion, it must be recognized that his intention was not to belittle or dismiss the importance of baptism itself but was motivated instead by his concern about the situation in Corinth. In the context of the passage, Paul is not specifically addressing the relevance of baptism or providing instruction regarding its proper administration. His focus, rather, is on the divisions that had become prevalent in the community. Tragically, a practice that celebrates and testifies to a believer's new spiritual life, a life that entails fellowship in God's spiritual family, appears to have been used as an instrument for further division. We may surmise that those who were baptized by certain individuals were naturally inclined to regard themselves to be closely aligned or associated with them. Some many have been drawn to the teaching of Apollos, for example, and were later baptized by him, while others regarded themselves to be "of Paul" and may have been converted through his ministry or simply drawn to his teaching. Paul's response clearly demonstrates a concern about these unhealthy factions. From his perspective, the identity of the individual who administers a baptism is not the basis of its importance or legitimacy. One does not become part of a particular tribe or tradition within Christianity through baptism. To the contrary, those who have experienced spiritual regeneration, a reality demonstrated and pictured by the practice of water baptism, are part of the one unified body of Christ. Consequently, it would be much better, he reasons, for individuals to have been baptized by someone other than himself than for those he baptized to regard themselves as part of a particular movement within the broader Christian world.

Paul's concern about the factions that had developed in Corinth is evident in this passage, but how might we account for the limited role that he seems to have played in baptizing new converts? Rather than conclude that Paul was indifferent to the practice of baptism and that he rarely encouraged or instructed new converts to be baptized—an inference that is inconsistent with the passages in Acts referenced above—we might assume that members of his apostolic circle and leaders of local churches often administered the practice. Paul's writings and the various accounts in Acts indicate that he often worked closely with a number of close colleagues and leaders of local churches. Rather than personally baptizing each convert in each location he visited, Paul may have left this task largely to those who belonged to the local churches and possibly with members of his apostolic circle who ministered alongside of him. It is possible that members of Paul's apostolic team (e.g., companions such as Barnabas, Silas, and Timothy) may have often taken a leading role in baptizing converts when ministering in a new location and that this responsibility was later passed on to members of local churches once they had been established.

Paul also refers to the practice of baptism in 1 Corinthians 15:29, a passage that is notoriously difficult to interpret. Dozens of unique proposals regarding the interpretation of this verse have been offered, with many scholars concluding that it is simply impossible to fully understand Paul's point, or at least some of the details in the passage. In the midst of his lengthy treatment of Christ's resurrection, Paul rhetorically asks, "Otherwise, what do people mean by being baptized on behalf of the dead? If the dead are not raised at all, why are people baptized on their behalf?" If there was no basis for being confident in the promise of resurrection, Paul reasons, why would individuals be baptized "on behalf of the dead?" The overarching point of Paul's reference seems clear: there would be no reason for individuals to offer themselves in baptism apart from the hope of a future resurrection. What is unclear, however, is how the words "on behalf of the dead" are to be understood." Paul clearly did not affirm the legitimacy of some type of vicarious baptism in which individuals are baptized for the sake of those who had passed away before they were baptized. This understanding of the passage would contradict what Paul makes clear elsewhere about the doctrine of salvation throughout his writings and is further challenged by the lack of historical evidence in early Christian literature that such a practice was common or widely recognized.

One might possibly conclude that Paul was referring to a vicarious baptism merely as an illustration or to make a broader point, but even this does not appear to be a wholly satisfying explanation of the passage. It has also been suggested that individuals were being baptized in honor of the dead or in response to their testimony, perhaps those who were faithful Christians or who had recently given their lives to martyrdom.[4] In contrast to a reading that entails some type of vicarious baptism, this interpretation would understand the preposition (Greek *hyper*) not in the sense of "for" or "on behalf of," language that implies some type of substitution, but in the sense of "on account of" or "in response to." Understood in this way, we might understand the passage as referring to individuals who responded favorably after hearing the gospel proclaimed by faithful believers who had since died.

It is perhaps more likely that Paul was not making reference to either a vicarious baptism or to those who came to faith through the testimony of those

---

4. For a survey of the major interpretations of this passage, see Anthony C. Thiselton, *The First Epistle to the Corinthians*, NIGTC (Grand Rapids: Eerdmans, 2000), 1242–49.

who had recently died, but that he was simply emphasizing the important point that baptism is performed with the hope of a future resurrection, that is, with the assurance of what God promises about the ultimate fate of those in Christ who have passed away (i.e., "the dead"). Often overlooked is the fact that baptism serves as a witness not only to what God *has* done for believers, but to what God *will* do "on behalf of the dead." Understood in this sense, we might loosely paraphrase the passage as follows: "In light of this, what will be done for those who are baptized with the hope that relates to the dead in Christ? If the dead are not all raised, why do people keep being baptized for what God promises about them?" Read in this way, Paul is not making a reference to some obscure or misguided practice known only to the Corinthians, but is instead emphasizing the central hope of a physical resurrection, a hope he discusses at length in the letter. When individuals receive baptism, they do so with the assurance and conviction that they will one day rise from the dead. Without this assurance, there is no hope, Paul argues, and thus no point of being baptized in the first place.

Tying all of this together, we find that Paul regarded baptism as a vivid picture of Christ's death, burial, and resurrection and the regenerating work of the Holy Spirit. Consequently, public identification with Christ through water baptism entails the proclamation of one's eschatological hope of a future resurrection and witness to the "washing of regeneration" (Titus 3:5) accomplished by the Spirit. We might further observe that Paul recognized an ecclesial dimension to the practice of baptism. Those who are "in Christ" bear a special relationship to one another, not just with Christ. This point is often missed in western culture where religion is often regarded as a private and individual experience. For Paul, to be "in Christ" was to be part of the greater family of God. As he explains to the Galatians, "as many of you as were baptized into Christ have put on Christ." This is then followed with his assertion that those in Christ "are all one in Christ Jesus" (Gal. 3:27–28).

Summary

Although references to the practice of baptism in Paul's writings are limited and appear primarily in contexts in which Paul was correcting misbehavior and misunderstandings, it is evident that it was regularly administered in the local churches where Paul ministered and that he regarded it as a public demonstration of the profound spiritual work that had been accomplished in the life of the believer. For Paul, baptism serves as a public witness to the regenerating work of the Spirit, one's fellowship with Christ and the greater body of believers, and to the eschatological hope of a future resurrection.

REFLECTION QUESTIONS

1. In your experience, what are some misunderstandings about the practice of baptism that you have observed?

2. What might be some of the reasons that the importance of baptism is not always recognized?

3. From your perspective, what is the possible relationship between spirit baptism and water baptism?

4. What do you consider to be the most plausible interpretation of Paul's reference to baptism in 1 Corinthians 15:29?

5. In your estimation, how important is the mode of baptism? Is this an inconsequential aspect of the practice or one that is closely tied to its meaning and significance?

What Is Paul's View of the Lord's Supper?

The Lord's Supper has been a central component of Christian worship for centuries. In keeping with the instructions of Christ on the night of his betrayal, believers have gathered together since the inauguration of the church to "proclaim the Lord's death" as they await his return (1 Cor. 11:26). Despite this long history, Christians have not always understood the Lord's Supper in the same manner or practiced it in the same way. At times, these differences have led to sharp divisions. In the early church, there were disputes about the degree to which it corresponds to the Passover Seder and the particular manner in which it is to be administered. Such disputes were not limited, of course, to the early centuries of church history. During the Protestant Reformation, for example, disagreement between Martin Luther and Ulrich Zwingli over the subject of the Lord's Supper became so intense that it eventually resulted in a separation between their respective movements. Even today there is a lack of consensus on how the Lord's Supper is to be practiced, what transpires at the event, who is permitted to participate, the purpose of the Supper, and a host of additional issues.

With so many conflicting viewpoints, modern believers may be tempted to conclude that the Scriptures offer little direction or instruction regarding the practice of the Lord's Supper. Others may even be tempted to question its importance altogether. If scholars and various Christian communities continuously struggle to find agreement on fundamental subjects related to the Supper, how certain can we be in our own understanding of the practice? And are these disputed matters even that important? It is only natural to question the importance of something that seems to be a perpetual source of confusion, division, and conflict. Rather than fighting about the specifics of the practice, would we not be better off to place less emphasis on it? Surely there are more important matters to debate, one might conclude.

With such widespread viewpoints on a number of matters related to the Lord's Supper, it is crucial that we examine what Paul's writings and his teachings recorded in Acts reveal about the nature and purpose of the practice.[1] The fact that Christians have understood the Supper differently should be recognized as a reason for more intensive study and reflection of what the Bible reveals about this practice, not less. Consequently, we will make some brief observations regarding the reference in Acts to Paul's gathering with the believers in Troas before examining the direct references to the Lord's Supper in 1 Corinthians. Our consideration of these subjects will enable us to better appreciate the importance of the Supper and to make some general conclusions about its general character and function in the church.

The Lord's Supper in Troas

The majority of the references to the Lord's Supper in Luke's narrative describe the activities of early Christians in Jerusalem, yet a passing reference to the Lord's Supper in Troas may suggest that it was commonly practiced in Christian communities in Gentile areas. Luke records in Acts 20:7 that Paul joined believers in Troas "to break bread," what appears to be an early euphemism for the observance of the Supper. Grammatically, a case could be made that the infinitive *klasai* is used in this context to denote purpose, thereby suggesting that the church in Troas met on this occasion with the intention of partaking in the Supper. Rather than one activity of many that might take place from time to time, the language used by Luke indicates that Christians gathered regularly on "the first day of the week" with the purpose of celebrating the Lord's Supper. This would not have been the only purpose, of course, but it is treated as a purpose nonetheless. It is often charged that the narratives in Acts describing early Christian activities are descriptive in nature and should therefore not be regarded as binding prescriptions for each congregation. Care should certainly be made to avoid extracting more from a narrative in Acts than was originally intended, yet it is striking how frequent the Lord's Supper appears to have been observed in the early church and the central role that it served in local gatherings.

---

1. For additional treatment of Paul's understanding of the Lord's Supper, see "Lord's Supper," in *DPL* 569–75; Ralph P. Martin, *Worship in the Early Church* (Grand Rapids: Eerdmans, 1995) 121–29; I. Howard Marshall, *Last Supper and Lord's Supper* (Vancouver: Regent College Publishing, 2006), 107–23; James M. Hamilton, "The Lord's Supper in Paul: An Identity-Forming Proclamation of the Gospel," in *The Lord's Supper: Remembering and Proclaiming Christ until He Comes*, eds. Thomas R. Schreiner and Matthew R. Crawford (Nashville: B&H, 2010), 68–102. For a compilation of early Christian writings addressing the Lord's Supper, see Steven A. McKinion, ed., *Life and Practice in the Early Church: A Documentary Reader* (New York: New York University Press, 2001), 99–114.

The Lord's Supper in Corinth

In addition to the brief reference in Acts discussed above, Paul's first canonical epistle to the Corinthians makes important references to the Lord's Supper. As readers will quickly observe, Paul does not offer a thorough introduction to the practice or offer basic instructions on various aspects of its observation like we may observe in later Christian writings such as the Didache. What we find, rather, are Paul's corrections of some of the primary ways that the Corinthians were misguided in their practice and understanding of the event. In 1 Corinthians 10:14–22, Paul warns of the dangers of sins such as idolatry, sexual immorality, and grumbling, sins that were common among those of ancient Israel (1 Cor. 10:1–13) and were likewise a concern in Corinth. In his warning about these sins, Paul emphasizes the necessity of God's people removing themselves entirely from sinful practices and abstaining from all forms of pagan worship. This may not seem all that revolutionary to believers today, but it should be recalled that Greco-Roman religion tended to place little emphasis on moral transformation.[2] In addition, it was common for Greeks and Romans to worship a variety of household gods, local deities, and a number of gods that were worshiped throughout the empire, with the worship of one god often thought to be entirely compatible with the worship of others. In contrast to the pagans of Corinth who were known to engage in unrestrained feasting and illicit behavior while worshiping a number of false gods—worship that in Paul's view was demonic—Paul emphasizes that believers enjoy a partnership (Greek *koinōnia*) with Christ (1 Cor. 10:16) that is incompatible with participation in sinful activities and false worship. Rather than participate in idolatry and the behavior that was often associated with pagan worship, Paul instructs the Corinthians to separate themselves from these practices and to "do all to the glory of God" (1 Cor. 10:31).

In addition to Paul's overriding point that the worship of Christ is contrary to the worship of false gods, a link between the Jewish Passover and Christian communion may be observed. The "cup of blessing" and the "bread" (1 Cor. 10:16) were, of course, elements of the Passover meal. Paul now relates these elements to the observance of the Lord's Supper and reminds his readers of their significance. The Supper is of great importance, he explains, because of the fact that it involves participation in both the blood and body of Christ (1 Cor. 10:16). He then asserts that "Because there is one bread, we who are many are one body, for we all partake of the one bread" (1 Cor. 10:17). The unique sense in which Paul describes the nature of the Lord's Supper in this passage may be easily overlooked. Rather than stating that one loaf is to be consumed at the Supper because it is a fitting representation of the oneness of God's people, Paul observes that God's

---

2. For further elaboration on these points, see Larry W. Hurtado, *Destroyer of the Gods: Early Christian Distinctiveness in the Roman World* (Waco, TX: Baylor University Press, 2016).

people are "many," but that unity and a sense of oneness are cultivated by joining together to partake of the one loaf. To state the matter differently, the practice of the Lord's Supper does not simply remind believers that they are part of a single spiritual body. In addition to this, it serves as a practical means by which Christians are to build and foster their unity with each other. As Christians come together to celebrate the spiritual blessings made possible through the redemptive work of Christ, they become more aware not only of the significance of Christ's redemptive work, but the bond they have with each other. Given the natural proclivity of believers to engage in disputes, to form factions, and to devote themselves to their own interests, this particular role of the Supper is of great importance.

Paul's most detailed treatment of the Lord's Supper appears in 1 Corinthians 11:17–34, a passage that includes a stern rebuke of the misguided ways in which the Corinthians were observing the practice. While not designed to serve as an instructional manual, Paul's critique of the Corinthians' behavior offers important insight relating to his understanding of the purpose and importance of the event. His discussion begins with the sobering observation that the Corinthians were coming together "for the worse" (11:17) and that it was indicative of the divisions that had become so frequent (11:18–19). So confused and misguided was their observance of the Supper, Paul contends, that it could not legitimately even be regarded as the Supper (11:20)! What was it that Paul found so shameful about their conduct? Simply put, their behavior was exacerbating the factions that had formed in their community. Rather than coming together as one unified body to celebrate the fellowship they enjoyed with Christ and with each other, the Corinthians were only deepening the divisions that had taken root. At the beginning of the epistle, we find that many of the divisions had developed on the basis of allegiance to prominent figures such as Cephas or Apollos. Here we find that divisions also appear to have formed on socioeconomic lines and that the Supper was being used to further these divisions rather than to foster unity among those of different backgrounds and places in society.

As is widely recognized, it was uncommon in the Greco-Roman world of the first century for those of different social standings to share a meal with each another. We would not expect, for example, slaves or freedmen to share a meal with prominent figures who were of noble birth. This separation on social lines was consistently applied in all areas of life, even in pagan worship. Meals in honor of pagan deities often took place in cities such as Corinth. Even when these types of events took place, members of the upper classes would commonly celebrate together, indulging in the finest food and wine and being waited upon by their servants. Those of the lower classes, in contrast, often participated separately and had far less food and drink to enjoy. In short, pagan worship often did little to overcome the social divisions in society.

To the shame of the Corinthians, the way that they were observing the Supper closely resembled the manner in which worship was often conducted in pagan settings. In addition to the drunkenness and gluttonous behavior referenced in this passage, Paul's reference to the separation of individuals into various groups on the basis of their socioeconomic status is also reflective of pagan worship. In all likelihood, there would not have been a single table at which the Supper was celebrated. We cannot be certain how many individuals belonged to the Corinthian church or how many would have typically participated in the Supper on each occasion. Because of the large size of Corinth, however, we might assume that local gatherings may have been fairly large and that it was therefore necessary to separate each congregation into multiple tables. In such a scenario, we might imagine the wealthy and prominent members of a congregation sitting at their own tables and enjoying the best of the food and drink among themselves while those from the lower classes were relegated to other tables which may have been located in different locations.[3] Richard Hays helpfully explains how meals were often conducted in gatherings at private homes:

> The host of such a gathering would, of course, be one of the wealthier members of the community. It is reasonable to assume, therefore, that the host's higher-status friends would be invited to dine in the *triclinium*, while lower-status members of the church (such as freedmen and slaves) would be placed in the larger spaces outside. Furthermore, under such conditions it was not at all unusual for the higher-status guest in the dining room to be served better food and wine than the other guest.[4]

Despite the fact that they had apparently gathered at a single home to observe the same meal, the manner in which it was administered ran counter to the purpose that the meal was to serve in unifying the congregation.[5]

---

3. Commentators such as Mark Seifrid are likely correct "that the consumption of the meal—or the lack of a meal to consume—took place simultaneously." Mark Seifrid, "Gift of Remembrance: Paul and the Lord's Supper in Corinth," *Concordia Journal* 42 (2016), 122.
4. Richard B. Hays, *First Corinthians*, IBC (Louisville: Westminster John Knox, 1997), 196. A *triclinium* was a formal dining area in larger Roman homes. As the name implies, it included three couches on which guests could recline while eating together. For additional background, see Barry D. Smith, "The Problem with the Observance of the Lord's Supper in the Corinthian Church," *BBR* 20 (2010): 517–44; Ben Witherington III, *Conflict & Community in Corinth: A Socio-Rhetorical Commentary on 1 and 2 Corinthians* (Grand Rapids: Eerdmans, 1995), 241–52.
5. In the early church, the Lord's Supper appears to have been part of a larger meal, a full meal sometime referred to as the *agapē* or love feast (see 2 Peter 2:13; Jude 12). The fact that the

What was Paul's solution to this fiasco? He first reminds them of the gravity of the situation. The Lord's Supper is not to be regarded simply as an opportunity for individuals to engage in feasting and inappropriate behavior. To the contrary, this event was inaugurated by Christ himself the night before he was betrayed and serves as a perpetual reminder of the salvific work he accomplished (11:23–26). Participating in the Lord's Supper in "an unworthy manner" (11:27), therefore, is a serious matter that leaves one vulnerable to God's judgment. But what exactly does it mean to participate in an "unworthy manner"? In the context of this passage, it would appear to be precisely what Paul rebuked the Corinthians of doing—in this case, behaving in a manner that further divides God's people and brings reproach upon the name of Christ. When believers partake of the Lord's Supper, they are to do so while "discerning the body" (11:29). In view of the immediate context, the "body" in this verse likely refers to Christ's body, which, of course, is symbolized by the elements. Understood in this sense, behavior that is inconsistent with the person and work of Christ is not to be tolerated at the Supper. Finally, Paul reminds them of the importance of partaking of the Supper together (11:33–34). This instruction may seem almost unnecessary to modern readers but was important on this occasion given that the Corinthians were observing the Supper in a manner that was only deepening the various factions and divisions that had taken hold. Because a major purpose of the Supper is to foster unity in the body of Christ, it is paramount that God's people do so not only at one gathering but in a manner that encourages unity. For Paul, the Lord's Supper is not a rite designed to provide spiritual nourishment to individuals, but a unifying event designed to remind believers of their fellowship with both Christ and with each other.

Summary

The references to the Lord's Supper in Acts and Paul's epistles indicate that the practice was frequently observed and that it was a central component of Christian worship. Despite the importance that was placed on the practice, it is clear from Paul's response to the Corinthians that it was not always practiced in a healthy or appropriate manner. Rather than serving a unifying role in the body of Christ, it was practiced in a way that only furthered division and conflict. For Paul, the Lord's Supper is a uniquely Christian event that, when properly observed, serves both an evangelistic and ecclesial function. It is during this occasion that believers from diverse backgrounds have the opportunity to come together and celebrate the redemptive work of Christ and to celebrate the unity that is the result of the atonement of Christ.

Lord's Supper was based upon the last supper that Jesus shared with his disciples provides further indication that it was part of a larger meal shared between believers.

REFLECTION QUESTIONS

1. From your perspective, is there any type of connection between baptism and the Lord's Supper? Might there be an occasion in which you would advise or encourage an individual who has not been baptized as a professing believer to partake of the Lord's Supper?

2. To what extent do you believe it is necessary or beneficial for modern believers to follow the manner in which the Lord's Supper was practiced in the early church (i.e., weekly observances, part of a full meal, etc.)?

3. How meaningful has the observance of the Lord's Supper been in your own spiritual life?

4. Paul made several criticisms of the manner in which the Corinthian believers were celebrating the Lord's Supper. If he were to assess your church, what might he observe about the manner in which the Supper is practiced?

5. What is your understanding of Paul's warning about participating in the Lord's Supper in an "unworthy manner"? What does Paul seem to be referring to?

How Does Paul Understand the Relationship of Law and Gospel?

Debates on the relationship between law and gospel go back to church fathers such as Augustine, who expounded on these themes in his response to Pelagius.[1] While Augustine's views strongly influenced the Reformers, the Reformers themselves have had the most profound influence on how Protestants understand the relationship between law and gospel. Two of the most significant influences among the Reformers have been Martin Luther and John Calvin.[2]

Luther famously drew a sharp distinction between law and gospel, arguing that the former condemns, while the latter saves.[3] When someone believes the gospel, Luther contended that they are freed from the demands of the law. Calvin, on other hand, recognized a much greater degree of continuity between law and gospel, asserting that the Spirit works through the gospel to free Christians to obey the law's commands.[4] For Calvin, Christ is the example of one who fulfilled the law. While Calvin and Luther have significant differences, they agree that no one can be righteous through obedience to all that the law demands—this is legalism.[5] Still, their differences on

1. See Saint Augustine, "Anti-Pelagian Writings," in *NPNF*, ed. Phillip Schaff, vol. 5 (repr., Grand Rapids: Eerdmans, 1987).
2. On the law-gospel views of Luther and Calvin, see Donald G. Bloesch, *Freedom for Obedience: Evangelical Ethics in Contemporary Times* (Eugene, OR: Wipf & Stock, 1987), 108–13.
3. E.g., Martin Luther, *Lectures on Galatians*, Luther's Works, ed. Jaroslav Pelikan, vols. 26, 27 (St. Louis: Concordia, 1963); "The Distinction between Law and Gospel: A Sermon by Martin Luther, January 1, 1953," trans. Willard L. Bruce, *Concordia Journal* 18 (April 1992): 153–63.
4. E.g., John Calvin, *Institutes of the Christian Religion*, The Library of Christian Classics, ed. John T. McNeill (Louisville: Westminster John Knox, 2006), 340–427, 802–20.
5. Thomas R. Schreiner notes that "Luther and Calvin agreed that legalism posed a great problem, both in Paul's day among the Jews and in their day among Roman Catholics" (*The*

the relationship between law and gospel are substantial enough that they continue to influence the thinking of Pauline interpreters in different ways. For instance, Luther's emphasis on the discontinuity between law and gospel may be observed in the thinking of Rudolf Bultmann,[6] while Calvin's emphasis on continuity appears to have influenced the thinking of Karl Barth.[7]

The New Perspective on Paul is a more recent interpretive stream to address the relationship between law and gospel.[8] Proponents like N. T. Wright and James Dunn dissent from the Reformers' understanding that, in letters like Romans and Galatians, Paul combats Jewish legalism with the gospel of righteousness through faith. Instead, they argue that Paul opposes those who insist that covenantal membership requires obedience to ethnic boundary markers such as circumcision, food laws, and Sabbath keeping. From what we have noted, it is only natural to perceive an interpretive chasm between the Reformers' and New Perspective proponents' views on law and gospel. But if we press beyond these differences, we see commonality between the Calvinistic stream of the Reformed tradition and the New Perspective on Paul—that the Spirit empowers those who trust in the gospel of Jesus Christ to obey the law.[9] Dunn puts it this way: "This outworking [of faith through the Spirit] may be conceived in terms of the law, but not the law focused in such Jewish distinctives as circumcision, but focused rather in love of neighbor (Gal. 5:6, 13–14) as exemplified by Christ (Gal. 6:1–4)."[10] Wright sees obedience to the law as the necessary covenantal obligation of those who have believed the gospel of the Messiah.[11] All of this is possible through the work of the Spirit, who enables believers to exemplify the love of neighbor expected of God's people.

Since the Calvinistic stream of the Reformed tradition and New Perspective on Paul proponents share the view that faith in the gospel of Jesus Christ empowers believers for Spirit-driven obedience to the law, we consider both of these interpretive streams the "continuity view" on the relationship between law and gospel. Since Luther envisions a break between law and

---

   Law and Its Fulfillment: A Pauline Theology of Law [Grand Rapids: Baker Academic, 1993], 15). See also his broader discussion on Luther and Calvin (*Law*, 14–16).

6. E.g., Rudolf Bultmann, *Theology of the New Testament*, trans. Kendrick Grobel (Waco, TX: Baylor, 2007), 1:259–69.

7. E.g., Karl Barth, *The Word of God and the Word of Man*, trans. Douglas Horton (Boston: Pilgrim, 1928).

8. We will discuss the New Perspective on Paul in Question 33.

9. For a helpful work on reconciling Reformed and New Perspective views on Paul, see Stephen J. Chester, *Reading Paul with the Reformers: Reconciling Old and New Perspectives* (Grand Rapids: Eerdmans, 2017); Stephen Westerholm, *Perspectives Old and New on Paul: The "Lutheran" Paul and His Critics* (Grand Rapids: Eerdmans, 2004).

10. James D. G. Dunn, *The Theology of Paul the Apostle* (Grand Rapids: Eerdmans, 1998), 177.

11. E.g., N. T. Wright, *What Saint Paul Really Said: Was Paul of Tarsus the Real Founder of Christianity?* (Grand Rapids: Eerdmans, 1997), 110–20, 159–79.

gospel, we will refer to his perspective as the "discontinuity view." We will keep both of these views in mind as we examine the relationship between law and gospel in Paul's letters.[12] Our study of this relationship will conclude by reflecting on whether there is "continuity" or "discontinuity" between these significant Pauline themes.

Gospel

Paul uses the term "gospel" or "good news" (*euangelion*) quite flexibly in his letters, using terms and expressions such as "gospel" (Gal. 2:2, 5; Rom. 10:16), "my gospel" (Rom. 2:16; 16:25; 2 Tim. 2:8), "our gospel" (1 Thess. 1:5) the "gospel of God" (Rom. 1:1; 15:16), the "gospel of his Son" (Rom. 1:9), and the "gospel of Christ" (Rom. 15:19). While each use of the term "gospel" may have its own nuance, the basic content of Paul's gospel is found in texts such as 1 Corinthians 15:1–11. In this passage, he reminds the Corinthians of the gospel he personally received and proclaimed, the basic content of which is Christ's death, burial, resurrection, and appearances to his followers (1 Cor. 15:1–9). Also important is 2 Timothy 2:8, where Paul exhorts his audience: "Remember Jesus Christ, risen from the dead, the offspring of David, as preached in my gospel." These two passages cohere around the notion that the gospel is centered on the proclamation of Jesus's death and resurrection.

Yet, there is more to the gospel than what lies on the surface of 1 Corinthians 15 and 2 Timothy 2. We must also consider that each of these passages grounds the gospel in Israel's Scriptures. Paul makes this obvious in 1 Corinthians 15, where he explicitly asserts that his gospel is "according to the Scriptures" (v. 3). The primary Scripture to which Paul alludes is likely Isaiah 53, which foresees the suffering servant crushed for the people's iniquities. Following his "offering for guilt," the servant "sees his offspring" and "prolongs his days" (Isa. 53:10). This much is consistent with what we have already affirmed about the gospel: the servant, who prefigures Jesus, dies and later rises to life. We may observe this broader message when we read Isaiah 53 in the larger context of Isaiah 40–66, which anticipates God's rule over the nations in a new heavens and earth (Isa. 40–55; 61; 65–66). A consideration of the wider context of Isaiah 53 thus broadens our horizons and reveals that Paul's gospel encompasses the death and resurrection of Jesus and his rule over the nations.

Paul does not mention the word "Scripture" in 2 Timothy 2, but does draw from Israel's sacred writings, linking the risen Jesus with the "offspring of David" (2 Tim. 2:8). This association evokes the Davidic covenant recorded

---

12. For more expansive treatments on law and gospel in Paul's letters, see Brian S. Rosner, *Paul and the Law: Keeping the Commandments of God*, NSBT 31 (Downers Grove, IL: InterVarsity Press, 2013); Thomas R. Schreiner, *40 Questions About Christians and Biblical Law* (Grand Rapids: Kregel, 2010).

in 2 Samuel 7 and later recalled in 1 Chronicles 17. In this passage, the covenant anticipates a king who will establish an eternal monarchy. It also recalls Psalm 2, which anticipates God's son ruling over the nations of the earth. The resonance of such Old Testament passages in 1 Timothy 2, as well as the broader context of Isaiah 52–53 in 1 Corinthians 15, supports a robust understanding of Paul's gospel: that Jesus is the once-crucified-now-resurrected Messiah who will reign over Jews and Gentiles in a new creation.

Paul also evokes the aforementioned Scriptures of Israel in Galatians, where he makes it his aim to take the kingdom gospel to the Gentiles (2:2, 5, 7) with the hope that the nations would be incorporated into the people of God, making them recipients of the salvific promises to Abraham (3:1–14). Paul sees himself fulfilling the vocation of Jeremiah, who was called to announce the reign of God to the nations (Gal. 1:15; cf. Jer. 1:5; Rom. 1:1). Despite his call, Paul is well aware of the barriers to incorporating Gentiles into the community of God. That is why, in Galatians, he argues passionately against those who demanded that Gentiles take on the Jewish boundary marker of circumcision in order to be considered full members of the people of God (chaps. 2–5). Their trust in the Messiah is *the* distinguishing marker needed to make them beneficiaries of all God swore to Abraham and his descendants (Gal. 2:15–3:29).

In Ephesians, Paul also argues against barriers to gospel inclusion, emphasizing that all who believe in the "gospel of salvation"—both circumcised and uncircumcised, Jew and Gentile—are sealed with the promised Holy Spirit and together comprise one people who should no longer live in enmity and division (Eph. 1:13–14, 2:11–22). Paul stresses that Gentiles are no longer strangers to the saving promises of Israel (Eph. 2:11–13), but "fellow heirs, members of the same body, and partakers of the promise in Christ Jesus through the gospel" (Eph. 3:6; cf. Phil. 1:27–38).

Texts such as Galatians and Ephesians, and arguably Romans, reveal Paul's struggle to fulfill the hope of the gospel sourced in Israel's sacred writings: that Jews and Gentiles would be equal participants of God's kingdom and recipients of all the benefits thereof, a reality that is only possible through the death and resurrection of Jesus (also Rom. 1:1–6). All this gives us a better understanding of Paul's gospel—which includes Jesus's death and resurrection, as well as his rule over the nations. We will now examine Paul's understanding of law in relation to gospel.

Law

Paul articulates his understanding of the law in relation to gospel in Romans 8:3–4: "By sending his own Son in the likeness of sinful flesh and for sin, he condemned sin in the flesh, in order that the righteous requirement of the law might be fulfilled in us, who walk not according to the flesh but according to the Spirit." Although Paul does not mention the word "gospel," the death of the Son of God is at the heart of the good news. In addition, Paul insinuates that the Spirit aids believers in fulfilling "the righteous requirement of the law." When we consider the imagery of "walking" in this passage, which is used as a metonymy for "obedience," we see an allusion to Ezekiel 36:25–27, which anticipates the day when God would indwell his new covenant people with the Spirit, causing them to "walk in his statutes" and "obey his rules." Such obedience to God's "statutes" and "rules" associated with God's law is what people found difficult under the old covenant. This all changes with the arrival of the Spirit, who enables believers in the gospel of Jesus Christ to fulfill their covenantal obligations.

Paul makes a similar argument in Galatians 5:16–26. Also alluding to Ezekiel 36, he calls his readers to "walk by the Spirit," which entails obedience to the decrees associated with the law (Gal. 5:16). Those led by the Spirit will live out "love, joy, peace, patience, kindness, goodness, faithfulness, gentleness, self-control" in keeping with the law (Gal. 5:22–25). Such behavior is in contrast to those led by the flesh, who display their disregard for the law in "sexual immorality, impurity, sensuality, idolatry, sorcery, enmity, strife, jealousy, fits of anger, rivalries, dissensions, divisions, envy, drunkenness, orgies, and things like these" (Gal. 5:19–21). Paul makes clear that such people "will not inherit the kingdom of God" (Gal. 5:21), a point he also makes in 1 Corinthians 6:9–11. When we consider that the kingdom is associated with the gospel of Jesus the Messiah, as well as the allusion to Ezekiel 36, we find that those whom the Spirit leads into obedience enjoy the hope of being raised to dwell in the messianic kingdom.[13]

Thus far, then, we may observe that Paul sees significant "continuity"—rather than "discontinuity—between law and gospel. The essential link between the two themes is the Spirit, who empowers believers' obedience, giving them hope of dwelling in the promised kingdom. What we have yet to explain is what kind of obedience Paul expects of those who have been incorporated into the people of God. Does he expect obedience to Jewish boundary markers associated with the law? Or does Paul have something else in mind?

Paul's argument in Galatians, and to a lesser extent in Romans, rejects the idea that Gentiles must adopt Jewish markers of ethnicity to be members of the covenant people and partakers of the promises to Abraham's descendants. This is why he rebuffs Jewish believers who sought to enforce circumcision on the Galatians, going so far as to wish that those troubling the Galatians would emasculate themselves (Gal. 5:1–12). Paul, instead, emphasizes fulling the law by "loving your neighbor as yourself" (Gal. 5:14). He therefore expects Gentiles to work out their faith by exhibiting Spirit-led love for others (Gal. 5:5–6, 22–23). This, after all, is what prophets like Isaiah, Ezekiel, and Jeremiah expected—that God would ultimately bring Jews and Gentiles into one people whom the Spirit

---

13. See the helpful discussion in Michael J. Gorman, *Reading Paul* (Eugene, OR: Cascade, 2008), 111–31.

would empower to obey the law's requirement to love one another. Paul is keenly aware of both his calling and what the prophets foretold, and makes certain that the Gentiles are not hindered from partaking in the hope of the gospel.

In short, Paul expects that all who have been incorporated into the people of God through the gospel of the resurrected king Jesus will work out their faith through Spirit-empowered obedience to the law. Those who "walk" in such obedience have the hope of dwelling in the future kingdom of the Messiah. No markers of ethnicity are required—only faith in the God who enables the love for neighbor he has always expected of his people.

Summary

From our discussion in this chapter, we conclude that the relationship be-tween law and gospel according to Paul is one of remarkable "continuity." This is in keeping with what the Calvinistic stream of the Reformed tradition and what New Perspective proponents argue about the relationship between these twin Pauline themes. We find in Paul's writings that those who have been brought into the family of God through the work of Christ obey the law by the power of the Spirit. Such obedience fulfills the expectations of Old Testament prophets who anticipated the day when Jews and Gentiles would exhibit the love for others expected of the participants of God's kingdom. The important link between law and gospel—as scholars and influential figures such as Calvin, Wright, and Dunn have observed—is the Spirit who empowers obedience. While Luther and his followers have much to contribute to Pauline theology, we would argue that "discontinuity" between law and gospel does not cohere with the fact that Paul expects followers of Jesus to "fulfill the law" (Rom. 13:10; Gal. 5:14).

REFLECTION QUESTIONS

1. What is the "continuity view" of Paul's understanding of the relationship between law and gospel?

2. What is the "discontinuity view" of Paul's understanding of the relation-ship between law and gospel?

3. From your view, is the continuity or discontinuity view most consistent with Paul's perspective on the relationship between law and gospel? Why?

4. Can you think of any biblical passages outside of Paul's writings that artic-ulate a viewpoint of law and gospel that is similar to the viewpoint of Paul?

5. What are some possible dangers of placing a sharp distinction between law and gospel?

How Does Paul Understand the Role of Faith and Works in Salvation?

Protestants have a tendency to contrast faith and works, elevating the importance of the former while dismissing the latter as unessential.[1] Yet such separation conflicts with Paul's portrayal of faith and works as he sees them as having complementary roles in the process of salvation. While he emphasizes faith over works in letters such as Romans and Galatians, he does so in response to opponents placing disproportionate priority on works for salvation. His intent is not to diminish works, but to reorient his readers to the proper roles of faith and works in salvation (e.g., Gal. 2–5).

The perception that Paul elevates "faith over works" and that James emphasizes "works over faith" has led some to conclude that they hold contradictory views on salvation or that Paul's writings are to be given a more prominent voice. Martin Luther, for one, famously referred on one occasion to James as an "epistle of straw."[2] This remark would suggest that he regarded James to be of lesser value than writings such as Romans and Galatians that provide a more robust articulation of the doctrine of justification by faith. Yet, despite what might appear to be a contradiction in how Paul and James understand the role of works, we should not quickly assume that they present contrary perspectives. We should read Paul's and James's arguments in their situational contexts to discern whether their views on faith and works are at odds. We will address the relationship between Paul and James more fully

---

1. For a treatment on the role of works in the Christian life, see Thomas H. McCall, Caleb T. Friedeman, and Matt T. Friedeman, *The Doctrine of Good Works: Reclaiming a Neglected Protestant Teaching* (Grand Rapids: Baker Academic, 2023).
2. These words appear in his preface to the New Testament writings in the original edition (1522) of his German translation of the Bible. Later editions of the Luther Bible did not contain this remark.

later in this chapter. Before we do so, we must first examine Paul's view of faith and works in salvation.

Faith in Paul

"Faith" language in Paul's letters is expressed by the verb *pisteuō* and the related noun *pistis*. The semantic range for these terms includes senses like "faith" and "belief" (Rom. 6:8; 1 Cor. 13:7; 1 Thess. 1:8).[3] The semantic range for *pistis* in particular may extend beyond cognitive faith and into the realm of obedience, suggesting translations such as "loyalty" or "faithfulness" (Gal. 5:22; 2 Thess. 1:4).[4] Although these terms span a range of possible meanings, Paul often restricts their meaning to "faith" or "belief" in God's salvific work in the death and resurrection of Christ, i.e., the gospel. We see several examples in Paul's letters to the Thessalonians: "your faith (*pistis*) in God has gone forth everywhere" (1 Thess. 1:8); "For since we believe (*pisteuomen*) that Jesus died and rose again . . ." (1 Thess. 4:14); "when he comes on that day to be glorified in his saints, and to be marveled at among all who have believed (*tois pisteusasin*), because our testimony to you was believed (*episteuthē*)" (2 Thess. 1:10); "God chose you as the firstfruits to be saved, through sanctification by the Spirit and belief (*pistei*) in the truth" (2 Thess. 2:13).

We especially see this use of *pisteuō* and *pistis* in passages where Paul contrasts "faith" and "works." In such contexts, Paul often restricts the semantic range of these words to "faith" or "belief" to counteract his opponents who emphasize works as the proper response to the gospel. Romans and Galatians offer several prominent examples. In Romans: "And to the one who does not work but believes (*pisteuonti*) in him who justifies the ungodly, his faith (*pistis*) is counted as righteousness" (4:5); "It [righteousness] will be counted to us who believe (*tois pisteuousin*) in him who raised from the dead Jesus our Lord" (4:24); "because, if you confess with your mouth that Jesus is Lord and believe (*pisteusēs*) in your heart that God raised him from the dead, you will be saved" (10:9). In Galatians: "so we also have believed (*episteusamen*) in Christ Jesus, in order to be justified by faith (*ek pisteōs*) in Christ and not by works of the law, because by works of the law no one will be justified" (2:16);[5] "Does he who supplies the Spirit to you and works miracles among you do so by works of the law, or by hearing with faith (*pisteōs*) . . . ?" (3:5).

Also important is the way Romans and Galatians use the example of Abraham as one who was justified by "faith" as opposed to "works" (Rom. 4:3, 11, 17, 18; Gal. 3:6–9). That is to say, "faith" is what brings Abraham into the

---

3.   See the full discussion of *pistis* and *pisteuō* in BDAG, 816–820; Moisés Silva, "πιστεύω," in *NIDNTTE* (Grand Rapids: Zondervan, 2014), 6:759–72.

4.   For an excellent work on faith terminology in Paul's letters, see Nijay K. Gupta, *Paul and the Language of Faith* (Grand Rapids: Eerdmans, 2020).

5.   We are following the ESV's translation of *pistis Christou*. See Question 35 for a discussion of this contested phrase.

realm of resurrection life, i.e., salvation (Rom. 3–4). Other passages display how Paul emphasizes "faith" or "belief" as the proper response to the gospel (e.g., 1 Cor. 1:21; 15:11; Eph. 1:13, 19). It is this faith which justifies believers apart from works (Rom. 4:5), making them recipients of the promises of salvation (Rom. 3–4; Gal. 2–3).

Moreover, Paul emphasizes that faith is not something humans produce on their own—it is a gift (1 Cor. 12:8) and a fruit of the Spirit (Gal. 5:22). Elsewhere, Paul simply affirms faith as something God grants to the believer (Phil. 1:29). Thus, the proper response to the gospel through "faith" or "belief" comes through the work of God's Spirit—it is this Spirit-produced faith which justifies a person, bringing them into the realm of salvation.

Works in Paul

We now come to Paul's view of works. Douglas Moo defines "works" as "deeds that are performed," which can be good or evil.[6] Paul expects that Christians will perform good works, which compliment faith in the process of salvation. Ephesians 2:8–10 is an excellent example. In verses 8–9, Paul stresses faith for salvation: "For by grace you have been saved through faith. And this is not of your own doing; it is the gift of God, not a result of works." Then, in verse 10 he follows with the importance of works: "For we are his workmanship, created in Christ Jesus for good works, which God prepared beforehand, that we should walk in them." In its entirety, Ephesians 2:8–10 teaches that those who have received the gift of salvation through faith are to "walk" or "live" in "good works." This corresponds to passages in which Paul exhorts God's people to exhibit holy lives (Eph. 4:24), to be "zealous for good deeds" (Titus 2:14) and to "bear fruit in every good deed" (Col. 1:10).[7] Taken together, Ephesians 2:8–10, Titus 2:14, and Colossians 1:10 display an important link between those saved by faith and the good works expected of them.

Philippians 2:12–13 shows why works are important for the salvation of the believer: "Therefore, my beloved . . . work out your own salvation with fear and trembling, for it is God who works in you, both to will and to work for his good pleasure." In these verses, Paul has the totality of salvation in view, which includes a person's progressive holiness, often referred to as sanctification.[8] Good works are therefore an essential component of the process by which God makes believers holy. Furthermore, just as God empowers faith, he also strengthens believers "to will and to work for his good pleasure"

---

6. Douglas J. Moo, "'Law,' 'Works of the Law,' and Legalism in Paul," *WTJ* 45 (1983): 90–99. Thomas R. Schreiner, *The Law and Its Fulfillment: A Pauline Theology of Law* (Grand Rapids: Baker Academic, 1993), 51–52.

7. See the discussion in Francis Foulkes, *Ephesians*, TNTC 10 (Downers Grove, IL: InterVarsity Press, 1989), 85.

8. See the helpful discussion in Moisés Silva, *Philippians*, BECNT (Grand Rapids: Baker Academic, 1992), 134–42.

(Phil. 2:13). The striving for holiness will culminate when, as Paul argues in the related context of Philippians 3:7–16, believers are resurrected from the grave. At the resurrection, Christians will experience the fullness of their salvation, when they will at last be holy. Paul makes it his goal to know Jesus "and the power of his resurrection, and . . . share his sufferings, becoming like him in his death, that by any means possible I may attain the resurrection from the dead" (Phil. 3:10–11).

Paul stresses works to the point that he claims: "For it is not the hearers of the law who are righteous before God, but the doers of the law who will be justified" (Rom. 2:13). Moo rightly argues that the "doing of the law" in this passage refers to "faith-oriented obedience to God."[9] Believers who obey God will receive a favorable verdict at the final judgment, declaring them justified at the resurrection. When we consider passages such as Romans 3–4 and Galatians 2–3, we have a more complete picture of justification: the justification we receive by "faith" anticipates the final verdict of justification based on "works" to which Paul refers in Romans 2:13 and elsewhere in passages such as Galatians 2:16, 5:5, and Ephesians 5:5. Consequently, we can think of justification through an "already–not yet" paradigm: believers are "already" justified by faith but they have "not yet" received final justification in the eschaton. Believers will receive future justification after completing a life of "faith-oriented obedience to God." This coheres with the entirety of salvation Paul envisions, which will be realized when believers are made holy at the resurrection.[10]

In sum, Paul believes one is justified by "faith." Yet, one exercises faith through "good works." All of this is empowered by God, who initiates a person into salvation by justification through faith (Eph. 2:5, 8; Titus 3:5) and sees to their progressive holiness through good works (Phil. 2:12–13). This process will then culminate with the believer obtaining the fullness of their salvation at the resurrection (Phil. 3:7–16). Appropriately, then, we argue that for Paul, faith and works have complementary roles in the process of salvation.

Paul and James

We noted earlier that some find that Paul and James have presented contrary views on faith and works.[11] The critical passage for comparison is James 2:14–26. Here, James stresses that faith without works is "dead" and "useless," just like a dead a corpse (2:14–16, 20, 26). So, both faith and works are

---

9. Douglas J. Moo, *The Letter to the Romans*, 2nd ed., NICNT (Grand Rapids: Eerdmans, 2018), 157.
10. In response to his opponents, Calvin argues: "They cannot deny that justification of faith is the beginning, cause, proof, and substance of works righteousness" (*Institutes of the Christian Religion*, The Library of Christian Classics, ed. John T. McNeil [Louisville: Westminster John Knox, 2006] 1:812).
11. For an evaluation of four views on Paul and James, see C. Ryan Jenkins, "Faith and Works in Paul and James," *BSac* 159 (2002): 62–78.

necessary for justification (James 2:24). Like Paul, James draws on the story of Abraham to make his point on justification: "Was not Abraham our father justified by works when he offered up his son Isaac on the altar? You see that faith was active along with his works, and faith was completed by his works" (2:21–22). Yet, unlike Paul, he emphasizes the role of works in Abraham's justification, whereas Paul emphasizes his faith. James also draws on the story of Rahab to stress the role of works in justification: "In the same way was not also Rahab the prostitute justified by works when she received messengers and sent them out by another way?" (2:25). In this passage, then, we notice that James emphasizes the role of works along with faith for justification, which appears to contradict Paul in Romans 3:28: "one is justified by faith apart from works of the law." James also uses the Abraham story to support the argument that faith and works are essential for justification, whereas Paul uses Abraham as an example of one who was justified by faith apart from works (Rom. 4; Gal. 3).

What are we to think of this apparent contradiction? We suggest that any conflict between Paul and James is superficial. A synthetic reading of Paul—one that considers passages from various letters—coheres well with James's emphasis on the importance of faith and works for justification. Paul, after all, never argues that works are unrelated to justification or that they are unimportant. As we observed in Romans 2:13, Paul argues that the "doers of the law . . . will be justified." Here, Paul refers to final justification at the resurrection based on a life of "faith-oriented obedience to God."[12] We should also recall the importance that Paul places in Philippians 2–3 on a person "working out" their salvation in order to be resurrected in holiness. Such works are subsequent to initial justification by faith and are central to the work of sanctification and final justification.

So, when James emphasizes the need for faith and works for justification, particularly in the way Abraham's "faith was active along with his works, and faith was completed by his works" (James 2:22), we should not envision disagreement with Paul. James, after all, stresses the importance of faith—but faith is never mere belief, as he argues in 2:19: "You believe that God is one; you do well. Even the demons believe—and they shudder!"[13] True faith is always accompanied by works, such as providing clothing and food for the destitute (James 2:15–16). For James, then, as for Paul, works are important for justification—not for only for initial justification, but for working out one's faith, i.e., for sanctification. What is more, we find that Paul uses the Abraham tradition to emphasize that it is faith rather than works that serves as the basis for initial justification (Rom 4; Gal. 3). Because of this, Paul naturally does not discuss Abraham's later acts of faith. James, on the other hand, addresses

---

12. Moo, *Romans*, 243–46.
13. Schreiner, *The Law and Its Fulfillment*, 206.

those who disregard the role of works.[14] It is therefore necessary for him to emphasize the importance of works in relation to Abraham's faith, because faith is perfected through works, something which his readers underestimate. In sum, we find that when the writings of Paul and James are considered in their proper context that there is remarkable coherence in the manner in which they understand the role of faith and works.

Summary

Paul holds that faith and works have complementary roles in salvation—the former serves as the basis of initial justification while the latter is closely tied to the final justification at the resurrection. Nevertheless, Paul emphasizes the importance of faith over against works when responding to those who stress works for justification (Rom 3–4; Gal. 2–3). Although Paul's teaching on faith in such contexts may appear on the surface to contradict that of James, it is clear that James emphasizes works to counter those over-emphasizing faith for salvation. When we examine their writings in context, we find that Paul and James both recognize the importance of faith and works in the process of salvation and their integral relationship to one another.

REFLECTION QUESTIONS

1. What is Paul's view on the role of faith in salvation?

2. What is Paul's view on the role of works in salvation?

3. How does Paul portray the complementary roles of faith and works in salvation?

4. How does Paul's view of faith and works cohere with James?

5. How does Paul's view of faith and works relate to the viewpoint of other New Testament authors?

---

14. See Mark A. Seifrid, *Christ, Our Righteousness: Paul's Theology of Justification*, NSBT 9 (Downers Grove, IL: InterVarsity Press, 2000), 183.

What Is Paul's Eschatology?

Paul's eschatology centers on the arrival of the eschatological age. This is the age that prophets like Isaiah and Ezekiel envisioned, when God would abolish the old age and make all things new. While discussions about the expectation of a millennium are important, they are more relevant to the book of Revelation. Paul is more concerned about the advent of the new age. In his view, this age has "already" arrived but has "not yet" been consummated. This chapter will provide an overview of Paul's "already–not yet" eschatology.[1] After discussing this concept, we will then transition to more practical concerns. We will consider if Paul believed Jesus would return during his lifetime, and how his eschatology influenced his mission.

The Two Ages

Paul's eschatology is in keeping with the Jewish distinction between the present age and the age to come.[2] A couple of exemplary Jewish texts include *4 Ezra* and *2 Baruch*. The former claims that "the Most High has not made one age but two" (7:49). The present age is characterized by ungodliness, while the coming age is characterized by righteousness (*4 Ezra* 8:1).[3] *Second Baruch* presents a similar distinction between two ages, claiming that the righteous "will leave this world without fear and are confident of the world" which

---

1. For fuller discussions of Paul's eschatology, see Constantine R. Campbell, *Paul and the Hope of Glory: An Exegetical and Theological Study* (Grand Rapids: Zondervan, 2020); Geerhardus Vos, *The Pauline Eschatology* (Phillipsburg, NJ: P&R, 1994).
2. See Brant Pitre, Michael P. Barber, John A. Kincaid, *Paul, A New Covenant Jew: Rethinking Pauline Theology* (Grand Rapids: Eerdmans, 2019), 69–73; James D. G. Dunn, *Unity and Diversity in the New Testament: An Inquiry into the Character of Earliest Christianity* (London: SCM Press, 2006), 337–71.
3. See the brief discussion in George W. E. Nicklesburg, *Jewish Literature between the Bible and the Mishnah: A Historical and Literary Introduction*, 2nd ed. (Minneapolis: Fortress Press, 2005), 271–72.

the Lord "has promised to them with a full expectation of joy" (14:13).[4] The present world is difficult and temporary and the future world is the eternal home of the righteous (*2 Bar.* 16:1; 44:2–9, 12–13; 51:3; 84:2). We also see the distinction between two ages in Isaiah 65–66, which anticipates a transition from the present age of sin to the new heavens and earth.

Similarly, we may observe Paul's distinction between two ages in the following passages. With regard to the present age, Paul exhorts his readers to "not be conformed to this age" in Romans 12:2, and in 1 Corinthians 2:6 he affirms that "we do not impart wisdom of this age" (also 1 Cor. 1:29; 2 Cor. 4:4). He describes the current age as "evil" in texts such as Galatians 1:4 and Ephesians 5:16 (cf. Phil. 2:15) and hints at the transitory nature of the present world in 1 Corinthians 2:6–9 and Ephesians 2:1–3. In Ephesians 1:21, Paul contrasts "this age" with "the one to come." In Romans 8:18, he even compares "the present time" with the "glory that is to be revealed." The coming time is not a spiritualized existence devoid of matter, what is often called "heaven." Rather, it is the age in which creation is freed from its bondage to the curse of sin, which is better described as a new creation (Rom. 8:18–23). This is in line with Isaiah's vision of a new heavens and earth and the ideal world of *4 Ezra* and *2 Baruch*. In short, the Jewish expectation of two ages is the foundational distinction for Paul's eschatology, the former age understood as wicked and temporary and the one to come as glorious and eternal.

Yet, Paul envisions an overlap in the two ages, which is a development his forefathers, and many of his Jewish contemporaries, did not foresee. For Paul, the old age is in the process of passing away while the new one is now breaking in (2 Cor. 5:17; cf. Gal. 4:4; 2 Cor. 6:2). God's people therefore live "between the times," awaiting the day when the old age of sin and death will completely give way to the renewed world.[5] This overlap corresponds to an "already–not yet" eschatology.

Signs of the New Age (Already)

The prophets associate the resurrection and the Spirit's arrival with the eschatological age. These are the very same signs Paul associates with the onset of the eschaton.

Resurrection

Paul's eschatology is in keeping with the expectation of Daniel 12 and Ezekiel 36–37, that the resurrection signals the arrival of the new age. Still,

---

4. See the discussion of *4 Ezra* and *2 Baruch* in Miguel G. Echevarría, *The Future Inheritance of Land in the Pauline Epistles* (Eugene, OR: Pickwick, 2019), 90–95. See also the relevant work of Liv Ingeborg Lied, *The Other Lands of Israel: Imaginations of the Land in 2 Baruch* (Leiden: Brill, 2008).

5. Craig G. Bartholomew and Michael W. Goheen, *The Drama of Scripture: Finding Our Place in the Biblical Story* (Grand Rapids: Baker Academic, 2014), 204–07.

there are significant developments in his thinking. First, whereas Daniel 12 and Ezekiel 36–37 envision the new age ensuing with a corporate resurrection, Paul narrows the arrival of the eschaton to the resurrection of Jesus Christ. Second, Paul envisions the resurrection occurring in two stages. The initial one is linked to the resurrection of Jesus, who is the "firstfruits of those who have fallen asleep" (1 Cor. 15:20–23). Through the lens of his resurrection, Paul retrospectively understands that Jesus bore the curse of sin and death (Gal. 3:1–14) and triumphed over the principalities and powers that ruled over the fallen world (Col. 2:14–15).[6] The subsequent stage is when all the dead will "be made alive" (1 Cor. 15:22). This is the time when death will be eradicated, and the new age will arrive in all its fullness. Paul's vision of a two-stage resurrection therefore encompasses the initial resurrection of Christ, which initiates the new age that will triumph over the old, and a subsequent resurrection associated with the fulfillment of the eschatological age.

The Arrival of the Spirit
The prophets anticipated that the coming age would be marked by the arrival of the Spirit (Ezek. 11:19; 36:25–27; Isa. 44:3; Joel 2:28).[7] In keeping with the prophets, Paul envisions that the manifestation of the Spirit is another mark of the "firstfruits" of the new age, in anticipation of one day enjoying full deliverance from the present cursed age (Rom. 8:23). So strong is Paul's connection between the Spirit and the new age that he reminds his readers that the Spirit empowers and works miracles (Gal. 3:1–5; 1 Cor. 12:4–11). Paul also speaks of the Spirit as the guarantee that believers will one day dwell in the inheritance promised to God's people (Eph. 1:14).[8] Thus, for Paul the Spirit also signals the arrival of the new age.

Signs of the Consummation of the New Age (Not Yet)

The resurrection of the Messiah and the presence of the Spirit do not on their own indicate that the new age has arrived in all its fullness. There are certain eschatological expectations associated with the final resurrection that have "not yet" been fulfilled, among which include notable events such as the second coming of Christ, the restoration of creation, and the final judgment.[9]

Second Coming of Christ
Following his resurrection, Christ ascended into the heavens, leaving believers to anticipate the day when he would return to raise the dead and make

---

6. Our thought on this matter has been influenced by Bartholomew and Goheen, *Drama of Scripture*, 206.
7. James D. G. Dunn, *The Theology of Paul the Apostle* (Grand Rapids: Eerdmans, 1998), 416–19.
8. See the discussion in Echevarría, *Future Inheritance*, 176–78.
9. See Larry J. Kreitzer, "Eschatology," in *DPL*, 253–65.

all things new. Paul demonstrates his anticipation of Christ's return when he prays in 1 Corinthians 16:22: "Our Lord, come!" For Paul, Christ's return will be physical: "For the Lord himself will descend from heaven with a cry of command, with the voice of an archangel, and with the sound of the trumpet of God" (1 Thess. 4:16). Paul sometimes refers to the Lord's "coming" as a shorthand way of describing the second coming of Christ (1 Cor. 15:23; cf. 1 Thess. 2:19; 3:13; 4:15).[10] Other times, he describes this event with phrases such as the "day of the Lord" (1 Thess. 5:2; 2 Thess. 2:2), the "day of the Lord Jesus" (1 Cor. 5:5), or the "day of Jesus Christ" (Phil. 1:6). There are also occasions in which he uses the word *parousia* to express his expectation of Jesus's future coming (1 Cor. 15:23; 2 Thess. 2:1, 8–9).[11] When Jesus returns, the age will be consummated, and God will be "all in all" (1 Cor. 15:28).

Final Judgment

When Jesus returns to consummate the age, humanity will give an account before him (Rom. 2:1–11; 14:10–12; 2 Cor. 5:10). In view of this event, Paul encourages believers to live in holiness, knowing that they will appear before the judgment seat of Jesus Christ (1 Thess. 3:13). He also explains that the future judgment will reveal the quality of one's work (1 Cor. 3:12–15). Paul even speaks of his own aspiration to hold onto "the word of life," so that in the "day of Christ" his efforts will not have been in vain (Phil. 2:16). It is important to note that Paul does not envision the final judgment resulting in the believer's condemnation, but rather their vindication as sons and daughters of God (Rom 5:16; 8:1, 23). On the other hand, the final judgment will mean condemnation for Satan and hostile powers (Rom. 8:38–39; 16:20; 1 Cor. 5:5; 7:5; 2 Cor. 2:11; Eph. 6:12; Col. 2:8, 20). They are the ones who should fear the wrath associated with the judgment (Rom. 1:18; Eph. 5:6; Col. 3:6).

Restoration of Creation

For Paul, the restoration of creation includes the resurrection of human beings and the renewal of the created order. Since both humans and the creation were cursed because of Adam and Eve's sin (Gen. 3), both anticipate the day when they will be delivered from bondage, marking the consummation of the age. We see this in Romans 8:12–25, where Paul affirms that creation eagerly awaits "the revelation of the sons of God," which is another way to speak of the resurrection (v. 19). Then, he sums up the entire creation's eschatological hope for release from bondage: "For the creation was subjected to futility, not willingly,

---

10. In response to those who argue for a spiritualized *parousia*, Thomas R. Schreiner notes that in the New Testament the "word coming always has the idea of physical presence (cf. 2 Cor. 10:10; Phil. 1:26, 2:12), confirming the notion of a physical return of Christ" (*Paul, Apostle of God's Glory in Christ: A Pauline Theology*, 2nd ed. [Downers Grove, IL: InterVarsity Press, 2020], 505).
11. Kreitzer, "Eschatology," 259.

but because of him who subjected it, in hope that the creation itself will be set free from its bondage to corruption and obtain the freedom of the glory of the children of God" (Rom. 8:20–21; cf. Ezek. 36–37). Philippians 3:20–21 also ties the return of Jesus Christ to the time when Jesus "will transform our lowly body to be like his glorious body, by the power that enables him even to subject all things to himself." We should note that the "transformation of our lowly body" and the "subjection of all things" will take place at the return of Jesus Christ. The latter is when Jesus delivers creation from its bondage to sin and subjects it to his liberating rule (also Col. 1:15–20; Eph. 1:10). All in all, Paul envisions the consummation of the eschaton when Jesus returns to renew humanity and the created order, at which time he will also initiate the final judgment.

The Timing of Christ's Return

It is reasonable to wonder whether Paul believed that Jesus would return during his lifetime to bring judgment and restore the created order.[12] Those who argue that Paul anticipated the second coming of Jesus in his lifetime often point to 1 Thessalonians 4:15–17, where the apostle affirms that "we who are alive, who are left until the coming of the Lord, will not precede those who have fallen asleep" (v. 15). They also point to 1 Corinthians 15:51–52, where Paul contends that "We shall not all sleep, but we shall all be changed. . . . For the trumpet will sound, and the dead will be raised imperishable, and we shall be changed." In both of these passages, Paul may be including himself along with those who expect the return of Jesus Christ before their death. But it is unnecessary to read the passages this way. We could argue that Paul is simply reassuring his readers of the physical return of Christ, at which time there will be people alive on the earth.[13]

Obviously, Jesus never actually returned during Paul's lifetime. So, at some point Paul had to come to grips with a delay in the arrival of Christ (2 Cor. 5:1–10; Phil. 1:20–24).[14] Whatever stance we take on Paul's expectation of the return of Jesus Christ, we should note that he never argues for the timing of the *parousia*. Paul emphasizes the certainty of the event (1 Cor. 7:29; Phil. 4:5) without elaborating on its precise timing (1 Thess. 5:1–2). So, we are on safer ground to argue that Paul held to the imminent return of Christ, without speculating on his understanding of the timing of the event.

Eschatologically Driven Mission

Since the consummation of the eschatological age was imminent, Paul was on mission to gather the nations into the people of God. Paul saw himself

12. See Udo Schnelle, *Theology of the New Testament*, trans. M. Eugene Boring (Grand Rapids: Baker Academic, 2009), 345–49.
13. See Roy E. Ciampa and Brian S. Rosner, *The First Letter to the Corinthians*, PNTC (Grand Rapids: Eerdmans, 2010), 829.
14. Schnelle, *Theology of the New Testament*, 347–48.

living out the eschatological vision of Isaiah 49:6: "I will make you as a light for the nations, that my salvation may reach to the end of the earth," which itself is grounded in the Abrahamic covenant promises: that all the peoples of the earth would be blessed (Gen. 12, 15, 17, 18). These salvific promises extended to the nations through the true descendent of Abraham, Jesus Christ (Gal. 3:15–29). Armed with this conviction, Paul sought to fulfill his call as an apostle and minister to the Gentiles (Gal. 2:9; Rom. 15:15–16), so that they would also become sons and daughters of Abraham who would inherit the eschatological world (Rom. 4:13; Gal. 3:15–18; Eph. 3:6).[15] Though Paul is zealous for his work, he knows that Christ is the one working through him "to bring the Gentiles to obedience, in word and in deed, through signs and wonders, in the power of the Spirit of God" (Rom. 15:18–19).

Although he senses a distinct call to the Gentiles, Paul desires for his fellow Jews to trust in Jesus as the Messiah, making them recipients of the promises (Rom. 9–11).[16] We see this in how he organizes his argument in Romans 4–8 and 9–11. In the former, he contends that those who have the faith of Abraham—Jew or Gentile—inherit the promises that belong to God's people (Rom. 4:13; 8:18–30). Then, in Romans 9–11 he further reveals the fulfillment of the promises to the Gentiles in hopes of a future gathering of Israelites who will receive the promises to their ancestors. With that, the arrival of the eschatological age and its imminent fulfillment are what motivate Paul's mission to fulfill Isaiah's vision of gathering Gentiles into the community of God's saving promises, while maintaining hope that his Jewish kin will ultimately trust in Jesus.

Summary

Paul's eschatology follows a Jewish, dualistic understanding of two ages. Yet, his thought also develops beyond this basic schema—for he holds to an overlap between the old age, which is in the process of passing away, and the new age, which has not fully arrived. In other words, we may conclude that he holds to an "already–not yet" eschatology. Furthermore, for Paul the resurrection of Jesus Christ and the arrival of the Spirit indicate that the new age has arrived. When Jesus returns, he will judge humankind and restore the creation. Though he is not privy to the timing of Jesus Christ's return, Paul believes his arrival is imminent. His mission is therefore to take the message of Jesus to the Gentiles so that they would become recipients of the saving promises to Abraham, while holding out hope that his Jewish kindred would trust in the Messiah before the consummation of the eschaton.

---

15. Romans 4:13 clearly shows that the content of the inheritance of Abraham's children is the cosmos.
16. See Question 40 for the relevant discussion on Romans 11:26 ("all Israel will be saved").

REFLECTION QUESTIONS

1. How would you summarize Paul's eschatology?

2. What signaled to Paul that the new age had arrived?

3. What did Paul believe would signal the consummation of the new age?

4. What did Paul understand about the timing of Christ's return?

5. How did Paul's eschatology influence his understanding of mission?

Specific Questions

What Is the New Perspective on Paul?

The New Perspective on Paul diverges in key respects from the traditional Protestant reading of the Pauline epistles. The traditional reading is associated with Protestant Reformers such as Martin Luther, whose voluminous sermons, treatises, and commentaries on Paul's letters underscore that righteousness is through faith rather than by Jewish works of the law. Luther's influential interpretation mirrors his own struggle with the Roman Catholic Church to be right before a holy God apart from legalistic requirements. But did Luther rightly understand Paul, and did he accurately depict the Judaism of Paul's day? Such questions received little attention until the end of World War II.

Protestants generally accepted the traditional reading of Paul until the conclusion of World War II, when the world was awakened to the unchecked effects of antisemitism and ethnic partiality.[1] Only then was there a renewed interest among scholars in reassessing the nature of first-century Judaism

---

1. An example of prevalent antisemitism in early to mid-twentieth century scholarship is Gerhard Kittel's *Theological Dictionary of the New Testament* (*TDNT*; *TWNT* in the original German version). Hans Förester notes that Kittel was a member of the Nazi Party, whose anti-Judaism should raise caution when using his *TDNT* ("What to Do with the TDNT?" *Didaktikos: Journal of Theological Education* 4 [2021], 40–42; see also Robert P. Ericksen, *Theologians Under Hitler: Gerhard Kittel, Paul Althaus, and Emanuel Hirsch* [New Haven, CT: Yale University Press, 1985], 28–78). Although antisemitism is not an inherent property of the traditional reading of Paul, it is unmistakable that, from the period from the Reformation to World War II, Pauline scholars had associated Judaism with "the wrong sort of religion," representing "legalism, prejudice, and self-pride" (N. T. Wright, *What Saint Paul Really Said: Was Paul of Tarsus the Real Founder of Christianity?* [Grand Rapids: Eerdmans, 2007], 8–9). It was not until after the post-war period that scholars realized how such a negative view of Judaism could be tied to the antisemitism that fueled the Holocaust, awakening them to the need for a reassessment of first-century Judaism. Wright makes a similar argument, linking "the post-war reaction against the vile anti-Semitism which caused the Holocaust" to a change in perception about Judaism (*What Saint Paul Really Said*, 9).

and the notion that it was inherently legalistic, a caricature that was all too common in ecclesial and academic settings. Scholars such as W. D. Davies and Krister Stendahl began challenging various assumptions that have been thought to support a legalistic understanding of Judaism.[2] But it was not until E. P. Sanders's landmark study *Paul and Palestinian Judaism* in 1977 that a number of Pauline scholars began to abandon centuries of negative Jewish stereotypes. After examining a large sampling of Second Temple Jewish sources, which included Rabbinic texts, Dead Sea Scrolls, Apocrypha, and Pseudepigrapha, Sanders argued that first-century Judaism was not fundamentally legalistic—it was a religion of grace.[3] According to this viewpoint, Jews believed that God had graciously elected and made a covenant with his people. Later, he gave them the Mosaic law. Keeping the law was Israel's proper response to the God who had delivered them from slavery in Egypt. If the Jews transgressed the law, the sacrificial system provided a means of atonement and restoration. Jews were therefore already in a gracious relationship with God. So, keeping the law was not about attaining covenantal status, but maintaining it. In other words, it was not about "getting in" but "staying in." Sanders called this understanding of Judaism "covenantal nomism"—a term which encompasses God's gracious relationship with his people ("covenant") and the expectation of their obedience ("nomism").

It was not long before scholars began to recognize that such viewpoints on Judaism and the role of the law have notable implications for how Paul's letters are understood. In his 1982 Manson Memorial lecture, James D. G. Dunn used the designation "New Perspective" to describe the fresh reading of Paul's writings that is based on the general premise of Covenantal Nomism.[4] While proponents of the New Perspective disagree on various details, they are in general agreement that (1) Judaism was not a legalistic religion driven by works-righteousness—it was based instead upon God's electing grace; and that (2) Paul was a Jew whose writings should be understood in light of Jewish literature and not exclusively through Hellenistic categories.[5] In recent decades, scholars such as Dunn and Wright have pressed beyond Sanders and

---

2. See W. D. Davies, *Paul and Rabbinic Judaism: Some Elements of Pauline Theology* (repr., Minneapolis: Fortress, 1980); Krister Stendahl, "The Apostle Paul and the Introspective Conscience of the West," *HTR* 56 (1963): 199–215.

3. E. P. Sanders, *Paul and Palestinian Judaism: A Comparison of Patterns of Religion* (Minneapolis: Fortress, 1977).

4. James D. G. Dunn, "The New Perspective on Paul," *Bulletin of the John Rylands Library* 65 (1983): 95–112. This lecture is included in a volume of collected essays by Dunn, *The New Perspective on Paul*, 2nd ed. (Grand Rapids: Eerdmans, 2008).

5. For instance, Rudolf Bultmann, *Theology of the New Testament*, trans. Kendrick Grobel (repr. Waco, TX: Baylor, 2007), 1:63–352. One of the earliest twentieth-century arguments against reading Paul in light of Hellenistic categories came from Albert Schweitzer, *Paul and His Interpreters: A Critical History*, trans. William Montgomery (London: A & C Black, 1912).

modified some of his arguments, offering new proposals on concepts such as the "works of the law" and the "righteousness," concepts that we will explore in the remainder of the chapter. While most proponents of the New Perspective agree with the basic principles laid out by Sanders, it is far from a monolithic movement. Our discussion, therefore, will not represent the viewpoints of all New Perspective scholars on the nature of first-century Judaism. Our aim, rather, will be to examine the views of some of the more prominent scholars associated with the movement, which will allow us to differentiate the New Perspective from traditional readings of Paul.

Works of the Law

Dunn acknowledges that the phrase "works of the law" has been traditionally understood as the works done to achieve a right standing before God.[6] Proponents of this reading argue from passages such as Romans 4:4–5, where works lead to a reward, and Ephesians 2:8–9, where works in general are associated with boasting.[7] Rather than associating works with legalism, Dunn contends that works of the law should be understood in the context of God's covenant with Israel. Within a covenantal framework, Jews performed various works of the law in order to be holy before God and to separate themselves from their pagan neighbors. As a result, the law functioned as a way to separate Jews who were "in" the covenant from Gentiles who were "out." The particular works that visibly distinguished clean Jews from unclean Gentiles were circumcision (Gen. 17:9–14), dietary laws (Lev. 20:22–26; *1 Macc.* 1:62–63), and the observation of the Sabbath. (Exod. 31:12–17; Isa. 56:6).[8] Dunn argues that these "boundary markers"—the visible markers of Jewish identity—are what Paul has in mind when he uses the phrase "works of the law" (Num. 23:9; *Mos.* 1:278).[9] Others such as Wright and Richard Hays have understood the nature of the "works" Paul describes in a similar fashion.[10]

Jews would have expected Gentiles to adopt the ethnic boundary markers of Judaism in order to be considered genuine members of the people of God. With that, Paul's opponents in Galatia were not encouraging Gentiles to become righteous by keeping all the works of the law. They were instead urging Gentiles to adopt the markers of Jewish identity to be considered members of

---

6. James D. G. Dunn, *The Theology of Paul the Apostle* (Grand Rapids: Eerdmans, 1998), 354. For a more thorough understanding of Dunn's contributions, see N. T. Wright, *Paul and His Recent Interpreters: Some Contemporary Debates* (Minneapolis: Fortress, 2015), 89–96.
7. Dunn, *Theology of Paul*, 354.
8. Dunn, *Theology of Paul*, 354–58.
9. See also "works of the law" in Dead Sea Scrolls, e.g., 4QFlor.1:1–7 and 1QS 5:20–24.
10. See N. T. Wright, *Paul and the Faithfulness of God,* Christian Origins and the Question of God, vol. 4 (Minneapolis: Fortress, 2013); Richard B. Hays, "The Letter to the Galatians: Introduction, Commentary, and Reflections," in *New Interpreter's Bible Commentary*, vol. 10, ed. Robert W. Wall (Nashville: Abingdon, 2015), 1019–73.

the covenant and recipients of all God had promised to his people.[11] In other words, Paul was opposed to the notion that one must become Jewish in order to be part of God's people.

To combat the influence of his opponents, Paul exhorts his Gentile audience to reject Jewish circumcision as a means of gaining covenantal status (Gal. 2:11–3:14). Adopting works of the law would only lead to the curse pronounced in Deuteronomy 27:26 (Gal. 3:10). After all, the only requirement necessary for inclusion in the covenant community is faith in the Messiah (Gal. 3:15–29; 6:14). Paul so opposes those urging Gentiles to adopt covenantal boundary markers that he wishes they would "emasculate themselves" (Gal. 5:12). For him, there is no room for boasting in ethnic markers of privilege—in works of the law—only in the Messiah who was crucified for sinners (Gal. 6:14). Proponents of the New Perspective argue that Paul makes a similar argument when he refers to the works of the law in letters such as Romans and Philippians.

Righteousness

N. T. Wright argues against the traditional understanding of righteousness as "being in a right relationship with God."[12] First-century Jews, he suggests, had a more tangible covenantal expectation association with righteousness. Before explaining how people become righteous, Wright discusses the Pauline phrase "the righteousness of God" (e.g., Rom. 1:16–17; 3:21–4:25; 9:1–10:21; Gal. 2:15–16).[13] Septuagint texts such as Isaiah 40–55 would have shaped Paul's understanding of the phrase as "God's faithfulness to the covenant with Israel, as a result of which he saves her from exile in Babylon."[14] Appealing to the Abrahamic covenant in Genesis 17, Wright argues that God's faithfulness to Israel ultimately results in the salvation of the world—this includes people and the entire created order, which lies in bondage to the curse of sin and death. So, when Paul speaks of God's righteousness, he refers to God's covenant faithfulness, which is revealed in the death and resurrection of Jesus Christ, through whom he will redeem Israel and the entire world.[15] The revelation of God's righteousness is good news for the entire created order.

After discussing God's righteousness, Wright explains how people are declared righteous.[16] Being righteous (or justified) does not have to do with being "right with God" or how "people get saved." It has everything to do with humans being "in covenant" with their faithful God. Read in this fashion,

---

11. See Dunn, *Theology of Paul*, 359–62; See also Dunn's *The Epistle to the Galatians*, BNTC (Peabody, MA: Hendrickson, 2002). Hays, "Galatians," 1062–1107.

12. N. T. Wright, *What Saint Paul Really Said*, 131–48.

13. Wright, *What Saint Paul Really Said*, 110–15.

14. Wright, *What Saint Paul Really Said*, 111.

15. Wright, *What Saint Paul Really Said*, 109–130.

16. Wright, *What Saint Paul Really Said*, 131–58.

texts that refer to being declared righteous such as Philippians 3, Galatians 2–4, and Romans 3–4 signify that a person is a member of God's covenant people through faith in Jesus the Messiah, making them beneficiaries of the saving promises of eschatological vindication and resurrection (Rom. 8:12–25). With the arrival of the Messiah, Jewish boundary markers of ethnicity no longer function as badges of covenant membership. Gentiles can therefore become members of God's family without adopting a Jewish identity. All that is required is trust in Jesus the Messiah. Wright puts it succinctly: "'Justification' is the doctrine which insists that all those who have this faith belong as full members of this family, on this basis and no other."[17]

We noted above that Wright associates righteousness with eschatological vindication. He argues for eschatological vindication against traditional understandings of the imputation of the moral quality of God to the believer. Acknowledging the background of a Jewish lawcourt, Wright suggests that righteousness has to do with God's eschatological vindication of his covenant people at the end of history, distinguishing them from those who serve false gods. The imputation of God's moral quality, which is often argued from passages such as Romans 4:6 and 2 Corinthians 5:21, has nothing to do with the concept of righteousness. That is not what would have been expected in a Jewish law court, only the verdict of acquittal. Wright contends the declaration of righteousness is issued in the present for those who trust in the Messiah, an act anticipating the final verdict.

For Wright, then, and others who follow his view, being declared righteous means that a person is a member of the covenant through faith in Jesus the Messiah. No markers of Jewish ethnicity are required to be members of God's people and beneficiaries of eschatological vindication and resurrection.

Summary

Sanders's *Paul and Palestinian Judaism* has altered the face of Pauline studies. No longer do the majority of scholars follow the traditional reading of Paul's letters, which is highly influenced by Luther's legalistic understanding of first-century Judaism. Dunn's Manson lecture in 1982 coined the term the "New Perspective" to describe those who follow Sanders's thesis that Second Temple Judaism is a religion of grace.

While the New Perspective is by no means monolithic, scholars such as Dunn and Wright have made some popular developments to Sanders's argument. Most notably, they have argued: (1) Paul's opponents compelled Gentile believers to adopt boundary marks such as circumcision—works of the law—to be considered genuine members of the covenant. (2) Since the arrival of Christ, faith in Jesus Christ is the only covenantal badge that matters. All other marks of identity are obsolete. (3) The phrase "God's righteousness"

---

17. Wright, *What Saint Paul Really Said*, 158.

refers to God's covenant faithfulness, which he manifested in the death and resurrection of Jesus Christ to redeem Israel and the entire created order. (4) People can be declared righteous through faith in the Messiah, making them covenant members who will experience eschatological vindication and full deliverance from the curse that envelops the entire cosmos. All in all, the New Perspective maintains the central tenants of Sanders's seminal work while providing important modifications.

REFLECTION QUESTIONS

1. What does the traditional reading of Paul assume about the nature of first-century Judaism?

2. What specific conclusions does Sanders make about the nature of first-century Judaism?

3. Who coined the term the "New Perspective"?

4. What does Dunn argue about the nature of the "works of the law"?

5. What does Wright argue about the "righteousness of God" and God's declaration of individuals as "righteous"?

What Are the Strengths and Weaknesses of the New Perspective on Paul?

A s discussed in the previous chapter, the New Perspective has shifted the accepted framework for reading Paul. No longer do scholars widely assume that letters like such as Romans and Galatians present faith in Christ as the necessary alternative to Jewish legalism. In place of this once dominant interpretation, the New Perspective argues that Judaism was fundamentally a religion of grace. Keeping the law was Israel's response to the God who had graciously called them into a covenant relationship, what E. P. Sanders called "covenantal nomism."

James Dunn has argued that the Jewish works of the law refer to covenantal boundary markers such as circumcision, Sabbath observance, and food laws that Paul's opponents were enforcing on Gentile converts. Consequently, Gentiles were being pressured into assimilating into Judaism in order to be considered equal members of the people of God. N. T. Wright also argues that God's righteousness refers to his covenant faithfulness to deliver his people and the entire cosmos from the curse of sin and death. People become righteous—members of the covenant—when they trust in Jesus, the one through whom God displays his faithfulness to redeem his people and grant them eschatological vindication. Such interpretations of works and righteousness distinguish the New Perspective from traditional readings of Paul's letters.

Strengths of the New Perspective on Paul

Our discussion will now transition to some of the possible strengths and weaknesses of the New Perspective. This is by no means a definitive evaluation and we expect that others will discern their own strengths and weakness of reading Paul through the lens of the basic premise of covenantal nomism. We begin our evaluation with three strengths of the New Perspective.

Emphasis on Second Temple Jewish Literature

A significant strength of the New Perspective is its grounding in Second Temple Jewish literature. Texts such as 4QMMT, *Sirach*, *1 Enoch*, and *Jubilees* are windows into the Judaism of Paul's first-century context. We are not denying the benefits of commentaries, lectures, and theological treatises written by Protestant Reformers such as Martin Luther. But the reality is that Luther composed his writings centuries after the apostle Paul composed his epistles. More to the point, Luther's "faith over against works" polemics against the Roman Catholic Church are centuries removed from Paul's struggles against Jewish opponents. As a result, the chronological proximity of Second Temple texts to the apostle Paul makes them the primary sources for understanding topics such as "righteousness" and "works of the law" in Romans and Galatians. The New Perspective has done interpreters of Scripture a great service in appealing to Second Temple literature as the appropriate backdrop for reading Paul's letters. Even those who disagree with its conclusions owe the New Perspective a debt of gratitude—for they are compelled to reassess traditional interpretations of Paul in light of Jewish literature.

A Positive Portrayal of Judaism

A second strength of the New Perspective is its decidedly more positive portrayal of Judaism. The tables have turned on the assumption that Judaism is the "wrong sort of religion," the kind that can be described as legalistic. The New Perspective has now painted Judaism in a more positive light, revealing a more gracious Jewish soteriology. One of the clearest examples is found in Sanhedrin 10:1: "All Israelites have a share in the world to come."[1] Another example is found in *4 Ezra*, which asserts that the coming world belongs to Israel (6:59; 7:11). In other words, God has *graciously* sworn that his people will dwell in the coming world, a promise which is grounded in the Abrahamic covenant contexts of Genesis 17 and 24. The aforementioned texts are not unlike Romans 4:13 and 8:17–23, where Paul argues that Abraham's descendants are the beneficiaries of a cosmic inheritance (cf. Pss. 2, 110).

Yet, we must still question whether *all* of Second Temple Judaism should be described as a gracious religion. A number of essays in the two-volume work *Justification and Variegated Nomism* argue that Second Temple Judaism was too variegated to be subsumed under the rubric of covenantal nomism. As a result, we are free from reading Paul through "the restraints imposed by a too narrowly and controlled 'background.'"[2] We can use the same line

---

1. See discussion in E. P. Sanders, *Paul and Palestinian Judaism: A Compromise of Patterns of Religion*, 40th anniversary ed. (Minneapolis: Fortress Press, 2017), 147–50.

2. From the preface to D. A. Carson, Mark A. Seifrid, and Peter T. O'Brien, eds., *Justification and Variegated Nomism*, vol. 2, *The Paradoxes of Paul*, eds. D. A. Carson, Peter T. O'Brien, and Mark A. Seifrid, WUNT 2/181 (Grand Rapids: Baker, 2004), v.

of reasoning, however, to argue that the New Perspective has freed readers from perceiving Judaism solely through the "too narrowly and controlled 'background'" of Jewish legalism. Whatever our conclusion about the New Perspective, we should at least acknowledge the positive movement away from legalistic caricatures of Judaism, which scholars have linked to centuries of antisemitism.[3] What is more, we should credit the New Perspective for expanding our interpretive horizons to reexamine whether texts like Romans and Galatians argue against legalism or ethnic boundary markers that mark the true members of the covenant community.

The Interpretation of Paul in His Jewish Context

A final strength of the New Perspective is that it rightly places Paul within his Jewish world. Paul did not break with Judaism once he became a follower of the Messiah. Although some will argue that Paul's experience on the road to Damascus marked his break from Judaism (Acts 9, 22, 26), we argued in Question 27 that this event marked the point when he came to understand that Jesus is the promised Messiah (Gal. 3:16), whose crucifixion brought an end of the old age of sin (Rom. 6:1–11; Col. 2:15) and whose resurrection inaugurated a new age of life (2 Cor. 5:17). Reading Paul in his proper Jewish setting enables us to read his letters in light of the Judaism that enveloped him.[4] More to the point, it opens our vistas to envision how he embeds Jewish Scriptures into his own writings, often showing how Jesus fulfills Old Testament types and patterns. In Question 23, we referred to this phenomenon as intertextuality. Interpreters such as Rudolf Bultmann misunderstood Paul in large part because they read him in strictly Hellenistic categories. We can avoid the same mistake when we read Paul as a Jew who was transformed by an encounter with Jesus the Messiah.

Weaknesses of the New Perspective on Paul

Having discussed possible strengths of the New Perspective, we now consider three of its possible weaknesses.

Strict Assumptions of Jewish Soteriology

Earlier, we noted that some question the New Perspective's assumption that Second Temple Jewish Judaism was a religion of grace. This begs the following questions. Should we really subsume all of Judaism under the rubric of covenantal nomism? Or should we apply this paradigm more selectively, allowing for the possibility that some strands of Judaism were legalistic? *Second Baruch* is a text that appears to have legalistic leanings, suggesting

---

3. See the brief discussion in footnote 1 of page 253.
4. See Richard Hays, *Echoes of Scripture in the Letters of Paul* (New Haven, CT: Yale University Press, 1989), 19.

that keeping the Torah leads to the inheritance of the eschatological world (44:12–13). This writing also contends that "those who are proved to be righteous on account of my law" will receive the promised future world (51:3; cf. 84:2).[5] Another important text is 4QMMT, which stresses the observance of the law, especially "works of the law" (e.g., 4QMMT 109–113).[6] We see this emphasis in the following statement: "And it shall be reckoned to you as justice when you do what is upright and good before him, for your good and that of Israel" (4QMMT 117).[7] Such texts certainly give the impression of a more legalistic soteriology.[8]

Some argue against seeing legalism in such documents because Jewish obedience should be understood within the larger context of God's gracious election of his people.[9] So, texts that on the surface appear legalistic (e.g., 4QMMT) presuppose a gracious covenant within which works were performed.[10] We find an example of this argument in Sanders's observations on Tannaitic literature: "Only by overlooking this large pattern can the Rabbis be made to appear as legalists in the narrow and pejorative sense of the word. Their legalism falls within a larger context of gracious election and assured salvation. In discussing disobedience and obedience, punishment and reward, they were not dealing with how a man is saved, but with how a man should act and how God will act within the framework of covenant."[11]

While Sanders's argument for a covenantal framework should give us pause before rushing to conclude that Judaism was legalistic, we also cannot ignore possible legalistic strands in texts such as *2 Baruch* and 4QMMT, which may be regarded as a weakness of the New Perspective.[12] The reality is that the complexity of Second Temple Jewish literature resists generalizations about a grace-oriented soteriology—just like it also resists legalistic ones.

---

5. This translation is from A. F. J. Klijn, "2 (Syriac Apocalypse of) Baruch: A New Translation and Introduction," in *Old Testament Pseudepigrapha: Apocalyptic Literature and Testaments*, ed. James H. Charlesworth, vol. 1 (Garden City, NY: Doubleday, 1983), 615–52.

6. See Craig A. Evans, "The Old Testament in the New," in *The Face of New Testament Studies: A Survey of Recent Research*, eds. Scott McKnight and Grant R. Osborne (Grand Rapids: Baker Academic, 2004), 142–43.

7. This translation is from Florentino García Martínez, *The Dead Sea Scrolls Translated: The Qumran Texts in English*, trans. Wilfred G. Watson (Leiden: Brill; Grand Rapids: Eerdmans, 1996), 79.

8. For further discussion of Jewish source that betray a more legalistic soteriology, see Robert J. Cara, *Cracking the Foundation of the New Perspective on Paul* (Fearn, UK: Christian Focus Publications, 2017).

9. Sanders, *Paul and Palestinian Judaism*, 180–82.

10. See Charles H. Talbert, "Paul, Judaism, and the Revisionists," *CBQ* 63 (2001): 1–22. See also Kent L. Yinger's arguments against those who attempt to "rediscover" legalism in Judaism ("The Continuing Quest for Jewish Legalism," *BBR* 19 [2009]: 375–91).

11. Sanders, *Paul and Palestinian Judaism*, 181.

12. Legalism—i.e., works-oriented salvation—in the NT is normally associated with James. See the discussion of James in relation to Paul in Question 31.

Consequently, we should be open to the possibility that the Jewish soteriology of Paul's day was, in fact, "variegated."

An Overemphasis on the Role of Covenant in Pauline Thought

Another possible weakness of the New Perspective is that its endorsement of covenantal nomism runs the risk of making covenant an omnipresent theme in the Pauline epistles.[13] A. Andrew Das points out that there are relatively few references to covenant in Paul's letters to Gentiles and Paul's preference for the promises to Abraham rather than covenantal instruments (Gal. 3:15–17).[14] Das also notes that Paul does not give preference to a single, overarching covenant—sometimes he speaks of a single covenant associated with Israel's salvation (Rom. 11:26), other times he speaks of a new covenant of which Gentiles are also beneficiaries (2 Cor. 3). We do not need to agree *in toto* with Das's reservations to call for restraint in seeing a single covenant as a pervasive theme throughout Paul's letters.

Emphasis on the Works of the Law

A final possible weakness is that the New Perspective focuses its discussion of works of the law primarily on Jewish boundary markers. Certainly, in Galatians Paul emphasizes circumcision more than any other legal requirement. Paul's confrontation with Peter also suggests that, to a lesser extent, food laws separating Jews and Gentiles are also important to Paul's argument (Gal. 2:11–14). These boundary markers therefore are clearly at the forefront of Paul's understanding of works of the law.

But is it possible that Paul's opponents were emphasizing boundary markers such as circumcision and food laws as the ethnic markers of covenantal membership, which would then require individuals to keep the entire law? If so, it might be suggested that Paul refutes *some* particular "works of the law," works that might be described as boundary markers, precisely because they obligate a person to adhere to *all* that the law requires. This seems to cohere with Paul's point in Galatians 3:10, where he quotes Deuteronomy 27:26: "Cursed be everyone who does not abide by all things written in the Book of the Law, and do them." This view of works of the law also corresponds with Paul's use of the phrase in Romans 2–3, where boundary markers designate God's covenant people who are expected to keep the law's requirements. In light of passages such as this, we should recognize that while the

---

13. See N. T Wright's *The Climax of the Covenant: Christ and the Law in Pauline Theology* (Minneapolis: Fortress, 1993). Also see Peter T. O'Brien, "Was Paul a Covenantal Nomist," in *Justification and Variegated Nomism: The Paradoxes of Paul*, 2:249–96; See G. K. Beale's helpful review essay of *Justification and Variegated Nomism*, "The Overstated 'New' Perspective," *BBR* 19 (2009): 85–94.
14. See A. Andrew Das, "Rethinking the Covenantal Paul," in *Paul and the Stories of Israel: Grand Thematic Narratives in Galatians* (Minneapolis: Fortress, 2016), 65–92.

New Perspective is right to emphasize the role of boundary markers, we may have warrant to go beyond their limited scope—to argue that works of the law such as circumcision identify those who are obligated to perform all of the law's demands, lest they suffer the judgment associated with Deuteronomy's curse (Gal. 3:10).

Summary

The New Perspective on Paul has shifted the paradigm for reading the Pauline writings. Like any other movement, it has its strengths and weaknesses. We have suggested that its strengths include its emphasis on Second Temple literature, its positive view of Judaism, and its reading of Paul in a manner that places an emphasis on his Jewish background. On the other hand, it might be argued that the New Perspective often fails to recognize the variegated nature of Jewish soteriology, that it overemphasizes the covenantal nature of Paul's letters, and that it tends to limit the extent of the "works of the law" to Jewish boundary markers. Such critiques are from our limited vantage point. We assume readers will likely recognize additional strengths and weaknesses as they discern ways in which the New Perspective possibly contributes to or distracts from our effort to be more faithful readers of Paul's letters.

REFLECTION QUESTIONS

1. What are the aforementioned strengths of the New Perspective on Paul?

2. What are some other possible strengths of the New Perspective on Paul?

3. What are the aforementioned weaknesses of the New Perspective on Paul?

4. What are some other possible weaknesses of the New Perspective on Paul?

5. How has your study of the New Perspective changed or influenced the way you read Paul's letters?

Should *Pistis Christou* Be Translated as "Faith in Christ" or "Faithfulness of Christ"?

A major debate in Pauline studies is whether the phrase *pistis Christou* that appears throughout Paul's writings should be translated "faith in Christ" or "faithfulness of Christ." A couple of significant issues are at stake. Does Paul emphasize human "faith" in Jesus, or does he stress Christ's "faithfulness" to his people? The "faith in Christ" translation is based on an objective genitive reading of *pistis Christou*, whereas the "faithfulness of Christ" translation is based on a subjective genitive reading. The debate cannot be solved by relying on linguistic factors alone, as the head noun *pistis* carries an implicit verbal quality, making it possible for the modifying genitive *Christou* to serve as either the object of "faith" or the subject that expresses "faithfulness."[1] Because of the inconclusive nature of the grammatical and syntactical factors, we must also consider other factors such as the immediate context of the phrase in order to discern the most appropriate reading of *pistis Christou*.

We should note that the stock phrase *pistis Christou* may appear in alternative forms such as *pistis Christou Iēsou, pistis Iēsou Christou, pistis Iēsou, pistis tou huiou tou theou,* and *pistis autou.* The various modifiers of *pistis* all refer to the person of Jesus Christ. We should also note that "faith in Christ" and "faithfulness of Christ" are not the only translations for *pistis Christou.*

---

1. See the discussion in Daniel B. Wallace, *Greek Grammar beyond the Basics* (Grand Rapids: Zondervan, 1996), 113–19. As Stanley E. Porter and Andrew W. Pitts argue, the lexical, grammatical, and syntactical factors alone are enough to prove the objective genitive reading ("Πίστις with a Preposition and Genitive Modifier: Lexical, Semantic, and Syntactic Considerations in the πίστις Χριστοῦ Discussion," in *The Faith of Jesus Christ: Exegetical, Biblical, and Theological Studies*, eds. Michael F. Bird and Preston M. Sprinkle [Peabody, MA: Hendrickson, 2009], 33–53).

Preston Sprinkle, for instance, argues for an eschatological "Christ-faith" translation.[2] While arguments such as Sprinkle's are worth considering, we limit our discussion to the translations "faith in Christ" and "faithfulness of Christ" most associated with the *pistis Christou* debate. Although the debate is almost exclusively centered on the seven occurrences of the phrase in the undisputed Pauline epistles (Rom. 3:22, 26; Gal. 2:16a, 16b; 2:20; 3:22; Phil. 3:9), we will also include occurrences of *pistis Christou* in his other letters (Eph. 3:20). Regardless of which conclusion interpreters prefer, we should remember that both the objective and subjective genitive readings represent the views of faithful scholars whose conclusions are well within the bounds of Christian orthodoxy.

The Objective Genitive Reading

The objective genitive translation of *pistis Christou* ("faith in Christ") stresses the anthropological element in Paul's letters, making Christ the object of human faith. Scholars such as James Dunn and Gordon Fee are strong proponents of this reading.[3] The following are objective genitive translations of *pistis Christou* phrases.[4]

Rom. 3:22	the righteousness of God "through faith in Jesus Christ" (*dia pisteōs Iēsou Christou*) for all who believe
Rom. 3:26	so that he might be just and the justifier of the one who has "faith in Jesus" (*ex pisteōs Iēsou Christou*)
Gal. 2:16a	yet we know that a person is not justified by works of the law but "through faith in Jesus Christ" (*dia pisteō Iēsou Christou*)
Gal. 2:16b	so we also have believed in Christ Jesus, in order to be justified "by faith in Christ" (*ex pisteōs Christou*) and not from works of the law
Gal. 2:20	And the life I now live in the flesh I live "by faith in the Son of God" (*en pistei tou huiou tou theou*)
Gal. 3:22	so that the promise "by faith in Jesus Christ" (*ex pisteōs Iēsou Christou*) might be given to those who believe

---

2. Preston M. Sprinkle's reading has been called a "third view." See Sprinkle's "Πίστις Χριστοῦ as an Eschatological Event," in Bird and Sprinkle, *The Faith of Jesus Christ*, 165–84. See the short, but helpful, overview of the arguments of significant players in the *pistis Christou* debate in Jeanette Hagen Pifer, *Faith as Participation: An Exegetical Study of Some Key Pauline Texts*, WUNT 2/486 (Tübingen: Mohr Siebeck, 2019), 18–29.
3. James D. G. Dunn, "Once More, *PISTIS CHRISTOU*," in Richard B. Hays, *The Faith of Jesus Christ: The Narrative Substructure of Galatians 3:1–4:11* (Grand Rapids: Eerdmans, 2002), 249–71; *The Theology of Paul the Apostle* (Grand Rapids: Eerdmans, 1998), 379–85. Gordon D. Fee, *Pauline Christology: An Exegetical-Theological Study* (Peabody, MA: Hendrickson, 2007), 223–26.
4. We follow the ESV for objective genitive translations of *pistis Christou*.

Phil. 3:9	and be found in him, not having a righteousness of my own that comes from the law, but that which comes "through faith in Christ" (*dia pisteōs Christou*)
Eph. 3:12	in whom we have boldness and access in confidence "through our faith in him" (*dia tēs pisteōs autou*)

A common argument in favor of the objective genitive translation of *pistis Christou* is that *pistis* without the article suggests that the construction is objective.[5] This would suggest that *pistis Christou* statements in Galatians 2:20 (*en pistei tou huiou tou theou*) and Ephesians 3:12 (*dia tēs pisteōs autou*) are clear instances of objective genitive phrases. Still, this argument has been rejected by scholars on both sides of the debate. Moisés Silva, who advocates for an objective genitive reading, asserts: "the presence or absence of the definite article is of no help whatever in determining the force of the genitival construction. . . . The presence or absence of the article . . . is no clue to the semantic import of the genitival relationship."[6] That scholars on both sides of the debate have rejected this argument should caution against relying on *pistis* without the article to justify a "faith in Christ" translation.

Another argument for the objective genitive reading is that *pistis Christou* is in keeping with the function of equivalent phrases in the New Testament, where a verbal noun is followed by a modifying genitive.[7] The phrase *ho gnōsis Christou Iēsou* ("the knowledge of Christ Jesus"), for instance, is commonly understood as an objective genitive (Phil. 3:8–9). Dunn contends that "no one would think to take 'the knowledge of Christ Jesus's as any other than an objective genitive.'"[8] Other examples are the phrases *zēlos theou* ("zeal for God," Rom. 10:2) and *pistei alētheias* ("faith in the truth," 2 Thess. 2:13). While observing that similar constructions are important, we should keep in mind that the flexibility of verbal noun phrases suggests they can also be taken as subject genitives. We should therefore not assume that the similarity of *pistis Christou* to other New Testament phrases necessarily suggests it should be read as an objective genitive construction.

---

5. E. D. Burton, *Galatians*, ICC (Edinburgh: T&T Clark, 1921), 482; Dunn, "*PISTIS CHRISTOU*," 253; Fee, *Pauline Christology*, 224–25. Dunn argues Ephesians 3:12 and Romans 4:16 are exceptions to the pattern ("*PISTIS CHRISTOU*," 254).

6. Moisés Silva, "Faith Versus Works of Law in Galatians," in *Justification and Variegated Nomism*, vol. 2, *The Paradoxes of Paul*, eds. D. A. Carson, Peter T. O'Brien, and Mark A. Seifrid WUNT 2/181 (Grand Rapids: Baker, 2004), 227 n.27; see 227–34 for a fuller discussion. We originally noted this quote in Matthew C. Easter, "The *Pistis Christou* Debate: Main Arguments and Responses in Summary," *CBR* 9 (2010): 34–47.

7. See Dunn, "*PISTIS CHRISTOU*," 251–52. See also Ian G. Wallis, *The Faith of Jesus Christ in Early Christian Traditions*, SNTSMS 84 (Cambridge: Cambridge University Press, 1995), 122–23.

8. See Dunn, "*PISTIS CHRISTOU*," 251.

A further argument in favor of the objective genitive translation is that, in the very context of *pistis Christou* phrases, there are verbal constructions that clearly express the need for "faith in Christ."[9] As a result, it might be argued that we should translate *pistis Christou* in a manner consistent with clear references to believers' "faith." Against this view is the danger of making reference to faith redundant. Galatians 3:22, for example, if taken as an objective genitive, would mention faith/belief twice in the very same verse ("so that the promise 'by *faith* in Jesus Christ' [*ex pisteōs Iēsou Christou*] might be given to those who *believe*"). A similar conclusion could be made of Philippians 3:9. One could argue, then, that redundancy is a major challenge for this position.

The arguments we have surveyed reveal that there is a rebuttal for every case in favor of the objective genitive translation of *pistis Christou*. While this does not invalidate the objective genitive translation, it does mean that we should not blithely assume the validity of the traditional rendering of *pistis Christou* as "faith in Christ." It is important that we also consider arguments for the subjective genitive translation.

The Subjective Genitive Reading

The subjective genitive reading emphasizes Christology rather anthropology, arguing that *pistis Christou* should be translated "Christ's faithfulness." Since Richard Hays's *Faith of Jesus Christ: The Narrative Substructure of Galatians 3:1–4:11*, the subjective genitive view has seen a rise in acceptance among New Testament scholars. Morna Hooker and Dan Wallace are other proponents of this reading.[10] The following are subjective genitive translations of the same *pistis Christou* phrases that appear in the previous chart.[11]

Rom. 3:22	the righteousness of God "through the faithfulness of Jesus Christ" (*dia pisteōs Iēsou Christou*) for all who believe
Rom. 3:26	so that he might be just and the justifier of the one "from the faithfulness in Jesus" (*ex pisteōs Iēsou Christou*)
Gal. 2:16a	yet we know that a person is not justified by works of the law but "through the faithfulness of Jesus Christ" (*dia pisteōs Iēsou Christou*)
Gal. 2:16b	so we also have believed in Christ Jesus, in order to be justified "from the faithfulness of Christ" (*ex pisteōs Christou*) and not from works of the law
Gal. 2:20	And the life I now live in the flesh I live "in the faithfulness of the Son of God" (*en pistei tou huiou tou theou*)

---

9. Dunn, "*PISTIS CHRISTOU*," 256–58.
10. See Morna D. Hooker, "Another Look at Πίστις Χριστοῦ," *SJT* 69 (2016): 46–62; Wallace, *Greek Grammar*, 113–16.
11. We here provide our own subjective genitive translations of the relevant verses.

Gal. 3:22	so that the promise "from the faithfulness of Jesus Christ" (*ex pisteōs Iesou Christou*) might be given to those who believe
Phil. 3:9	and be found in him, not having a righteousness of my own that comes from the law, but that which comes "through the faithfulness of Christ" (*dia pisteōs Christou*)
Eph. 3:12	in whom we have boldness and access in confidence "through his faithfulness" (*dia tes pisteōs autou*)

A notable argument for the subjective genitive rendering is that *pistis Christou* phrases should be understood in light of the story of "Jesus's faithfulness." Hays describes this story, which becomes the interpretive backdrop for reading *pistis Christou*:

> The narrative structure of the gospel story depicts Jesus as the divinely commissioned protagonist who gives himself up to death on a cross in order to liberate humanity from bondage (Gal 1:4; 2:20; 3:13–14; 4:4–7). His death, in obedience to the will of God, is simultaneously a loving act of faithfulness (πίστις) to God and the decisive manifestation of God's covenant faithfulness to Abraham. Paul's uses of πίστις Ἰησοῦ Χριστοῦ and other similar phrases should be understood as summary allusions to this story, referring to Jesus' fidelity in carrying out his mission.[12]

Hays notes the correlation between the story of "Jesus faithfulness" and the centrality of covenant in Paul's letters.[13] The key for seeing this connection "is to recognize that Paul's defense of God's faithfulness to Israel in Romans 3:3–5 is linked . . . to his affirmation that the righteousness of God (δικαιοσύνη θεοῦ) has been manifested through the faithfulness of Jesus Christ (διὰ πίστεως Ἰησοῦ Χριστοῦ)."[14] Hays's observations about the subjective genitive (Christological) reading are an especially attractive to proponents of the New Perspective, who argue for an interpretive backdrop for reading themes such as the "righteousness of God" and "the faithfulness of Christ."[15] Although it is helpful to be aware of a possible background for understanding *pistis Christou*, we should be weary of superimposing a narrative on Paul's letters.

---

12. Richard Hays, "Πίστις and Pauline Christology: What Is at Stake?" in *The Faith of Jesus Christ*, 275.
13. Hays, "Πίστις and Pauline Christology," 294.
14. Hays, "Πίστις and Pauline Christology," 294.
15. Dunn is a notable exception.

We must discern interpretive frameworks for reading *pistis Christou* directly from evidence in Paul's writings.

Another argument for the subjective genitive reading is that *pistis* followed by a personal genitive never suggests "faith in a person."[16] George Howard is one of the earliest proponents of this view. Not counting *pistis Christou* phrases, he identifies twenty-four cases in the Pauline corpus where *pistis* is followed by a genitive of person or a personal pronoun (e.g., Rom. 3:3; 4:12, 16).[17] Every case, he explains, "refers to the faith of the individual, never faith in the individual."[18] Some of the passages normally cited against this argument are Mark 11:22, James 2:1, and Revelation 2:13, where "faith" is directed at a personal objective genitive.[19] Yet, none of these passages are examples from authentic or even disputed Pauline epistles. One of the only rebuttals from Paul's letters comes from occurrences of *pistis* followed by an impersonal objective genitive (Col. 2:12; 2 Thess. 2:13).[20] Again, however, this does not directly contradict what scholars such as Howard argue: that *pistis* followed by a *personal* genitive in the Pauline corpus is never objective. While the lack of direct rebuttals may suggest the merits of the argument, the *pistou Christou* construction is syntactically flexible enough to allow for a variety of views and opinions. Thus, one should avoid simplified conclusions. We would be on more stable ground to argue that *pistis* followed by a personal genitive is "almost never objective."

A further argument in favor of the subjective genitive is that it avoids making the phrase "faith in Christ" superfluous.[21] We see this in key texts such as Romans 3:22 and Galatians 2:16, where Paul already uses the verb *pisteuō* to stress the importance of trusting in Jesus Christ. In such contexts where faith is already clearly emphasized, it arguably makes sense to take *pistis Christou* phrases as a subjective genitive. The priority in such readings remains on the Christological sense ("faithfulness of Christ") without forfeiting the anthropological element ("faith in Christ"). With this in mind, it is important to note that proponents of the objective genitive translation contend that Greek repetition is not negative, for (1) it shows consistency with verbal expressions of "faith" already in the context and (2) Paul uses repetition to emphasize the importance of "faith in Christ."[22] While these objections do not negate a subjective genitive translation of *pistis Christou*, they do caution against assuming that repetition, which is more distasteful to modern authors

---

16. Wallace, *Greek Grammar*, 116.
17. George Howard, "On the 'Faith of Christ,'" *HTR* 60 (1967): 459–84.
18. Howard, "Faith of Christ," 460.
19. See Wallace, *Greek Grammar*, 116.
20. Wallace, *Greek Grammar*, 116.
21. N. T. Wright, *Justification: God's Plan and Paul's Vision* (Downers Grove, IL: InterVarsity Press, 2009), 122–36; Morna D. Hooker, "πίστις χριστοῦ," *NTS* 35 (1989): 321–42.
22. Dunn, "*PISTIS CHRISTOU*," 262.

than it was to ancient ones, is enough of a reason to reject an objective genitive translation in favor of a subjective one.

As we saw with the objective genitive arguments, the arguments we have surveyed show that there is a rebuttal for every case made for the subjective genitive translation. Consequently, we should not assume that these arguments are impervious and that they decidedly point to the subjective genitive understanding of *pistis Christou* as "the faithfulness of Christ."

Summary

If our discussion of the main arguments for the objective and genitive readings of *pistis Christou* has revealed anything, it is that there is no foolproof argument for translating *pistis Christo* as either "faith in Christ" or "faithfulness of Christ." What we have, then, are two plausible readings for the syntactically flexible *pistis Christou* phrase in Paul's letters.[23] As a result, we will not argue for an objective or subjective translation of *pistis Christou* in all cases. We encourage readers to carefully consider the respective arguments before choosing a preferred translation. While doing so, we should remind ourselves that there are faithful scholars on both sides of the debate who are well within the bounds of orthodoxy. Given the complexities of the subject, a large dose of interpretive humility is in order.

REFLECTION QUESTIONS

1. Why are linguistic factors alone incapable of providing clarity about the proper understanding of *pistis Christou*?

2. What are some possible strengths and weaknesses of the "faith in Christ" (objective genitive) rendering of *pistis Christou*?

3. What are possible strengths and weaknesses of the "faithfulness of Christ" (subjective genitive) rendering of *pistis Christou*?

4. Which translation of *pistis Christou* do you generally find most persuasive?

5. What contextual factors may support either the "faith in Christ" or "faithfulness of Christ" renderings?

---

23. See Easter, "The Pistis Christou Debate," 44.

What Is Paul's View Regarding Marriage, Singleness, and Divorce?

Paul's "already–not yet" eschatological framework shapes his view of marriage, singleness, and divorce. As we argued in Question 32, Paul understood that the new age has "already" arrived but has "not yet" been consummated, awaiting the day when Christ returns to judge humankind (2 Cor. 5) and restore the creation (Rom. 8). The present state of believers is therefore one of living "between the times." In this chapter, we will examine Paul's view on marriage, singleness, and divorce, showing how his perspective on these matters is shaped by his concerns about the present age, while also stressing the importance of service to the one who will soon consummate all things, Jesus Christ.

Marriage

Some have accused Paul of having a low or ascetic view of marriage.[1] Their support for this conclusion comes from a text like 1 Corinthians 7:1: "Now concerning things about which you wrote: 'It is good for a man not to have sexual relations with a woman.'" The problem with this reading is that 1 Corinthians 7:1 represents the view of the Corinthians—not Paul. More to the point, Paul is responding to a Corinthian slogan, which promotes the notion that sexual abstinence was the preferable state for Christians, for, so they argue, it brings one closer to God. Paul devotes the remainder of 1 Corinthians 7 to reorienting the Corinthians' perception of sexual relations and marriage in view of the imminent arrival of the eschaton (vv. 26, 29, 31). In so doing, he

---

1. See discussions on the asceticism of Paul in Dale B. Martin, *The Corinthian Body* (New Haven, CT: Yale University Press, 1995), 209–12; Vincent L. Wimbush, *Paul, the Worldly Ascetic: Response to the World and Self-Understanding according to 1 Corinthians 7* (Eugene, OR: Wipf & Stock, 1987).

affirms that marriage is the proper context for sexual relations (1 Cor. 7:1–4). If couples are going to abstain, they should do so for the sake of prayer, and only for an agreed-upon period of time, lest Satan tempt them into sexual immorality (1 Cor. 7:5). Once more, Paul is anything but ascetic. He realizes that people have strong sexual desires for which marriage is the proper outlet (1 Cor. 7:6–9). Elsewhere, he argues that marriage is good and that anyone who forbids this institution, as well as other ascetic practices like forbidding certain foods, is nothing short of demonic (1 Tim. 4:1–4).[2] We can certainly claim that Paul envisions marriage as a gift from God (1 Cor. 7:7).

The nearness of Christ (1 Cor. 7:29) and the passing of the present age (1 Cor. 7:31), however, restrain Paul from having an overly enthusiastic view of marriage. He prefers for believers to be free from anxieties related to their spouse and the many responsibilities that come with marriage, so that they can be singularly devoted to serving the Lord (1 Cor. 7:32–35). In what we have observed, Paul balances the tension between the dangers of sexual immorality of the present age and devotion to Jesus who will soon consummate the new age. In this period "between the times," he sees marriage (while not for everyone) as the proper avenue for sexual fulfillment, while also warning that those who undertake this institution will be divided between pleasing their spouse and serving Jesus.

Still, Paul envisions an even greater purpose for marriage. In Ephesians 5:31–32, he cites Genesis 2:23–24 to underscore that marriage is grounded in the one-flesh union between a husband and wife, which reflects the permanent union between Christ and his church. Thus, for Paul, marriage is for more than just sexual fulfillment or procreation. He understands that the larger canonical vision for marriage is to reflect the loving relationship between Christ and his church. Since the time is short, those who participate in marriage should take seriously the responsibility of revealing—by loving their spouses and seeking their good—the loving relationship that the church will enjoy with Jesus in the new creation (cf. Rev. 22).

Singleness

Modern readers may be surprised to learn that Paul prefers singleness over marriage (1 Cor. 7:7–8, 26, 28, 32–35, 37–38, 40). This does not mean he is given to asceticism or a low view of marriage, however. We have already argued that Paul understood marriage as a reflection of love that Christ has for his church. His preference for singleness is driven by the fact that "the appointed time has grown short" (1 Cor. 7:29). Soon the distress of the present age will come to an end and the new age will arrive in all its fullness (1 Cor. 7:26, 31). Thus, it is preferable for a person to be free from the concerns of

---

2. See Thomas R. Schreiner, *Paul, Apostle of God's Glory in Christ: A Pauline Theology*, 2nd ed. (Downers Grove, IL: InterVarsity Press, 2020), 459–61.

marriage so that they can devote themselves to serving Jesus without distraction (1 Cor. 7:31–35).

Paul reveals his own singleness when he speaks to widows, encouraging them to remain "as I am," (i.e., unmarried, 1 Cor. 7:8).[3] As discussed in Question 2, the fact that Paul places himself in the same class as widowers would suggest to some that he was once married.[4] If he was married, his marriage would have been in keeping with a high view of marriage in Judaism, which we see in *Sirach* 36:29: "He who acquires a wife makes a beginning of a possession, a helper corresponding to him and a pillar of rest."[5] Paul, then, may possibly speak out of his own experience with marriage, knowing how difficult it is to please a spouse and the Lord. In light of the fact that the consummation of the new age is at hand (1 Cor. 7:17–24), he suggests that it would be better for those who are single—including widowers—to remain as they are, for the consummation of the new age is at hand (1 Cor. 7:17–24).

Nevertheless, Paul understands that singleness is not for everyone. For those who desire a spouse, it is acceptable for them to marry (1 Cor. 7:6–8). That Paul permits marriage as a "concession," so that believers might not be tempted into sexual immorality, should reorient the way churches think about marriage (1 Cor. 7:6). All too often marriage is elevated above singleness—a position that is contrary to Paul's thinking. In light of the principles emphasized by Paul, it should be recognized that single people have a unique opportunity to devote their entire lives to the undivided service of Jesus. If we view life in view of the eschaton, as Paul does, perhaps we would see the incredible gift that single people are to the church.

Divorce

Paul's preference for singleness over marriage may lead some to think that divorce is an acceptable practice. After all, divorce would allow someone to dedicate their life to serving Jesus, without the added burden and responsibility of pleasing their spouse. Yet, nothing could be further from the truth. In principle, Paul holds that a husband and wife are bound to one another so long as they are both alive (Rom. 7:2; 1 Cor. 7:39).[6]

As with marriage and singleness, the most direct information on divorce is found in 1 Corinthians 7. Paul's authority for his instruction comes

---

3. See the helpful discussion in Richard B. Hays, *First Corinthians*, IBC (Louisville: Westminster John Knox, 2011), 119.

4. Hays, *First Corinthians*, 119.

5. Translation from Benjamin G. Wright, "Sirach," in *A New English Translation of the Septuagint*, eds. Albert Pietersma and Benjamin G. Wright (Oxford: Oxford University, 2007), 749.

6. See Schreiner, *Paul*, 473–75.

from the very teachings of Jesus[7]: "To the married I give this charge (not I, but the Lord): the wife should not separate (*chōrizthēnai*) from her husband (but if she does, she should remain unmarried or else be reconciled to her husband), and the husband should not divorce (*aphienai*) his wife" (1 Cor. 7:10–11). It is important to note that first-century Mediterranean societies did not distinguish "separation" from "divorce."[8] Thus, Paul uses the verbs *chōrizō* and *aphiēmi* to prohibit the wife and husband from pursuing divorce.[9] Separation apart from marriage would not have been in the mind of Paul.

The dilemma facing many of the Corinthians was that they were married to unbelieving spouses. It is probable that they considered themselves to be in an "unholy" union. Would it not be preferable, then, as some may have thought, to free themselves from such marriages? Would it not be better, as Paul would later suggest in 2 Corinthians 6:14, to have no association between righteousness and lawlessness or fellowship between light and darkness? Would it not be more advantageous for them to no longer be "yoked" to an unbeliever (2 Cor. 6:14–15)?[10] Paul offers a direct response based on his own apostolic authority ("I, not the Lord"), forbidding husbands and wives from divorcing unbelieving spouses so long as the latter consents to remain in the marriage union (1 Cor. 7:12–13). His reasoning is the opposite of the Corinthians: the unbelieving spouse is "made holy" in a sense by the believing spouse (1 Cor. 7:14); that is, the believer has the power to be a sanctifying influence on the household. If the believer were not in the home, there would be no such influence on the spouse and children. As it stands, their godly influence may lead to their family's deliverance from the realm of sin and death (1 Cor. 7:16).

Although Matthew's gospel makes an exception for divorce in the case of sexual immorality, Paul makes no appeal to this tradition (Matt. 5:32; 19:9). He, instead, focuses on the unbeliever's willingness to remain in the marriage union. Once more, if they desire to remain in the marriage, the believer is to exercise a sanctifying influence on the household. But if the unbeliever no longer desires to be married, the believer should free them from the commitment (1 Cor. 7:15). In such cases, Paul argues that a Christian is no longer bound to their spouse (1 Cor. 7:15). Paul may envision here that abandoned spouses are free to remarry. Even in such cases, we should assume that Paul

---

7. This is an instance of Paul appealing to the Jesus tradition. See James D. G. Dunn, "Jesus Tradition in Paul," in *Studying the Historical Research: Evaluations of the Current State of Research*, eds. Bruce Chilton and Craig A. Evans (Leiden: Brill, 1994), 155–78.

8. Richard B. Hays, *The Moral Vision of the New Testament: A Contemporary Introduction to New Testament Ethics* (New York: Harper Collins, 1996), 358.

9. See BDAG, 156–57, 1095.

10. See the helpful discussion in Hays, *Moral Vision*, 359.

would prefer that the widowed person remain single, if fitting, in order to devote themselves fully to serving Christ.[11]

Summary

Paul's "already–not yet" eschatological framework drives his view of marriage, singleness, and divorce. If Christ is returning soon, then singleness should be preferred over marriage, so that believers can dedicate themselves to serving Jesus Christ without the responsibilities and concerns of marriage. Paul's position does not suggest that he has a low view of marriage, however. He understands the necessity of marriage for those who do not have the gift of singleness which he possesses. While the marriage union provides an appropriate context for individuals to fulfill their sexual desires, its main purpose is to reflect the eschatological relationship Christ will enjoy with his church. Moreover, the marriage union is intended to be permanent, even if one's spouse is an unbeliever. In such relationships, Christians are a sanctifying influence on the household, whom God may use to deliver their family members from darkness to light. If the unbeliever chooses to abandon the marriage union, however, Paul recognizes that believers are free from their marital obligations and are free to remarry. Paul would prefer, however, that divorced and widowed persons remain unmarried so as to devote their lives more fully to the work of the gospel.

REFLECTION QUESTIONS

1. What are some of the reasons Paul prefers singleness over marriage?

2. What is Paul's twofold purpose for marriage?

3. Why does Paul advise unbelievers to remain married to unbelievers?

4. Under what circumstances is a believer free from their union to an unbeliever?

5. In what ways has the church elevated the status of marriage over singleness, despite Paul's preference for the latter? How might the church benefit from a more biblically informed perspective on singleness?

---

11. In 1 Timothy 5:14, Paul advises "younger widows" to marry. While this verse may appear to contradict our conclusions, Paul's admonition is related to his earlier comments in 5:11 ("for when their passions draw them away from Christ, they desire to marry"). Many "younger widows" will desire marriage over singleness. In their case, Paul would prefer they marry than to succumb to sexual desires and commit immorality. His admonition, then, is a concession to an existing reality, which does not negate his preference for the status of singlehood in devotion to Christ.

What Does Paul Teach Regarding the Role of Women in the Home and in the Church?

Only a handful of passages in the New Testament address the role of women in the home and church. Most of these are found in Paul's epistles. Interpretations of these passages may be broadly grouped into complementarian or egalitarian positions. Complementarians argue that God has created men and women in his image and designed them to have "complementary" roles in domestic and ecclesial settings.[1] Egalitarians, on the other hand, contend that the "equality" men and women have before God is to be reflected in the full exercise of their gifts, with no restraints on how they can serve in Christian contexts.

We will now explain how complementarians and egalitarians share different perspectives on Paul's teaching about the role of women in the home and church. In what follows we will consider some of the key characteristics of each position. While a detailed discussion of all nuances associated with each view is not be possible, we will present the general contours of each position and consider what Paul teaches regarding women's domestic and ecclesial roles.[2]

The Complementarian Position

Wayne Grudem, John Piper, Denny Burk, and Thomas Schreiner are among the most notable complementarians. All have published works

---

1. We should note that complementarians have not always argued for the ontological equality of the sexes. See William G. Witt, *Icons of Christ: A Biblical and Systematic Theology for Women's Ordination* (Waco, TX: Baylor, 2020), 11–38.
2. For a fuller treatment of the issues addressed in this chapter, see Sue Edwards and Kelley Mathews, *40 Questions About Women in Ministry* (Grand Rapids: Kregel, 2023).

addressing complementarian gender roles and have been involved with the Center for Biblical Manhood and Womanhood (CBMW), an organization dedicated to the promotion of complementarian values. We will interact with such authors as we overview the complementarian position on the role of women in the home and in the church.

Women in the Home

Complementarians argue that the household codes (German: *Haustafeln*) in Ephesians 5:22–6:9 and Colossians 3:18–4:1 support their view on women in the home. Household codes addressed the relationships between husbands and wives, fathers and children, and masters and slaves, and were common in Greco-Roman literature.[3] A complementarian reading of Paul's household expectations assumes that the apostle is in step with the instructions in texts such as Aristotle's *Politics* and Plato's *Laws*, which call wives to submit to their husbands. Yet, they recognize that Paul departs from the way Greco-Roman authors view women as ontologically inferior to men.

Paul's most extensive household code is found in Ephesians 5–6, within which he situates his exhortation to wives: "Wives, submit to your own husbands, as to the Lord" (Eph. 5:22). Paul links a wife's submission to her husband to the church's submission to Christ (Eph. 5:23–24). Grudem contends that the comparison to the church's submission to Christ, and not the other way around, makes mutual submission between husband and wife incompatible with Paul's instructions.[4] Burk argues similarly: "In the home, wives are called to submit to their husband's leadership. The pattern for her submission is the church's proper submission to Christ (Eph. 5:22–24)."[5]

Paul's household code in Colossians also calls each wife to submit to their husband's leadership (3:18). While the nature of his instructions in Colossians is the same as that in Ephesians, the former is more succinct and omits the husband/wife and church/Christ comparison. Importantly, most complementarians narrow down the application of Paul's domestic instructions in Ephesians and Colossians to a wife's submission to her own husband, not all men in general.

Beyond the Pauline household codes, complementarians also appeal to 1 Corinthians 11:2–16 for insight related to Paul's teaching on gender roles. They contend that when Paul says "the head (*kephalē*) of every man is Christ, the head (*kephalē*) of a wife is her husband, and the head (*kephalē*) of Christ is God" (1 Cor. 11:3), the word "head" (*kephalē*) refers metaphorically to the "authority" that the first member of the pair has over the second. According

---

3. See Aristotle, *Politics* 1.2.1; Plato, *Laws* 781b.
4. Wayne Grudem, *Evangelical Feminism and Biblical Truth: An Analysis of More Than 100 Disputed Questions* (Colorado Springs: Multnomah, 2004), 190.
5. Denny Burk, *What Is the Meaning of Sex?* (Wheaton, IL: Crossway, 2013), 168.

to this reading, a husband's authority over his wife is like that of the Father over the Son. The comparison also suggests that, as the Father and Son are coequal in deity, so also the man and the woman are coequal in personhood. Additionally, since the Son's submission to the Father does not mean he is ontologically inferior, the woman's submission to her husband does not indicate she is inferior to her husband.[6]

Also in 1 Corinthians 11, Paul instructs women to wear head coverings in worship (1 Cor. 11:4–16). According to Thomas Schreiner, the head covering likely refers to a shawl or a way of wearing hair that displays a wife's submission to her husband, her authority (1 Cor. 11:4–16).[7] A hairstyle that does not follow such guidelines disgraces the husband (1 Cor. 11:5–6). In short, complementarians point to 1 Corinthians 11, as they would Ephesians 5 and Colossians 3, to argue that Paul expects wives to submit to their own husbands.

Women in the Church

Complementarians argue that 1 Timothy 3 and Titus 1 limit the office of elder (known variously as pastor, overseer, or bishop) to qualified males, as Paul requires that an elder be the "husband of one wife" (1 Tim. 3:2; Titus 1:6). Since only a man can be a husband, complementarians claim that the role of elder is limited to a male. Consequently, women are not eligible to hold an authoritative office associated with church leadership.

A related point is that complementarians limit corporate teaching roles (where the majority of the church is assembled) to men. Grudem appeals to 1 Timothy 2 to argue that in corporate gatherings women "are not to teach or to exercise authority (*authentein*) over a man" but "to remain quiet" (v. 12).[8] Although the use of the word *authenteō* is heavily debated, the parallelism between "teaching" and "exercising authority" suggests a teacher exercises authority over a congregation. And since only males can exercise ecclesial oversight, a woman should not teach in corporate settings (also 1 Cor. 14:33–36). Moreover, Paul ties his reasoning to the creation account ("Adam was formed first, then Eve"), which insinuates the timeless, universal scope of his instructions (1 Tim. 2:13). While women should not teach authoritatively in

---

6. See the arguments of Burk, *What is the Meaning of Sex?*, 166–67. See also Wayne Grudem's discussions on the "Creation of Man" and "Man as Male and Female" in *Systematic Theology: An Introduction to Bible Doctrine*, 2nd ed. (Grand Rapids: Zondervan, 2020), 463–99.
7. See Thomas R. Schreiner, "Head Coverings, Prophecies, and the Trinity: 1 Corinthians 11:2–16," in *Recovering Biblical Manhood & Womanhood: A Response to Evangelical Feminism* (Wheaton, IL: Crossway, 2006), 127–30.
8. Grudem, *Evangelical Feminism*, 65–74. See also Andreas J. Köstenberger and Thomas R. Schreiner, eds., *Women in the Church: An Interpretation and Application of 1 Timothy 2:9–15*, 3rd ed. (Wheaton, IL: Crossway, 2016).

the church, many complementarians make concessions for settings such as women's Bible studies and children's Sunday school.

For complementarians, then, Paul's view of women in the home and the church is one of submission to their own husbands and pastors respectively. A strength of this view is the attention to what Paul expects of his first-century audiences. A possible weakness, however, is that complementarians often fail to locate the place of Paul's instructions within the redemptive storyline of Scripture. If all things are moving toward their ultimate fulfillment in Christ, should this not also nuance our view of gender roles in Christian contexts?

The Egalitarian Position

Gordon Fee, Richard Hays, Aída Besançon Spencer, Craig Keener, Linda Belleville, William Webb, Nijay Gupta, and Cynthia Westfall are some of the more prominent egalitarian voices in recent or contemporary evangelicalism. Evangelicals of a prior generation, such as John Stott, F. F. Bruce, and I. Howard Marshall, also contended for an egalitarian view of gender roles. While we recognize the nuance in their arguments they all share a common concern for gender equality in the home and in the church, a perspective that we will briefly survey below.

The Home

Egalitarians emphasize that the Pauline household codes call for mutual submission between a husband and wife. In the Ephesians code, they argue that Paul's instructions to husbands and wives begin in Ephesians 5:21, not in 5:22. As a result, in 5:21 the participial phrase *hypotassomenoi allēlois* ("submitting to one another"), which modifies the imperatival sentence in 5:18 ("be filled with the Spirit"), is assumed in 5:22.[9] This suggests that mutual submission in marriage is a manifestation of how believers are to be "Spirit-filled."[10]

Addressing the parallels between the husband/wife and Christ/church relationships (Eph. 5:21, 22, 24), Michael Gorman places the instructions to husbands and wives in the broader context of Ephesians 5, which call believers to "walk in love, as Christ also loved us" (5:2) and husbands to love their wives (5:25).[11] This underscores that "wives and husbands alike are

---

9. Lynn H. Cohick, *The Letter to the Ephesians*, NICNT (Grand Rapids: Eerdmans, 2020), 348–49. See also Cohick's "Loving and Submitting to One Another in Marriage: Ephesians 5:21–33 and Colossians 3:18–19," in *Discovering Biblical Equality: Biblical, Theological, Cultural & Practical Perspectives*, eds. Ronald W. Pierce and Cynthia Long Westfall, 3rd ed. (Downers Grove, IL: InterVarsity Press, 2021), 185–204.

10. Craig S. Keener, *Paul, Women, & Wives: Marriage and Women's Ministry in the Letters of Paul* (Peabody, MA: Hendrickson, 1992), 159; Michael J. Gorman, *Cruciformity: Paul's Narrative Spirituality of the Cross* (Grand Rapids: Eerdmans, 2001), 265, cited in Witt, *Icons of Christ*, 109.

11. Gorman, *Cruciformity*, 264.

being called to act out in marriage the same type of self-sacrificing, respectful, submissive love they would in any and all relationships within the believing community."[12] Marshall argues that this kind of mutual submission is not unlike the selfless attitude that believers are to have toward one another in Galatians 5:13 and Philippians 2:3–4.[13]

Against the egalitarian reading is Peter Gurry's strong claim for the presence of the imperative verb *hypotassesthōsan* ("let them be submissive") in Ephesians 5:22. Gurry observes that the imperative is found in early witnesses such as Codex Sinaiticus and Codex Alexandrinus, early Latin and Coptic versions, and the patristic versions of Tertullian and Origen.[14] The exegetical implications for his argument is that Ephesians 5:21 ("submitting to one another") would be the final statement in the section describing how to be a Spirit-filled community. Ephesians 5:22 would then start the household code, calling wives to "be submissive to their own husbands as to the Lord." Gurry's argument presents a serious problem for those who argue the participle in Ephesians 5:21 has controlling influence over Paul's instructions in 5:22.[15]

But the egalitarian argument does not depend solely on the continuation of thought between Ephesians 5:21 and 22. Egalitarians also contend that the word *kephalē* in Ephesians 5:23 should be translated as "source" or "origin," not "authority."[16] William Witt notes that the use of *kephalē* as "authority" is limited to select examples in the Septuagint and Philo, as well as there being little evidence of its use in Greek literature prior to the first century.[17] Although *kephalē* is used in the sense of "authority" in contemporary political and military literature, it is never used in the context of a relationship between a husband and wife. Consequently, the meaning of *kephalē* should derive from Paul's context, suggesting that his husband/wife and Christ/church comparison means that the husband is the "source" of a wife's love and care, just as Christ is for the church.[18] Thus, Ephesians 5:23 is about nourishment rather

---

12. Gorman, *Cruciformity*, 265.

13. I. Howard Marshall, "Mutual Love and Submission in Marriage: Colossians 3:18–19 and Ephesians 5:21–33," in *Discovering Biblical Equality: Complementarity without Hierarchy*, eds. Ronald Pierce and Rebecca Merrill Groothuis (Downers Grove, IL: InterVarsity Press, 2004), 197.

14. Peter J. Gurry, "The Text of Eph 5.22 and the Start of the Ephesian Household Code," *NS* 67 (2021): 560–81. Gurry's article provides far more evidence than we are able to provide in this chapter.

15. See also Benjamin L. Merkle, "The Start of Instruction to Wives and Husbands: Ephesians 5:21 or 5:22?" *BSac* 174 (2017): 179–92.

16. Linda L. Belleville, "Women in Ministry: An Egalitarian Perspective," in *Two Views on Women in Ministry* (Grand Rapids: Zondervan, 2005), 31–32. See also Cynthia Long Westfall, *Paul and Gender: Reclaiming the Apostle's Vision for Men and Women in Christ* (Grand Rapids: Baker Academic, 2016), 79–102.

17. Witt, *Icons for Christ*, 128.

18. Witt, *Icons for Christ*, 113–14.

than hierarchy. Egalitarians make similar arguments for Paul's use of *kephalē* in 1 Corinthians 11:2–16.

With regard to the Colossian household code, egalitarians interpret Paul's instructions for wives to "submit to their husbands, as is fitting in the Lord" (3:18) along with his admonition for husbands to love their wives (3:19). The paired instructions to husbands and wives suggest that Paul expects mutual submission. Keener concedes that Paul's expectations "would have been unheard of" and "rarely attempted" in the patriarchal culture of the first century.[19] But that does not make them less significant for marital unions.

While agreeing with the egalitarian conclusions of the aforementioned passages, Hays and Webb present important, nuanced arguments. Hays reads the household codes in view of their eschatological *telos*: that the arrival of Jesus Christ initiates a new creation in which the Spirit is moving all things, including marriage, to their proper redemptive goal. For the Ephesian code, which he claims is an elaboration of the one in Colossians, Hays argues:

> [I]f marriage is a metaphor for the relationship between Christ and the church, the exalted ecclesiology of Ephesians must deconstruct static patriarchal notions of marriage. The church, in Ephesians, is not dominated by Christ; rather, in unity with Christ, it is nurtured into full maturity, into "the measure of the full stature of Christ." What then should the *telos* of marriage be?[20]

Webb's redemptive-movement hermeneutic is similar to Hays's approach. Webb argues for reading Paul's domestic instructions with an eye towards the redemptive direction to which the texts point. He emphasizes the "redemptive spirit" of Scripture, which extends the application of a text beyond its original audience. According to Webb: "A sense of the biblical or redemptive spirit can be obtained by listening to how texts compare to the broader cultural milieu and how they sound within the development of the canon."[21] Webb's redemptive hermeneutic leads him to conclude that the patriarchal assumptions of the ancient world no longer exist in the Western world. Consequently, the modern application of submission commands in verses such as Ephesians 5:22 and Colossians 3:18 "must push beyond the ladder of abstraction, beyond patriarchal customs and toward a mutual deference relationship between men and

---

19. Craig S. Keener, "Mutual Submission Frames the Household Codes," *Priscila Papers* 35 (Summer 2021), 12.

20. Richard B. Hays, *The Moral Vision of the New Testament: A Contemporary Introduction to New Testament Ethics* (New York: Harper Collins, 1996), 65.

21. William Webb, *Slaves, Women, and Homosexuals: Exploring the Hermeneutics of Cultural Analysis* (Downers Grove, IL: InterVarsity Press, 2001), 30.

women."[22] Although egalitarian arguments are not monolithic, they do agree that Paul's instructions promote gender equality, not hierarchy. Submission is therefore a mutual posture between men and women.

The Church

Egalitarians dispute that Paul's instruction in 1 Timothy 3 and Titus 1 prohibit a woman from holding the authoritative office of elder or pastor. Just because these passages say an elder should be the "husband of one wife" does not mean the office is limited to men (1 Tim. 3:2; Titus 1:6). Linda Belleville argues that elsewhere the Pastoral Epistles *do* permit women to hold the office of elder. In 1 Timothy 5:2, for instance, Paul uses the feminine plural form of *presbyteros* with the sense of "elder," as in church leader, as it used elsewhere in the New Testament.[23] Spencer contends that in Titus 2:3 Paul's use of *presbytis* can mean "female elder," rather than "old woman."[24] Thus, there may have been female elders in Crete, "especially in light of the fact that they are called 'teachers' (*didaskalos*), 'teachers of the good.'"[25] In addition, Belleville argues that the widows in 1 Timothy 5:3–16 were likely female elders, for the qualifications for such women in this passage parallel those for men in other passages, such as the wife of one husband, raising her children well, and a reputation for hospitality.[26]

Egalitarians also hold an alternative perspective regarding Paul's instruction in 1 Timothy 2. First, they argue that 1 Timothy 2:11, which calls them to be "silent," does not forbid women from teaching or speaking in corporate gatherings. According to Keener, Paul is concerned about women who were not yet taught properly, so they were to remain quiet (also 1 Cor. 14:33–36).[27] The universal principle applies to both men and women: "those who do not understand the Scriptures and are not able to teach them accurately should not be able to teach others."[28] Secondly, egalitarians argue that in 1 Timothy 2:12 the verb *authenteō* should not be translated as "exert authority" but as "usurp authority" or "domineer." "Paul's intention is not to prohibit women from speaking altogether, but simply to emphasize that it should be done in a manner that does not "usurp" or "domineer" men.[29] He would have forbidden men from doing the same.

---

22. William Webb, "Gender Equality and Homosexuality," in *Discovering Biblical Equality*, 411.

23. Belleville, "Women in Ministry," 39–45.

24. Aída Besançon Spencer, *Beyond the Curse: Women Called to Ministry* (Nashville: Thomas Nelson, 1985), 107.

25. Spencer, *Beyond the Curse*, 107.

26. Belleville, *Women in Ministry*, 39–45.

27. Keener, *Paul, Women & Wives*, 109.

28. Keener, *Paul, Women & Wives*, 120.

29. See Linda L. Belleville's detailed study in "Teaching and Usurping Authority: 1 Timothy 2:11–15," in Pierce and Westfall, *Discovering Biblical Equality*, 205–27.

Another important point is that egalitarians draw attention to the significance of the eschaton for the place of women in the church. Fee, for example, contends that the arrival of the new age signals a new equality among believers.[30] Paul may be understood to make such a claim in Galatians 3:28: "There is neither Jew nor Greek, there is neither slave, there is no male and female, for you are all one in Christ Jesus." Also linked to the new age is the arrival of the Spirit, who makes men and women equal sons and daughters of Abraham (Gal. 3:2–4:7). This is the very Spirit that the prophets associate with a new creation (Ezek. 36:25–28), who would enable "sons and daughters" to prophecy (Joel 2:28–32). As a result, it is understood that the Spirit has now gifted both men and women to speak on behalf of God, so women should not be barred from authoritative teaching or leadership in the new covenant community.

According to egalitarians, then, Paul calls for mutual submission in the home and permits women to teach authoritatively and to hold the ruling office of elder. An arguable strength of the egalitarian reading is the eschatological trajectory with which some interpret Paul's instructions to women and men. If the Spirit is in the process of restoring relationships and healing broken structures, then it may be argued that this should influence the way we understand gender roles. Yet, a weakness of the egalitarian position may be the way it appears to stretch interpretations beyond their plain readings. Does *authenteō* in 1 Timothy 2 really mean that women should not "usurp authority" in the church? Do the Pastoral Epistles really advocate for women elders? Or is Paul just addressing widows and older women? Another challenge is that egalitarians must reckon with Gurry's argument for the inclusion of the imperative verb *hypotassesthōsan* in Ephesians 5:22, which calls women to "submit" to their husbands.

Summary

A handful of New Testament passages on women's roles in the home and in the church have garnered significant and ongoing attention. From our discussion, we have shown how the complementarian and egalitarian positions on these matters are sourced in Scripture. This does not mean that both views are correct in all that they address—it simply means that both claim a biblical basis for their arguments. Our own conclusion is that Paul taught that women should submit to their husbands and male ecclesial authorities—that much is clear from the aforementioned passages. Yet, there are still questions that complementarians and egalitarians must answer. Can complementarians make a more convincing case for how Paul's instructions extend beyond the first century? How does the complementarian position cohere with the

---

30. See Gordon D. Fee, "Male and Female in the New Creation, Galatians 3:26–29," in *Discovering Biblical Equality*, 179.

redemptive trajectory of Scripture? Are egalitarians too quick to reinterpret instructions that offend modern sensibilities? Do their arguments address variant textual readings that challenge their views on gender roles? And since no one is free of interpretive bias, a final question for readers: How do our ecclesial and social environments predispose us to prefer either the complementarian or egalitarian position, before even seriously weighing the respective arguments?

REFLECTION QUESTIONS

1. What is the complementarian position on the role of women in the home and in the church?

2. What are the possible strengths and weaknesses of the complementarian position?

3. What is the egalitarian position on the role of women in the home and in the church?

4. What are the possible strengths and weaknesses of the egalitarian position?

5. Do you find the complementarian or egalitarian view of women's roles in the home and in the church to be more compelling? Why?

Did Paul Teach That Certain Spiritual Gifts Would Cease?

Paul taught that the Holy Spirit distributes a variety of spiritual gifts to believers (1 Cor. 12–14) for the edification of the church (Rom. 12:6–8; Eph. 4:12). His teaching is consistent with Joel's eschatological expectations: "And it will come to pass afterword, that I will pour out my Spirit on all flesh; your sons and daughters will prophesy, your old men shall dream dreams, and your young men shall see visions" (Joel 2:28). Paul uses several words to refer to the eschatological "gifts" of the Spirit, such as *pneumatika* (1 Cor. 12:1; 14:1), *pneumata* (1 Cor. 14:32), *charismata* (1 Cor. 1:5, 7), and *dōrea* (Eph. 4:7). Among such gifts are those commonly referred to as "extraordinary" or "miraculous," such as healing, prophecy, and tongues (1 Cor. 12:8–11), which were characteristic of the earliest Christian churches.

Some scholars argue that the miraculous practices of the earliest churches gave way to a more organized, hierarchical church structure in the second century. Evidence for this shift is found in the progression from Paul's charismatic instructions in 1 Corinthians to the more structured guidelines of the Pastoral Epistles, which many claim point to a post-Pauline origin. While this is one way to frame the argument, most evangelicals prefer to speak of miraculous gifts in terms of "cessationist" or "continuist" perspectives. Cessationists argue that miraculous gifts ceased shortly after the arrival of the new age. Continuists, on the other hand, claim that miraculous gifts will continue until the consummation of the eschaton.

The remainder of this chapter will consider the cessationist and continuist positions on whether Paul taught that miraculous gifts would cease before the consummation of the new age. To be clear, both positions agree that the Spirit still distributes spiritual gifts such as teaching, evangelism, or exhortation. What is disputed is whether the Spirit continues to bestow miraculous or extraordinary gifts to believers such as healing, prophecy, and tongues.

Cessationism

A popular argument for the cessation of spiritual gifts is grounded in 1 Corinthians 13:8–13. In this passage, Paul says that prophecies "will pass away" and tongues "will cease" (v. 8). He goes on to say that such gifts will cease "when the perfect comes" (1 Cor. 13:10). Some argue that "the perfect" refers to the completion of the New Testament canon, when God's revelation is complete, making obsolete miraculous gifts like prophecy and tongues. Others are not convinced of this interpretation. Thomas Schreiner, who is not a continuationist, suggests that Paul was not aware that his letters would later be collected and included in the canon.[1] Consequently, it would have been nearly impossible for him to have used "the perfect" in reference to the New Testament canon. Neither is it evident that his readers would have understood that he was referring to the completion of the Scriptures, which would have required far more explanation.[2]

Richard Gaffin has another take on 1 Corinthians 13:10. He claims that Paul's reference to the arrival of "the perfect" asserts that tongues and prophecy will cease at an unspecified point.[3] Paul is not affirming *when* they will cease, but simply that they *will*. Paul's main point, according to Gaffin, is to contrast the transitory quality of prophecy and tongues with the permanent quality of faith, hope, and love (1 Cor. 13:13). While they disagree on *when* they would cease, cessationists agree that 1 Corinthians 13 teaches that extraordinary gifts *will* end. Determining approximately when this will occur depends largely on other Pauline passages.

Schreiner presents one of the most balanced claims for the cessation of prophecy, grounding his perspective in Paul's claim that the church was "built on the foundation of the apostles and prophets" (Eph. 2:20).[4] He notes that many continuationists argue that the office of apostle ceased after the foundation of the church. Consequently, we no longer have apostles like Paul, James, and John, who received an apostolic commission and were witnesses to the resurrected Jesus. Paul saw himself as the last person to whom Jesus appeared, "showing there would be no apostles appointed after the apostle Paul."[5] What remains of the apostolic office is authoritative teaching, which has been preserved in the New Testament documents (Acts 2:42). His observation begs the question: If the gift of apostleship has passed away, should we not also insinuate the same for the role of prophet?

---

1. Thomas R. Schreiner, *Spiritual Gifts: What They Are and Why They Matter* (Nashville: B&H, 2018), 150.
2. Schreiner, *Spiritual Gifts*, 150.
3. Richard B. Gaffin's "A Cessationist View," in *Are Miraculous Gifts for Today? Four Views*, ed. Wayne Grudem (Grand Rapids: Zondervan, 1996), 55n81.
4. See Schreiner, *Spiritual Gifts*, 157–68.
5. Schreiner, *Spiritual Gifts*, 158.

Schreiner argues that the apostles and the prophets, the foundation upon which the church was built, spoke authoritatively and infallibly.[6] And if it is the case that the apostles who spoke the authoritative and infallible Word of God do not exist today, then we may conclude that prophets, whom God gifted to speak in a similar way, are likewise no longer active. The foundation of the church has been laid and there is no longer a need for prophecies. This took place gradually as the matter of canon was being settled in the early centuries of the church. Schreiner suggests that the authority of Scripture would be undermined if people still claimed to speak on behalf of God as their words might be thought to have a similar authority.

In addition to prophecy, Schreiner notes that other miraculous gifts were necessary in the early period of the church to attest to the message that Jesus is the Messiah and God's Son (Heb. 2:4), as well as to encourage and bring comfort to God's people.[7] Since miraculous gifts have served their purpose in the life of the church, gifts such as tongues and healings are no longer normative. Schreiner's position does not deny that God may still heal or do something miraculous; it simply denies that miraculous gifts are normative for the church today. Schreiner calls this a *modified* cessationist position.

Strict cessationists contend that miraculous gifts like tongues, prophecies, and healings have served their purpose and are no longer in existence *at all*. An argument for this view is that, for Paul, miracles were the "signs of an apostle" (2 Cor. 12:12). Consequently, miraculous gifts ceased with the close of the apostolic era. Another argument is that miraculous gifts once served a purpose, attesting to the message of Jesus Christ. The Scriptures are now the only attestation we need to the life, death, and resurrection of Jesus Christ. While there are different contours to their views, cessationists share the conviction that Paul teaches miraculous gifts would cease after the apostolic age.

Continuationism

Continuationists unanimously reject the notion that 1 Corinthians 13 affirms the cessation of miraculous gifts, arguing instead that Paul expects miraculous gifts will pass away *only* when believers "know" and see Christ "face to face" at his second coming (1 Cor. 13:12). This is what Paul means by the arrival of "the perfect" (1 Cor. 13:10). As a result, extraordinary gifts will continue until Christ returns to consummate the eschaton. Contrary to some cessationist readings, continuationists claim Paul would not have envisioned a New Testament canon, so he would not have taught that miraculous gifts would cease after the formation of the canon.[8]

---

6. Schreiner, *Spiritual Gifts*, 159–60.
7. Schreiner, *Spiritual Gifts*, 166–68.
8. Craig S. Keener, *Gift and Giver: The Holy Spirit for Today* (Grand Rapids: Baker Academic, 2001), 75.

Jack Deere provides an argument for continuationism from the wider context of 1 Corinthians 12–14.[9] He notes that gifts are for the "common good" (1 Cor. 12:7) and for the strengthening of the church (1 Cor. 14:26). Deere poses the following suggestive questions: "Since edification is the primary purpose of spiritual gifts, how can anyone conclude they have been taken away from the church? If they built up the church in the first century, why wouldn't they build up the church in the twenty first century."[10] These questions suggest that Paul envisioned that spiritual gifts would continue to edify the church until the return of Jesus.

Another important passage is Ephesians 2:20. Earlier, we observed Schreiner's argument that prophecies, which were once associated with the apostles and prophets, gradually ceased gradually once the canon was settled. Gaffin also argues that apostles and prophets, and the gifts associated with their offices, ceased with the completion of the canon.[11] Gordon Fee, however, contends that Ephesians 2:20 does not indicate that Paul anticipated a future time in which certain gifts would become unnecessary. Consequently, it should be assumed that he envisioned spiritual gifts remaining active beyond the apostolic era.[12]

A further passage of importance is Ephesians 4. Craig Keener contends that verses 11–13 reveal that spiritual gifts are necessary to equip the church for the task of ministry.[13] These gifts include miraculous ones like prophecy and normative ones like pastor and teacher, which are necessary so long as "the church needs more maturity and unity."[14] Since the church will continue to grow in maturity throughout the present age, we should assume that both miraculous and normative spiritual gifts will be necessary until Jesus returns to bring all things to their "full stature."

A final point to consider is how the continuationist perspective addresses the expectations and worldview of the apostle Paul. Undoubtedly, miraculous gifts were a regular part of Paul's ministry (Rom. 15:18–19; 2 Cor. 12:12) and those of his churches (Gal. 3:5). As a result, Fee argues that the apostle would not have understood the presence of the Spirit without evidence of miraculous deeds such as prophecies and healings.[15] Fee goes

---

9. Jack Deere, *Surprised by the Power of the Spirit: A Former Dallas Seminary Professor Discovers That God Speaks and Heals Today* (Grand Rapids: Zondervan, 1993), 134–35.

10. Deer, *Surprised by the Power of the Spirit*, 135.

11. See Richard B. Gaffin, *Perspectives on Pentecost: Studies in the New Testament Teaching on the Gifts of the Holy Spirit* (Phillipsburg, NJ: P&R, 1979). Craig Keener notes that Gaffin bases almost his entire argument for the cessation of certain spiritual gifts on Ephesians 2:20 (*Gift and Giver*, 77).

12. Gordon D. Fee discusses Ephesians 2:20 in his discussion of *charismata* (*Paul, the Spirit, and the People of God* [Peabody, MA: Hendrickson, 1996], 111–19).

13. Keener, *Gift and Giver*, 78–79.

14. Keener, *Gift and Giver*, 79.

15. Gordon D. Fee, *Paul, the Spirit, and the People of God* (Grand Rapids: Baker Academic, 1996), 112.

on to note how cessationist evangelicals balk at how scholars like Rudolf Bultmann dismiss the miraculous events described in Paul's writings, associating them with a "primitive" worldview.[16] Yet, they fail to see that, by limiting the work of the Spirit to the age of the apostles, they practice a rationalism similar to that of Bultmann. Paul, on the other hand, believed in an all-powerful God, whose Spirit would continue performing miraculous deeds among his people. Consequently, those "who believe in God as creator and sustainer, but who balk at the miraculous both past and present, have created theological positions for themselves difficult to sustain and quite removed from the biblical perspective."[17]

While there are different emphases in their arguments, what unites continuationists is the belief that God continues to endow believers with extraordinary gifts such as prophecy, tongues, and healings. Scripture does not explicitly state that the extraordinary has come to an end, as continuationists often note. To argue that some gifts have ceased puts one in the company of rationalists like Bultmann, rather than those with a biblical cosmology like Paul.

Summary

Cessationists and continuationists disagree on whether Paul teaches that miraculous gifts have ceased. Cessationists claim miraculous gifts were only necessary until the closure of the canon and/or the establishment of the church. In contrast, continuationists claim that God still bestows gifts like prophecy, tongues, and healings on his people for the sake of ministering to and building up the church. While both views are within the boundaries of evangelicalism, we would be hard-pressed to identify a passage where Paul clearly asserts that miraculous gifts either have ceased or would shortly cease. Scholars like Deere and Keener rightly emphasize that Paul envisions God *continuing* to empower believers with miraculous gifts until the second coming of Christ.

Of the cessationist arguments, Schreiner's nuanced perspective is perhaps the most reasonable, arguing that God may still perform extraordinary deeds, even if they are no longer normative. On the whole, however, it might be said that cessationism goes beyond what Paul actually articulates in his writings, for he never explicitly states that miraculous gifts would cease shortly after the apostolic era and the establishment of the church. Consequently, Fee is warranted in his conclusion that rationalism may be at the heart of some cessationist arguments. Cessationism, after all, flourishes in Western countries like the United States, Canada, and Great Britain. Areas that have been less influenced by enlightenment ideals, like Latin American and Africa, are more likely to recognize the continuation of extraordinary spiritual gifts, even

---

16. Fee, *Paul, the Spirit*, 112.
17. Fee, *Paul, the Spirit*, 112.

testifying to God's miraculous works of healing and tongues. Their perspective on the supernatural is arguably closer to Paul's—a perspective that recognizes that God's Spirit empowers his people to perform wondrous deeds, like healing the sick and speaking in tongues that testify to the mighty works of God in Christ.[18]

REFLECTION QUESTIONS

1. What is the cessationist position on miraculous spiritual gifts?

2. What is Schreiner's modified cessationist position?

3. What is the continuationist position on miraculous spiritual gifts?

4. Do you find the continuationist or cessationist view on miraculous gifts more convincing? Why?

5. What role might our social context play in our view of miraculous gifts?

---

18. See also Graham H. Twelftree, *Paul and the Miraculous: A Historical Reconstruction* (Grand Rapids: Baker Academic, 2013).

Did Paul Address Slavery and Racial Division?

Paul was well acquainted with slavery and racial division. It has been esti-mated that up to twenty percent of the population of first-century Rome was comprised of slaves.[1] Although Roman slaves were often allowed privi-leges such as a daily wage and the possibility of freedom by the time they were thirty, they were still considered property of the male head of house-hold, commonly called the *paterfamilias*. The *paterfamilias* could do what he pleased with slaves, such as beat or sexually abuse them, with little fear of repercussion. It is right to wonder what Paul thought of such a dehumanizing institution.

Racial division was prevalent in the tension between Jews and Gentiles. Jews considered themselves God's covenant people, beneficiaries of the law and the saving promises. No other group had such ethnic privileges. This led to centuries of hostilities between Jews and Gentiles that did not disappear with the arrival of the messianic age. With the inclusion of Gentiles into the reconstituted community of God, Paul directly addressed the longstanding racial tension between Jews and Gentiles (Gal. 2–5; Eph. 2). We will now ex-amine how Paul addresses slavery and racial tension. Though we are centu-ries removed from the social circumstances of Paul's historical audiences, his teaching on slavery and racial hostility is no less relevant today than it was in the first century.

Slavery

Paul would never have imagined that those who claim to follow Jesus would use his writings to justify the enslavement of human beings. Yet, this

---

1. See the helpful discussion of John Madden, "Slavery in the Roman Empire Numbers and Origins," *Classics Ireland* 3 (1996), 109–12.

is exactly what happened in North America, as self-professing Christians appealed to Paul's letters to justify stealing men, women, and children from their homes in Africa and selling them to slave owners.[2] Such flagrant misinterpretation of Paul's letters cuts against the grain of his anthropology: that all people are created in the image of the God who never intended for them to be treated as expendable property. That Paul does not directly condemn slavery does not mean he condoned the practice. Nor does it mean he envisioned slavery as a permanent institution. A glance at the relevant passages in his letters reveals that he subtly usurps a system that is already in the process of passing away, along with all other systems associated with the age of sin and death.

1 Corinthians 7:17–33

Paul's overarching concern in 1 Corinthians 7:17–33 is for believers to "lead the life the Lord has assigned" to them (v. 17). Regardless of social distinctions like circumcision and uncircumcision or slave and free, believers should exercise their primary identity as followers of Christ (1 Cor. 7:18–21). What this means for slaves is that, despite their bondage, they are actually free in the Lord (1 Cor. 7:22). So, they should be unconcerned about attaining their freedom (1 Cor. 7:21). Just as well, free people should not seek the social station of slaves (1 Cor. 7:22–23). While this may sound awkward to modern ears, in the Roman world persons were known to sell themselves into slavery to pay off debts. Since Jesus has already died to redeem believers from slavery to sin and death, selling oneself into slavery is contrary to believers' true identity as "free persons" (1 Cor. 7:23–24). So, in whatever social station a person has been called, Paul encourages them to live out their free status in Christ.

Nevertheless, Paul was still concerned about the status of slaves. In the very context of Corinthians 7, he supplies a qualifying remark immediately after he instructs slaves to be unconcerned about their social station: "But if you can gain your freedom, avail yourself of the opportunity" (1 Cor. 7:21). Paul was well aware that slaves lived a contradictory existence: though they were "already" free from the dominion of sin, they were "not yet" free from bondage. The Christian slave therefore exemplified the tension of an "already–not yet" existence. But if there was an opportunity for slaves to "gain their freedom," and thereby come closer to full deliverance from sin's dominion and all its tangible repercussions, Paul encouraged slaves to take advantage of it.

Ephesians 6:5–9 and Colossians 3:22–4:1

In the household codes recorded in Ephesians 6:5–9 and Colossians 3:22–4:1, Paul encourages the freedom of slaves by subverting an institution that expected their unwavering submission to their masters. We see this when

---

2. See the excellent work of Lisa M. Bowens, *African American Readings of Paul: Reception, Resistance and Transformation* (Grand Rapids: Eerdmans, 2020).

Paul calls slaves and masters to treat one another in a manner that honors their common master, the Lord Jesus Christ (Eph. 6:5–9; Col. 3:18–4:1). The implications are that slaves should only obey their earthly masters as long as their actions are in keeping with their devotion to Jesus Christ. In addition, masters should only require of their slaves that which Christ would approve. The result is that God restrains the actions of both parties, which leads to a more Christ-honoring dynamic.

What is more, Paul's instructions to slaves initiates a redemptive trajectory, which has immediate and long-term implications.[3] Initially, his instructions redefine slave-master relations, creating more ideal circumstances than those promoted in the Greco-Roman household codes. Beyond the first century, Paul's words set into motion the expectation that, at some point in the eschatological future, slaves and masters will be primarily concerned with honoring God, rather than living out slave-master dynamics associated with the old age of sin. Christ therefore recalibrates the slave-master relationship.

Since we are twenty centuries removed from the apostolic age, Paul would expect us to be closer to the full eradication of slavery. While the forces of the old age are continuously at work to prevent this reality, Christians are new creations who should work toward the elimination of slavery and all its lingering effects, anticipating the day Jesus returns to eradicate sin and all its vestiges. Consequently, using the household codes in Colossians and Ephesians to support slavery misses the subversive nature of Paul's instructions and the eschatological reality to which they point.

Philemon

Paul's instructions to Philemon also subvert the Roman institution of slavery. We see this in the way Paul redefines Philemon's relationship to Onesimus. Although their relationship was previously governed by a slave-master dynamic, Paul appeals to their now common relationship in the Lord: "no longer a slave, but more than a slave, as a beloved brother—especially to me, but how much more to you, both in the flesh and in the Lord" (Philem. 16).[4] Thus, their new status as "brothers in the Lord" should change Philemon's treatment of Onesimus—no longer as a slave, but as members of a family. Consequently, Onesimus and Philemon are free from the expectations of a slave-master dynamic that no longer applies to members of the family of Jesus.

While Paul's letter to Philemon was used to justify slavery in contexts such as the American South, the apostle never intended for this letter to keep

---

3. Our hermeneutic for reading slave-master passages in Paul benefits from William J. Webb's *Slaves, Women, and Homosexuals: Exploring the Hermeneutics of Cultural Analysis* (Downers Grove, IL: InterVarsity Press, 2001).

4. We dissent from the ESV's translation of *doulos* as "bondservant." "Slave" more accurately reflects Philemon's former relationship to Onesimus.

people in chains or to justify bringing runaway slaves back to their earthly masters.[5] Just the opposite: it was intended to deliver slaves from bondage and all claims that people belong to anyone other than Jesus Christ.[6] When we also consider 1 Corinthians 7:21–33 and household code passages such as Ephesians 6:5–9 and Colossians 3:22–41, we envision how Paul's instructions subverted the system of slavery.[7] A redemptive reading of his letters sets a trajectory for the abolishment of slavery and the full dignity of human beings in the eschaton.

Racial Strife

In addition to his treatment of the subject of slavery, Paul also addresses racial strife between Jews and Gentiles. We noted in Question 33 that Jews emphasized their distinctiveness from Gentiles by stressing boundary markers such as Sabbath-keeping, circumcision, and food laws (e.g., *1 Macc.* 1; 6; *Jub.* 50), distinguishing themselves as the genuine people of God (*4 Ezra* 7; *Sir* 44). The hostility that arose from such beliefs and practices did not necessarily disappear when Jews and Gentiles began worshiping a common Messiah. In response to such matters, Paul pens his most helpful instructions on racial strife in Galatians and Ephesians.

Galatians

In Galatians, Paul combats a group of Jews pressuring Gentiles to adopt "works of the law" (e.g., 2:16, 19; 3:2, 4, 10). The context of his letter reveals that the "works" he emphasizes are those that historically distinguished Jews from Gentiles—circumcision (Gal. 4:6, 11; 5:1, 3) and, to a lesser extent, food laws (Gal. 2:11–13). Since the Jewish group who went to Galatia "came from James," a pillar and head of the Jerusalem church, we may assume that they were followers of Messiah who were enforcing Jewish boundary markers on Gentile converts (Gal. 2:12).[8] As a result, the markers of the *old* covenant were rousing *old* frictions in the *new* Messianic community (Gal. 5:20–21, 26).

Paul would have none of this. So, he passionately argues that stressing boundary markers as a necessary requirement for membership in God's people amounts to "another gospel," and that its proponents should be "accursed"

---

5. See Bowens, *African American Readings of Paul*, 113–24.
6. See Esau McCaulley's insightful reading of Philemon (*Reading While Black: African American Interpretation as an Exercise in Hope* [Downers Grove, IL: InterVarsity Press, 2020], 152–57).
7. We also see Paul's disdain for slavery in 1 Timothy 1:8–11, where he includes "enslavers" in his list of lawbreakers.
8. For helpful studies on Paul's Jewish opponents in Galatia, see Craig S. Keener, *Galatians: A Commentary* (Grand Rapids: Baker Academic, 2019), 27–36; James D. G. Dunn, *The Theology of Paul's Letter to the Galatians*, New Testament Theology (Cambridge: Cambridge University Press, 2004), 8–12.

(Gal. 1:8–9). He is so upset that he wishes his opponents would "emasculate themselves" (Gal. 5:12). For Paul, it is only through faith in Jesus that Jews and Gentiles are recipients of the Spirit and equal members of God's family (Gal. 3:15–4:7). No markers of ethnicity are required—for both groups are "one in Christ Jesus" (Gal. 3:28). With that, Paul eliminates any grounds for ethnic hostility based on the unity that all believers—regardless of race—have in the same Messiah.

Ephesians 2

In Ephesians 2, Paul reminds readers that they were once "strangers to the covenants of promise, having no hope and without God in the world" (2:12). Being outsiders to the promised covenants was synonymous with the label "the uncircumcision," whereas Jews within the covenants considered themselves "the circumcision" (2:11). Paul highlights "circumcision" as a clear boundary which separated Jews, who considered themselves the true beneficiaries of the covenant promises, and Gentiles, who were regarded as strangers to such salvific privileges. The pride Jews took in their ethnic status, as evidenced through circumcision, was a major source of ethnic strife.

But all this was to change through the "blood of Christ," which brought Gentiles near to the God from whom they were once "far off" (Eph. 2:13). As result, they are now beneficiaries of the covenant promises that originally belonged to Israel; they too are the people of God in whom the Spirit dwells (Eph. 2:19–22). The work of Christ has removed all markers of ethnic privilege that once brought hostility between Jew and Gentile. In light of these realities, there should be peace between two groups who were once bitterly divided, for they are now "one people" who worship the same God (Eph. 2:14, 17).

From our discussion of Paul's teaching in Galatians and Ephesians, we see that he does not tolerate ethnic strife. The person and work of Jesus Christ has nullified markers of ethnic privilege that once identified the genuine people of God. Jewish and Gentile believers have a common faith in Jesus, who makes both groups members of the one covenant people of God and beneficiaries of his saving promises. This leaves no room for division based on racial superiority.

Summary

Paul was by no means satisfied with traditional slave-master roles and Jew-Gentile ethnic strife. For him, the arrival of Jesus Christ meant that slaves and masters are both accountable to the same Lord, who expects that they would treat one another as members of the same family (Col. 3:22–4:1; Eph. 6:5–9; Philem.). His expectations were radically different than those found in Roman society, setting a redemptive trajectory that would culminate in the elimination of abusive hierarchies and the full humanity of all people in the eschaton. In the interim, Paul encourages slaves to take hold of their freedom, if they are able (1 Cor. 7). He also exhorts masters to no longer treat or regard their slaves as property, but as free members of God's family (Philem. 16). For Paul, the spiritual bond between believers is antithetical to the master-slave relationship that was common in Roman society.

The arrival of Christ also eliminated any grounds for ethnic strife. In Paul's letters to the Galatians and Ephesians, both Jews and Gentiles share a common faith in the Messiah, who has made them members of the people of God and recipients of the salvific promises. Consequently, boundary markers such as circumcision and food laws, which traditionally distinguished Jews from Gentiles, are no longer relevant. The only distinguishing marker of God's people is their faith in Jesus.

Paul's words on such matters are no less relevant for us today. His instructions on slave-master relations demonstrates that there are no grounds for any form of slavery. God has never intended for people to be enslaved to other human beings, but to be free from sin and all its repercussions, including slavery. As a result, Christians should work toward the eradication of an institution that has its origins in the passing age of sin and death. Additionally, Paul's words on Jew-Gentile ethnic strife reveal that all believers, regardless of their background, have equal standing in the people of God. No ethnic group should claim superiority over another, for we all worship the same Lord who has made believers equal members of his family, eliminating any grounds for friction or pride among races.

REFLECTION QUESTIONS

1. How do Paul's instructions to slaves and masters challenge the institution of slavery?

2. Why does Paul expect that Christians will work toward the eradication of slavery and all such oppressive systems?

3. What are some of the reasons that racial strife took place between Jews and Gentiles?

4. Why is there no reason for ethnic strife or ethnic superiority between followers of Christ?

5. What are some ways you have witnessed ethnic strife or ethnic superiority among believers?

Did Paul Believe the Church Replaced Israel?

God swore the salvific promises to Abraham, the father of ethnic Israelites (Gen. 12; 15; 17). He later reaffirmed them to posterity such as Isaac, Jacob, and David. When the New Testament records the arrival of Jesus Christ, the offspring of Abraham, it should come as no surprise that his earliest followers and recipients of the promises were Jewish.

Soon after Pentecost, the ethnic makeup of the people of God began to change, as Gentiles increasingly trusted in Jesus (Acts 8; 10).[1] This happened to fulfill the promises to Abraham, among which was the promise that he would be a blessing to the nations (Gen. 12:3; 17:1–8). As the church grew in the second and third centuries, it became composed primarily of Gentiles, many of whom questioned or outright rejected the place of Jews in the salvific plan of God. For example, the second-century *Epistle of Barnabas* argued that the Jewish covenant with Moses was "shattered," resulting in the Gentiles becoming recipients of "the covenant of the beloved Jesus" (4:8).[2] The third-century theologian Tertullian argued that grace has been taken from the Jews and handed to the Gentiles.[3] We could argue that the rise of Gentile Christians, and the waning decline of Jewish influence in the church following the apostolic period, was a major factor in the belief that the church had replaced Israel.

---

1. Paul draws his understanding of the "church" (e.g., 1 Cor. 1:1; 10:32; 2 Cor. 1:1; Gal. 1:13) from Israel's self-identity as the "congregation of Yahweh/Lord" (e.g., Num. 16:3; 20:4; Deut. 23:1–3; 1 Chron. 28:8) and the "congregation of God" (1QM 4:10; James D. G. Dunn, *The Theology of Paul the Apostle* [Grand Rapids: Eerdmans, 1998], 537–43). Since the "congregation of Israel" is equivalent to the "people of God," we equate the new covenant people of God with the church.
2. Michael W. Holmes, ed., "The Epistle of Barnabas," in *The Apostolic Fathers: Greek Texts and English Translations*, 3rd ed. (Grand Rapids: Baker, 2007), 389.
3. Tertullian, *An Answer to the Jews*, 2–3.

But not all Christians have adopted "replacement theology" or "supersessionism." Many have genuinely struggled to discern a place for Israel in the story of redemption. Paul himself wrestled with the relationship between his kinspeople, the Israelites, and the church. With that in mind, we will now explore Paul's view of Israel and the church. Our discussion will center around whether (1) the church has replaced Israel, (2) whether there is continuity between Israel and the church, and (3) whether there are distinct salvific plans for Israel and the church.

The Church as the Replacement of Israel

Paul never argues that the church has replaced Israel. Instead, he affirms the rich blessings that God has graciously bestowed upon the Jewish people such as "the covenants, the receiving of the law, the temple worship, and the promises" (Rom. 9:4). He even traces their ethnic lineage to the patriarchs and ultimately the Messiah (Rom. 9:5). He mentions all this to argue that the people of Israel have not been replaced or superseded in the plan of God, which goes back to the covenant he made with Abraham.

To argue that the church replaced Israel would be to misinterpret Paul's sentiments on a very personal subject. Lest we forget: Paul experienced "great sorrow and unceasing anguish in his heart" for his fellow Israelites (Rom. 9:2), even wishing he were "cursed" and "cut off from Christ" for their sake (Rom. 9:3). If anyone could be accused of supersessionism, it was the arrogant Gentiles in Romans 11:13–25, whom Paul reminds of how God can again "graft" believing Israelites into the people of God.[4] Although many Jews failed to believe in the Messiah, seeking to establish their own righteousness (Rom. 10:3), Paul acknowledges that God's purposes for Israel are still unfolding, meaning there is still hope for his ethnic kinspeople (Rom. 11:25–32).[5] Although the phrase is much debated, Paul speaks of Israel's future hope in Romans 11:26, arguing that "all Israel will be saved."

The Continuity Between Israel and the Church

In Romans 11:17–24, Paul uses an olive-tree metaphor to argue for an organic connection between Israel and the church. He draws this metaphor from Jewish literature, which uses an olive tree to symbolize Israel (Jer. 11:6; Hos. 14:5–6; *1 En.* 10:16; *Jub.* 16:26; 1QS 8:5).[6] Yet, he expands the olive tree metaphor to include both Jews and Gentiles (Rom. 11:22–23; cf. Rom. 10:8–13). What is more, Paul uses the metaphor in a way that negates ethnic

---

4. Douglas J. Moo, *A Theology of Paul and His Letters: The Gift of the New Realm in Christ*, BTNT (Grand Rapids: Zondervan, 2021), 572.
5. James D. G. Dunn, *The New Perspective on Paul*, 2nd ed. (Grand Rapids: Eerdmans, 2008), 252.
6. For a fuller discussion of the olive tree metaphor, see Douglas J. Moo, *The Epistle to the Romans*, 2nd ed. NICNT (Grand Rapids: Eerdmans, 1996), 719–21.

privilege—for both Jews and Gentiles are grafted into the tree, which is representative of all the people of God, through faith in Jesus the Messiah.

Since faith in Jesus makes Gentiles partakers of the saving promises, their salvation depends on the rich history of Israel, which should remove any sense of arrogance on their part, or any sense that they have replaced Israel in the saving purposes of God (Rom. 11:17–18). God's mercy extends to both Israelites and Gentiles only through their common faith in the Messiah, bringing both groups into the one people of God, the church.

Paul even informs his readers in Romans, as we noted earlier, that "all Israel will be saved" (11:26). Although ethnic Israel is currently experiencing a "partial hardening," Paul anticipates a *future* salvation for Israel, after "the fullness of the Gentiles has come in" (Rom. 11:25–26). Some hold that Paul uses "all Israel" to refer to all believers, both Jew and Gentile.[7] While this would be consistent with the way Paul has described the people of God in the preceding section (Rom. 11:17–24), he makes a distinction in the present passage between ethnic Israelites, who are currently experiencing hardening, and Gentiles, who are coming to faith in greater numbers (Rom. 11:25–26). Consequently, we narrow the interpretive options to those that address the salvation of ethnic Israel.

Another viewpoint is that "all Israel" refers to all ethnic Israelites who have ever lived, regardless of whether they have trusted in Christ.[8] Others claim that Paul refers to all elect Jews throughout history.[9] Still others argue that Paul refers to the conversion of many Jews at the end of history.[10] Of these options, the future eschatological context of Romans 11, which emphasizes the importance of faith in the Jewish Messiah, precludes the possibility that all Israelites will be saved, regardless of whether they trust in Jesus. Moreover, it also makes it improbable that Paul refers to all believing Jews throughout history—for the two uses of the future tense verb *enkentristhēsontai* ("they [Israel] will be grafted in," Rom. 11:23–24) make the passage undeniably eschatological. Instead, the context points to a future conversion of many Jews at the return of Christ. This group of believing Jews will be "grafted in" to the people of God at the end of history, in keeping with Paul's argument in Romans 11:23–24.[11]

---

7. N. T. Wright, "The Letter to the Romans," in *The New Interpreters Bible Commentary*, vol. 9 (Nashville: Abingdon, 2015), 590–93.

8. Krister Stendahl, *Paul Among the Jews and Gentiles and Other Essays* (Philadelphia: Fortress, 1976), 3.

9. Benjamin L. Merkle, "Romans 11 and the Future of Ethnic Israel," *JETS* 43 (2000): 709–21; Merkle, "A Typological, Non-Future–Mass-Conversion View," in *Three Views on Israel and the Church: Perspectives on Romans 9–11*, eds. Jared Compton and Andrew David Naselli (Grand Rapids: Kregel, 2018), 161–208.

10. Moo, *Paul and His Letters*, 571.

11. That the first clause in Romans 11:23 is a conditional clause ("if they do not continue in unbelief") does not negate our point. Since the context points to a future conversion of Jews, we may assume that Jews will not "continue in unbelief."

God will certainly keep his promises to Israel (Gen. 12; 15; 17). We see how this unfolds in texts like Romans 11, where Paul explains that the promises made to ethnic Israelites are fulfilled through Jesus Christ, making both Jews and Gentiles members of the people of God and beneficiaries of the saving promises to people like Abraham, Isaac, and Jacob. For Paul, then, there is clear continuity between Israel and the church.

Israel and the Church Are Distinct

Some Christians object to the notion of continuity between Israel and the church based on the argument that these are distinct groups in the economy of God's salvation. They point to the notion that the covenant promises were originally sworn to ethnic Israelites, requiring their literal fulfillment when the nation of Israel is restored to the original Promised Land, likely during the millennial reign of Christ. While this view is popular with traditional dispensationalists, it might be objected that it runs counter to Paul's argument in Romans 11. As we have seen, Paul uses an olive tree analogy to contend that believing Jews and Gentiles are members of God's one people and partakers of the rich blessings promised to ethnic Israelites, like the promised Spirit (Gal. 3:14; cf. Ezek. 36–37; Isa. 44:3) and the inheritance of the coming world (Rom. 4:13; cf. Ps. 2; Isa. 65–66). The promises to Israel, then, are not exclusive to ethnic Israelites. God always intended for all nations—Jews and Gentiles—to partake of the promises to Abraham, without regard to ethnic distinction (Gen. 12:3; 15:6; Rom. 4:11–12; Gal. 3:7–9).

There is at least one other passage that presents difficulties in seeing continuity between Israel and the church. In Galatians 6:16, Paul says, "And as for all who walk by this rule, peace and mercy be upon them, and (*kai*) upon the Israel of God." Here, Paul seems to mark out "the Israel of God" as a distinct group, which some scholars take as either ethnic Israel or Jewish believers.[12] Although the latter is the most plausible of the two readings, there are still challenges with this view. First, Paul has taken pains throughout the letter to include Gentiles into the one people of God who receive the promises to Abraham (Gal. 3:1–4:7). Second, he has argued that ethnic distinctions between Jews and Gentiles are eradicated among those who are "one in Christ" (Gal. 3:28). He says as much in Galatians 6:15, arguing that "circumcision" and "uncircumcision" do not define the recipients of the Abrahamic promises, which culminate in a new creation. Thus, it is highly unlikely that Paul

---

12. Craig S. Keener provides a list of the plausible options for "Israel of God" in *Galatians: A Commentary* (Grand Rapids: Baker Academic, 2019), 578–79. For the sake of simplicity, we simply noted Jewish believers as an alternative interpretation to all ethnic Jews. Keener provides more nuanced options: law observant Jewish believers, Jewish people who come to faith at the end of history (cf. Rom. 11:26), and Jewish believers who do not impose circumcision on Gentiles.

distinguishes ethnic Israel as a unique entity at the end of his letter right after he argues in 6:15 against the value of ethnic distinctions.

But we still have to address the grammar of the passage. Though the ESV translates the conjunction *kai* as "and," which lends itself to making Israel a distinct group, we have reasonable grounds to translate *kai* with an explanatory sense ("that is"), clarifying the identity of "those who walk by this rule" as the "Israel of God."[13] In keeping with the message of Galatians, "the Israel of God" includes both Jewish and Gentile believers who "walk by the rule." While the translation "and" is grammatically possible, the explanatory sense coheres with the message of Galatians, which includes both Jews and Gentiles in the one people of God. The unity of Jew and Gentile is also consistent with 2 Corinthians 6:16, where Paul calls all believers the "temple of God," and is similar to Titus 2:14, where he refers to all believers as God's "possession."

In short, Paul does not distinguish Israel and the church in the plan of God. Rather, believing Israelites are members of the people of God, along with believing Gentiles. All God's people are participants in the singular plan of God, making them equal participants in a new creation.

Summary

Paul does not argue that the church has replaced Israel. Nor does he argue that Israel and the church are distinct entities. What he claims, rather, is that the promises God made with ethnic Israelites are fulfilled through Christ and are now made available to all those, whether Jew or Gentile, who belong to Christ. Consequently there is no room for Jews to take pride in their ethnic privilege, nor for Gentiles to assume that they have replaced Israel in the salvific plan of God. Through faith in Jesus, both groups are grafted into the one people of God, the church, and together partake in the rich blessings promised to Israel. We argue, then, that there is continuity between Israel and the church.

REFLECTION QUESTIONS

1. Why do some interpreters hold that the church has replaced Israel?

2. Do you see a connection between replacement theology/supersessionism and antisemitism?

3. Why do some believe Israel and the church are distinct entities in the plan of God?

---

13. A revised translation of Galatians 6:16 reads: "And as for all who walk by this rule, peace and mercy be upon them, that is (*kai*), upon the Israel of God."

4. On what basis does Paul argue for continuity between Israel and the church?

5. How do you understand Paul's assertion that "all Israel will be saved" (Rom. 11:26)?

Select Resources for Further Study

Bird, Michael F. *An Anomalous Jew: Paul among Jews, Greeks, and Romans.* Grand Rapids: Eerdmans, 2016.

Bird, Michael F., ed. *Four Views on the Apostle Paul.* Grand Rapids: Zondervan, 2012.

Bruce, F. F. *Paul: Apostle of the Heart Set Free.* Grand Rapids: Eerdmans, 2000.

Campbell, Douglas A. *Framing Paul: An Epistolary Biography.* Grand Rapids: Eerdmans, 2014.

Capes, David, Rodney Reeves, and E. Randolph Richards. *Rediscovering Paul: An Introduction to His World, Letters and Theology.* 2nd ed. Downers Grove, IL: InterVarsity Press, 2017.

Dunn, James D. G. *The Theology of Paul the Apostle.* Grand Rapids: Eerdmans, 1998.

Fee, Gordon D. *Pauline Christology: An Exegetical-Theological Study.* Peabody, MA: Hendrickson, 2007.

Gorman, Michael J. *Apostle of the Crucified Lord: A Theological Introduction to Paul & His Letters.* Grand Rapids: Eerdmans, 2004.

Hawthorne, Gerald F., Ralph P. Martin, and Daniel G. Reid, eds. *Dictionary of Paul and His Letters: A Compendium of Contemporary Biblical-Scholarship.* Downers Grove, IL: InterVarsity Press, 1993.

Longenecker, Bruce W., ed. *The New Cambridge Companion to St. Paul.* Cambridge: Cambridge University Press, 2020.

Longenecker, Bruce W. and Todd D. Still. *Thinking through Paul: A Survey of His Life, Letters, and Theology.* Grand Rapids: Zondervan, 2014.

McKnight, Scot and B. J. Oropeza. *Perspectives on Paul: Five Views*. Grand Rapids: Baker Academic, 2020.

McRay, John. *Paul: His Life and Teaching*. Grand Rapids: Baker Academic, 2003.

Moo, Douglas J. *A Theology of Paul and His Letters: The Gift of the New Realm in Christ*. BTNT. Grand Rapids: Zondervan, 2021.

Novenson, Matthew V. and R. Barry Matlock, eds. *The Oxford Handbook of Pauline Studies*. New York: Oxford University Press, 2022.

Porter, Stanley E. *Paul the Apostle: His Life, Thought, and Letters*. Grand Rapids: Eerdmans, 2016.

Quarles, Charles L. *Illustrated Life of Paul*. Nashville: B&H, 2014.

Sanders, E. P. *Paul: The Apostle's Life, Letters, and Thoughts*. Minneapolis: Fortress, 2015.

Schellenberg, Ryan S. and Heidi Wendt, eds. *T&T Clark Handbook to the Historical Paul*. London: T&T Clark, 2022.

Schnabel, Eckhard J. *Paul the Missionary: Realities, Strategies and Methods*. Downers Grove, IL: InterVarsity Press, 2008.

Schnelle, Udo. *Apostle Paul: His Life and Theology*. Translated by M. Eugene Boring. Grand Rapids: Baker Academic, 2005.

Schreiner, Thomas R. *Paul, Apostle of God's Glory in Christ: A Pauline Theology*. 2nd ed. Downers Grove, IL: InterVarsity Press, 2020.

Witherington III, Ben. *The Paul Quest: The Renewed Search for The Jew of Tarsus*. Downers Grove, IL: InterVarsity Press, 1998.

Witherington III, Ben and Jason A. Myers. *Voices and Views on Paul: Exploring Scholarly Trends*. Downers Grove, IL: InterVarsity Press, 2020.

Wright, N. T. *Paul and the Faithfulness of God*. 2 vols. Minneapolis: Fortress, 2017.

Scripture Index

1 Corinthians

2 Corinthians

40 QUESTIONS SERIES